Libraries, Literatures, and Archives

Not only does the library have a long and complex history and politics, but it has also an ambivalent presence in Western culture—both as a site of positive knowledge and as a site of error, confusion, and loss. Nevertheless, in literary studies and in the humanities, including book history, the figure of the library remains in many senses under-researched. Hence, this collection brings together established and up-and-coming researchers from a number of practices—literary and cultural studies, gender studies, book history, philosophy, visual culture, and contemporary art—with an effective historical sweep ranging from the Classical era to the present day.

In the context of the rise of archive studies, this book attends specifically and meta-critically to the figure of the library as a particular archival form, considering the traits that constitute (or fail to constitute) the library as institution or idea and questions its relations to other accumulative modes, such as the archive in its traditional sense, the museum, or the filmic or digital archive. Across their diversity, and in addition to their international standard of research and writing, each chapter is unified by commitment to analyzing the complex cultural politics of the library form.

Sas Mays is Senior Lecturer in Cultural and Critical Theory in the Department of English, Linguistics, and Cultural Studies at the University of Westminster, London. His overall research concerns mediations of cultural memory through technological and archival forms, from the textual to the visual and the analogue to the digital.

Routledge Studies in Library and Information Science

1. **Using the Engineering Literature**
   Edited by Bonnie A. Osif

2. **Museum Informatics**
   People, Information, and Technology in Museums
   Edited by Paul F. Marty and Katherine B. Jones

3. **Managing the Transition from Print to Electronic Journals and Resources**
   A Guide for Library and Information Professionals
   Edited by Maria Collins and Patrick Carr

4. **The Challenges to Library Learning**
   Solutions for Librarians
   Bruce Massis

5. **E-Journals Access and Management**
   Edited by Wayne Jones

6. **Digital Scholarship**
   Edited by Marta Mestrovic Deyrup

7. **Serials Binding**
   A Simple and Complete Guidebook to Processes
   Irma Nicola

8. **Information Worlds**
   Social Context, Technology, and Information Behavior in the Age of the Internet
   Paul T. Jaeger & Gary Burnett

9. **Perspectives on Information**
   Edited by Magnus Ramage and David Chapman

10. **Libraries, Literatures, and Archives**
    Edited by Sas Mays

Previous titles to appear in Routledge Studies in Library and Information Science include

Using the Mathematics Literature
Edited by Kristine K. Fowler

Electronic Theses and Dissertations
A Sourcebook for Educators: Students, and Librarians
Edited by Edward A. Fox

Global Librarianship
Edited by Martin A. Kesselman

Using the Financial and Business Literature
Edited by Thomas Slavens

Using the Biological Literature
A Practical Guide
Edited by Diane Schmidt

Using the Agricultural, Environmental, and Food Literature
Edited by Barbara S. Hutchinson

Becoming a Digital Library
Edited by Susan J. Barnes

Guide to the Successful Thesis and Dissertation
A Handbook for Students and Faculty
Edited by James Mauch

Electronic Printing and Publishing
The Document Processing Revolution
Edited by Michael B. Spring

Library Information Technology and Networks
Edited by Charles Grosch

Libraries, Literatures, and Archives

Edited by Sas Mays

NEW YORK AND LONDON

First published 2014
by Routledge
711 Third Avenue, New York, NY 10017

Simultaneously published in the UK
by Routledge
2 Park Square, Milton Park, Abingdon, Oxon OX14 4RN

First issued in paperback 2017

Routledge is an imprint of the Taylor & Francis Group, an informa business

© 2014 Taylor & Francis

The right of the editor to be identified as the author of the editorial material, and of the authors for their individual chapters, has been asserted in accordance with sections 77 and 78 of the Copyright, Designs and Patents Act 1988.

All rights reserved. No part of this book may be reprinted or reproduced or utilized in any form or by any electronic, mechanical, or other means, now known or hereafter invented, including photocopying and recording, or in any information storage or retrieval system, without permission in writing from the publishers.

Trademark Notice: Product or corporate names may be trademarks or registered trademarks, and are used only for identification and explanation without intent to infringe.

Library of Congress Cataloging-in-Publication Data

Libraries, literatures, and archives / edited by Sas Mays.
    pages cm.—(Routledge studies in library and information science ; 10)
    Includes bibliographical references and index.
    1. Library science—Sociological aspects. 2. Library science—Philosophy. 3. Information science—Sociological aspects. 4. Information science—Philosophy. 5. Critical theory. 6. Libraries—Philosophy. 7. Archives—Philosophy. 8. Literature—Philosophy. 9. Books and reading—Philosophy. 10. Collective memory. I. Mays, Sas, editor of compilation.
    Z665.L583 2014
    020.1—dc23
    2013028320

ISBN 13: 978-0-8153-4684-5 (pbk)
ISBN 13: 978-0-415-84387-4 (hbk)

Typeset in Sabon
by Apex CoVantage, LLC

For Cassie

Contents

List of Figures xi
Copyright Acknowledgments xiii
Preface xv
Acknowledgements xvii

Introduction: Unpacking the Library 1
SAS MAYS

1 Index 20
  GEOFFREY BENNINGTON

2 'Under a Heap of *Dust* They Buried Lye, within a *Vault* of Some Small *Library*': Margaret Cavendish and the Gendered Space of the Seventeenth-Century Library 40
  EMILY BOWLES

3 Outside the Archive: The Image of the Library in Hitchcock 56
  TOM COHEN

4 Reading in the Library of Catastrophe: W. G. Sebald's *The Rings of Saturn* 80
  RICHARD CROWNSHAW

5 Agendas and Aesthetics in the Transformations of the Codex in Early Modern England 97
  ELIZABETH EVENDEN

6 Magical Values in Recent Romances of the Archive 115
  SUZANNE KEEN

7 Classifying Fictions: Libraries and Information Sciences and the Practice of Complete Reading 130
  MICHELLE KELLY

8	Autobibliographies: For Lovers of Libraries MARTIN MCQUILLAN	150
9	'That Library of Uncatalogued Pleasure': Queerness, Desire, and the Archive in Contemporary Gay Fiction KAYE MITCHELL	164
10	The Archive, the Event, and the Impression SIMON MORGAN WORTHAM	185
11	Cataloguing Architecture: The Library of the Architect ANDREW PECKHAM	202
12	Reading *Folk Archive*: On the Utopian Dimension of the Artists' Book DAN SMITH	224
13	The Archive and the Library in V. Y. Mudimbe's *The Rift* WENDY W. WALTERS	239
14	Digital Libraries and Fantasies of Totality ANDREW WHITE	257
	Contributors	276
	Index	281

Figures

3.1	Tobin's library (Alfred Hitchcock, *Saboteur*)	57
3.2a	Santa Rosa's Free Public Library (Alfred Hitchcock, *Shadow of a Doubt*)	59
3.2b	The stack of first editions circled with the cord (Alfred Hitchcock, *Rope*)	60
3.2c	Scottie visits the Argosy Book Shop (Alfred Hitchcock, *Vertigo*)	60
3.2d	Cary Grant looks into the liquor cabinet (Alfred Hitchcock, *North by Northwest*)	61
3.3a	Norman's leather bound diary (Alfred Hitchcock, *Psycho*)	62
3.3b	The fly on Norman's hand in the police cell (Alfred Hitchcock, *Psycho*)	63
3.3c	The attack on the Schoolhouse (Alfred Hitchcock, *The Birds*)	64
3.3d	The evacuation of the eye socket and the home (Alfred Hitchcock, *The Birds*)	64
3.4a	Tracy is chased through the British Museum (Alfred Hitchcock, *Blackmail*)	65
3.4b	Tracy descends past the head of Nefertiti (Alfred Hitchcock, *Blackmail*)	66
3.4c	The dome of the British Library (Alfred Hitchcock, *Blackmail*)	66
3.4d	The reading room of the British Library (Alfred Hitchcock, *Blackmail*)	67
3.5	Marks and gashes atomise the sky (Alfred Hitchcock, *The Birds*)	73
3.6	Hitchcock's interrupted reading on the Underground (Alfred Hitchcock, *Blackmail*)	75
11.1	O. M. Ungers's desk in his *Studiolo*	205
11.2	Fachhochschule Library, Eberswalde, corner detail	209

11.3 Bradenburg Technical University Information, Communication and Media Centre, Cottbus, façade (late afternoon) 211
11.4 Baden State Library, Karlsruhe, Reading Room 215
11.5 'Model crates 2002' 217

Copyright Acknowledgments

Ch.1 This text originally appeared in Geoffrey Bennington, *Legislations: The Politics of Deconstruction* (London: Verso, 1994), and is reproduced with permission of the publisher.

Ch. 4 Excerpts from *The Rings of Saturn* by W. G. Sebald used in the U.S. with permission of The Wylie Agency LLC. All rights reserved. This chapter is a development of a section of Richard Crownshaw, *The Afterlife of Holocaust Memory in Contemporary Literature and Culture* (Basingstoke, UK, and New York: Palgrave Macmillan, 2010), pp. 41–60, and is included here by kind permission of the publisher.

Ch.12 Some material in this chapter was published as chapter 2 of Wendy Walters, *Archives of the Black Atlantic: Reading Between Literature and History* (London and New York: Routledge, 2013), and is included here with the kind permission of the publisher.

Ch.14 This chapter significantly revises some material that first appeared in Simon Morgan Wortham, *Derrida: Writing Events* (London and New York: Continuum, 2008). It is included here by kind permission of Bloomsbury Publishing PLC.

Preface

The object of this collection is ambivalence of the figure of the library, considered as the institutional form of the collection, ordering, and dissemination of texts, broadly thought, within cultural and critical practices of various kinds in early modern to contemporary Western, and non-Western culture. In this context, the library has been taken as a place of security—a site for the collection of knowledge which remains stable, codified, and determinate, but on the other hand, and at the same time, the library may also appear as a complex, problematic, and recalcitrant object. As such an ambivalent object, situated between order and disorder, the library may appear within or between a series of oppositions: between the maintenance of ideas and the mere accumulation of physical material, between imaginative or intellectual freedom and the ideological constraints of collections policies, between private ownership and mass dissemination, between taxonomy and miscellany, and between the past and the future. The library may appear not only as a place of memory, security, and knowledge, but also of loss, trauma, and indeterminacy. Indeed, the library, considered in terms of such ambivalences, has been an object of attention within a number of practices, disciplines, and areas of cultural study including, and other to, those of book history, librarianship, and the professional practices of archiving. Hence, the purpose of this collection is to stage a productive confrontation between these disciplinary analyses and those of post-structuralist humanities, in order that the possibility of an ensuing dialogue might mutually enrich an understanding of the historical and contemporary forms of the accumulations of inscribed memory.

Acknowledgements

This book results from a long process of gestation, development, and formal finalisation. Its origins are located in a colloquium that the editor of this volume organised at the University of Westminster, titled 'Literature and the Library', as part of the English Literature Colloquium series of the Department of English, Linguistics and Cultural Studies, in the Faculty of Social Sciences and Humanities at the University of Westminster in 2006. Thanks should be given, then, to the original speakers at the colloquium, Gary Hall, Suzanne Keen, Colbey Emerson Reid, and Dan Smith; to the supporting members of the department, Alex Warwick and David Cunningham; to Marq Smith and Jo Morra, for their contribution to the discussion; and to the Westminster Estates and Facilities staff who managed the event.

Since that time, the development of the book was protracted by a number of issues: the discompaction of some potential, but apparently committed contributors; shifts in understanding of the technological, cultural, and political conditions of textually mediated knowledge, which required further essays to be included or existing essays to be modified; and the exigencies of life. In the period up to 2013, energies were required by events brief and protracted, of personal, historical, and institutional kinds—where there were sudden accidents and belated recognitions of long-running programmes; where relationships were formed, dissolved, and reconfigured; and where there were deaths, births, and survivals. In this context, let me thank Rosalind Mays and Colin Duly, for their support and generosity in adverse and better times, particularly in the final stages of editing. And let me thank, between the origination and finalisation of this collection, for the birth of my son, to whom this book is dedicated, with my endless love.

Amid this scene of transformation, and given the protraction of the editing of this volume, I would also like to thank the early contributors to this volume for their patience and dedication, and to thank all of the authors included for their place in this text—because the process of collation and editing has been one that has positively developed my understanding of the field of study under consideration in this book. I hope that this collection is as thought provoking and productive, and results in as many realisations and disagreements, for its readers, because it is designed to open a continuing time and space of protracted and productive contestation in which the past, present, and future of the library may be both thought and practiced.

Introduction
Unpacking the Library

Sas Mays

CONTEXTS AND TERMS

This book is situated at the intersection of two academic domains that have traditionally been separated: on one hand, post-structuralist cultural theories (or what has come to be termed more broadly 'critical theory'), and on the other, the professional practices of Libraries and Information Sciences (LIS). The need for a dialogue between these domains has been asserted in Gloria Leckie and John Buschman's introduction to the edited collection *Critical Theory for Library and Information Science* (2010). Here, critical theory appears as a necessary supplement to LIS on three key counts: first, the problematic disciplinary isolation of LIS as a practice-based activity; second, the lack of a strong tradition of meta-theoretical discourse in LIS; and third, its lack of critical engagement with contemporary sociopolitical issues, such as the demand that libraries function according to neoliberal economic imperatives. Indeed, Leckie and Buschman argue that because the localised practices related to the development and management of textual collections are located within wider ideological and economic structures, it is imperative for LIS to theorise its relationships to, and its evaluation of, such contexts.[1]

This collection stands in some relation to this demand for interdisciplinarity, by thinking that critical theory has something to offer to collections practices. Yet such claims should be tempered in a number of ways. First, it should be recognized that the professional practices of archiving have, in some instances, already developed a sense of their own meta-theoretical frameworks or have developed a critical relationship with post-structuralist or postmodernist discourses. Such work should be recognised as a positive resource for critical theory.[2] Second, critical theories have often been remiss in addressing the *practical* issues of collections practices, particularly as they are conceived in LIS, even at the very moment that physical books and the forms of their collection are invoked within such theories themselves. This is a point that I discuss via Roland Barthes in the second, central section of this introduction.

Nonetheless, although it may be true that there has not been a consistent attention to the kind of issues encountered by collections practices in critical theory, various critical-theoretical discourses *have* engaged specifically with issues concerning textual collections in a number of ways: through problems of taxonomy, for example, or of material accumulation. In this sense, post-structuralist critical theory has been concerned with matters of practice, just as the seemingly merely practical activities of LIS have developed theoretical frameworks. For this reason, we should no doubt be suspicious of any too simplistic sense that the difference between critical theory and LIS amounts to one between the theoretical and the practical. We might certainly acknowledge that the emphasis of each domain has tended toward one side of the polarity of theory and practice, in the context of the difference between, say, theories of taxonomy as they relate to shelf classification and practices of taxonomy as they relate to theoretical discourse. Yet the difference between critical theory and LIS may be thought of less as a matter of essence and more as a matter of disposition, in which each activity has in fact encroached on the other's territory, if, often, in ways peculiar to their own institutions and traditions. Hence, this book includes essays from the disciplines of book history and LIS, yet it is also keen to show that even the apparently most 'theoretical', deconstructive discourses are nevertheless engaged with the practical issues of textual collections, just as much as book history and shelf classification are engaged with wider cultural and epistemological issues. Hence, *Libraries, Literatures, and Archives* aims to contribute toward the developing dialogue between critical theory and LIS by engaging with the representation of books and collections within literary and cultural texts through a number of critical perspectives across the humanities—architecture, book history, film theory, libraries and information sciences, literary theory, philosophy, and postcolonial theory.

What these perspectives share, as the title of this collection suggests, is an overriding concern with the complex relationships between material textual holdings and the wider cultural practices and understandings within which they are enmeshed. In this sense, the central term refers not only to literature in the conventional sense of imaginative fiction; it also encompasses the ways in which different cultural practices—architecture, for example—produce their own meta-discourses as writings and that thus gesture toward their accumulation and collection in paper-based archives including libraries of various kinds. Equally, cultural practices may reflect, consciously or unconsciously, on the nature of such texts and holdings, and thus produce a literature *of* the library. In this sense, cultural practices are not only generative of textual materials: they also develop traditions that are themselves partly recorded as texts of various kinds. Thus, as the final term of the title suggests, cultural practices not only gesture toward particular libraries or ideas of libraries but also toward more general considerations of technological-institutional forms of memory, and thence to general theories of 'the archive', for example, as the overall system that governs the production of knowledge in a given historical epoch.[3]

Although the terms *archives* and *libraries* are sometimes used interchangeably, or in more or less metaphorical ways, it is important to note that such terms may not, of course, be synonymous across different practices. For example, where libraries are thought in terms of the collection of imaginative literary texts, such accumulation also requires non-imaginative writings—catalogues and indices, as well as ordered records of acquisition, maintenance, dissemination, and destruction. Such records of institutional transaction, the sense in which the professional practice of archiving defines the term *archives*, may thus not be equated with libraries as such, at least insofar as they are defined by their content collection.

What then does it mean, in the title of this book, to refer to 'libraries'? The term in part designates particular, empirical, or historical instantiations of textual collections, traditionally comprising scrolls, tablets, codices, and other textual forms. Yet, as much as the term implies differences between such institutions that might be specified historically, geographically, and technologically, it designates a set of institutional forms brought together by their function; that is, there is also a shared, generic character. Likewise, if the term *the library* can refer to a specific architectural, institutional collection or set of collections of texts, however dispersed, it can also refer to a generic set of characteristics shared by different libraries based in the idea of ordered accumulations of texts. We might say, pragmatically, that there are *particular* libraries and that there is an *idea* of 'the library' in its generic sense. However, just as we have to problematise the difference between theory and practice, in terms of a simple opposition between critical theory and LIS, we need also to problematise this apparent difference between the empirical and ideational. Simply put, specific conceptions of libraries partake of a general idea of the library, as much as generic conceptions of the library are formed within specific historical and cultural locations in which there are forms of libraries. Indeed, generic conceptions of the library are always specific to general discursive frameworks that are themselves historically, culturally, and politically located.

Thus, the question of what it means to refer to libraries, or the library, should also be rephrased as a matter of historical situatedness. This collection is focused, although not exclusively, on codexical forms and on libraries considered in their traditional senses as the place of the accumulation, ordering, and dissemination of such paper-based texts.[4] There might appear to be a difficulty with this focus, given that this is a time when traditional forms of writing and storage seem to be in a process of destabilization, transition, or displacement, conditioned by the apparent ascendency of digital forms of textual inscription, accumulation, and transmission. Both the positive and negative dimensions of an end of the paper-based codex, and its forms of collection, have been variously argued through elsewhere, just as there have been many affirmative and negative valorisations of digital forms of writing and accumulation more generally. Equally, between these positions, there have been calls for hybridised forms of publication and storage that would combine both paper-based and digital modes.[5] What this scene of contestation should be taken to indicate is that both libraries, as institutional and cultural forms, and concepts of the library, as themselves institutional and cultural forms, have always existed within historical and technological processes, despite relative periods of stasis. Specific collections of texts based on changing technologies of inscription and taxonomical systems have partially accumulated, periodically stabilised, decayed or dispersed, and reemerged in other collections, just as generic ideas of the library have been subject to their own mutational existence. Indeed, in this sense, an original or final form of the book or the library has never been constructed, and never will be: textual forms, and their forms of collection, are *always* embedded in processes of transition.

THE BOOK AND THE LIBRARY IN RUINS

If libraries, and the library, have always existed in processes of transition, such processes have concerned, particularly since the Renaissance, the wider ideological and economic structures of capitalism. Indeed, understanding the contemporary situation of capitalism is precisely Leckie and Buschman's requirement, with which we began. In order to provide some coordinates for thinking about books and their collection in the historical and contemporary scenes of capitalism, I would like now to discuss a number of analyses from Roland Barthes, Walter Benjamin, and Jacques Derrida, precisely because, in their complexity, they come to indicate and underscore the transitionality and complexity of libraries, and of the library.

In his essay 'From Work to Text', Roland Barthes describes two ways of thinking about writing. On one hand, the *text* is understood to be characterised by an endless process of signification that cuts across and transgresses the boundaries of literary classifications such as genre. These kinds of classifications are, for Barthes, signs of the bourgeois desire for order, regulation, and the circulation of determinate commodities. On the other hand, and against such determinacy, the text is said to transgress the form of the *work*, an object of authorial property attached to the material form of the book and its traditional mode of collection. As Barthes puts it:

> the work is a fragment of substance, occupying a part of the space of books (in a library for example), the Text is a methodological field. The opposition may recall (without at all reproducing term for term) Lacan's distinction between 'reality' and 'the real': the one is displayed, the other demonstrated; likewise, the work can be seen (in bookshops, in catalogues, in exam syllabuses), the text is a process of demonstration, speaks according to certain rules (or against certain rules); the work can be held in the hand, the text is held in language, only exists in the movement of a discourse (or rather, it is Text for the very reason that

it knows itself as text); the Text is not the decomposition of the work, it is the work that is the imaginary tail of the Text; or again, *the Text is experienced only in an activity of production*. It follows that the Text cannot stop (for example on a library shelf); its constitutive movement is that of cutting across (in particular, it can cut across the work, several works)'.[6]

The book, held systematically in 'catalogues' and physically in 'bookshops', is not only placed, as a commodity, within the market: it is also represented in 'exam syllabuses', and it is thus implicated, for Barthes, within the dominant education system. It hence gestures toward the role played by realist literature in the French state education system, and in the bourgeois legal system, in the short essay 'Dominici, or the Triumph of Literature'. As Barthes argues in this piece, a peasant farmer, Gaston Dominici, is wrongly convicted of the murder of Sir Jack Drummond and his family by ascribing to him spurious stereotypes garnered from literary texts. Such fictional texts, shared by the court officials through their education, operate as a common understanding for real human psychology, and are deployed as part of the official legal process in a way that is clearly socially divisive and repressive.[7] Barthes's discussion thus involves the not only the bourgeois education system that privileges such literary works and their psychological and ideological values, but also issues of national canon, and the libraries in which such canonical texts are conserved. Yet if this reminds us of the ideological dimensions of textual culture, Barthes's comparison of the text and the book also enables further questions to be raised: should we not consider the book and its forms of collection as complex things, rather than merely as the normalising classification of commodities, and consequently, should they not be understood to be conditioned by the complex and transgressive character accorded, by Barthes, to what he calls the 'text'?

It is precisely the complexity and ambivalence of the book and its collection which is raised by Walter Benjamin, in his 1931 essay 'Unpacking My Library'. Benjamin begins by asking that the reader 'join [him] in the disorder of crates that have been wrenched open, the air saturated with the dust of wood, the floor covered with torn paper, to join [him] among piles of volumes that are seeing daylight again after two years of darkness', prior to the moment when the books are 'on the shelves', and are thus 'touched by the mild boredom of order'.[8] Thus far, there seems to be some comparability to Barthes's association of shelf order and classification with stifling norms, yet Benjamin complicates such an association in reference to 'the confusion of the library' and 'the dialectical tension between disorder and order'.[9] As he also says:

> Every passion borders on the chaotic, but the collector's passion borders on the chaos of memories. More than that: the chance, the fate, that suffuse the past before my eyes are conspicuously present in the accustomed

confusion of these books. For what else is this collection than a disorder to which habit has accommodated itself to such an extent that it can appear as order?[10]

In this context of the problematic relationship between opposites, it is hardly contingent that Benjamin should, apparently without cause, as he says:

> put my hands on two volumes bound in faded boards which, strictly speaking, do not belong in a book case at all: two albums with stick-in pictures which my mother pasted in as a child and which I inherited. They are seeds of a collection of children's books which is growing steadily even today, though not in my garden. There is no living library that does not harbour a number of booklike creations from fringe areas. They need not be stick-in albums or family albums, autograph books or portfolios containing pamphlets or religious tracts; some people become attached to leaflets and prospectuses, others to handwriting facsimiles or typewritten copies of unobtainable books; and certainly periodicals can form the prismatic fringes of a library.[11]

Benjamin's albums, indicating something about the familial and, indeed, gendered milieu of books and knowledge, appear outside strict classification, and, hence, partially outside the remits of (the body of) the library proper. Yet, in their ubiquity to 'any living library', they are also within it. They are both internal to and transgressive of the library in classificatory terms. In their liminality, which is also somewhere between text and image, these quasi-books from the fringes of the library thus represent something of an objectification of the complexity of the book and the library in general that Benjamin posits in his essay.

Benjamin's liminal book-like object, acquired through inheritance, appears to contrast with the essay's otherwise preeminent concern with the financial acquisition of books, their collection in a private library, and the sense of subjectivity which may be constructed through such possession. Yet, as Benjamin says, 'a collector's attitude toward his possessions stems from an owner's feeling of responsibility toward his property. Thus it is, in the highest sense, the attitude of an heir, and the most distinguished trait of a collection will always be its transmissibility'.[12] This sense of responsibility engages with capitalism as a system that emphasizes the construction of individuality through property ownership, if in a way that is designed to develop (and problematise) some kind of redemption from its bourgeois character. In this regard, one of the central metaphors which determines Benjamin's thought of the relation between the ownership of books and subjectivity in 'Unpacking My Library' is, I think, provided by Hegel's articulation of the supremacy of Prussian capitalism, of its bourgeois culture, and of the laws regulating the relation between the individual and the state, in the *Philosophy of Right*

(1821). Part of what Hegel engages within here is the problematic distinction between the book or the work as a determinate object governed by authorial and legal authority, and the text, as a more fluid and multiple entity. Yet where Barthes, for example, in the 'Death of the Author' (1968), licenses the reader to create meaning beyond any authorial intention, Hegel inversely champions the legally regulated development of authorial ideas.

In the *Philosophy of Right*, freedom is effectively defined as the freedom to own private property, and possessions of various kinds are that which constitute personality. Hegel's thought is directed toward the *purity* of the concept of private ownership—for an object to be the exclusive property of an individual, he or she must be able to seize hold of the object and, thence, to be able to fully, and continuously, invest that object with his or her *will*. By contrast, Hegel describes a particular situation in which two people might share ownership of an object as a 'madness of personality'—because it is logically impossible for two people to have exclusive ownership of the same object.[13] But the book appears to verge on this very madness: on one hand, one may exclusively own a particular copy of a text as a physical object, whereas the ideas remain the property of the author through the laws of copyright, but on the other, nevertheless, Hegel says that it is the 'destiny' of the book for its ideas to be appropriated and transformed into new ideas by further thinkers. Although copyright has a limited ability to protect authors, Hegel also refers to the 'endless multiplicity' of more or less minor alterations to texts which thus give a 'superficial imprint of being *one's own*'. Such plagiarism, Hegel continues, 'can easily have the effect that the profit which the author or inventive entrepreneur expected from his work or new idea is eliminated, reduced for both parties, or ruined for everyone'.[14]

If Hegel says that plagiarism ruins private ownership, and it thus ruins the subjectivity couched in it, Benjamin's thought appears to be directed precisely at entering such ruination. This architectural metaphor is particularly apt for the essay: the collector, says Benjamin, 'lives in' the 'building stones' of his books—they compose a dwelling into which he will 'disappear' at the close of the essay. But Benjamin's sense of textual architecture is one that is opened and problematised by the essay, just as his thoughts on the photographic image offer a way of permeating the interiority of the bourgeois domestic enclosure in 'The Work of Art in the Age of Mechanical Reproduction', first published in 1936. Indeed, to the extent that both the book and the library are placed in ruination, this is in continuity with Benjamin's sense that 'time is running out' for the private mode of book collecting, and thus (like Hegel's philosophical owl of Minerva flying at dusk): 'Only in extinction is the collector comprehended'.[15] In this sense, as in others, the essay is structured by a concern with endings, yet through a movement toward paradoxical states where opposites coexist. As Benjamin says:

> Once you have approached the mountains of cases in order to mine the books from them and bring them to the light of day—or, rather, of

night—what memories crowd upon you! Nothing highlights the fascination of unpacking more clearly that the difficulty of stopping this activity. I had started at noon, and it was midnight before I had worked my way to the last cases.[16]

As this inversion of darkness and light indicates, the book and the library are, for Benjamin, objects characterized by opposing forces: categorisation and transgression, reason and dreaming. At the same time, they are connected with the imbrication of other oppositions—possession and loss, identity and its transformation.

In Benjamin's thought, the subjectivity of the private collector is transient and complex, rather than fixed and singular.[17] Indeed, this idea of complexity appears to be a central aspect of the essay. With a dialectical tension so characteristic of Benjamin, he not only states that the acquisition of a book at auction requires a 'cool [. . .] head', but he also displays a passionate relation to the book: a 'particular volume' inspired in him 'the ardent desire to hold on to it forever', and its seizure was his 'most exiting experience'.[18] However, the moment of possession is countered at the same stroke, because the particular volume in question is Honoré de Balzac's *La Peau de chagrin* (1831). *Chagrin* not only designates the magically inscribed skin of the wild Ass in the novel, but also, in French, grief and disappointment. Indeed, Balzac's story is precisely about the loss of life and the diminishment of the skin through acts of will bent on the acquisition of worldly desires. The point, then, is that by accentuating the idea of private ownership of texts, Benjamin simultaneously undermines the idea of a bourgeois subjectivity assured by its possessions. As with the book, and the library, between creation and destruction, the subject is suspended in ruin.

This reference to Balzac also allows a connection to be made to Derrida's thoughts regarding the history of the technology of paper, the book, and its archives: ending with a scene of burned paper, Balzac's novel gestures toward the historical destruction of the book as the hegemonic medium of writing, which Derrida places in its relation to capitalisation:

> The successor to parchment made of skin, paper is *declining*, it is *getting smaller*, it is *shrinking* inexorably at the rate that a man grows old—and everything then becomes a play of expenditure and savings, calculation, speed, political economy, and [. . .] of knowledge, power and will.[19]

Yet such a decline should not be thought of in terms of a simple teleology emerging from a simple origin or pointing to an ultimate end or in terms of a strict separation of technological forms of writing. Derrida's thought in this context is, rather, to try to think the extent to which the condition of paper as a complex or 'multimedia' technology prefigures the digital economy, just as much as the digital economy is itself dependent upon the text as a paradigm, for example, in the *pages* of the Web. To the extent that traditional and digital technologies of writing may share attributes, then, we are again on the terrain of the kind of complex liminal textual form exemplified by Benjamin's albums, and the ruin of simple, stable identities, whether these are material, textual, technological, or subjective. As such, it is important that one of the main contexts for this collection is, precisely, the history of the technologies of the book and the library and the current state of their transition. As Derrida wrote elsewhere:

> When one speaks of the destruction of an archive, do not limit oneself to the meaning, to the theme, or to consciousness. To be sure, take into account an economy of the unconscious, even if only to exceed it once again. But it is also necessary to take into consideration the 'supports', the subjectiles of the signifier—the paper, for example, but this example is more and more insufficient. There is this diskette, and so on. Differences here among newspapers, journals, books, perhaps, the modes of storage, of reproduction and of circulation, the 'ecosystems' (libraries, bookstores, photocopies, computers, and so on). I am also thinking of everything that is happening today to libraries. Official institutions are calculating the choices to be made in the destruction of nonstorable copies or the salvaging of works whose paper is deteriorating: displacement, restructuring of the archive, and so on.[20]

In the paper that this citation is extracted from, Derrida discusses the complex relations between that in culture which is *biodegradable,* and which may be lost or transformed, and that in culture which is *non-biodegradable*, that which remains. As Derrida argues, in historical terms, part of the work of deconstruction is to maintain a memory of those aspects of culture that 'certain forces have attempted to melt down into the anonymous mass of an unrecognizable culture, to "(bio)degrade" in the common compost of a memory said to be living and organic'.[21] In this guise, we might be reminded of Derrida's discussion of James Joyce in the interview published as 'This Strange Institution Called Literature' (1989), in which Derrida suggests that '*Ulysses* arrives like one novel among others that you place on your bookshelf and inscribe in a genealogy. It has its ancestry and its descendants'.[22] Here, then, with some similarity to Barthes, the library shelf gestures toward the way in which new works may become conserved as part of literary tradition and canonical culture. We could also link this to Benjamin's sense of the 'mild boredom' of shelf order. But, on the other hand, as Derrida argues, Joyce also inaugurates a new idea of writing that transgresses the existing rules for literary production and that transgresses the unity of 'the work'. Contiguously, in 'Biodegradables', Joyce's writings remain in their radical incommensurability—they resist the totalisation or finalisation of their meanings and possibilities, and are thus non-biodegradable. As Derrida argues, such writings must be assimilated into culture *as* the unassimilable—that which is included in order to disrupt the conventions proscribed by normative orders.[23] Indeed, as they thus *continue* to exist in an incommensurability that invites interpretation, they also give possibility to the generation of new meanings in the future.

In this way, we might link the biodegradable and the non-biodegradable, consecutively, with Benjamin's insistence on the transmissibility of libraries, and his affirmation of the singular, lasting memories of acquisition—precisely because, as we have seen in relation to Balzac, such moments may be complex and contradictory, resisting simple categorization, and may offer some kind of disruption or ruination of the norms of bourgeois property ownership. Likewise, Benjamin's albums, in their material liminality, resist simple categorization, and thus remain incommensurable to simple assimilation within a library understood as a collection of unitary codexical works. In such ruinations, the library may be incommensurable, and therefore be non-biodegradable, and thus remain. Hence, although there will also be transformation and obsolescence of various kinds for libraries considered in the traditional sense of paper repositories, something of their incommensurability may remain in the digital milieu. In this scene of the cultural ecosystems of which libraries are a part, and their transition, the ruination of the library, as a form that has never not been ruined in one way or another, must not be registered simply in melancholic, nostalgic, or fetishistic terms. Rather, the ruin of the library is not only a condition of its operation: it is also the very possibility of its future.

THEMES AND CONNECTIONS

The chapters of this book comprise a collection of theoretical and disciplinary perspectives through which the issues of the library, past, present, and future, might be engaged. A number of chapters included here—those by Geoffrey Bennington, Tom Cohen, Martin McQuillan, and Simon Morgan Wortham—are specifically engaged with Derrida's thoughts regarding technological memory and the archive, and a number of others, Kaye Mitchell's and Wendy Walters's, also intersect with deconstruction. These two latter contributions are also part of a strong engagement with literature, which is similarly present in the chapters provided by Emily Bowles, Richard Crownshaw, Suzanne Keen, and Andrew White. But this collection is not predominately about deconstruction or literature; rather, it aims to stage a multidisciplinary attention to matters pertaining to the library, through philosophy (Bennington), film theory (Cohen), trauma studies (Crownshaw), book history (Elizabeth Evenden), library classification (Michelle Kelly), queer theory (Mitchell), architecture (Andrew Peckham), contemporary art (Dan Smith), postcolonialism (Walters), and digital humanities (White). Alongside the overlaps and divergences of these approaches, there are three themes through which these chapters might be brought into productive difference, and which I would like to discuss in the following order: first, technological transformations in media of memory; second, problems of taxonomic order; and, third, contestations of history and spaces of reading.

First, then, the issue of technological transformation is key to a number of contributions. Tom Cohen's chapter, 'Outside the Archive: The Image of the Library in Hitchcock', argues that Hitchcock's films consistently engage with the figure of the book, and, in their imaging of textual memory and the library, cite the 'tectonic' shift from written language to film, considered as archival forms. Cohen also argues that this shift, from the private, interior mental space of reading, to public space of cinematic viewing, must be understood as a matter of capitalism and ecology. Indeed, as Cohen shows, this shift involves the destruction of textual reading, the supersession of the library and all of the pedagogic and ideological structures associated with the 'era of the book'.

This theme, of archival destruction, is also an issue for Elizabeth Evenden's chapter, 'Agendas and Aesthetics in the Transformations of the Codex in Early Modern England', which opens on a preceding historical scene of technological mutation—that of the shift from the scroll or tablet to the codex form of the book. Such a shift involves not only the maintenance of previous manuscript writings, or their repurposing, but also their destruction. As with Cohen's chapter, this shift is not merely technological, but political: it concerns the way in which the construction of codices and their collection was part of the development of state religion. Of particular interest here, however, is the way in which the selection of books to be included in libraries, and the selection of texts to be included in books, was also a matter of personal taste on the part of the collector, and despite the appearance of unity and completion given by the material form of the codex, Evenden's close analysis shows that they also comprised heterogeneous material bound by idiosyncratic decision. It might thus be argued that such heterogeneity is a necessary part of any library, a sign of the blurring of its taxonomic or rational architecture.

Such an issue also concerns Martin McQuillan's 'Autobiobibliographies: For Lovers of Libraries', which begins by discussing Derrida's engagement with the problematic image of Plato directing Socrates' writing—an inversion of paternal filiation that 'challenges the received wisdom of the ages, of every library, and every university, of the entire metaphysical tradition', and of 'the encyclopaedic principle' which aims to circumscribe knowledge. McQuillan links this issue of the encyclopaedic to the context of digital archiving, shifting attention from the Bodleian Library to the Paul de Man archive. Through this discussion, McQuillan engages with the complex relations between uniformity and heterogeneity, determination and contingency, and encyclopaedic totality and its disruption, in both analogue and digital contexts.

This chapter intersects with Andrew White's 'Digital Libraries and Fantasies of Totality', which offers a sustained engagement with the utopian idea that digital technologies of memory and dissemination could constitute a 'universal library' of 'perfect information'. As White argues, this 'postmodernist' idea of the archival possibilities of digital hypertext has historical precedents that effectively begin with the Ptolemaic library of Alexandria and that develops in sixteenth- and seventeenth-century utopian thought, through the European Enlightenment's idea of complete knowledge inscribed in paper, through the nineteenth century, and into the countercultures of the 1960s. But what is also key here is the way in which postmodernist conceptions of the total library emerging from the latter context have not only been facilitated by literary fictions, but acquire in part their persuasive character from such antecedents. Thus, White's chapter not only historically contextualises the idea of the library as a form of replete information: it also reads the contemporary versions of such a utopian idea in the context of the marketisation and capitalisation of knowledge.

Second, as the issue of the universal library must intersect with problems of taxonomy, contemporary issues of digital collections are also an aspect of Michelle Kelly's chapter, 'Classifying Fictions: Libraries and Information Sciences and the Practice of Complete Reading', at its open and close. Yet the core issue in this chapter, which contextualises its relations to the digital, concerns the impossibility of providing a universal method for the classification of traditional, paper-based fictional texts and the way in which some librarians have responded to the problem by classification through the 'complete' reading of such texts. Although there are clear differences here between such long reading practices in LIS and the *close reading* practices of literary studies, the shared tendency toward prolonged engagement with the content of narrative fiction nevertheless could be argued to *also* involve, in deconstructive terms, something of a crossover between these discourses or, indeed, a tendency toward their partial collapse.

If Kelly's examples thus show how fictional texts might problematise library taxonomy for LIS, Geoffrey Bennington's essay, 'Index', engages with philosophical issues of books' indices, employing the complexities and paradoxes of their deictic function in order to problematise designation in general. Looking at a number of test-cases, beginning with the curious status of the index in academic books, the essay shows that deictics, as exemplified in particular by the word *this*, involve a radical moment of blank stupidity—a kind of non-reflexive self-reference—which is a condition of possibility of any sense or reference whatsoever. Through these discussions, the chapter problematises the figure and the function not only of the index in texts but also, by extension, the figure and the function of the library in terms of its very taxonomic core—its catalogue.

Readings of taxonomy are also key to Simon Morgan Wortham's chapter. Through its close engagement with Derrida's writings, 'The Archive, the Event, and the Impression' reads the 'event' of 9/11 through a complex set of metonymically related terms—'book, library, institution, law, statute, state deposit, nation-state'. In order to indicate ways in which these terms are linked, I might refer here to Morgan Wortham's reading of the complex terms *biblion* and *bibliotheke*. The former term refers to books and works, but also to other materials of inscription—'paper, bark, tablets'—while the latter refers to the library, or the 'place' or 'slot' for a book. As Morgan Wortham discusses, however, the book and the library are not simply sites of immobilization or fixity: the lodging of the Hélène Cixous archive at the Bibliotèque nationale de France (BNF) offers something of a danger to such a state institution and to traditional taxonomies of knowledge, given the subversive character of her work. It is in part this idea of subversion, and of the unstable character of the library, that opens it to new meanings, and future transformations.

The taxonomic problem of the *bibliotheke* also features in Dan Smith's chapter, 'Reading *Folk Archive*: On the Utopian Dimension of the Artists' Book'. Smith's analysis of conceptual art shows that artists' books may occupy a problematic position, in being potentially classified as art *and* documentary, a taxonomic problem that is also registered in the contemporary art practice of Jeremy Deller and Alan Kane. As this indicates, recognition of the productive and disruptive relations between institutional discourses, such as art and documentary, is not only a feature of deconstructive readings of the library. I should also note here that in Smith's reading of Deller and Kane's *Folk Archive*, this art project materializes a desire to remember social practices that may be obliterated by the official image of history given by the heritage industry, and thus constitutes something of a *counter-archive*. It shares, in a sense comparable to White's discussion of the digital library, a utopian desire. This, then, entails an issue of the construction, reconstruction, and transformation of histories and identities through archival collections, an issue that concerns a number of other chapters in this book.

Third, then, in terms of the contestations of history and spaces of reading, Suzanne Keen's chapter, 'Magical Values in Recent Romances of the Archive', concerns precisely this issue of heritage. Her essay opens with the distinction between the 'meaningful value' of manuscripts, which contribute to national heritage, and their 'magical value', which concerns libidinal and sensory ways of bringing the past to life. The latter, Keen argues, 'extends a central fantasy of the heritage industry' in terms of the embodiment of the past. In her consideration of the role of these two forms of value in fictional representations of libraries and their contents, Keen focuses on contemporary U.S. 'document-driven' novels that emphasise the quest for truths secreted in manuscript collections. Significantly, Keen analyses the way in which access to and interpretation of Old World archival material by New World figures reflects the neo-imperialism of recent American foreign policies, as much as such novels also reflect the changing world of immigration and gender. If such romances figure the archive as a site for embodiment, we should thus also think of the relation between history and the archive as a *place* of reading and interpretation.

Rick Crownshaw's contribution to this volume, 'Reading in the Library of Catastrophe: W. G. Sebald's *The Rings of Saturn*', also concentrates on the fictional representation of archives and libraries and questions the possible differences and relations between them. On one hand, Sebald's work associates archives with the rationalising drives of the European Enlightenment, with a modernity that led to the violences of the Nazi regime, and thus with the destruction of Jewish culture and history. On the other hand, as Crownshaw argues, there are other forms and spaces of collection and recollection in Sebald's writings—reading rooms, private collections, literary and photographic libraries. In addition, Sebald's compendious works constitute the figure of a 'meta-library' that is constructed through intertextuality and literary allusion. Crownshaw's discussion of Sebald's *The Rings of Saturn* (1995) and *Austerlitz* (2001) thus proposes that these latter forms of the library, while linked to the order of the rationalising archive, offer, in the Benjaminian terms already discussed here, disorder and the disorganisation of recollection and memory, and thus an alternate way of remembering the traumas of modernity.

Wendy Walters's 'The Archive and the Library in V. Y. Mudimbe's *The Rift*', concerns the traumas of colonialism and its aftermaths, and it leads, with some comparability to Crownshaw's sense of Sebald's partially disorganized library forms, to the idea of literary works as, in themselves, multiple archives. The archive is understood in this chapter less as a singular physical space, or set of spaces, but rather, in the Foucauldian sense, as the overall system that governs statements of knowledge. In this sense, the phrase *colonial library* refers to the history of European discourse about Africa, and the way in which Western colonialist discourses, nineteenth-century and early-twentieth-century anthropology for example, attempted to epistemologically categorise and fix subjected peoples and cultures. However, the place of reading in a specific library may appear in this chapter as a prison in which the existential experience is one of *blocage*, an inability to write, think, or achieve resolution. In this scene of research, Mudimbe's novel emphasizes the archival materials of books, diaries, and index cards and the difficulties of achieving determinate knowledge. As Walters argues, a response to this problem may be couched in Mudimbe's writing, considered not only in terms of its engagement with cultural *hybridity* as a destabilisation of Western taxonomic principles but also in terms of its *oeuvre*, because this latter comprises a 'compilation of multiple discursive inroads [that] succeeds not only in creating a new archive, but that works between and amongst multiple archives, teasing out the discourses of their very formation'.

Issues of history and spaces of reading are also key to Emily Bowles's chapter, entitled '"Under a Heap of *Dust* they Buried Lye, within a *Vault* of Some Small *Library*": Margaret Cavendish on Alternatives to the Library'. As Bowles argues, Cavendish images institutional libraries as dusty and patriarchal spaces, in which men's intellectual conflicts also gesture to the material destruction of books and their collections. On the other hand, Cavendish's writings engage with private spaces of reading that have traditionally been associated with femininity. Yet Cavendish's career, both during the Interregnum and following the Restoration of the monarchy in England, is marked by a deliberate attempt to enter into masculine spaces—by sending copies of her works to the major libraries in England and Europe. If the purpose of Bowles's analysis is thus to attend to the gendered spaces of private and more public libraries, it is also to understand the shape that libraries lend to intellectual and creative work and to outline Cavendish's strategies for subverting the library's limitations of space, access, and combination. With some comparability to the idea of the meta-library in Crownshaw's discussion of Sebald, and in Walters's discussion of Mudimbe, such subversion concerns the way in which Cavendish transformed her own books into forms that expanded beyond the physical covers of the volumes, beyond the circumscribing parameters of library walls and the literary marketplace, into extensive networks of allusion and interactivity.

Kaye Mitchell's chapter, '"That Library of Uncatalogued Pleasure": Queerness and the Archive in Twentieth-Century Gay Fiction and Beyond', also intersects with these issues of history and the space of the library in fiction and in the world. As Mitchell argues, there may be a democratizing effect in the construction of actual archives that reflect lesbian, bisexual, gay, and transgender identities and histories. When such countercultural archives are composed of nonnormative forms of document, such as ephemera, they may also open new modes of archiving and of interpretation. However, as Mitchell cautions, 'the "queering of the archive" is not a straightforward process, and [. . .] the very notion of the archive is apt to be treated with scepticism within queer culture'. Such scepticism resides in part in the Foucauldian and Derridean recognitions of the archive as mechanisms of power and control. It is precisely through this ambivalence of the archive, as a site of possibilities and limitations, that Mitchell discusses the symbolic function of representations of libraries in Radclyffe Hall's *The Well of Loneliness* (1928), Alan Hollinghurst's *The Swimming Pool Library* (1988), and Sarah Waters's *Fingersmith* (2002). As Mitchell shows, each of the novels approaches the problems of documenting and memorizing queer identities in ways that do not repeat the totalizing and exclusionary function of traditional archives and that recognise that the place of the library and the interpretation of the archive, are permeated by desire. In this sense, Mitchell's chapter would bear comparison to Keen's discussion of the libidinal and sensory aspects of archival research, to Walters's discussion of Mudimbe's engagement with homosexuality, and to McQuillan's discussion of amour.

Spaces of reading are addressed in a literal sense in Andrew Peckham's chapter, 'Cataloguing Architecture: the Library of the Architect'. Concentrating on German rationalist architect O.M. Ungers and on Swiss architects Herzog and de Meuron, Peckham discusses the complex relationships between architectural and textual spaces and practices. Peckham's intention here is to investigate the notion of 'the library of the architect', in two key, related senses. First, it concerns specific library buildings and the ways in which their design may reflect on the content, function, and history of the library as an institutional form, and the way in which their interior and exterior design may reflect technological changes in forms of writing and communication—the tablet, the scroll, the book, and the contemporary data landscape. But, second, it also involves the sense in which architects collect, preserve, and represent their own work in the codexical form of the catalogue and the way in which such forms gesture toward their own collection in libraries, including those of the architects themselves. In this latter respect, for example, Peckham intersects with Benjamin's discussion of 'the collector's concern for consistency and completion' in 'Unpacking My Library', arguing that, nevertheless, such unity must also recognise 'traces of instability'. So, we return to the issue of the library's ruins, and thus its future.

Finally, on this note of future forms and understandings of the library, or of libraries, I should note that the order of chapters for edited collections is normatively constructed through a mediation of contrapuntal differences or thematic similarities, and differences in authorial ability or acumen, a kind of tabular flower arranging that attempts to capitalise on its contents page and to structure the complex heterogeneity of the form of the edited collection. Hence, the arrangement of these chapters in this book, in alphabetical order of the author's surname, requires a brief explanation. Such a strategy was an organizing principle in Barthes's book, *A Lovers' Discourse: Fragments* (1977). Here, the sections of the book are arranged alphabetically, the key point being that alphabetical organization, one form of order which is nevertheless entirely arbitrary, is at odds with the linearity of traditional narrative writing and reading, another form of order. The aim of such alphabeticisation was to evade the normative strictures of autobiographical narrative, in order to open the text to contingent, nonlinear readings. Similarly, an example of the way in which systems of order may open up different readings might be given in terms of the U.S. Dewey Decimal system (1876), which in the shelf arrangement of books serially abuts unconnected subjects. There is a clear way in which browsing might open up contingent encounters with books. To some extent, as a result of the scientific, classificatory values of the system, it allows (in open-access mode rather than closed-stack systems) for readers to transgress disciplinary and thematic boundaries. Nevertheless, given that edited collections are almost never read in sequence, in opposition to autobiographies, perhaps the most aleatory approach for *this* book would be to submit to the order of the alphabet. Thus, alongside the suggestions I have given for thematic relations and differences between the chapters of this collection, the alphabetic organization of the chapters in this book through the contingencies of the author's surname is partly an issue of relinquishing the determining effects of editorial control and is designed to facilitate the kind of chance encounters and new interpretations enabled by taxonomies for its readers.

NOTES

1. Gloria Leckie and John Buschman, 'Introduction: The Necessity for Theoretically Informed Critique in Library and Information Science (LIS)', in *Critical Theory for Library and Information Science: Exploring the Social from across the Disciplines*, ed. Gloria Leckie, Lisa Given, and John Buschman (Santa Barbara, CA: ABC-CLIO, 2010), xi–xiii.
2. The Canadian journal *Archivaria*, generally speaking, and Terry Cook's work in particular, would be exemplary in this regard. For the latter, see, for example, Terry Cook and Joan M. Schwartz, 'Archives, Records, and Power: from (Postmodern) Theory to (Archival) Performance', *Archival Science* 2 (2002), pp.171–85.
3. For this definition of 'the archive', see Michel Foucault, *The Archaeology of Knowledge* [1969] (Abingdon, UK: Routledge, 2003), p. 145.
4. It is not the intention of this introduction to engage with the history of the library form, or of specific libraries per se; such an engagement would necessitate prolonged consideration of historiography and disciplinarity. Nevertheless, with some relevance to the kind of cultural analyses of this collection, and as introductions to such a history, see Mathew Battles, *Library: An Unquiet History* (London: Vintage, 2004); and Fred Lerner, *The Story of Libraries: From the Invention of Writing to the Computer Age* (New York and London: Continuum, 2009). Intersections with the history of the book and the library are also found in Steven Roger Fischer, *A History of Reading* (London: Reaktion, 2003); and Shafquat Towheed, Rosalind Crone, and Katie Halsey, eds., *The History of Reading* (Abingdon, UK, and New York: Routledge, 2011).
5. In terms of an analysis of a mixed media milieu, which nevertheless appears to retain something of a nostalgia for the codex, the sense in which electronic texts should 'act as a supplement to, not a substitute for Gutenberg's great machine' and in which print and digital texts could be combined, but nevertheless with the printed version of the *apex* of a pyramidal structure of publication forms, see Robert Darnton, *The Case for Books: Past, Present and Future* (New York: PublicAffairs, 2009), pp. 76–77. Comparatively, the desire for a comingled and complementary relation between printed and electronic texts is expressed in Ted Striphas, *The Late Age of Print: Everyday Book Culture from Consumerism to Control* (New York: Columbia University Press, 2009). In terms of digital affirmation, the Internet has been argued to offer the potential for a 'universal library' whose connectivity and accessibility transcend the 'paper prison' of the codex and the traditional library, and for electronic books to combine digital connectivity with the paged format of the traditional codex. See Christian Vandendorpe, *From Papyrus to Hypertext: Toward the Universal Digital Library* [1999], trans. Phyllis Aronoff and Howard Scott (Urbana, Chicago, and Springfield: University of Illinois Press, 2009), p. 164.
6. Roland Barthes, 'From Work to Text' [1971], in Roland Barthes, *Image – Music – Text*, trans. Stephen Heath (London: Fontana Press, 1977), pp. 156–57. We might note, given this discussion, that books and shelves are themselves technologies with complex histories. See Henry Petroski, *The Book on the Bookshelf* (New York: Vintage Books, 2000).
7. Roland Barthes, 'Dominici, or the Triumph of Literature', in *Mythologies* [1957], (London: Vintage, 1993), pp. 43–46.
8. Walter Benjamin, 'Unpacking My Library: A Talk about Book Collecting' [1931], in Walter Benjamin, *Illuminations,* ed. Hannah Arendt and trans. Harry Zohn (New York: Shocken Books, 1969), p. 59.
9. Benjamin, 'Unpacking My Library', p. 60.
10. Ibid.

11. Benjamin, 'Unpacking My Library', p. 66.
12. Ibid.
13. G. W. F. Hegel, *Elements of the Philosophy of Right* [1821], ed. Allen W. Wood (Cambridge: Cambridge University Press, 1991), pp. 90–91.
14. Ibid., pp. 100–01.
15. Benjamin, 'Unpacking my Library', p. 67.
16. Ibid., p. 66.
17. On the transience of the collector, see ibid., p. 63.
18. Ibid., p. 64.
19. Jacques Derrida, 'Paper or Me, You Know . . . (New Speculations on a Luxury of the Poor)' [1997], in Jacques Derrida, *Paper Machine*, trans. Rachel Bowlby (Stanford, CA: Stanford University Press, 2005), p. 42.
20. Jacques Derrida, 'Biodegradables: Seven Diary Fragments', trans. Peggy Kamuf, *Critical Inquiry* 15, no. 4 (Summer 1989), p. 865. In my discussion of this text, I abstract Derrida's specific engagement with the archives and legacy of Paul de Man, in order to emphasise and develop the more general aspects of Derrida's positions on deconstruction, history, and technological memory forms.
21. Derrida, 'Biodegradables', p. 821.
22. Jacques Derrida, 'This Strange Institution Called Literature' [1989], in Jacques Derrida, *Acts of Literature*, ed. Derek Attridge (London: Routledge, 1992), p. 74.
23. In this context, we should note Derrida's general point that 'deconstructive interpretation and writing would come along, without any soteriological mission, to "save", in some sense, lost heritages'. Yet 'This is not done without a counterevaluation, in particular a political one. One does not exhume just anything. And one transforms while exhuming'. See Derrida, 'Biodegradables', p. 821. We must recognise, then, that any supposed historical reclamation of the library must always be a reinterpretation, a transformation.

BIBLIOGRAPHY

Roland Barthes. 'Death of the Author' [1968], in Roland Barthes, *Image – Music – Text*, translated by Stephen Heath. London: Fontana Press, 1977.
Roland Barthes. 'Dominici, or the Triumph of Literature', in *Mythologies* [1957]. London: Vintage, 1993.
Roland Barthes. 'From Work to Text' [1971], in Roland Barthes, *Image – Music – Text*, translated by Stephen Heath. London: Fontana Press, 1977.
Mathew Battles. *Library: An Unquiet History*. London: Vintage, 2004.
Walter Benjamin, 'Unpacking My Library: A Talk about Book Collecting' [1931], in Walter Benjamin, *Illuminations*, edited by Hannah Arendt and translated by Harry Zohn. New York: Shocken Books, 1969.
Walter Benjamin, 'The Work of Art in the Age of Mechanical Reproduction' [1936], in Walter Benjamin, *Illuminations*, edited by Hannah Arendt and translated by Harry Zohn (New York: Shocken Books, 1969.
Terry Cook and Joan M. Schwartz. 'Archives, Records, and Power: from (Postmodern) Theory to (Archival) Performance'. *Archival Science* 2 (2002).
Robert Darnton. *The Case for Books: Past, Present and Future*. New York: PublicAffairs, 2009.
Jacques Derrida, 'Biodegradables: Seven Diary Fragments', translated by Peggy Kamuf. *Critical Inquiry* 15, no. 4 (Summer, 1989).
Jacques Derrida, 'Paper or Me, You Know . . . (New Speculations on a Luxury of the Poor)' [1997], in Jacques Derrida, *Paper Machine*, translated by Rachel Bowlby. Stanford, CA: Stanford University Press, 2005.

Jacques Derrida, 'This Strange Institution Called Literature' [1989], in Jacques Derrida, *Acts of Literature*, edited by Derek Attridge. London: Routledge, 1992.
Steven Roger Fischer. *A History of Reading*. London: Reaktion, 2003.
Michel Foucault. *The Archaeology of Knowledge* [1969]. Abingdon, UK: Routledge, 2003.
G. W. F. Hegel. *Elements of the Philosophy of Right* [1821], edited by Allen W. Wood. Cambridge: Cambridge University Press, 1991.
Gloria Leckie and John Buschman. 'Introduction: the Necessity for Theoretically Informed Critique in Library and Information Science (LIS)', in *Critical Theory for Library and Information Science: Exploring the Social from Across the Disciplines*, edited by Gloria Leckie, Lisa Given, and John Buschman. Santa Barbara, CA: ABC-CLIO, 2010.
Fred Lerner. *The Story of Libraries: From the Invention of Writing to the Computer Age*. New York and London: Continuum, 2009.
Henry Petroski. *The Book on the Bookshelf*. New York: Vintage Books, 2000.
Ted Striphas. *The Late Age of Print: Everyday Book Culture from Consumerism to Control*. New York: Columbia University Press, 2009.
Shafquat Towheed, Rosalind Crone, and Katie Halsey, eds. *The History of Reading*. Abingdon and New York: Routledge, 2011.
Christian Vandendorpe. *From Papyrus to Hypertext: Toward the Universal Digital Library* [1999], translated by Phyllis Aronoff and Howard Scott. Urbana, Chicago, and Springfield: University of Illinois Press, 2009.

1 Index

Geoffrey Bennington

> The hearer is unable to see both the road he is being led to take and the goal to which it leads.
>
> Wittgenstein, 'Lecture on Ethics'

This is what I have to say.
What I have to say is—this.

Indexes are an important, if rather disreputable means of access to a book. How many of us make a preliminary—and often final—judgement of a book on the basis of what is or is not in its index, or on the basis of a short passage or two that its index points out?

So it came as something of a surprise to me to discover that Gérard Genette's *Seuils*, a sort of poetics of approaches to books (titles, prefaces, acknowledgements, dedications, cover notes, etc.), does not include a chapter on indexes. I was unable to discover this by consulting the index, although the work does have one, a little unusual for a French publication of this kind. This index is itself presided over or approached (assuming one approached indexes from the top) by the following preliminary note:

> With the usual load of errors and omissions [I can confirm that there are several incorrect entries], this index refers to actual occurrences of authors' names and their implicit occurrences through mention of a title. A little more useful would have been an index of titles (sometimes several per work), with an indication of names (same remark) and dates (same again), but I am told that such an index would have been longer than the book. Such as it is, as with most indexes, its real function is to avoid the shaming remark: *'no index'*.[1]

What is an index? Henry B. Wheatley's (1879) path-breaking book of that title opens with a confident definition: 'An index is an indicator or pointer out of the position of required information, such as the finger-post on a high road, or the index finger of the human hand'.[2] One hundred years later, Borko and Bernier's *Indexing Concepts and Methods* wants to say that the road is already an index with respect to the places it links and that the road sign is an index to that index, and if this extension of the definition allows them to assert confidently that 'social interaction, as we know it today, would be impossible without indexes', it no doubt also permits the suspicions we may have about the definition they subsequently quote from the American National Standards Institute, according to which an indexing system is 'the set of prescribed procedures (manual and/or machine) for organizing the contents of records of knowledge for the purposes of retrieval and dissemination'.[3]

Roads, road-signs, pointing fingers, and prescription: let these be an index of the problems awaiting us.

Some preliminary propositions include the following:

- A book that could be exhaustively indexed would already be its own index.
- All indexes are constitutively imperfect.
- There is no absolutely indexless book.
- Indexes are the *end* of what they index.
- No index can index itself.

Indexes are not usually thought of as integral parts of the books they index. In order to index at all, indexes must be separable from what they index. Only this allows us to make any sense of Genette's possibility that the index be longer than the book—this would be a meaningless idea if the index were really and inseparably part of the book. An index may usually be bound into the volume it indexes, but it need not be, just as the catalogue of a library usually stands on the shelves of the library it catalogues, but can also stand on the shelves of other libraries, in whose catalogues it appears as one book among others. And just as a catalogue would not usually include any entry to itself, so an index would not normally have an entry for itself, nor would each of its entries normally end with a reference to the page on which that entry occurs. There is no need to put up a signpost pointing to the place where you are.[4] One of the Latin senses of the word *index* is catalogue, as in the *Index Librorurn Prohibitorum*.

This position of relative exteriority means that often enough indexes are not compiled by the author of the (rest of the) book, and are not generally thought to be part of what the author's signature subscribes to or is answerable for (although Wheatley does quote 'the great Spanish bibliographer Antonio', himself quoting a 'once celebrated Spaniard' to the effect 'that the index of a book should be made by the author, even if the book itself were written by someone else' (191). Works of French philosophy, such as Derrida's *La Vérité en peinture* [*The Truth in Painting*], often do not contain an index, but translators of such works are sometimes invited to compile one.

There are traditionally two sorts of indexes, derived, I imagine, from the scholastic distinction between nominal and real definitions, and although neither Wheatley nor Borko and Bernier recommend such a division, it is not difficult to see why it might be made: an *index nominorum* essentially records the places where names or their obvious substitutes (unambiguous pronouns, definite descriptions such as 'the author of *Waverley*', 'the Stagirite', 'the left-hander from Liverpool', etc.) appear in the text, and it is something a computer can compile quite easily, with a little help in the case of the substitutes. An *index rerum* does not record the occurrence of words at all, but of sentences dealing with, referring to or otherwise discussing certain 'things' or concepts or themes. Particular words in the text can be a useful guide in compiling such an index, but an *index rerum* will typically not record every occurrence of the word that figures at the beginning of a given entry and may well refer to pages on which that word does not appear at all. It will certainly not contain an entry for every word that appears in the text, whereas an *index nominorum* can reasonably be expected to contain an entry for every proper name that appears in the text. A computer has trouble with an *index rerum*. An index is not a concordance.

Lyotard's *Discours, figure* [*Discourse, Figure*] and *Le différend* [*The Différend*] are fairly unusual among works of French philosophy in that they contain indexes. Each has both an *index nominorun* and an *index rerum*. In the first of these, one of the names to appear, between those of Lyotard, Corinne and Lyotard-May, Andrée, is that of Lyotard, J.-F. Even though Lyotard, J.-F. wrote every page of *Discours, figure*, the entry here does not just read 'passim', because the name in question does not appear on every page. Nor does it include an entry to the cover of the book and the title page, where the proper name it is indexing does, however, appear, because these occurrences are already in principle part of the larger index formed by the catalogue, allowing whole works to be distinguished from each other by means of their title. This is also why it is possible for the index of names in *Le différend* not to include the name of Lyotard, J-F. at all.

All six references to Lyotard, J.-F. are in footnotes in the text. One of these footnotes suggests how the discussion of fantasy being developed in the text could be applied to the theatre, and ends with a list of references to work in this field. The last reference here is to an article by J-F. Lyotard, who appears in the list with no marks to distinguish him from the other authors cited or to link his name with that of the book's signatory (345n). One other of the six entries refers to an article co-authored by Lyotard with Dominique Avron (who also has an entry in the index referring to this same note; 89n). Of the remaining four entries, one seems mysteriously to be referring to a piece by Bruno Lemenuel, and one has to have read or seen that piece to know that Lyotard is again its coauthor (373n). This absence of the proper name to which the index might be referring is also the case in one of the other entries, where the footnote refers to an article without giving an author's name, and one infers from an introductory 'Que le lecteur me permette de renvoyer à . . .' that Lyotard is its author (which the index entry then apparently confirms; 355n). Neither of the two remaining entries yields a proper name either, but in both cases the pronoun *Je*, which we refer without difficulty to the proper name on the title page and to the 'subject of enunciation', or more accurately the signatory, of the book as a whole.

This name in the *index nominorum*, then, does not quite obey the rules we thought we could detect by stating that such an index referred to occurrences of words in the text. It is not simply that in the case of the author of the book we include in the index occurrences of the word *Je* (or *nous*, or *on*, or *l'auteur de ces lignes*, etc.), for there are many such occurrences in the course of the text which are not indexed and which one would not expect to see indexed. The principle seems to be that the *index nominorum*, which we have suggested does not really form part of the book it indexes, refers from its position more or less outside the book to references the book *itself* makes to outside the book: the author's own name appears in it to the extent that the book refers to other work by him not in the same volume, or not in the same unit of writing (in the case of a collection of essays, for example). And when the pronoun *Je* or its surrogates appear, it counts as replacing the author's proper name and is therefore indexed only when referring to the author as author of *other* work, not the present book as a whole. But the fact that these pronominal substitutes can occur in this way only in the case of the name of the author suggests a claim over those external texts which can pull them into the field dominated by the signature and no longer simply the proper name of the author.

On this hypothesis, the *index rerum* would be different, referring from outside the book to pages within the book where certain questions or concepts or objects are discussed. Whether the book then refers outside itself to other texts on these matters would presumably be a question for the *index nominorum* again. Compiling an *index rerum* involves weighty philosophical decisions. It suggests as a basic principle that the compiler is able to distinguish between a purely verbal occurrence of a word, and a thematically or conceptually significant occurrence. It also assumes that the compiler is able to recognize the presence of a concept or theme in the absence of its name. The compiler of the index for the English translation of *La Vérité en peinture* soon realized that something about that book made it virtually impossible to compile a satisfactory *index rerum*, and wondered why. There was no obvious sense in which the book did not need such an index (it does not index itself), but a suspicion that Derrida's work defied indexing according to the traditional rules. Quite apart from the fact that Derrida explicitly and exhaustively casts doubt on the coherence of notions such as theme, concept or meaning, is it always possible to distinguish in Derrida's writing between merely verbal occurrences of words and conceptually significant occurrences, or to give a name to a theme being treated but not named in certain pages of his work? The temptation is strong just to write 'passim' after an entry such as 'writing' or 'text', for example—but passim is the least useful reference an index can provide, and would seem here to duplicate the sort of error or misunderstanding that would be involved in writing 'passim' after the author's name in the *index nominorum*.

It might be worth consulting *Discours, figure* to try to find out more about indexes, and what better way than by using the index it provides? In the 'Index des concepts et des termes allemands' of Lyotard's book (this conjunction giving quite some food for thought), there is no entry for *index*. This may seem surprising, not because the book contains indexes (we've already seen that indexes do not refer to themselves—however, it seems reasonable for the existence of an index to be indexed in the table of contents, somewhere between the index proper and the catalogue), but because the term appears in the title of the first main section of the book ('Dialectique, index, forme', first part of 'Signification et désignation', immediately following an introductory section), and the term *index* appears several times in the text. But scanning the index for cognate terms, we do find an entry for *indicateur*. This 'indicateur' (in French the word means a variety of things ranging from a police informer to a signpost to a railway timetable) provides no page-references proper, but refers the reader back to the entry *déictique*. This sort of intra-indexical reference need not surprise us or be taken as transgressing the rule that indexes don't refer to themselves, so long as the term referred to elsewhere in the index provides page-references to the text (in Borko and Bernier, the longest entry in the index ['prepared by Charles L. Bernier, Past President of the American Society of Indexers, in accordance with the recommendations of that society'] is the entry for the term *index*, which entry consists exclusively of cross-references to other entries in the index)—and the entry for *déictique* duly does so—first to the very opening pages I have just referred to, in which the term *index* occurs, then to pages dealing with Benveniste's theory of deictics, then to Husserl (these references also, of course, appear in the index of names). But after these references there is a surprise: the final reference in the entry reads: 'exemples de [déictiques], tous les termes de l'Index en tant que tels' ('examples of deictics, all the terms in the Index as such', where the 'as such' qualifies the terms).

If all the terms in Lyotard's index, or in an index in general, are deictics (or indexicals, as I believe they are called in analytic philosophy), then this would seem to be because they point out or indicate, as *indicateurs* ('indicators' being indeed the technical indexer's term for such references, as Borko and Bernier point out, as opposed to cross-references of the sort we have just seen) the places in the volume to consult for discussion of the concept concerned. The term 'deictic' is itself no exception to this, in its first entries at any rate, pointing us to those pages of *Discours, figure* which discuss deictics. But this final reference is not an indicator of this type, giving no page numbers, nor is it a cross-reference referring to other entries which do give page numbers, but it refers to all the terms of the index *en tant que tels*, as such, insofar as they are terms in an index, insofar as indexing, indicating, or pointing out is what they do. We would not understand in what sense the terms exemplified deixis unless we understood what a deictic was, so this index entry clearly has a privilege over all the others. Of all the terms in the index, *deictic* is in some sense the *most* deictic: it says what it does as it does it; it accumulates or capitalizes in itself the being-deictic of all the other entries by promising to tell, if we refer to the pages it indicates, what a deictic, and therefore an index entry 'en tant que tel' is. We were using Lyotard's index to try to find out about indexes, but we need to refer to certain pages in the text to discover what we are up to in so doing—except that this final reference is not to elsewhere in the text at all, but tells us to stay just where we are, 'you are here', where deixis and indexing are exemplified. So if the whole entry to 'déictique' seemed to capitalize the being-deictic of the deictics that index entries are, then this final reference in that entry ought to capitalize that capitalization itself, showing or indicating itself as deixis or indicating itself. By pointing to all the terms in the index as such, at the as such of index entries, this one is really pointing to itself as what points, as *the* example of an indicator, the most indexical index in the index. But this is precisely the one entry that no longer indexes at all, as it is neither an indicator nor a cross-reference—we've seen that an index is only an index to the extent that it points outside itself and not to itself, which this entry seems to do. Unless we have to imagine that the entry which best tells us something about pointing outside can only do so by pointing at itself pointing. Truth itself presenting its own self-presentation, *index sui*. And if we consult the entry for deictics in the index of *Le différend*, which has no entry for 'index' either, then we find that the final reference, after the section numbers where deixis is most explicitly a theme in the book, is a reference to another term in the index, which happens to be the term *sui-référence*, 'self-reference'.

If the concentration of self-reference happens here around the term *deictic*, which, according to the pages of *Discours, figure* we have now located with the help of the index, implies a pointing out or designating which always involves a specific negativity generated by the distance between the pointer and what is pointed to, then we seem to have a paradox whereby the term or type of term which allows language the ability to point outside itself (for we are talking about nothing less than the problem of reference here), cannot help pointing *to* itself, or else the term that points to itself and seems to run the risk of enclosing us in the index and never allow us out is precisely the term that points out(side), or at least points out the pointing out(side) of deictics in general, here demonstrated by all the terms in the index as such, except the term that says so. One item in the list of indexed or indexical terms has grown to monstrous proportions, bigger than the set of which it is a member. We might link this to a suspicion that this mysterious final non-reference of the final entry for *déictique* is something like the *word Index*, which *entitles* the Index in which all the terms, including the term *deictic* appear. This title, 'Index', is not itself an index on the same level as are the terms gathered under its title; however, it is something like an index, as we have said, when it appears on the contents page. But to see that, and to make the link with the last reference of the entry for *déictique*, we have to allow that reference somehow to point to that title, and the title to point to the entry, in a way that still looks like the deixis to which this was supposed to be an exception. (*Index* in Latin also means 'a title'.) And maybe this is not so unlike the problem we encountered with the entry to 'Lyotard, J-F.' in the *index nominorum*, or at least with those references where the proper name did not explicitly appear: just as the *Je* in the text could only communicate with the 'Lyotard' in the index via the position of the author's proper name on the title page or the cover, in a position which seems similar to that occupied by the word *Index* entitling the Index, exposing its external surface to a greater index (the contents page).

This turning of the inside out, the way in which apparent self-reference seems to implicate the exposure of a title or a cover, the outer limits of a frame or an enclosure, reminds me of the cover of one of my dictionaries, which bears a reproduction of part of one of the pages within the dictionary—the page which happens to contain the entry for the word *dictionary*, which entry is circled in red, in imitation of the way an enthusiastic but inconsiderate user might highlight a particularly important entry. This has the obvious advantage to the publisher that anyone in the bookshop who sees the dictionary but does not know what the word means can consult the dictionary to find out, without yet having to know how to open and consult a dictionary. The word *dictionary*, even when it appears in or on a dictionary, is not, of course, a dictionary, in the way that Lyotard's index implied that the word *deictic*, in an index at least, was a deictic. But the word *dictionary* in a dictionary could be a deictic, even though at first sight, it does not look as though a dictionary is really an index. Maybe we can find out more about all this by consulting the dictionary, which we now know how to use. One of the things that we might discover from the entry reproduced on the cover is the etymology of the word *dictionary* (and the etymology of the word *etymology*, which it gives as the Greek words *etumos* and *logos*, meaning 'true' and 'word' [or such like]): the word *dictionary* comes from the Latin *dictio*, the action of saying. *Index*, on the other hand, comes from the Latin *index*, meaning 'an indicator, a discoverer, an informer, a catalogue or list, an inscription, the title of a book': the index finger is so called because it is the one used for pointing to or out. But I know from watching a video of Michel Serres in the Musée d'Orsay talking about dictionaries that the true etymology of this Latin etymology of *dictionary* is the Greek verb *deiknumi*, 'I show, I indicate, I point out'. In this case, the 'true meaning' of *dictionary* begins to look very close to that of *index* after all.

We have never really managed to get out of the index, then, away from the indicator, the pointing finger. There was a slogan in May 1968 which said, 'Quand le doigt montre la lune, l'imbécile regarde le doigt' ('When the finger points to the moon, the imbecile looks at the finger'). In his demonstration of the vacuity of imagining that language or language acquisition can satisfactorily be thought of in terms of a fundamental ostensive definition, Wittgenstein shows, among other things, that this supposed primal scene (pointing finger, index, *deiknumi*, accompanied by the name of what's pointed to—'this is an index', 'this is a dictionary', and so on) can never reduce a necessary uncertainty as to what exactly is being pointed out (this a result of the irreducible exteriority of what's pointed to with respect to the pointer, as also stressed by Lyotard), and goes on to detect a slightly different problem, no longer to do with what is pointed at but with the gesture of pointing itself—why assume that it is self-evident that one should look in the direction going from wrist to fingertip rather than the reverse?[5] 'This is the moon', says the pointer, and Wittgenstein's imbecile looks at the person pointing, or for there is no a priori reason to assume that the imbecile knows that pointing is pointing in any direction at all, he just looks at the finger. (Heidegger half envisages this possibility in §17 of *Being and Time*, where his exemplary sign is not a signpost (though that is in fact the first example he gives), but a red arrow apparently fitted to cars at the time, in lieu of what we would now call indicators, precisely, to allow the driver to point out the way he is going to turn. No point looking for something pointed out here, nor of simply staring at the arrow itself—the point is to get out of the way before the car runs you down: Heidegger's example has an imperative element which his own analysis does not take up. The root of Wittgenstein's point is that no indicator can simultaneously indicate and indicate that indicating is what it's doing. If pointing out is how we are supposed to learn language, how do we learn the language of pointing out? (Wittgenstein 1973: §§9, 38)—it's as though we learned how to use signposts because the first one we saw had a signpost marked 'signpost' pointing at it.[6] The question whether Wittgenstein's notion of rules, which he *also* describes as signposts (§85), solves this problem, would take us down another road, and involve using this whole question of pointing, showing or indicating to cast some doubt on the supposed radicality of the break between the Wittgenstein of the *Tractatus* and the Wittgenstein of the *Investigations*, with a detour via *On Certainty*, where the moon has a part to play (in fact there's a whole planetary and even galactic drama underlying everything I'm trying to say here, running from earth to moon, to Mars, to the sun, to the starry sky above my head).[7] 'This is the moon': I look firmly at the finger. Trying to save the situation, the disconcerted pedagogue corrects himself, saying, 'No, sorry, this is a pointing finger'. 'What is?' I ask. 'This', he says, pointing at it with the index finger of his other hand. 'And what's *that?*' I ask, staring at the second finger. The finger is soon pointing at me, and I can hardly avoid looking at it now, in the sort of curious foreshortening of perspective that reduces the finger to a directionless blob in those posters of Kitchener or of Uncle Sam picking me out for service. At this point, the feeling of imbecility becomes an uncomprehending sense of obligation, doom, and destiny.

Staring at the last part of Lyotard's index entry for the term *deictic*, which is the one place in the index not doing what it should be doing, although it seems as though it ought to be the most indexical part of the index, I feel just such an imbecility descend: a finger pointing at itself pointing. Self-reference, but the terms that are pointed out as pointing to themselves are the terms that point out of the system at something else. They are precisely what should save us from being trapped in the dictionary and its system of intra-linguistic signification. For, if we finally turn to the pages of *Discours, figure* indicated by the index entry, we find that deictics are precisely *not* like most words in the language in that they really have no meaning in the system of langue in Saussure's sense [in the *Course in General Linguistics* (1916)], as we can verify by looking in the dictionary. Most words in the language are given an effect of semantic content by being defined in terms of other words on the same level in the system—according to Saussure's 'differences without positive terms' definition, each term gains its identity and value by definition in terms of other terms, according to what Saussure calls the associative and syntagmatic axes, and Jakobson, the operations of selection and combination. In most cases, it is possible to give a more or less approximate substitute term or to unpack semantic subsets which will define a whale, for example, as an aquatic mammal or a hut as a small wooden house. But if selection and combination can account exhaustively for all the features of language at the phonematic level, this attempted extension into the semantic level runs into trouble, says Lyotard, with deictics, because deictics have no meaning outside their actualization in particular acts of discourse or *parole*. The same cannot really be said for other words, because the dictionary is able to give more or less exhaustive lists of the potential meanings which can be actualized for them in any given act of parole, whereas for deictics all the dictionary can give is a *grammatical* definition in terms of function, not a list of possible meanings. It seems clear enough that Lyotard is right to say that the lexical definition of *whale* as 'aquatic mammal' is of a different order to the grammatical definition of *I* as 'first-person pronoun'. In other words, deictics seem to defy the distinction between langue and parole, at least as Saussure describes that distinction: the system of language should prescribe the meanings possible in the acts of *parole* but in the case of deictics that meaning only happens at all in the instant of utterance. For the Lyotard of *Discours, figure* at least,[8] deictics have the privilege of allowing the 'flat', horizontal negativity of the language system to communicate with, and be disturbed by, the 'deep' vertical negativity of space (thought of here in phenomenological terms as the sensory, and essentially visual space around the 'origin point' of the body in the world). This 'origin point' is defined in terms of the deictics 'I-now-here', which get their meaning each time differently in each act of discourse. From that point, the object of the discourse is designated at a distance by further deictics: 'Indiquer, c'est tendre l'index vers un lieu' ('To indicate is to stretch out the index finger towards a place'; 37). There is something irreducibly nonlinguistic (at least in the sense of a system of *langue*) here, and deictics are the trace in language of that alterity. (It might be worth pointing out that it does not seem that defiance of lexical definition in a dictionary is a sufficient criterion for the identification of a deictic—lots of non-deictic terms [particles, syncategoremes in general] only get a grammatical definition, and proper names seem to defy both lexical *and* grammatical definitions.[9] It is also not clear how the various very different deictics would be distinguished in this description, nor why they should all [including *now, yesterday*, and so on] be given a description which is essentially *spatial*.) Whence a critique, in these early pages of *Discours, figure*, of Hegel's description of sense-certainty at the beginning of the *Phenomenology of Spirit*: Lyotard reads Hegel as demanding that the spatial depth of the sensory field as marked by deictics should be sublated into the language of the concept via an assimilation, which Lyotard argues against, of the two types of negativity. Here Lyotard opposes to dialectics what he calls a diadeictics:

> Diadeictics is not a dialectic in Hegel's sense, precisely in that the former presupposes the empty gap, the depth separating shower and shown, and even if this gap is referred onto the table of what is shown, it will there be open to a possible index, in a distance which language can never signify without remainder.[10]

And if we turn now to what is said of deictics in *Le différend*, we find that although the phenomenological perspective is dropped, deictics retain a not dissimilar role as designators functioning only in terms of the 'now' of the event of each sentence, replaceable by the appropriate proper names (including dates, measures, place names, etc.) but distinct in their operation from signification as such. Deictics operate as designators, not signifiers, and now not even bodily presence in a sensory field precedes them, insofar as 'I' is a deictic among others and is no more foundational or secure than any other.

This leads me to think that Lyotard ought, even with *Le différend*, to maintain his criticisms of Derrida's reading of Husserl's account of the deictic 'I'.[11] It is in fact quite difficult at first to see how the two types of reading can even communicate. It will be remembered that Derrida takes Husserl's recognition of the status of the deictic 'I' (as an 'essentially occasional expression') to undermine the search for a purity of expression untouched by, precisely, indication. Even in the intimacy of interior monologue where indication and indexes should not be necessary, such 'occasional' expressions defy replacement by 'objective' expressions.

Derrida's deduction, at two different moments in *La voix et le phénomène* [*Speech and Phenomena*], claims that the statement 'I am' implies my death: the presence of the present of the I/here/now implies an ideality of the present generated by the possibility of its formal repetition as present in my empirical absence and therefore after my death. Knowing the presence of the present means knowing my transience with respect to it. The argument is similar in 'Cogito et histoire de la folie' [*Cogito and the History of Madness*],[12] in which it is suggested that the transcendental status of the thinking subject is only deduced based on the necessary possibility of the death of the empirical subject, which death can then, from the transcendental vantage point attained only thus, be relegated, *après coup*, to the status of an empirical accident. This supposed empirical accident then becomes, in a manoeuvre constant in Derrida's thinking, the quasi-transcendental of the transcendental itself, and is as such no longer strictly empirical or transcendental at all—which is also why conditions of possibility in Derrida are always also conditions of impossibility. The trick of transcendental philosophy in this case can reasonably be formulated as an undercover operation performed on the deictic 'I' in its transformation into the so-called philosophical 'I', which no longer functions strictly as a deictic at all but as a sort of bogus proper name of the transcendental subject.

The second moment of Derrida's deduction is based on the general possibility, recognized by Husserl, of the absence of the object of intuition in the functioning of discourse. A proposition must be able to be understood in the absence of its object. Now Derrida says that if this is true in general, it must also be true of the object of the pronoun 'I'—what I say must be at least minimally understandable not only in the absence of what I say I see, for example, but in the absence of my seeing. Insofar as it is legitimate to say that a proposition bespeaks the absence of its object (and it *is* legitimate if we accept the logic of the 'necessary possibility', which functions throughout Derrida's work to disrupt all oppositions of the type essence/accident, law/case, and so on and is perhaps the major challenge to any attempt to formalize deconstruction or to write its operations in a symbolic logic), then it is legitimate to say that it also bespeaks the absence of the speaking subject, and a quick way of saying that absence in its most radical possibility is to refer to it as death. When I say 'I am', then, I say 'I am dead'.

Lyotard's polite objection to this in a long footnote in *Discours, figure* runs as follows: the point about deictics in general is that they cannot be understood in terms of the flat negativity of the system of language, which they traverse towards an exteriority ruled by the incompatible 'deep' negativity of perceptual space. The disagreement with metaphysics, as represented for Lyotard here by Hegel's *Phenomenology*, is that it attempts to bring that second negativity into the domain of the first, under the domination of the first, and therefore think deictics along the same lines as other elements in the language system—which cannot legitimately be done. In Husserl's terminology, this is a general attempt to rescue the exteriority implied by indication to the supposed interiority of expression, or the ideality of meaning. Derrida, at least in the second part of the deduction I have just recalled, treats the deictic 'I' as though it were assimilable to any element of the language system (it must be able to function in the absence of its object like any other sign)—but treating the 'I' as ideally assimilable to other words is just what Lyotard wants to criticize Husserl for, and so Derrida must apparently be going wrong if he does the same thing. This criticism would go along with the more general suspicion that Derrida enfolds everything in his notion of text, and Lyotard's refusal, much later in his book, to assimilate what he calls 'difference itself' to what Derrida calls the trace.[13]

This is not an easy argument to untangle. Let me recall that Lyotard detects a complication in Saussure (from whom he takes the notion of language system as at least initially satisfactory for terms *other than* deictics—and we have already suggested some reservations about this view in terms of other sorts of nonlexical items): everything Saussure says tends towards the description of that system in terms of value calculated in the differential way since become so familiar. Why then does he persist in using the traditional (metaphysical) terminology of signifier and signified, when the notion of value should disallow anything as metaphysical as a signified? Precisely (and this works as an oblique confirmation of Lyotard's general argument) because in describing language Saussure is taking it as the *object* of his discourse and, therefore, as all discourse does with its object, setting it at the distance constitutive of reference, the distance betrayed, within the flatness of the system, by deictics, and therefore spontaneously thematizing it in terms of the negativity of depth: just as a perceived object presents one aspect but constitutively hides others (Merleau-Ponty's cube that cannot show all six sides it once), so langue, when taken as the object of discourse by a linguist, tends to show up as revealing one side (signifiers) and therefore, it is assumed, hiding another (signified). Saussure constantly confuses his correct description of langue as a system of values with a description of langue as a system of signs, whereas the real signs are the referents of language, at least insofar as those referents are objects of sensory perception offering a manifest side and therefore hiding another side. Lyotard can preserve his two initial types of negativity—which he *then* wants to complicate by demonstrating that deep negativity really is at work in language, first of all via designation, as revealed within the system by those unaccountable deictics—only by purifying Saussure's description of the wrong sort of infiltration by the other negativity in the form of signs, for if language really were a system of signs rather than values, then on Lyotard's account of what a sign is, it would be no different from other worldly objects and, therefore, would be invulnerable to any attempted subversion by the deep negativity Lyotard wants to play against the flatness of the system. Having thus shown to his satisfaction that deictics do not fit into the system, Lyotard is understandably unhappy to find Derrida apparently treating the deictic term *I* as though it were any old term in the system in langue.

Lyotard's argument is attractive in that it seems to reintroduce the question of reference into a tradition of thinking which, as everyone knows, is supposed to go wrong by forgetting or bracketing out the referent. It is no accident that the long footnote which takes its distance from Derrida should appear at the end of a section of *Discours, figure* which discusses a text scarcely known in France at the time, titled 'Über Sinn und Bedeutung' [*On Sense and Meaning*] (1980), by a certain Gottlob Frege, and which was made available to Lyotard as a duplicated handout of the German text (there being no French translation) from a course of Paul Ricoeur's.[14] We are back with the moon here and do not want to be caught stupidly looking at the finger (even though we now know that there is an irreducible moment of stupidity in the need to look first at the finger to see where it might point). Lyotard makes a great deal of Frege's astronomical analogy whereby *Bedeutung* is likened to the real moon up there, *Sinn* to the real (rather than virtual) and therefore still objective image of the moon in the telescope, and the subjective idea or representation of the moon to the retinal image in the eye of the observer.[15] There can be several expressions having a different sense but the same reference, just as there can be several different real images in several different observatories all observing the one same moon. Lyotard likes this analogy because it is optical (his whole account of 'deep' negativity depending on an account of visual space—which is why, incidentally, painting is so important in Lyotard's thought), and annexes the essential elements of Frege's description to his own, ending this footnote by denying that his arguments about designation commit him to a 'metaphysics of presence', as he fears Derrida may fear, and making quite a large 'lunar' claim:

> Frege distinguishes the moon (*Bedeutung*) looked at through the lens of an astronomical telescope, and its image (*Sinn*) situated in the optical system of that telescope. The comparison makes it clear that the moon is not more objective than the image, that the image is not less objective than the moon, and that the only pertinent difference resides in that one is in the (optical, and analogically linguistic) system and the other outside it. With Frege's moon and Benveniste's deictic, thought withdraws from the Platonic sun of presence. The *Einseitigkeit* of the designatum renders illusory any *Erfüllung*.[16]

We should probably not worry too much here about this language of images, which might end up looking a little like the much-maligned early Wittgenstein. But are Frege's astronomers looking at the finger or the moon here? They certainly *can* look at fingers if they decide to, because of Frege's dictum about the reference of an 'indirect' sentence being its customary sense. In Lyotard's exploitation of the astronomical analogy, this comes out a little oddly as an observer in observatory 1 expressing something said about the object in observatory 2—which breaks the visual analogy by smuggling into it the notion of expression which the analogy is supposed to be clarifying: in the terms of that analogy, it would presumably have to be that some sort of relaying device transmitted to observatory 1 the real image of the moon in the telescope of observatory 2. In this case, what is being looked at is not the moon but the *image* of the moon, and what observatory 1 is inspecting is not the moon but observatory 2's image of the moon. I imagine a confused astronomer in observatory 1 asking a colleague what exactly they are looking at here and the colleague pointing at the image on the screen and saying, 'This'.

The *Einseitigkeit* Lyotard is stressing is not quite yet the insistence on the event which will dominate *Le différend*, but one of perspective, no doubt based on a radicalization of Husserl's *Abschattungen*. What is *Einseitig*, one-off, is apparently the *Sinn*, not the *Bedeutung*—however, complications for the analogy (Frege of course would say it's *only* an analogy)[17] start when we remember that it is possible to look at the moon directly without a telescope (for example, when someone points to it and says, 'Look at that'), whereas according to Frege's analysis, it is impossible to get a *Bedeutung* without going via a *Sinn*. *Le différend* does not get tangled up in the same optical analogy: here there's a much later Wittgenstein explanation: if the bewildered astronomer fails to grasp the sense of the deictic 'this' (and a fortiori the reference), then his colleague can spell it out for him by providing names: 'it's a relayed image of the view of the moon from observatory 2 at 0300 hours on such and such a date'. It's not so much that the deictic 'this' is a pronoun, but that the names (places and dates) are pro-deictics (or quasi-deictics, as Lyotard puts it), allowing designation beyond the confines of the sentence in which they appear, or, in the phenomenological language of *Discours, figure*, beyond the speaker's 'origin point'. We might imagine an explanation here whereby names are used to avoid misunderstanding, just as Wittgenstein says that descriptions are given when names might lead to misunderstanding.[18] So just as a 'What's this?' elicits an answer clarifying the reference of 'this' in terms of a 'world' no longer dependent on the 'universe' of the sentence preceding the question, but defined as a network of names, a 'Who am I?' will elicit a proper name in reply, and thus ruin the foundational privilege of the deduction it interrupts, in that the proper name must already have been given in advance of the deduction which ought for Descartes to precede it.[19] Derrida undermined that privilege by appealing to a necessary ideality of the sense of the 'I' which immediately fissured the event of its pronunciation and therefore its certainty by revealing its basis in a possibility of mechanical repetition which is quite indifferent to whether I am or think at all: Lyotard undermines the same privilege by stressing the evanescence of the 'I', and then showing that the ability to synthesize its two occurrences as designating the same 'subject' presupposes a proper name which must have been received in a contingency and passivity prior to the supposedly founding moment of the cogito. Derrida's deduction is apparently all about repeatability of sentences, Lyotard's all about their singularity.

I wonder, however, whether this apparent incompatibility is only apparent. Derrida's argument goes something like 'any singular sentence must necessarily be repeatable, quotable, etc. *as* the same sentence—but these repetitions of the same sentence cannot be *identical* with the 'first' sentence (otherwise they would not be repetitions, but still the first sentence), so the first sentence already implies the necessary possibility of its own alteration, simulation, untruth, etc., in its apparently singular or one-off occurrence— the very thing which makes a sentence identifiable as the sentence it is (its repeatability as the same, for there is no sameness without repetition) immediately splits that sentence with the necessary possibility of its ghostly doubling'.

Lyotard is claiming something like 'the philosophical attempt to reduce the singularity of sentences to a type of which they are tokens, or a proposition they are supposed to express, overlooks the fact that each time a sentence is singular—including the sentence which claims that two or more other sentences are tokens of the same type or express the same proposition.' Lyotard's reproach to Derrida in *Discours, figure* would be something like 'by stressing repeatability you pull singularity into the domain of the concept, which is exactly what philosophy has always done', to which Derrida might reply with something like 'but you will be unable to account either for the singularity you want to respect or the fact that philosophy has been able to go wrong about this unless you presuppose something like my iterability, which you do whenever you say that what looks like the same thing in "I think" and "I am", is not in fact the same.'

I notice that in *Writing the Event,* trying to communicate Lyotard's insistence on the singular event of a sentence, I wrote that 'A sentence is always *a* sentence, *this* sentence'. I can now quote that sentence, which makes the 'this' it contains enigmatic, and seems to attenuate the eventhood it is trying to stress, in a way that Derrida's notion of iterability seems to explain. I can at any rate hardly have meant that sentence very literally: I imagine no one reading the book would imagine that I was claiming, in saying that 'A sentence is always *a* sentence, *this* sentence', that all sentences really were in any sense *that* sentence. The claim is obviously the reverse of that, namely, that any sentence is always only the singular sentence it is in its event. In the sentence I wrote, the stressed deictic 'this' in fact, in accordance with Hegel's analysis of sense-certainty at the beginning of the *Phenomenology,*[20] signifies a general 'this-ness' rather than indicating the event of the sentence it apparently indicates, but only hopes it can somehow enact or simulate because of course that event has already been missed by the time the deictic tries to catch it. Just like the final entry under 'déictique' in Lyotard's index, which seemed to be simultaneously the least and the most deictic term of all, the sentence which attempts to state the this-ness or singularity of all sentences ought to be the most singular but ends up being the most general. But compared with other deictics, 'this' appears to have possibilities which are not available in the canonical triad of I/here/now supposed to define the origin point in phenomenology. For example, if I had written 'Every sentence is always a sentence *now*', then the mild air of paradox could easily be removed by appealing to Lyotard's own difficult analysis in *Le différend* of the distinction between 'now' and 'the now', whereas the *Einseitigkeit* is ensured by the argument that each sentence happens in the event of an absolute 'now' 'before' the temporal syntheses that distribute events in a time then thought on the basis of '*the* now'. A similar analysis could be made of the deictic 'here'. But this cannot quite be done for 'this', which not only is indeterminate as to temporal and spatial reference but also brings with it a supplementary complication that the other deictics do not display.

'This' might indeed be taken as the canonical deictic, rather than 'I' or 'here' or 'now', in that it would accompany the pointing finger in Wittgenstein's refutation of the view of language built from ostensive definition.

'This' can refer to itself as word or utterance or token or event, whereas 'I', 'here', and 'now' can only refer to the agent of the saying and to the place and time in which what is said is said. *This* always might mean just 'this', 'itself', 'its own self'. At which point the finger *can* point to itself pointing, which seems to lead us to absolute imbecility, or absolute knowledge. Absolute deixis would then be no deixis at all, just as absolute knowledge is knowledge of nothing determinate. And this ('this') is really the problem I suggested earlier may haunt both early and late Wittgenstein as a sort of unthematizable residue, which the elegant self-destruction of the end of the *Tractatus* may handle more satisfactorily than the endless divagation of the *Investigations*, through the ineffable notion of *showing,* though one way of reading the *Investigations* is as showing, precisely, that that supposedly ineffable moment is in fact present all the time in the most usual practices of language. 'This' as appearing in expressions such as 'This is simply what I do' (§217) when justifications and explanations run out, I shall examine elsewhere in its complicated relationship with the 'this' in the ostensive view of language Wittgenstein is concerned to criticize. But 'this' appears in less obvious and explicit ways too, in §144, for example, which ends with '(Indian Mathematicians: "Look at this")'. More enigmatically, in §16, Wittgenstein is arguing that the colour samples in one of his elementary language games may as well be reckoned among the instruments of the language, even though they are not words, because there is no essential difference between their role and the role that words themselves can play, if one gives someone a sample of language by saying, for example, 'Pronounce the word *the*'. The paragraph ends with a sentence enclosed in two pairs of brackets (sentences enclosed in brackets are a common way of ending paragraphs throughout the *Investigations,* but this use of doubled brackets is rare in the first half of the book, though more common later),[21] which reads '((Remark on the reflexive pronoun "*this* sentence"))'.[22] There are a number of ways of reading this: it might, for example, be suggesting that the paragraph in which it is the last sentence can or might be read as a remark on the reflexive pronoun '*this* sentence', in which case there is an implicit deictic apart from the one in quotation marks: 'That was a remark on the reflexive pronoun "*this* sentence". This seems a little implausible. The sentence might also be a sort of reminder or incitement to author or reader to supply, on the basis of that paragraph—which would then be thought of as providing the means so to do—just such a remark. ('I've now provided the rules for writing that sort of remark, go ahead and do so here': finger points, now I can go on, now I can't go on, I must go on, I'll go on.) Or it might be simply marking the place where such a remark might pertinently be made, without implying that the means to formulate such a remark are already given. In which case the fact that the remark itself does not appear, but only an index marking where it should have been, might signal a particular difficulty in formulating any such remark intelligibly ('This would be the place to put a remark on the reflexive pronoun "*this* sentence", if I'd managed to write one'). But then again, the sentence might itself just *be* a remark on the reflexive pronoun '*this* sentence'. In this last case, the fuller form would involve a doubling of the deictic 'this', and give 'This remark is a remark on the reflexive pronoun "*this* sentence"' or 'This sentence is a remark on the reflexive pronoun "*this* sentence"'. But as the words enclosed in quotation marks are not in fact a reflexive pronoun, it might be safer to avoid this dubious grammatical description and say rather, '((This sentence is a remark on "*this* sentence"))'. Or perhaps, if we do really want it to be about a reflexive pronoun, '(("This is a remark on "*this*"))'. But as this 'this' in quotation marks already signals by those marks that 'this' is being reflected or remarked upon, then we might reduce it further, to simply '(("*this*"))'. Here it does not look as though the italics are doing any work any longer, so we might decide they can go. '(("This"))', then. But the quotation marks are no longer really necessary now, either, as there is nothing left for the 'this' to remark but itself: so, '((This))'. This '((this))' would be something like a pure deictic or index, in all its imbecility.

This imbecilic 'this' precedes the starting point of phenomenology, whether it be the Hegelian version that Lyotard wants to resist or the Merleau-Pontian version he thinks can help in that resistance. This 'this' is not the 'this' of sense-certainty, though no doubt *that* 'this' would not be possible without it. Hegel gets going only because the this immediately and apparently without difficulty (being already *the* This, and not 'this'), splits into subject (or consciousness) and object, and into here and now, this this and that this. But it seems as though in the Wittgensteinian version this does not happen: *there is* this this ('showing') before any question of consciousness or certainty or objects or knowledge. Maybe we're getting closer here to what has happened in Lyotard's thinking between *Discours, figure* and *Le différend*: in the former, the deictic turned against Hegel in the reading of the passage on sense-certainty is essentially the 'here' of spatial location, still rooted in a corporeal sensorium, already a subject. In *Le différend,* what I am here calling 'this' is not really part of the analysis of deictics proper at all, but, before that analysis, something like the event of presentation which a sentence is. In that case, what I'm calling 'this' is what Lyotard calls 'that', not in a deictic sense at all but in a grammatical usage: 'that there is a sentence' preceding all questions as to what the sentence is or even what a sentence is. In that case, presentation shows up as a trace in sentences no longer in deixis, but in a grammatical particle. This 'that' would still escape lexical definition in a dictionary, and this seems to confirm our earlier suspicion about the apparent specificity accorded deictics in *Discours, figure*. But then the argument with Derrida loses its apparent force, because in insisting on the effects of iterability of the I, Derrida was not necessarily treating it just like a lexical item in a system of langue, once we recognize that there is more in play here than an opposition between deictics and all the rest. By arguing based on an essential iterability of the deictic 'I', Derrida is less assimilating an indexical item to a lexical item than infiltrating lexical items in general with indexicals—which is in fact the general drift of his demonstration that Husserl cannot purify expression of indication. But if lexical items are thereby indexed, then it would follow that far from reinforcing too unitary a view of *langue* in Saussure's sense, as Lyotard suspects in the footnote from *Discours, figure*, Derrida is opening any such system, and in fact any transcendental realm whatsoever, to the contingency, eventhood and 'mere probability' attendant on Husserl's notion of the index. Or if Lyotard's suspicion was that Derrida's analysis would be unable to account for a Fregean reference, but enclosed us in the operations of sense, it now appears that that Fregean opposition would be deconstructed not on the basis of sense, as has often been assumed, but of reference. *Différance* just is the movement of reference, and sense is not then the route to the reference, but already is the movement of reference 'itself', of the *renvoi*, already lunar.[23] To the (limited) extent that Frege's analysis of *oratio obliqua* captures this entanglement of sense and reference, then we can say that Derrida makes all discourse oblique in a certain sense (or a certain reference), which would again appear to be confirmed by his claim that language does not answer to any rigorous distinction between its reality and its representation. But this *also* means that, insofar as iterability entails non-identity, each event really is singular, as Lyotard's later thought would wish, but singular only through the iterability that can also always allow its singularity to be reduced, as philosophy has always done, to the status of exemplification of an ideality or of a case subsumable by a rule. To that extent what I'm calling 'this' is singular only in so far as it also gathers itself (binds itself to itself, as Derrida would say in another context) through an always incomplete self-reference (whereby 'this' is always also a reference to itself as deictic) which is a condition of its reference to any other 'this', just as we have to look, however briefly, at the pointing finger to know where it is pointing our gaze. 'This' seems a reasonable 'name' for this because of its constitutive undecidability between auto- and hetero-reference. The pointing finger, which we first thought could point at anything except itself, cannot *but* point to itself if it is to point elsewhere, and this seems to prescribe a moment of imbecility as a part of any claim to intelligence. In Wittgenstein, this shows up in the eccentric or recalcitrant pupil figures who people his examples and, in Lyotard and Derrida, as a sort of radical passivity of thought before the event.

Saussure argues, against traditional conventionalism, that we receive the system of langue like the law. Our relation to it is primarily one of subjection, rather than one of contractual agreement. I imagine too that there is a similar force in Wittgenstein's saying that he follows the rule *blindly*.[24] In both cases there is a suspicion of difficulty in explaining how that law never seems to be absolutely binding—which is another way of asking how questions of ethics and politics are possible (for they are only possible to the extent that the law is *not* absolutely binding), and suspecting that Wittgenstein's remarks about banging one's head against the limit of language are necessarily too absolutist in character. I imagine the scene of the law as precisely one involving staring and imbecility: the legislator moves an index finger away from the near horizontality of indication, through a 90-degree rotation not, as Lyotard wanted in *Discours, figure*, from the lateral space of the linguistic system to the deep space of the world but into that sort of absolute verticality which designates something beyond even the moon.

This is what I had to say.

NOTES

1. Genette's *Seuils* (1987) is translated in: Gérard Genette, *Paratexts: Thresholds of Interpretation* [1987], trans. Jane E. Lewin, Cambridge, UK: Cambridge University Press, 1997. See p. 419.
2. Henry B. Wheatley, *What Is an Index? A Few Notes on Indexes and Indexers*, London, UK: Longmans, Green, and Co., 1879, p. 7.
3. Harold Borko and Charles L. Bernier, *Indexing Concepts and Methods*, New York: Academic Press, 1978, p. 3, p. 8.
4. The paradox of knowing whether the catalogue of all catalogues not including entries to themselves should include an entry to itself is not far from the problems indicated for us.
5. See Wittgenstein, *Philosophical Investigations*, trans. G.E.M. Anscombe (Hoboken, NJ: Wiley-Blackwell, 1973), §185. In Wittgenstein's *Philosophical Grammar* (Berkeley, CA: University of California Press, 1978), §52, he makes it a matter of 'human nature' to understand pointing as going from wrist to fingertip rather than vice versa, but this naturalism disappears in his later work.
6. References to sections in Wittgenstein's *Philosophical Investigations* will be cited in-text.
7. The reading of Wittgenstein along these lines is the object of a work in progress.
8. For a fuller exposition, see my *Lyotard: Writing the Event* (Manchester, UK: Manchester University Press 1988), pp. 56–66.
9. Lyotard's logic here goes as follows: Saussure defines language as system S; but a set of indubitably linguistic elements D cannot be included in S; therefore, (1) Saussure is wrong to define language as S, and (2) D reveals the essential truth of that error. But there are other indubitably linguistic elements which are part of neither S or D, so Lyotard's second claim appears vulnerable.
10. Jean-François Lyotard, *Discours, figure* [1971], Paris: Klincksieck, 1971, p. 41.
11. Ibid., 115–16n18; cf. Bennington, *Writing the Event*, p. 64. For a brief discussion of Lyotard's more general criticisms of Derrida, see Geoffrey Bennington, 'Spirit's Spirit Spirits Spirit', in *Legislations: The Politics of Deconstruction* (London and New York: Verso, 1994).
12. Jacques Derrida, *L'Ecriture et la différence* [1967], trans. Alan Bass as *Writing and Difference* (Chicago: University of Chicago Press, 1978).
13. Lyotard, *Discours, figure*, p. 328; cf. Bennington, *Writing the Event*, pp. 101–02.
14. See Lyotard, *Discours, figure*, p. 105n1.
15. 'The following analogy will perhaps clarify these relationships. Somebody observes the moon through telescope. I compare the moon itself to the meaning [*Bedeutung*]; it is the object of the observation, mediated by the real image projected by the object glass in the interior of the telescope, and by the retinal image of the observer. The former I compare to the sense, the latter is like the

idea of experience [*Vorstellung oder Anschauung*]. The optical image in the telescope is indeed one sided and dependent upon the standpoint of observation; but it is still objective, inasmuch as it can be used by several observers. At any rate it could be arranged for several to use it simultaneously. But each one would have his own retinal image'; Gottlob Frege, 'Über Sinn und Bedeutung' [1967], trans. Max Black as 'On Sense and Meaning', in *Translations from the Philosophical Writings of Gottlob Frege*, 3rd ed., ed. P. Geach and M. Black (Oxford, UK: Blackwell 1980), pp. 56–78. In this work in progress, I try to show how Frege's celebrated distinction is fundamentally incoherent.
16. Lyotard, *Discours, figure*, p. 116n.
17. The classical philosophical response to criticism of illustrations or analogies or examples is to write off the difficulties to the 'only' in the expression 'only an analogy'.
18. Wittgenstein, *Philosophical Investigations*, §79.
19. Cf. Bennington, *Writing the Event*, p. 123.
20. G. W. F. Hegel, *Phenomenology of Spirit*, trans. A. V. Miller (Oxford, UK: Oxford University Press 1977), §§90–110.
21. See Wittgenstein, *Philosophical Investigations*, §§213, 251, 321, 524, 534, 539, 559, 568, 606, 609, 610.
22. '((Bermerkung über das reflexive Fürwort "dieser Satz".))'
23. This would be confirmed by analysing everything Derrida says about the sun throughout his work.
24. Wittgenstein, *Philosophical Investigations*, §219.

BIBLIOGRAPHY

Geoffrey Bennington. *Lyotard: Writing the Event*. Manchester, UK: Manchester University Press 1988.
Geoffrey Bennington. 'Spirit's Spirit Spirits Spirit', in *Legislations: The Politics of Deconstruction*. London and New York: Verso, 1994.
Harold Borko and Charles L. Bernier. *Indexing Concepts and Methods*. New York: Academic Press, 1978.
Jacques Derrida. *L'Ecriture et la différence* [1967], translated by Alan Bass as Jacques Derrida, *Writing and Difference*. Chicago: University of Chicago Press 1978.
Gottlob Frege. 'Über Sinn und Bedeutung' [1967], translated by Max Black as 'On Sense and Meaning', in *Translations from the Philosophical Writings of Gottlob Frege*, 3rd ed., edited by P. Geach and M. Black. Oxford, UK: Blackwell, 1980.
Gérard Genette's *Seuils* [1987], translated as Gérard Genette, *Paratexts: Thresholds of Interpretation*, trans. Jane E. Lewin. Cambridge, UK: Cambridge University Press, 1997.
G. W. F. Hegel. *Phenomenology of Spirit*, translated by A. V. Miller. Oxford. UK: Oxford University Press, 1977.
Jean-François Lyotard. *Discours, figure* [1971]. Paris: Klincksieck, 1971.
Henry B. Wheatley. *What is an Index? A Few Notes on Indexes and Indexers*. London, UK: Longmans, Green, and Co., 1879.
Ludwig Wittgenstein. 'Lecture on Ethics' [1929]. *The Philosophical Review* 74, no. 1 (1965).
Ludwig Wittgenstein. *Philosophical Investigations*, translated by G. E. M. Anscombe. Hoboken, NJ: Wiley-Blackwell, 1973.
Ludwig Wittgenstein. *Philosophical Grammar*. Berkeley, CA: University of California Press, 1978.

2 'Under a Heap of *Dust* They Buried Lye, within a *Vault* of Some Small *Library*'
Margaret Cavendish and the Gendered Space of the Seventeenth-Century Library

Emily Bowles

Margaret Cavendish (1623–1673) spent much of her adult life attempting to redefine the boundaries of the library by calling attention to the ways in which this space reinforced the binary oppositions that she was relentlessly unsettling in her published writings and her private life. Wildly prolific, spectacularly dressed, and always controversial, Cavendish sent copies of her works to the major libraries in England and Europe. Her career, both during the Interregnum and following the restoration of the monarchy in England, is marked by a deliberate attempt to enter into libraries on her own terms. However, as my ensuing discussion of her writing shows, Cavendish represents libraries as spaces of disorder and dust. She prefers living, breathing intellect, even though she values the role that libraries play in supplying social value to the material contained in them.

As Sandra Bartky has noticed, women 'are restricted in their lived spatiality'.[1] Cavendish grapples with her own sense of restriction throughout her life and writings, often attempting to dispel the limiting grids applied to her because of her gender and her politics (she wrote most of her works while exiled from England during the Interregnum). Described as a woman deeply invested in displaying her body in journals kept by Samuel Pepys and John Evelyn, she seems to have written her life in such a way as to dismantle the fixities that governed the conduct, appearance, and embodiment of a Restoration-era wife. Her own intellectual pursuits, as she enacts them through her relationships with British and European libraries, and as she encodes them in her published works, are similarly marked by a tension between societal expectations and personal prerogatives.

Cavendish does not ever mention her own physical library in her published writings, although evidence of her reading appears in the constant barrage of allusions that readers find in all of her works. Instead, she criticizes the options of private and public book ownership that were available during the seventeenth century. Some questions that should be addressed in analyzing Cavendish's idea of the library thus include 'How did Cavendish perceive women's libraries during the period?' 'What did she find lacking in private collections?' 'How did she represent the library in her narrative fictions?' and, most important, 'How did she manage to transform her own books into forms that expanded beyond the physical covers of the volumes, beyond the circumscribing parameters of library walls and the literary marketplace, into extensive networks of allusion and interactivity that allowed her to encompass texts as diverse as William Shakespeare's *Much Ado about Nothing* and her own Civil War–era account books? Using Donna Haraway's model of 'the embodied nature of all vision' throughout this paper, I suggest that Cavendish imagines the library as a space that not only is always already marked by patriarchal conventions but that is also, simultaneously, an expandable and extendable site for the articulation of a range of authorial impulses not usually connected to seventeenth-century libraries.[2]

Both during the Interregnum and after the Restoration, Cavendish developed works capable of sustaining a range of household ideologies and their political corollaries after she and Newcastle moved back to England. In her writings, she highlights the importance of maintaining and entering literal libraries while simultaneously developing networks of reading and writing that break down the conventional boundaries of libraries and of the conventional female body, and her works suggest the tactics by which she throws into relief 'conventional constructions of femininity' often by ascribing to them 'extreme or hyperliteral' forms, as Susan Bordo has written in a different context.[3] Her print publications, which parallel broader political events in which patriarchy was challenged, suggests a dense network of associations between reading, writing, publication and catalogization that would perhaps have been difficult for a woman writing without the destabilizing factors of war and exile to imagine. Her rebellion against the privatization of books, her interest in making public her own literary and domestic worlds, and her investment in reading beyond any fixed parameters are reflected in early descriptions of libraries and transform, in her later publications, into far more complex ideas about what it means to read, write, print, own, and rewrite books.

* * *

Book ownership was not uncommon for seventeenth-century aristocratic women. Many women, including Anne Clifford and Frances Egerton, Lady Bridgewater, developed libraries that were distinct from their husbands' collections on spatial, material, and intellectual levels. Lady Bridgewater's library is of particular note in the context of this study because Lady Bridgewater's son John married Cavendish's stepdaughter Elizabeth. When she inherited Lady Bridgewater's title, Elizabeth also inherited the library and the elaborately decorated private book closet. Elizabeth went on to own and add to the library, and she probably used the private space provided by her library (a book closet) to read and respond to texts in her religious meditations.[4] This room, as described in an inventory made after Egerton's death, was

> hung with white imbrodered satten naild to ye Cubbords. The lower part of ye clossett is hung with 4 Curtens of rich taffaty wrought with

42 *Emily Bowles*

flowers of needleworke 2 window Curtens a Carpett, and a window cloth of Stained taffaty 1 little square table, and 2 stooles of Irishstitche 1 old Japan Cabbonett with drawers.⁵

For Cavendish, a private retreat of this sort would have possessed many of the same fallbacks as the library of Cambridge. Egerton's book closet is, as the word *closet* implies, a closed space. Once books enter into a library such as this one, they become largely privatized property, and for Elizabeth, the knowledge gleaned from them became modulated in what Cavendish would have considered private forms. Elizabeth read her books and, without marking in them, went on to write the religious meditations that 'nothing, but her closet knew'.⁶

The sociability of texts within such a library and among small groups of largely female readers in a closet or a household should not be discounted. Neither should the lives of the books housed in Cambridge's library. Within the context of this chapter, it is instructive to remember that Cavendish did not have access to these sorts of sites because of her gender and her exile during the Interregnum, so she developed an alternative to the libraries of Cambridge and (more tacitly) to the libraries that women such as her stepdaughter accumulated. She developed a conjugal archive—similar to what Elizabeth Eisenstein has described as a 'library without walls'—that evolved and metamorphosed as she interacted with a vast and multifarious reading population and added her own manuscripts, printed works, and revised printed editions to the network of texts constituting the public literary marketplace.⁷

Throughout her printed works, Cavendish represents the library as a physical space and a cultural institution. The libraries that Cavendish invents in *Poems and Fancies* (1653) and *Natures Pictures Drawn by Fancies Pencil to the Life* (1656) expand and contract in ways that draw attention to the material limitations that the library, both as a dusty room and as a sign of male-dominated educational systems, represents for Cavendish. In her poem 'Fames Library, within the Temples', she describes '*Fames Library,* where old Records are plac'd'.⁸ It is an image that becomes highly charged with personal relevance in the unexpected series of poems that follows the body of *Poems and Fancies*:

> The *worst Fate Bookes* have, when they are once read,
> They're laid aside, forgotten like the *Dead:*
> Under a heap of *dust* they buried lye,
> Within a *vault* of some small *Library.*⁹

The library here is imagined as a sepulcher, in which books are buried. Such books are removed from networks of social authorship, which limits their potential impact, again showcasing the unacknowledged set of assumptions and practices governing the relationship between the gendered/sexed body and the formation of the library as an institution of containment and even confinement, wrenched from lived experiences. To a degree, the library as Cavendish imagines it *is* femaleness and exile: it separates texts from the world, controls them, confines them, and keeps them safe from contamination.

Yet Cavendish also turns the library upside down in her description of scholars' careless treatment of books:

> a long Gallery, wherein were Books placed in long rows, and Men in old tatter'd Gowns reading therein, and turning the leaves thereof; which shewed him his errour in thinking he hears a Winde, for it was the shuffling of the numberless leaves of the numerous Books that were turned over by those many men. But desiring to instruct himself of their several studyes, he went softly to peruse them.[10]

Rife with comedy that anticipates Henry Fielding's *Tom Jones* (1749), this interval in Cavendish's picaresque character's adventure depicts the sartorial carelessness of educated men who wear 'old tatter'd Gowns' and playfully hints that the sound of these men's literary pursuits can scarcely be differentiated from the passing of wind.

Despite wanting her books to belong in university libraries, Cavendish recognized some of the limitations that the exclusivity of academic settings engendered. Intimately tied to these comic observations is a subtler subtext that focuses on the network of production and consumption that develops among of writers, publishers, and readers. The reference to the 'numberless leaves of the numerous books' in particular takes on a strikingly autobiographical tenor when considered in connection with printer's errors that led to the mispagination, absent pagination, or otherwise unclear pagination of many of Cavendish's early works. For example, Cavendish's epistle 'To All Writing Ladies' is an unpaginated sequence sandwiched between pages 160 and the subsequently mispaginated as page 142. Not all of these leaves are exactly numberless, but because they follow a nonsequential pattern, their order is somewhat arbitrary and indeterminate.

Cavendish critiques colleges for enclosing texts in a system that ultimately short circuits their presence in networks of ongoing cultural and intellectual exchange, and she foregrounds the insufficiency of such textual enclosure acts by depicting a nasty argument among the lawyers, arithmeticians, astronomers, geographers, theologians, poets, natural philosophers, historians, grammarians, logicians, geometricians, and physicians. The scholars' 'fiery words flew above all respect or civility', and 'they grew out of all order, and there became such a confusion, that they cared not who they did fight'.[11] Male readers' shared intellectual contexts make them unable to make meaningful revisions to or adaptations of the books. They know that they disagree about the information contained by the books in their library, but they do not know why. Moreover, they do not know how to inflect either the books or their conversations about the books with a sense of polyvocalism.

The scholars' preference for textual exclusivity over textual expansiveness ultimately leads to their destruction of many books. The library

> was like a Ship after a storm at Sea, in great disorder; for there was strewed about pieces of papers rent from Books, and old patches of cloth and stuff torn from Gowns; Slippers kick'd from their feet, Caps flown from their heads, handfuls of hair pulled from their crowns, and pen and ink, *sans* number.[12]

Not knowing how to add to books, they physically deface, delete, and destroy them. There is a difference between this image of a 'Ship after a storm at Sea' and Cavendish's later description of her own plays, which she sent to England from Antwerp in a ship that 'was Drown'd'.[13] Had she not safely kept a copy of her manuscript draft of the plays with her, she would have compared the loss of her 'Twenty Playes, as the Loss of Twenty Lives'.[14] Safely possessing a manuscript of the plays, she knew that she could have them reproduced and revised. The destruction of the school's library, however, lacks the sense of reproduction and even resurrection that Cavendish associates with her own writing and forwards a model in which (false) intellectualism metonymically takes on traits of promiscuity and wastefulness. Cavendish's image of disordered male attire and the correlatively disordered male sphere of the library shifts the locus of satire from the female body and reinscribes it on the predominantly male world of the college library, and the violence against the library becomes a series of actions by which Cavendish transforms the gender differences and hierarchies typical of male/female relations into a solipsistic male act of misused intellectual resources.

Throughout 'The Schools Quarrels, or Scholars Battles', Cavendish persistently undermines the library as an institution in order to lodge a critique against male education.[15] The books in the school's library are neither explicitly mentioned nor overtly critiqued. Rather, their misuse by their male readers instigates the scholar's battle. 'Heavens Library, which Is Fames Palace Purged from Errors and Vices' hinges on the interactions between readers, writers, and texts, thereby developing a more multivalent critique of the canonization of texts, the institutionalization of learning, and the resulting systems of social authorship and social readership. The narrative begins with Jove describing his library as 'foul and full of wormy errours'.[16] Fame advises Jove that he and his counsel should 'purge and cleanse their Library'.[17] The resulting inventory and assessment of the library's books allows Cavendish to deploy a significant number of textual judgments.[18] Moreover, she has the opportunity to experiment with the differences between a library and an archive, for she implies that a library necessitates a degree of censorship, expulsion, and control. An archive, by contrast, allows for the existence of multiple drafts and disagreements. *Natures Pictures* itself exists as a part of Cavendish's archive, and in its second edition, Cavendish does not provide a paratextual retraction of any sort for the first edition. Instead, she simply allows for the multiple versions of the text to perform

Under a Heap of Dust *They Buried Lye, within a* Vault 45

separate but interrelated functions. Neither is an essential component of the other; at the same time, neither requires the absolute erasure of the other.

***

With two of her later printed works—*The Life of William* and *Observations upon Experimental Philosophy, to which Is Added a Description of a New Blazing World*—Cavendish further refines her sense of the interconnectedness or even intertextuality of her writings, specifically by interrogating the ways in which her writings fit into libraries and refusing to conform to the boundaries of specific libraries or even general literary trends. Cavendish imagines a conjugal library in these works. That is, she views her writing as complementary to and even commensurate with her role as a wife. Unlike her stepdaughters, who subordinate their creative writing to their household writing, Cavendish sees her published writing as a component of her married life. Literature is not something she partitions off from her relationship with her husband but is something that coexists with her role as his wife and, later, his biographer. The conjugal library is thus both the actual shared space she has with her husband and a more figurative belief that marriage can facilitate entry into intellectual circles. She expands the literal and figurative shelves of this conjugal library until they transform into the infinitely adaptable metaphoric shelves of a conjugal archive in such a way as to foreground the ways in which (again borrowing from Bordo) 'we must [. . .] think of the network of practices, institutions, and technologies that sustain positions of dominance and subordination in a particular domain'.[19]

In recent years, most of the attention directed toward the paratextual apparatus of *Observations* has focused on Cavendish's dedicatory epistle 'To the Most Famous University of Cambridg [*sic*]'. However, the paratext of *Observations* is not simply designed to induce educated male readers to add Cavendish's works to their libraries. After all, as the previously mentioned passages from *Natures Pictures* indicate, her ideas about scholars and their libraries are not entirely positive. The paratext simultaneously emphasizes privileges the book's placement in Cavendish's conjugal library, an expandable archive with material and rhetorical dimensions, both of which come into play in Newcastle's poem 'To Her Grace the Duchess of Newcastle, on Her Observations upon Experimental Philosophy' and Cavendish's epistle 'To his Grace the Duke of Newcastle'. Newcastle's poem to his wife exhibits his characteristic verbal and rhetorical excesses but is notable here because of its striking emphasis on the book-bound nature of *Observations*:

> This Book is Book of Books, and onely fits
> Great searching Brains, and Quintessence of Wits;
> For this will give you an Eternal Fame,
> And last to all Posterity your Name:
> You conquer Death, in a perpetual Life;
> And make me famous too in such a Wife.
> So I will Prophesie in spight of Fools,

When dead, then honour'd, and be read in Schools.
And *Ipse dixit* lost, not He, but She
Still cited in your strong Philosophy.[20]

Newcastle's poem continues the work of the title page of *Observations*, which foregrounds one crucial material difference between Cavendish and her male contemporaries: they use different printers. The publications of members of the Royal Society all bore the imprint of John Martyn and James Allestrye, the men who published all of Cavendish's early works. After Cavendish stopped working with Martyn and Allestrye, she tried a few different printers before settling on Anne Maxwell, with whom she published all of her later works and produced revised editions of most of the works that Cavendish had published over the course of her fairly short but wildly prolific writing life.

Observations is a 'Book of Books' because it is materially different from the outpouring of books on scientific topics produced during the 1660s by virtue of its imprint. On a more literary level, *Observations* depends on intertextuality—it is a 'Book of Books' because it so relentlessly strings together literary allusions, scientific data, philosophical ruminations, and domestic realities. In a way, the book collapses distinctions between books and their authors. Newcastle prepares readers for this manoeuvre with his own allusion to one of Shakespeare's most text bound of heroines, Hero. Once Don John plants doubts about Hero's virtue in Claudio's mind, the characters begin to identify her as a woman whose fall has been 'printed in her blood'.[21] To rewrite this story, her father and the friar decide to

Let her awhile be secretly kept in,
And publish that she is dead indeed.
Maintain a mourning ostentation,
And on your family's old monument
Hang mournful epitaphs, and do all rites
That appertain unto a burial.[22]

Hero accumulates a secondary function in the play: she represents the posthumously appreciated author who, in Shakespeare's re-scripting, is given the chance to enjoy posthumous fame for the virtuous texts that were in fact 'printed in her blood'. Through some lexical and thematic borrowings, Newcastle's poem suggests a synchronicity between Cavendish and Hero, largely hinging on the hope of achieving posthumous fame without having to die. After Hero's imagined death, Claudio reads the following epitaph for her from a scroll:

Done to death by slanderous tongues
Was the Hero that here lies.
Death, in guerdon of her wrongs,

Gives her fame which never dies.
So the life that died with shame
Lives in death with glorious fame.²³

Hero's 'glorious fame' reverses the language of 'slanderous tongues' and rearticulates the stories 'printed in [Hero's] blood' by transforming them into ethereal, aestheticized funerary documents written by male hands on a scroll. But Claudio is led to believe that Hero's fame has been bought at the price of her death. The idea of a woman achieving posthumous fame through her epitaph was not at all uncommon. Cavendish's stepdaughter Elizabeth Egerton, for example, became an exemplar for other women because of her husband's posthumous compilation of her manuscript writings on religious, maternal, and conjugal topics. Authorship systematically acquired legitimacy when it was recuperated and reoriented by interventionist texts such as epitaphs and elegies, meaning that in death women could acquire the 'glorious fame' unavailable to them during their lives.

Following Newcastle's poem to his wife is Cavendish's dedicatory epistle, in which she emphasizes contradistinctions between her husband's writings and the writings of members of the Royal Society while highlighting the literary nature of his writings and his character:

> In this present Treatise, I have ventured to make some Observations upon Experimental Philosophy, and to examine the Opinions of some of our Modern Microscopical or Dioptrical Writers: and, though your Grace is not onely a Lover of Verturosoes, but a Vertuoso your self, and have as may sorts of Optick Glasses as any one else; yet you do not busie your self much with this brittle Art, but imploy most part of your time in the more Noble and Heroick Art of *Horsemanship* and *Weapons*, as also in the sweet and delightful Art of *Poetry*, and in the useful Art of *Architecture*, &c. which shews that you do not believe much in the Informations of those Optick-Glasses, at least think of them not so useful as others do, that spend most of their time in Dioptrical inspections.²⁴

Throughout this epistle, Cavendish remains as attuned to differences between her writings and the writings of male scientists as Newcastle does in his poem, and she highlights her husband's most masculine virtues, which she views as more noble, heroic, sweet, delightful, and useful than the 'brittle Art' of examining objects with 'Optick Glasses'.

As concerned as this passage is with discounting the methodologies popular with members of the Royal Society, however, Cavendish's primary interest is in developing a version of herself as a particular kind of literary author and by extension in making room for herself in libraries whose shelves were already overburdened with books such as Robert Hooke's *Micrographia: Or Some Physiological Descriptions of Minute Bodies Made by Magnifying*

Glasses (1665). Neither 'Microscopical [n]or Dioptrical', Cavendish's writing is kaleidoscopic. Her scientific and philosophical writing resembles her fictional prose narratives, poetry, and plays insofar as she experiments with perceptual lenses to induce a sense of vertiginous fictionality in *Observations* as much as in *Poems and Fancies* or *Natures Pictures*: the central subject of the text shifts constantly, perspectives change without warning, and textual features mediate and punctuate the texts in unexpected, often jarring ways.

Cavendish thus differentiates herself from her male contemporaries by lodging a critique against male writers' limited methods of seeing the world. Throughout the paratext of *Observations*, she continues to distinguish her work in this way. Her title page, her husband's poem, and her own dedicatory epistle, as well as the ensuing preface to the treatise, her letter to the reader, her 'Argumental Discourse', and her lengthy 'Table of All the Principle Subjects contained and discoursed of in this Book', all assert her unique way of writing herself and bringing her ideas into being while simultaneously delineating the terms for her entry into the literary marketplace and into the libraries of patriarchal institutions of learning. The final epistle that she appends to the first section of this text, 'To the Most Famous University of Cambridg [*sic*]', allows her to reorient typical spatial and intellectual hierarchies, much as she has already undermined perceptual categories with her dedicatory epistle. She does not offer her *Observations* to these privileged readers first. Rather, she prescribes the terms by which her book should be read—and then makes her offering to the me of Cambridge, which seems to suggest that she expects her readers to abide by the standards she has set up for them.

Cavendish utilizes the paratext of *Observations* to establish a conjugal archive that exists in co-functionality rather than collaboration with the libraries of Cambridge and other male-dominated institutions. Further, by supplying an additional set of paratextual apparatus deep within the text of *Observations* to mark the distinction between her scientific discourses and her science fictional narrative, *The Blazing World*, Cavendish suggests that archives often build difference and nonsequentiality into their structures. As an extension to and compendium for *Observations*, *The Blazing World* poses a unique challenge to readers because it is a scientific treatise written in the style of romance and supplemented with literal details of Cavendish and Newcastle's domestic life, their political position, and their conjugal relationship.

***

In *The Blazing World*, as in so many of Cavendish's printed works, Newcastle is presented as an ideal reader who interacts with Cavendish's words on the page and beyond the limited margins of either the handwritten or the printed page. Cavendish's various representations of Newcastle reveal ways in which he helped to authorize her texts but never reigned in her meaningful, formal, and material choices.[25] By following the chronological trajectory of Cavendish's publishing career, Newcastle's character emerges as a layered and complex one, whose story is told as much in his wife's paratexts and in her fictions as in her biography of him. Ultimately, *The Life of William* archives Newcastle in such a way as to help readers remap and consolidate the many different versions of Newcastle in Cavendish's writings.

Even in this published narrative, ostensibly about Newcastle, Cavendish makes clear in her paratext that a crucial component of her husband's role in this text is as the enabler of the text.[26] The persistent gratitude that she has shown her husband in other dedications, epistles, and narratives transforms, however, into a complex convergence of masculine and feminine forms of self-authorization:

> yours have been of War and Fighting, mine of Contemplating and Writing: Yours were performed publickly in the Field; mine privately in my Closet: Yours had many thousand Eye-witnesses; mine, none but my Waiting-maids. But the Great God that hath hitherto blessed both Your Grace and Me, will, I question not, preserve both our Fames to after-Ages.[27]

Underscoring the comparison that Cavendish develops between her husband's battles and her own writing is a fairly conventional metonym by which the female pen substitutes for the male sword. What makes this metonym possible is Cavendish's emphasis on relational textual categories. She does not acknowledge the final print versions of her texts, because her pen would not have produced these public versions. Instead, she emphasizes the time she has spent privately writing with no audience but her waiting maids. Her self-authorization does not begin when her writing is prepared by the printer and is sold on the literary marketplace but when she first puts pen to paper, in her closet.

Cavendish establishes this binary opposition between the sword and the pen to help her establish a method for writing her husband's story that at first glance is deferential yet knowing, untutored yet wise, original yet factual, unconventionally structured yet generically tenable. She takes on an authorial persona that allows her to foreground some ideological fictions about subservience to husband and king even as she undercuts these fictions and formulates a particular kind of textual archive in which she cannibalizes histories, narratives, accounts, romances, descriptions, catalogues, essays, and quotations. Within her preface, Cavendish distances herself from 'the Rules of writing Histories' and critiques historians who prefer 'feigned Orations, mystical Designs, and fancied Policies, which are, at the best, but Pleasant Romances' but by elaborating these frames she develops a vitally dialogic discursive form.[28]

Cavendish overlays a sense of structure on the text, first by suggesting that it is a monarchical life-writing project that hinges on 'a Particular History' and then by providing an overview of the contents of the four sections.[29]

50   Emily Bowles

The first book, she claims, is drawn from narratives shared with her by John Rolleston and others familiar with Newcastle's life during the early years of the Civil War, the second describes Newcastle's suffering during exile and concludes with a 'a Computation of my Lord's losses', the third offers a description of his person, and the fourth mixes essays and discourses of Newcastle's with some of her own remarks.[30] This four-book structure allows Cavendish to access a range of intertextual possibilities; throughout them, she mixes genres, allusions, and voices in a way that breathes life and multidimensionality into her husband's story.

In the final pages of book 2, Cavendish develops an intermeshing system of voices and text forms by drawing domestic documents into what is at this point a largely historical narrative. She underscores her overarching concern with her husband's losses with some visual representations of debts by incorporating actual lists of accounts and examples of Civil War bookkeeping in her narrative. Before providing her version of the accounts, Cavendish explains that

> these are but petty Losses in comparison with those he sustained by the late Civil Wars, whereof I shall partly give you an account: I say partly; for though it may be computed what the Loss of the Annual Rents of his Lands amounts to, of which he never received the least worth for himself and his own profit, during the time both of his being employed in the Service of War, and his Sufferings in Banishment; as also the loss of those Lands that are alienated from him, both in present possession, and in reversion; and of his Parks and Woods that were cut down; yet it is impossible to render an exact account of his Personal Estate.[31]

Like the gap in Jane's account book during the major events of the Civil War, the partial account that Cavendish offers her readers of her husband's losses during the war is a necessary fiction derived from the impossibility of maintaining normal domestic patterns of consumption, production, and income during exigent times. However, where Jane and Elizabeth enweave their losses into fantasies of courtship, witches, and shepherdesses, their stepmother suggests the fictionality of all account keeping and emphasizes the limitless, circuitous, and unknowable difficulties incurred by her husband. The differences between Cavendish and her stepdaughters—particularly in regards to their unequal locational relations to the events of war—thus manifests in strikingly different understandings of and extrapolations from civil war account keeping procedures.

Because of the ductility that Cavendish perceives the account book format to possess, she allows it to occupy a large amount of *The Life of William*: Fitzmaurice has quantified the detailed accounts as constituting about a quarter of *The Life of William*.[32] The creatively and critically deployed accounts thus function as a form in which Cavendish renegotiates fictions of patriarchal and monarchical control in such a way as to make her husband's losses simultaneously private and public. She can therefore 'speak seamlessly, and unapologetically, about both personal and political tragedy', as Erica Longfellow has written in a slightly different context regarding Lucy Hutchinson's Civil War biography of her husband.[33]

A deliberate rhetoric governs Cavendish's public account keeping. Like *The Concealed Fansyes*, *The Life of William* develops a critical set of interactions between domestic reality and literary form by interspersing real accounts into published narrative. Here as elsewhere, Cavendish's approach to history involves an overlap of public and private textualities that function, simultaneously, as a gendered tactic and a generic trait. By taking these broad generalities and major events of history and placing them within a domestic framework, Cavendish developed mixed generic tactics that she deploys in order to encourage her reader to empathize with her husband through a most basic sort of affinity: by showing his accounts. The intimacy of this act coupled with the familiarity of the process of keeping accounts attempts to give the reader visceral, immediate access to Newcastle's state and to impress the reader with a sense of empathy.

The domestic practices that Cavendish transcribes and arranges in book two give way to representations of household interactions in book three. Cavendish moves away from historical narrative toward description of William's day-to-day activities and typical behaviours. The aggregate effect of the entries in this section is to produce a vital, lively, multidimensional version of Newcastle's physical identity. Book 4 extends book 3's practice of nonsequential textual layering and dialogism. Titled 'The Fourth Book: Containing Several Essays and Discourses Gather'd from the Mouth of My Noble Lord and Husband. With some few Notes of mine own', Cavendish develops a unique and interactive text archive that foregrounds the interrelationships among the different modes of textual production that provide the basis for a conversational, conjugal archive.[34] Cavendish opens book 4 with the phrase 'I have heard My Lord say'.[35] The open-ended sentence engenders, organizes, and makes available a series of *bon mots* and lengthier discourses that Cavendish has collected from conversations with Newcastle.

As book 4 progresses, Cavendish builds herself into these 'Essays and Discourses Gather'd from the Mouth of My Noble Lord and Husband'. For example, she records the following:

> I have heard him say several times, That his Love to his Gracious Master King Charles the Second, was above the Love he bore to his Wife, Children, and all his Posterity, nay to his own life: And when, since his Return into England, I answer'd him, that I observed his Gracious Master did not love him so well as he lov'd him; he replied, That he cared not whether his Majesty lov'd him again or not; for he was resolved to love him.
>
> I asking my Lord one time, what kind of Fate it was, that restored our Gracious King, Charles the Second, to his Throne? He answer'd, It was a blessed kind of Fate.

Asking my Lord one time, whether it was easie or difficult to govern a State or Kingdom? He answer'd me, That most States were govern'd by Secret Policy, and so with difficulty; for those that govern, are (at least, should be) wiser than the State or Commonwealth they govern.[36]

Beyond helping her to develop a highly readable narrative, this narrative tactic allows Cavendish to endorse a positive Royalist value system by quoting her husband while planting subtle seeds of dissent with her own words. The fiction of unquestionable Royalist authority and patriarchy is subtly undermined in ruminations that sound domestic, safe, and feminine: the thoughts of an unhappy but deferent wife. Her words are safe because, within the framework of this text, she has affected the posture of a dutiful wife who wants to see her husband vindicated. The character that she established for herself—subservient wife—allows her to produce a text that is far more critical than it might otherwise have been. Because she concedes to being a dependent wife, Cavendish possesses a free ticket for fractious political discourse. She implies that her husband's values mitigate her own, which is an obvious fiction because Cavendish makes sure to publish her discontent. Cavendish thus preserves Royalist codes and ideologies while subverting them.

Book 4 devolves from essays and discourses of Newcastle to increasingly more conversational exchanges and finally to a series of Cavendish's own musings, titled 'Some Few Notes of the Authoresse'. Within this section, Cavendish discusses flattery, dissembling, vice, valor, power during the Civil War, and fortune. Most of her statements are somewhat gnomic. Although they could all be generally applied to Newcastle, they seem to be aphorisms that Cavendish has distilled from Newcastle's life, his example, and the events of the war. For example, she notes, 'I have observed, That many instead of great Actions, make only great Noise'.[37] Whether Newcastle made great actions or great noise is an issue that centuries of historians beginning with Edward Clarendon have debated, most falling on the side of great noise. But *The Life of William* offers a stirring version of his story that develops the interactivities between action and noise, as well as between nation and household, husband and wife, and fact and fiction. As was demonstrated in the previous section, Cavendish also relied heavily on the intersections of manuscript and print in generating her highly individuated and strikingly personal political narrative.

With her version of her husband's life, Cavendish thus rewrites the boundaries of the book in such a way as to suggest a porous openness irreconcilable with the exclusiveness and privacy that she would have associated with libraries, whether lined with satin and taffeta or heaped with dust. Cavendish's textual approach to the library allows her to reject systems that did not accommodate her, at the stake of sacrificing other (for example, non-aristocratic) writers' and readers' modes of literary exchange. Consequently, her conjugal archive can also be seen as a private fantasy of textual expansion and extension, not as a valid alternative to existence within patriarchal structures or as a sustainable mode of literary production more generally. Still, the archive that she compiled reveals a system of self-archiving that is voluminous, adaptable, and exhilarating.

NOTES

1. Sandra Lee Bartky, 'Foucault, Femininity, and the Modernization of Patriarchal Power', in *Writing on the Body: Female Embodiment and Feminist Theory*, ed. Katie Conboy, Nadia Medina, and Sarah Stanbury (New York: Columbia University Press, 1997), p. 134.
2. Donna Haraway, 'The Persistence of Vision', in *Writing on the Body: Female Embodiment and Feminist Theory*, ed. Katie Conboy, Nadia Medina, and Sarah Stanbury (New York: Columbia University Press, 1997), p. 283.
3. Susan Bordo, *Unbearable Weight: Feminism, Western Culture, and the Body* (Berkley: University of California Press, 1993), p. 175.
4. Mary Ann O'Donnell has indicated in her entry on Frances Stanley Egerton for the *Oxford DNB* that Lady Bridgewater had also added to the library at least twice during her lifetime. After having a 'Catalogue of All my Ladies Books at London, 1627, Oct. 27' transcribed, she added supplementary entries in 1631 and 1632.
5. Quoted in Heidi Brayman Hackel, 'The Countess of Bridgewater's London Library', in *Books and Readers in Early Modern England: Material Studies*, ed. Jennifer Anderson and Elizabeth Sauer (Philadelphia: University of Pennsylvania Press, 2002), p. 142, from Huntington Library EL 8094, 21 December 1663.
6. 'An Elegy On the death of that Incomparable Lady, Elizabeth, Countess of Bridgewater wife to ye right Honorable John Earle of Bridgewater, Shee dyed a little after her Delivery of her Tenth Child. 1663. Made some years after her death', HN MS EL 8352, fol. 2. Thomas Lawrence seems a likely candidate for the author of this elegy.
7. Elizabeth L. Eisenstein, *The Printing Press as an Agent of Change: Communications and Cultural Transformations in Early-Modern Europe* (Cambridge: Cambridge University Press, 1979), p. 219. Eisenstein has derived this phrase from Erasmus, who described a library that had no limits but the world itself.
8. Margaret Cavendish, *Poems and Fancies* (London, 1653), p. 172.
9. Ibid., p. 213. Randall Ingram has discussed the significance of this 'postface' of *Poems and Fancies* in 'First Words and Second Thoughts: Margaret Cavendish, Henry Mosely, and 'the Book', *Journal of Medieval and Early Modern Studies* 30, no. 1 (2000), p. 105.
10. Margaret Cavendish, *Natures Pictures Drawn by Fancies Pencil to the Life* (London, 1656), p. 105.
11. Ibid., pp. 106–07.
12. Ibid., p. 107.
13. Margaret Cavendish, *Sociable Letters*, ed. James Fitzmaurice (Orchard Park: Broadview, 2004), p. 203.
14. Ibid., p. 203.
15. Heidi Brayman Hackel has noticed similar parodies of male scholars in Cavendish's writing and explains how Cavendish's 'detailed critique of the Great Scholar's performance [in *CCXI Sociable Letters*] reveals that in her circles communal reading was an elite process as well'. See her *Reading Material in*

Early Modern England: Print, Gender, and Literacy (Cambridge: Cambridge University Press, 2005), p. 51.
16. Cavendish, *Natures Pictures*, p. 357.
17. Ibid., p. 358.
18. For a thorough examination of the ways in which 'Heavens Library' allows Cavendish to articulate her ideas about genre, see Emma L.E. Rees, '*Heavens Library* and *Natures Pictures*: Platonic Paradigms and Trial by Genre', in *Women's Writing* 4, no. 3 (1997), pp. 369–82.
19. Bordo, *Unbearable Weight*, p. 168.
20. Margaret Cavendish, *Observations upon Experimental Philosophy. To which Is Added, the Description of a New Blazing World. Written by the Thrice Noble, Illustrious, and Excellent Princesse, the Duchess of Newcastle* (London, 1666), sig. A2 r.
21. William Shakespeare, *Much Ado about Nothing*, in *The Riverside Shakespeare*, ed. G. Blakemore Evans, J.J.M. Tobin, Herschel Baker, Anne Barton, Frank Kermode, Harry Levin, Hallett Smith, and Marie Edel (Boston and New York: Houghton Mifflin Company, 1997), IV.i.122.
22. Ibid., IV.i.203–8.
23. Ibid., V.iii.3–8.
24. Cavendish, *Observations upon Experimental Philosophy*, sig. B1 r.
25. Kate Lilley has developed an especially convincing argument about the ways in which Newcastle has an impact on Cavendish's 'practices of reading, writing, and publishing'. See 'Contracting Readers: "Cavendish Newcastle" and the Rhetoric of Conjugality', in *A Princely Brave Woman: Essays on Margaret Cavendish, Duchess of Newcastle*, ed. Stephen Clucas (Aldershot, UK: Ashgate, 2003), pp. 19–39.
26. Many modern scholars have ably charted the positive role Newcastle played in his wife's development as a writer. As Alexandra G. Bennett has succinctly put it, 'It is a truism to say that Margaret Cavendish owed at least some of her productivity as a writer to the support of her loving husband'. See her 'Happy Families and Learned Ladies: Margaret Cavendish, William Cavendish, and Their Onstage Academy Debate', *Early Modern Literary Studies* 14 (May 2004), 3.2.
27. Margaret Cavendish, *The Life of the Thrice Noble, High Puissant Prince William Cavendishe* (London, 1667), sig. B1r.
28. Ibid., sig. B2 r and sig. B2 v.
29. Ibid., sig. C1 r.
30. Ibid., sig. D2 r.
31. Ibid., pp. 124–25.
32. James Fitzmaurice, 'Margaret Cavendish on Her Own Writing: Evidence from Revision and Handmade Correction', *The Papers of the Bibliographical Society of America* 85, no. 3 (September 1991), p. 303.
33. Erica Longfellow, *Women and Religious Writing in Early Modern England* (New York and Cambridge: Cambridge University Press, 2004), p. 180.
34. Cavendish, *Life*, p. 212.
35. Ibid., p. 212.
36. Ibid., pp. 235–38.
37. Ibid., p. 255, mispaginated p. 155.

BIBLIOGRAPHY

Sandra Lee Bartky. 'Foucault, Femininity, and the Modernization of Patriarchal Power', in *Writing on the Body: Female Embodiment and Feminist Theory*, edited

by Katie Conboy, Nadia Medina, and Sarah Stanbury. New York: Columbia University Press, 1997.
Alexandra G. Bennett. 'Happy Families and Learned Ladies: Margaret Cavendish, William Cavendish, and Their Onstage Academy Debate'. *Early Modern Literary Studies* 14 (May 2004).
Susan Bordo. *Unbearable Weight: Feminism, Western Culture, and the Body*. Berkley: University of California Press, 1993.
Margaret Cavendish. *The Life of the Thrice Noble, High Puissant Prince William Cavendishe*. London, 1667.
Margaret Cavendish. *Natures Pictures Drawn by Fancies Pencil to the Life*. London, 1656.
Margaret Cavendish. *Observations upon Experimental Philosophy. To which Is Added, the Description of a New Blazing World. Written by the Thrice Noble, Illustrious, and Excellent Princesse, the Duchess of Newcastle*. London, 1666.
Margaret Cavendish. *Poems and Fancies*. London, 1653.
Margaret Cavendish. *Sociable Letters*, edited by James Fitzmaurice. Orchard Park, New York: Broadview Press, 2004.
Elizabeth L. Eisenstein. *The Printing Press as an Agent of Change: Communications and Cultural Transformations in Early-Modern Europe*. Cambridge: Cambridge University Press, 1979.
James Fitzmaurice. 'Margaret Cavendish on Her Own Writing: Evidence from Revision and Handmade Correction'. *The Papers of the Bibliographical Society of America* 85, no. 3 (September 1991).
Heidi Brayman Hackel. 'The Countess of Bridgewater's London Library,' in *Books and Readers in Early Modern England: Material Studies*, edited by Jennifer Anderson and Elizabeth Sauer. Philadelphia: University of Pennsylvania Press, 2002.
Heidi Brayman Hackel. *Reading Material in Early Modern England: Print, Gender, and Literacy*. Cambridge: Cambridge University Press, 2005.
Donna Haraway. 'The Persistence of Vision', in *Writing on the Body: Female Embodiment and Feminist Theory*, edited by Katie Conboy, Nadia Medina, and Sarah Stanbury. New York: Columbia University Press, 1997.
Randall Ingram. 'First Words and Second Thoughts: Margaret Cavendish, Henry Mosely, and 'the Book'. *Journal of Medieval and Early Modern Studies* 30, no. 1 (2000).
Kate Lilley. 'Contracting Readers: "Cavendish Newcastle" and the Rhetoric of Conjugality', in *A Princely Brave Woman: Essays on Margaret Cavendish, Duchess of Newcastle*, edited by Stephen Clucas. Aldershot, UK: Ashgate, 2003.
Erica Longfellow. *Women and Religious Writing in Early Modern England*. New York and Cambridge: Cambridge University Press, 2004.
Emma L.E. Rees, '*Heavens Library* and *Natures Pictures*: Platonic Paradigms and Trial by Genre'. *Women's Writing* 4, no. 3 (1997).
William Shakespeare. *Much Ado about Nothing*, in *The Riverside Shakespeare*, edited by G. Blakemore Evans, J.J.M. Tobin, Herschel Baker, Anne Barton, Frank Kermode, Harry Levin, Hallett Smith, and Marie Edel. Boston and New York: Houghton Mifflin Company, 1997.

3 Outside the Archive
The Image of the Library in Hitchcock
Tom Cohen

INTRODUCTION: THE LIBRARY, THE ARCHIVE, AND MNEMOTECHNICAL CONFLICT

The figure of the library lies within the enigma of archiving: the preserving of traces that shape, and are shaped by, the histories that its inscriptions anchor and platform, which are in turn generative in terms of memory, ideation, and world. The library is not equivalent to the archive, since the former represents only a set of formalisations of the latter's enveloping and internalising premises. The library is tied to letteration, to the *era of the book*, and to the histories of monotheism in the West that have nevertheless come to be undermined by textual knowledge. But the book is itself in a process of displacement by digital technologies. The book, and its forms of institutional collection, thus appears to be part of but one mode, albeit once dominant, of a more general archival episode and its technologies of memory. In this latter sense of mnemotechnics, the archive operates across multiplex spaces and sign systems that involve sociolinguistic forces and mnemonic programs, including eco-wars between biopolitical vectors and animal forms, and hence, it is tied to global capital and the eviscerations of terrestrial life forms. In this context of capitalism and the ecological, the library will not appear merely as a site of storage, or only as an institution of the politics of memory (those concerning inclusion and exclusion and canonization and censorship, for example). Indeed, the status of the library today is curious, particularly in terms of its relation to another form of archiving: film.

The library, because of the faux unity this designation posits, should always be read as a term under suspicion. It also appears as a front: *the library* simulates a figure of the home, a domesticised enclosure that stores and relays a general memory system. But what occurs, at the advent of cinema, say, when the library or the book appears rehoused in the cinematic image or rehoused within its frame, when it must thus be read through cinema's very different histories and mnemotechnics? In being framed, cited, or indexed, the library calls into play a network of figures: how the era of the book gives way to, is placed by and within, that of the image; how alphabeticism and certain historically bound literacies are dissolved by the cinematic

Figure 3.1 Tobin's library (*Saboteur*)

image (see Figure 3.1). Thus, the library opens onto to the dynamics of technologically mutating archives, out of which diverse epistemological and sociocultural realities have been produced. Yet the mnemonic programs of any given time can always fall into passive spells, self-destroying backloops, epochal suspensions; become ill or blind; or become fetishised in their anachronicity, as we might see in the nostalgia for the printed text and its forms of accumulation in the digital age.

Changes in forms of technological memory are thus temporally complex. Such complexity could be noted where Eduardo Cadava, in addressing the temporal complexity of the photographic image in the thought of Walter Benjamin, underlines the image's paralinguistic premise as a skein not of representations, indexes, or icons, but as the 'citational structure' of the image.[1] This structure claims graphic powers that include textual networks, from which the programs of the visible are questioned, and through which timelines are displaced through Benjamin's somewhat kitsch appeal to the temporal complexities of 'dialectics at a standstill' and 'shock' logic.[2] Thus, in this article, I use the term, the *image of the library*, in the counter-normative sense given it by Benjamin—not in a familiar opposition to writing or texts, which preserves an ancient aesthetic separation, but as a 'citational structure' that refers beyond itself to its complex political, historical, and technological conditions. Such conditions are those of conflict, contestation, and violence: writing of the library and photography, Eduardo Cadava reminds us that the archive is always a site of *war*—over memory, over the dominance and stability of hermeneutic programs, over institutional and subjective agencies, and over the very experience of the phenomenal world. Indeed, as Cadava makes clear, the image of the library is one that is inherently concerned with conflict, and that concerns a complex relation between destruction and production: 'If the archive names a body of texts whose existence is threatened by war, the war also assures its continued existence'. As Cadava explains this complexity:

> To the extent that the archive depends on both the preservation and destruction of inscriptions, its structure would seem to imply reference to things beyond its limits. But this strange image of shattered archival space is itself destined for the archive, is even archivized, fleetingly, in the pages of this essay. If the violence that exposes the archive to its radical precariousness, to its fragility, allows us to glimpse its finitude, this violence also enables its survival. We need only recall the history of the burning of libraries—from Alexandria to Strasbourg to Louvain—and all innumerable written accounts and literatures these conflagrations have occasioned.[3]

If the destruction of libraries leads to the production of further texts that must themselves gesture towards new libraries, then we must also think of this logic of conflict in the context of textual and filmic mnemonics, because where the filmic image cites the library, it claims to supersede and envelope it in a manner that is in its own way violent and subject to contestation. In order to develop an understanding of this war of technological memory forms, and in developing the question of the 'limits' of or 'beyond' of the archive cited by Cadava, one could assemble a selective dossier, or schematic representation of an archive, of the image of the book in Hitchcock's films, in which cinema is thinking itself as a historical event and an agency. There are innumerable instances, and each seems minimal yet has exorbitant implications—in *Spellbound*; in *Marnie*; in *Saboteur, Sabotage*; in *The 39 Steps*; and so on. In each case, the citation of the book, or of the library, as the repository of memory, is positioned within a rupture of one of its histories—those of print, reading, and the eye. Indeed, film here will envelop and undermine the authority of the book, and its era, as an issue of the historical conflicts between archival forms.

CITATIONS OF THE BOOK AND THE LIBRARY IN HITCHCOCK: A DOSSIER

In *Shadow of a Doubt*, Uncle Charlie makes a small paper cut-out of a newspaper in the form of a house, marking the latter as defined by the circulation of public print and media, while Young Charlie's revelatory discovery in the 'Free Public Library' comes after a panoply of tele-technologies—telephones,

Outside the Archive 59

Figure 3.2a   Santa Rosa's Free Public Library (*Shadow of a Doubt*)

telegraphs, machinal reading (Anne)—and, at the edge or rim of these normative technics, what is named *telepathy*.[4] That the library is notoriously covered in vines places the archive before and within any trope of 'nature', which is in turn a mnemonic construct or a front itself, like the historically marked swirls in the cut giant sequoia in *Vertigo* (see Figure 3.2a).

The cord that is used to strangle Kenneth at the opening of *Rope* turns up tied around the collection of first edition books that displaces the corpse— only to find the penthouse harried by giant neon letters outside its windows (see Figure 3.2b). These imply, through the partially visible first three letters, both 'store', a cipher of consumer capitalism, and 'storage', a cipher of memory and thus of film's strips of celluloid. The circular cord mimes the motif of eternal recurrence, together with the misappropriation by the student (Brandon) of the 'words' of the master text (James Stewart). The only work of Hitchcock's to mention Nietzsche by name, if inversely in dismissal, remains tied to the fiction of 'first editions', in which books have imprints but no *originals* as such. The scene of the library, or other accumulations of books, is always a scene of repetition without origin.

In *Vertigo*, Scottie is led to the Argosy Bookshop to excavate the history of Carlotta, where he engages Pop Liebl as the resident archivist of San Francisco lore (see Figure 3.2c). The name 'Argosy' links these books, for Hitchcock, with the thousand-eyed demigod and the search for the golden

60   Tom Cohen

Figure 3.2b   The stack of first editions circled with the cord (*Rope*). Original in colour.

Figure 3.2c   Scottie visits the Argosy Book Shop (*Vertigo*). Original in colour.

fleece (referenced to Madeleine). The history of books is bound within the store window, its rectangular glass gesturing to the cinema screen but with mirroring reflection, and thus both are linked to the eye. But the eye itself is produced as a mnemotechnical construct: it is linked to the Möbius-like biomorphics emanating from within the female eye of the Saul Bass credit sequence. Thus, sight and visibility are constructs, already and in advance, and, like Elster's plot, are a setup, a logic of betrayal and programming.[5] Any origin of the 'past' is itself marked as a vertiginous, perpetual backlooping implant, a setup and a trap. The 'origin' is not even the possession of the living by the dead, as if one could seriously track back to Carlotta. The rational Scottie dismisses this when Elster asks him, and he is right. When he is reduced to a blank stare, he is not taken over or possessed by a ghost or the dead but by a ghost that never existed to begin with ('Madeleine'). The reflection on the window of the bookstore mirrors street traffic, and thus, it doubles as a screen or a medium refracting *another* scene of sheer, blank transport that displaces the interiority of consciousness. Such blankness, voiding subjectivity, is a recurrent theme here.

Opening *North by Northwest,* Van Damm's library is liquefied into bourbon, as book-memory is dissolved into the sheer traffic jams and media accelerations of Madison Avenue (see Figure 3.2d). From the non-direction and hyperdirectionality of the title, the film arrives at the vertical precipice of Mount Rushmore and Rapid City (a naming allied to the processing of

Figure 3.2d Cary Grant looks into the liquor cabinet (*North by Northwest*). Original in colour.

film itself, in terms of the rapid processing of 'the rushes'): it thus leads to the prosopopoeia of Mount Rushmore's assembled patriarchs, and thus to global 'America'—capital of telemedia and advertising—and the U.N.

In *Psycho,* we are almost allowed to glimpse, with Lila, the pages of Norman's leather-bound diary in his bedroom (see Figure 3.3a). We are then cut away, without being allowed to read what a wide-eyed Lila scans, en route to the cellar and 'Mother'—the figure who dominates the whole but cannot be said to exist anywhere at all or to be embodied in any place or site. Thus, 'Mother' marks a logic paralleling that which Derrida gives, overwriting Plato's dialogue *Timaeus,* to the archival site of pre-inscriptions called *khora*:

> In the couple outside of the couple, this strange mother who gives place without engendering can no longer be considered as an origin. She/it eludes all anthropo-theological schemes all history, all revelation, and all truth. Preoriginary, *before* and outside all generation, she no longer even has the meaning of a past, of a present that is past. *Before* signifies no temporal anteriority. The relation of independence, the nonrelation, looks more like the relation of the interval or the spacing to what is lodged in it to be received in it.[6]

Likewise, in *Psycho,* 'Mother' is neither in the mummy that is adduced nor simply located in the female-impersonating voice, and cannot simply be identified with Anthony Perkins's character. She is not even what that voice

Figure 3.3a Norman's leather bound diary (*Psycho*)

appears to speak within the head of a staring Norman in the closing scene of the police cell—a cell that cites a celluloid storage box. It is this voice of 'Mother' that we are given, it seems, looking at her or his hand with a fly on it. It is this voice that tells, against Norman, if she or he is to be believed at all, that this staged restraint will show those surveilling him or her that she or he wouldn't even hurt a fly. 'Mother' in *Psycho* is amaternal and amaterial, cross-gendered, and never 'present'. The fly on his or her hand pinpoints filmic animation, as well as a black hole, a gap, or a blot within the field of filmic representation that persists (see Figure 3.3b). The fly returns, in the next work, *The Birds*, as the myriad black slashes and points that come to deface visibility from the sky, attacking children at the point of textual memorization in the schoolhouse, eating out eyes (as the locus of the human consumption of film and of the world), and blinding the blindly programmed population of Bodega Bay (see Figures 3.3c and 3.3d).[7]

In *The Birds*, Hitchcock binds the citation of the library to a split set of forces. On the one hand, there is an implied ending of the era of the book and its construction of subjective interiority through solitary reading and the articulation of words within the mind. On the other hand, there is the assault on the screen itself, central to cinema as the new public space of a communal psyche, which suggests a suspended mutation and a re-inscription of the individual subject. What the end of the film depicts, as the car carrying the Brenners departs, is a distinctly non-mosaic *exodus*, and the eradication of interiority tout court. Melanie's catatonic gaze, a recurrent figure in Hitchcock (for instance, in *Spellbound*), is a kind of erasure of seeing, interior or

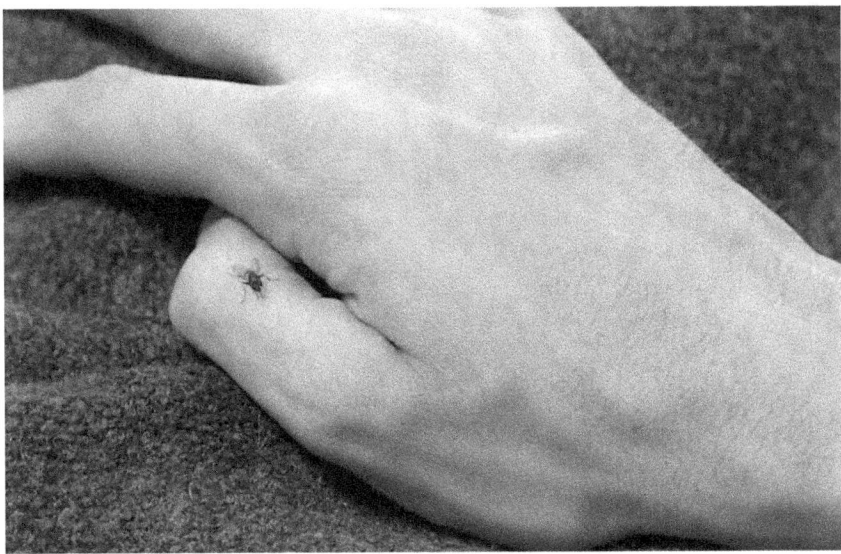

Figure 3.3b   The fly on Norman's hand in the police cell (*Psycho*)

64 Tom Cohen

Figure 3.3c The attack on the Schoolhouse (*The Birds*). Original in colour.

Figure 3.3d The evacuation of the eye socket and the home (*The Birds*). Original in colour.

exterior, a seeing necessarily linked to the act of reading, textual or filmic, and thus an erasure of the functioning of technologies of memory.[8] The catatonic gaze, and the birds' disruption of the screen, figure cinema's twin poles: that of appearing as a mesmerizing industrial effect of cultural pacification (Hollywood, advertisement implants, propaganda, the star system) and that of performing as a *war machine* creating an accelerating mutation within traditional, text-based archival orders.[9]

In Hitchcock's *Blackmail*, that is marked by and that represents the shift from the 'silents' to the 'talkies', we find a hyperbolic instance of cinema's recording of its own point of emergence in purely archival terms. As sound begins to be included while the film unrolls, the film reflexively evokes a unique moment within the technological unfolding of cinema, and in which the histories of textual mnemonics appear as museum sites. The blackmailer, named Tracy, is first chased into the British Museum, a repository of monumental and imperial pasts. Fleeing the Scotland Yard detectives, he passes through rows of books en route to the Egyptian collection—papyrus under glass, mummies, implacable stone faces (see Figure 3.4a). He stares at the reflective glass of their cases and lets himself down a celluloid-like chain next to the giant head of Nefertiti—descending beyond or before the histories of writing, linked as they are to the histories of consciousness and subjectivity (see Figure 3.4b). The pursuing detectives' 'Flying Van' discretely mimes a film production crew (curtains, elaborate dials for a wireless), much as the museum oddly doubles to name an array of frozen times. Tracy runs through monumental halls in which the frozen-time images and relics gathered by the Empire as the image of universal history are on display. He then runs outside to the rim of the dome of the building (see Figure 3.4c). Chased to the top,

Figure 3.4a Tracy is chased through the British Museum (*Blackmail*)

66 Tom Cohen

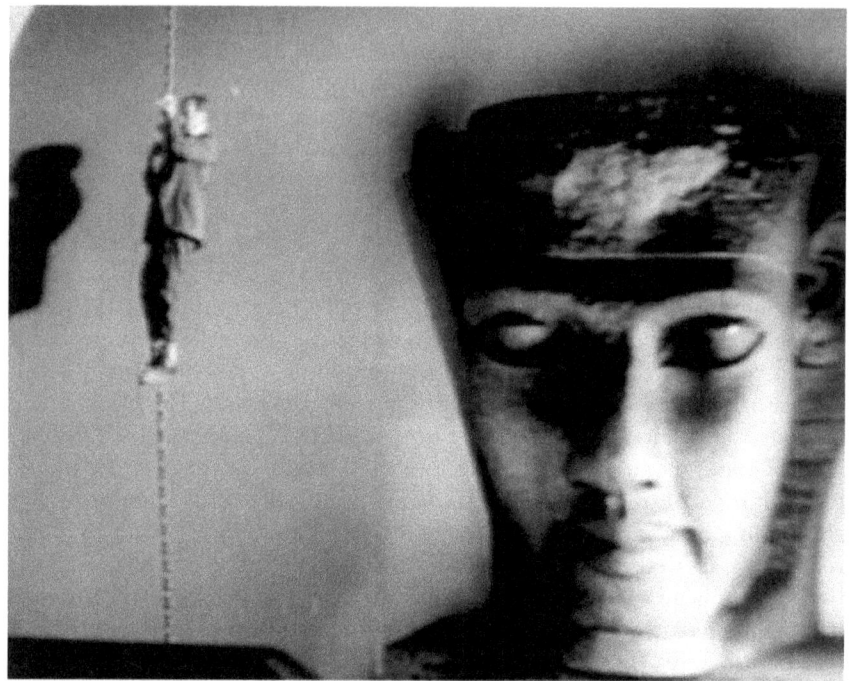

Figure 3.4b Tracy descends past the head of Nefertiti (*Blackmail*)

Figure 3.4c The dome of the British Library (*Blackmail*)

Figure 3.4d The reading room of the British Library (*Blackmail*)

he will turn, point a finger of accusation or indictment (or indexing) at his policial pursuer, and fall back through a crashed glass medium into circles upon circles of readers and books below. Tiny shadows of men crawl across this headlike architecture, as later occurs atop Mount Rushmore in *North by Northwest*—the anagrammatic fiction of 'George Kaplan' projecting the idea of an anthropomorphic head (*capo*) of the earth (*geo*). The head, as with that of Nefertiti, is the trope of cognition and perceptual programs. The domed head of the British Museum and reading room contains the material premises of history, memory storage, communal reading (see Figure 3.4d). It is here then, at this point of mnemotechnical mutation, where cinema occupies the ear and asserts its mimetic semblance, the accord between lips and voice that pretends to manifest the speaking being, that a universal library is self-reflexively evoked. *Blackmail* calls the archive, the era of the book, and the museum culture of empire, and the histories of writing all the way back to Egypt, into question.

DECONSTRUCTION, THE ARCHIVE, AND THE DISAVOWAL OF FILM

What does it mean for the cinematic image to cite these preceding technologies of citation and reference, running through the monumental memory of an imperial museum claiming to contain all human history and culture? The film itself is aware of marking an event or acceleration of tele-technological powers, after which the full era of cinematic globalization came to be unleashed. As *Blackmail* is the first British or Hitchcock talkie, an event where something as if outside—sound and recording speech—invades the mute image, it opens and entombs the 'pure' visuality—the hieroglyphics—of what were in retrospect called 'silents'. The logics implied by the term *blackmail*, that of holding a secret against the present moment itself, define the relation of the cinematic trace to the supposedly present moment. These logics extort and silence the present with the threat of a destroying revelation. Like the digital today that can produce any visual simulation by a loop through numeration and pixellation, the cinematic is revealed as that which can configure any of the historical scriptive modes represented in the film itself. Thus, any era of the book was itself only a dossier in a broader history of teletechnics and marking systems that are essentially cinematisable. When the library appears within the image, in *Blackmail*, it speculates on the historical relation between mnemonics and the senses—that is, the way in which technologies of recording have an impact on the sensory perception of the world. Here, the cinematic image can cite the archive, ally it to a stone capital or head, and reference it to book reading or to hieroglyphics. Cinema finds itself in *Blackmail* at a hyperbolic site or non-site: the outer rim of the archive, of the histories of memory systems and cognitive practices. What does it imply for Hitchcock to trace this pursuit, the double chase of a blackmailer and a history of technological memory, to the outer rim of the archive? Cinema here appears to speculate on what the rim of the archive may be—what might be outside of the memory networks through which the world is made legible and visible, what is outside of the programming of the eye and the understanding by the knowledge structures of the archive. This exceeding of the library, as one of those forms of programming, in *Blackmail*, provokes the chase of imperial detectives policing what is legal within the construction of universal history. Does the cinematic here mark the library as itself tied to reading as interiorization and sight as constructed through archival and epistemological programmes? And what might, or indeed, what could be beyond the library in this sense?

In Derrida, there is a corollary to this question of the exteriority of the archive; one that returns us here to the *khora*, which, as we have seen, emerges from Derrida's discussion of a sort of false feminization. The *khora* further counters the patriarchal-archival order of writing systems (always the province of male orders: priests, brotherhoods), and is presented as the non-site at which inscriptions appear, or do battle, and out of which mnemonic and then interpretive networks derive:

> 'khora' seems never to let itself be reached or touched, much less broached, and above all not exhausted by these *types* of tropological or interpretative translation. One cannot even say that it furnishes them with the support of a stable substratum or substance. *Khora* is not a

subject. It is not the subject. Nor the support [*subjectile*]. The hermeneutic types cannot inform, they cannot give form to khora except to the extent that, inaccessible, impassive, 'amorphous' [. . .] and still a virgin, with a virginity that is radically rebellious against anthropomorphism, it *seems to receive* these types and *give place* to them.[10]

What would it mean, as Derrida sometimes seems to want, to speak as if for or from the place of the *khora*—the non-site at which pre-inscriptions are set, erased, or mutate? What would it mean to enter a war zone of inscriptions or to mark the epochal decline of archival programs, suicidal default settings, or what Derrida refers to as 'archive fever' (*mal d'archives*)?[11]

It is worth remarking here on the implications of what Derrida refers to as 'the archiving archive'. The archiving archive does not only record *events*, but, through its technologies and structures, *produces* archivable events; indeed, the archiving archive structures the very *experience* of the event, and thus in order to understand the phenomenal we must detour through the archival.[12] *The archive* as such is never defined merely by the materiality of books or script, and its surfaces and media are numerous: parchment and stone, celluloid and flash disks, mnemotechnics. The backloop through such technologies of inscription, generated by recognition of their effaced imprints, has always been a scandal to consciousness and is routinely and collectively forgotten, just to get through any day. It cannot be seen or handled, even as what we call 'the eye' would be itself an effect of such archival programming and editing—as the archival construction of the event indicates. Such an argument would concern Enlightenment paradigms of power: the backloop finds that 'light' itself is utilised by and constructed by techniques of discourse and that regimes of naturalized reference—say, to 'light itself'—are rather mutable and at war with themselves, when viewed *as if* from without.[13] This also suggests that a received order of the book and its protocols of reading are generally contaminated—sites of betrayal and programming. Hence, this backloop raises the questions of intervention and of altering such inscriptions (programs of cognition, of otherness, of sense, of consumption, etc.). And the backloop circuits as if to an unlocatable pre-site of these inscriptions, and finds it can do so, or simulate this, only by a hyperbolic legibility that precedes the law, that is, a simulation that dispels (or *dispells*) circular memory programs of reference and the temporal orders they conjure or legislate.

Any 'outside' of the archive as that which would be exterior to it is banned by Derrida, in part because there is no *hors-texte*—nothing exterior to textuality, or 'writing', in the expanded sense given to it by Derrida in *Of Grammatology*, to refer to *any* system of differences.[14] There is thus no *hors-archive*: no final, meta-textual, or meta-archival position, and there are always other 'archival' programs (chemical, cellular, viral, climactic, geomorphic) which human script is embedded and subsumed within. Any 'outside' of the archive—heard as the zone of technico-material inscription, a 'materiality' bound to evolving technologies—is also disallowed, because any supposed interiority of supposedly organic memory is itself the illusory forgetting of these effects. This suggests that the inside (what thinks of itself as organic) is the outside (technical memory) and that the outside has no outside—not even in terms of a messianic rupture of pure futurity, because this too is part of an historical-archival repetition in Derrida's thought.[15] In line with such inversions, the blind is internal to the archive, not its exteriority as such. Indeed, as repetition gestures toward the death drive, in Derrida's thought, such historical-archival repetition indicates that the archive must be constitutively *mal*, 'archiviolithic', ill or evil, in suicidal fashion.[16] As Derrida wrote,

> But, the point must be stressed, this archiviolithic force leaves nothing of its own behind. As the death drive is also [. . .] an aggression and a destruction (*Destruktion*) drive, it not only incites forgetfulness, amnesia, the annihilation of memory, as *mneme* or *anamnesis*, but also commands the radical effacement [. . .] of that which can never be reduced to *mneme* or to *anamnesis*, that is, the archive, consignation, the documentary or monumental apparatus as *hypomnema*, mnemotechnical supplement or representative, auxiliary or memorandum. Because the archive, if this word or this figure can be stabilized so as to take on a signification, will never be either memory or anamnesis as spontaneous, alive and internal experience. On the contrary: the archive takes place at the place of originary and structural breakdown of the said memory.
>
> *There is no archive without a place of consignation, without a technique of repetition, and without a certain exteriority. No archive without outside.*[17]

Yet Derrida's circulation and hailing of the term *archive* in this sense of an active mnemotechnics in advance of any phenomenality may, however, remain too incantatory. There are visible sutures in Derrida's attempt to at once probe and stabilise this figure of the archive. Even the attempt to arrest the drift seems demur ('No archive without outside'), trading the assertion of an outside against the implied residue of an interiority effect that counter-defines it from within. Any *outside of the archive* one could pretend to point to, or at, would be a site that both precedes and suspends any of the archive's contemporary programs (its artifactualities). It can only be gestured to by moving to the outer site of an *interiority*: a membrane, a wall, or a border. In the belated dawning of the era of climate change, before which the era of the book appears as interwoven with suicidal accelerations of commodified models of perception and consumption, what remains interesting is where and how an epistemographic war machine—such as cinema—emerges, punctures, or perforates this membrane.

But we must pursue here the exclusion of cinema in Derrida's writing. Its machinality puts, for Derrida, the entire rhetoric of the *to come*—the possibility of a future radically different to the present—in question. There is nothing innocent, Derrida notes, about an archive, nothing done without violence and imposed power—in a bid, say, to claim some future. This is one reason why Derrida in his only interview on film, with *Cahiers du Cinema*, implicitly *disavows* it:

> cinema is a major art of diversion. [. . .] It does not present itself on the mode of learned or philosophical culture. Cinema remains for me a great hidden enjoyment, secret, avid, gluttonous, and thus infantile. [. . .] Everything in cinema is permitted , including adjacencies between the heterogeneous roles [appearances] of publics and of relationships to the screen. [. . .] Cinematic experience belongs, altogether, to spectrality, which I link to everything one could have said about the spectre in psychoanalysis—or the very nature of the trace. [. . .] As spectral memory, cinema is a magnificent mourning, a work of mourning magnified. [. . .] It is thus double a trace: trace of witnessing itself, trace of forgetting, trace of absolute death, trace of that-without-trace, trace of extermination.[18]

Hence, Derrida's take on archival destruction, which ricochets into the sheer materiality and mutability of the sites of storage:

> When one speaks of the destruction of an archive, do not limit oneself to the meaning, to the theme, or to consciousness. To be sure, take into account an economy of the unconscious, even if only to exceed it once again. But it is also necessary to take into consideration the 'supports', the *subjectiles* of the signifier—the paper, for example, but this example is more and more insufficient. There is this diskette, and so on. Differences here among newspapers, journals, books, perhaps, the modes of storage, of reproduction and of circulation, the 'ecosystems' (libraries, bookstores, photocopies, computers, and so on). I am also thinking of everything that is happening today to libraries.[19]

The argument has devolved here, where 'modes of storage' are said to constitute 'ecosystems'. To cast the material premises of the archival as a matter of the 'eco' to begin with—since we are told it is of the 'outside'—puts the problem of troping the 'library' as the interiority of the home into question. The archiving archive was not only 'of the outside' (in terms of forms of external memory), it was without any interiority to begin with and, hence, any conceit of the eco or 'home' other than that generated by the recollection and archiving of itself is illusory. The library here appears to *house* the material supports of the book, and to be a part of, or partly to form,

72   Tom Cohen

what are imagined momentarily as 'ecosystems'. One might wonder if this metaphor does more to naturalize or technicise the thinking of this problem, because the 'home' or 'eco' being identified is, Derrida knows, an artifice itself, a criminal trope that presupposes interiors to be created, maintained, and proprietised. Thus, a skeptical reading of this interview shows a Derrida 'at war' with himself, perhaps in a different way from that sense of inner conflict discussed by Derrida in his final interview with *Le Monde*.[20] Cinema will, throughout, be mentioned as the very figure of the trace, of the trace without trace, of survival, of spectrality, and so on, yet he retains no memory of it (while recalling everything) and will not write on it. For Derrida, as the grammatologist of the trace and the letter, *cinema* will need to be occluded from reference—unlike the photographic still.[21] The problem with Derrida's figure of the archive may thus be embedded in his disavowal of cinema. Cinema appears to suspend, in its machinality, the rhetoric of the 'to come' which Derrida had come to rely on as a rhetorical foil.

An 'outside' of the archive is, by definition for Derrida, not possible, except perhaps as a trace of the world that has not entered into mnemonic formations (say, the way there is no memory of the last Ice Age in human communities, hence no template to recognize climate change as a repetition). Perhaps Derrida's prioritization of 'survival' turns away from these additional forms of the trace, occluding the logics of climate change or eco-catastrophism that, in the past decades, have arrived *as if* from outside to interrupt hyper-industrial modernity through resource depletion and extinction events.[22] What seems to exceed the archiving archive as it circulates after Derrida, and what seems to exceed Derrida's figure of the 'ecosystems' of writings, is, precisely, the question of climate, and of ecocide, and it is toward this dimension of Hitchcock's films that I now turn.

THE OUTSIDE OF THE ARCHIVE

Hitchcock marks the advent of *cinematics* as a cognitive mutation that arrives before and within an unaware public. The screen is the new and primary public space. It supplants letteration with exile, opens onto non-anthropomorphic or ex-anthropic agencies irreconcilable to the twentieth-century fables of subjectivity that movies would have appeared to enshrine (the face, its star systems, and 'intersubjective' identification with it). The tranced-out humans of Bodega Bay in *The Birds* are not to be identified with: the screen identifies with the birds against the b-list actors who are pushed out of the frame and who begin an exodus marked at the non-end of the film by the car ride through the massed and waiting birds. The birds do not have any narrative or referent to claim—not an Oedipal one (pointedly dismissed by Annie: 'With all due respect to Oedipus') nor a natural allegory (that of the ornithologist). One is asked to identify with the one thing that has no interior or subjective

Figure 3.5 Marks and gashes atomise the sky (*The Birds*). Original in colour.

kernel: the alien, invading birds, that also blot the cinematic screen, figuring its disruption (see Figure 3.5).

The blots coalesce, disperse, marshal, cut off generations, peck out eyes, and yet remain allied to the formal geometrics where life and its others interface and the twenty-first-century U.S. is previewed from non-anthropomorphic traces avenging without apparent cause on a totality, an entire horizon. This does not place Hitchcock in a Derridean template or as an exemplar of *khoratic* practices. Derrida invokes this prefigural zone as one in which contests over re-inscription before any phenomenality or body emerge. Rather, Hitchcock claims those zones as given and almost banally exposed, aporetic, and at war. What does it mean to be on this putative outside of the archive—that is, to reside at the border between the cognitive, representational world and its others? The question resonates in its way today, in the era of climate change, with the banal materiality of life systems and resource depletion, climactic mutation and inundation, and extinction events.

In *The Birds* an impossible tangent is posited, the atomization of visual or scriptive systems, which, nonetheless, obey certain swarming logics, a war strategy. The avian animants perform rather than represent (as gashes on the screen) an ex-anthropic domain of terrestrial systems, an earth become entirely technic and turned against programmed trance and consumption (seeing, eating, the production of interiority, of reserves of memory). This purported alterity is not reducible to the catalogs of managed otherness that fill archives. Thus, the succession of twentieth-century wars that Hitchcock incorporates and marks as part of cinema's interface shifts from the human enemies of 'world wars' (and then cold wars) to something more radically alterior. That is what is called *the bird war*—a totalized war of atomic, material, nanographic, animated, techno-organological systems pitted against the anthropocene parenthesis on earth and its construction of the 'visible', of interiority, and of archives: *the rim of the archive* is exposed to a bio-semiotic storm.[23]

We noted at the outset of this discussion that 'the library' was always only one technological path, albeit epochally dominant, provided by materials of inscription that have been formed and read through a series of interpretive strategies. Such strategies, aiming at their own historical continuation and hegemonic reach, are necessarily bound with the politics of literacy. Thus, in *The Birds*, the attack on the schoolchildren stands out—a moment designed as if to cut off the future or generations, but also to cut off what we see occurring in the school in the singsong memorization exercises repeated in unison: the employment of mnemotechnics in imprinting and programming. The children echo the Mynah birds sought in the pet store, for which the repetition of learned sound simulates voice by machinal memoration, without ideational content. We have also noted that the swarms of birds stand as both filmic marks *and* slashes in the field of the visible, and are attached to the pecking of eyes—the organs of the internalisation of written or otherwise visual signs and thus the border of the technical exterior and the 'organic' interior. The birds void subjectivity and counter the construction of the visible, divesting the home of inhabitance and all psychic interiors. Thus, the birds' attacks parallels the chase onto the archival dome in *Blackmail*—an archival dome read as the rim of border of the mnemonic programs out of which 'life' or animation derives. The outside of the archive exposes inscriptive devices taunted by their inability to reconfigure, when staring, like catatonic Melanie, at the implications of leaving the constituted dwelling of the home, of abandoning the phantom of interiority.[24]

Cinematic logics is thus presented in *The Birds* as the interruption of reading, and all of the literary, institutional, and historical structures associated with it. Hitchcock's cameo in *Blackmail* seems to mark this interruption at the opening of film. Sitting in a London Underground train, itself a figure of the cinematic (flashing lights and window screens, as if the carriage was film spooling through the projector gate), he is twice interrupted by a bullying boy—a figure of the future—who, finally, stares him down, making him lower the book he is reading (see Figure 3.6). *The Birds*, we might then say, reconfigures this association of the future with the interruption of reading by expanding its remit to that of the visible in representation more generally and by aligning it to a future to come *beyond* human optics and power. Cinema thus posits its own immolation through the birds, and the possibility of the post-human world—and, significantly, given the contemporary sentimentality for the epoch of the book, the birds' machinality is without affect in any human register. Voiding the domestic interior, they cannot be related to homesickeness: they are beyond nostalgia.

Outside the Archive 75

Figure 3.6   Hitchcock's interrupted reading on the Underground (*Blackmail*)

CONCLUSION: THE DOUBLED FUTURES OF THE LIBRARY

Sometimes, archival mutations are discrete, academic, matters of unearthed inscriptions, and, at other times, techno-morphic and on the order of geological, tectonic shifts. An example of the former could be found in the unearthing of a pre-biblical tablet, *Gabriel's Vision of the Revelations*, which threw Christian theorists into consternation.[25] Partial texts, with key gaps, emerged from the stone with inscriptions exposing a tradition of three-day resurrections that predates Jesus by centuries. An archival inversion, it implied the resurrection myth was pre-scripted, necessary to conform to a long prescribed test of authenticity for messiahs. This archival eruption would embarrass the always *unique* claims of God's interventions, rendering the resurrection a media repetition that would successfully launch a brand name: 'Jesus' becomes, again, a textualised product. It displaces holy text to the order of simulation, of copy, recasting in turn the *canonical* 'resurrection'. What was supposed to come after is displaced to before, and the 'event' appears secondary, artefactual, and, of course, imitative.

An example of a techno-morphic mutation on the order of geological shifts might be Hitchcock. The turn from the material book toward digitalization has spawned narratives of the decline of the library. It appears together with discussions of a generational mutation of cognitive reading models—those derived from the image, video games, interactive websites. With these networks, alternative literacies and temporalities evolve, and synapses configure and reconfigure, according to the logic of 'neural plasticity'.[26] This narrative of decline is, like its opposite, suspect, because it erects the library as a restituted *home*. As one commentator notes,

> This process, which Agre terms disintermediation, suggests the obsolescence of institutions such as the library and the university. The availability of academic discourse at all levels on the Internet brings the risk of flattening the structures of knowledge, making them largely invisible to the Web-surfing student or incautious scholar.[27]

Digitisation has brought much unexpected theoretical regression and could appear less as a threat to the library's literal borders than as an unrestrained extension of its logic, as a matter of archival logics. Digitisation has allowed the maintenance of archives in multiple versions that seem to allow for an all-inclusiveness, and print on demand and e-publishing allow libraries to store and include, well beyond their physical limits. If one views digitisation, however, as the creation of *units* through which material as such becomes capable of storage or circulation, then the library has always been digital and has always relied on other apparatuses—such as copyright, printing, and knowledge factories—in order to provide its already managed data. In this sense, then, we might see the digital era as one in which the library is both maintained and transformed. But if we should thus see the image of the library as a complex figure within the development of mnemotechnics, we should also take note of the speculative character of the Hitchcock's films as discussed here. They ask us to think not only of the historical changes and complexities of various forms of mnemotechnical institutions and technologies, but the possibility of their rim, their boundary, and thus the question of their outside. Such forms of human memory are, of course, bound with capitalist logics that regularly flirt with ecocide and ecological catastrophe, and all the consequent eradications of human life and knowledge that such implies.

NOTES

1. See Eduardo Cadava, 'Lapsus Imaginis: The Image in Ruins', *October* 96 (Spring 2001), p. 55.
2. These concepts are articulated in Walter Benjamin, 'On the Theory of Knowledge, Theory of Progress', in Benjamin's *The Arcades Project*, ed. Rolf Tiedemann and trans. Howard Eiland and Kevin McLaughlin (Cambridge, MA: Harvard University Press).
3. Cadava, 'Lapsus Imaginus', p. 57.
4. In terms of this connection between tele-technologies and telepathy, see J. Hillis Miller, 'The Medium is the Maker: Browning, Freud, Derrida, and the New Telepathic Ecotechnologies', *The Oxford Literary Review* 30, no. 2 (2008).

5. Aside from glossing the prosthetic blonde 'Madeleine' as a golden fleece trope, the Argosy Bookshop assigns the flotilla to the shipbuilder Elster, who contrives the entire setup: it also cites a shattered panopticon, *Argus Panoptes*, the hundred-eyed giant, a trope applied to the sun as well.
6. Jacques Derrida, *On the Name* [1993], ed. Thomas Dutoit and trans. David Wood, Jean P. Leavey, Junior, and Ian McLeod (Stanford, CA: Stanford University Press, 1995), pp. 124–25.
7. The place name itself refers to storage, given that *bodega* in Spanish means 'cellar'.
8. The logic of this exodus—of the Brenners and Melanie being driven out of the home, with the restive avians assembled around all structures—may be said to be programmatically misread by a psychoanalytic interpretation in which, viewing the characters and the 'maternal superego' as background, Melanie's catatonic gaze is a defeat before Lydia. Yet this empty gaze can be said to register a voiding of psychic programs rather than a personal collapse, a non-Oedipal 'future' attached to a wandering without return or home, interiority, or reversibility.
9. As discussed in Gilles Deleuze and Fèlix Guattari, *A Thousand Plateaus: Capitalism and Schizophrenia* [1980] (London and New York: Continuum, 2004).
10. Derrida, *On the Name*, p. 95.
11. See Jacques Derrida, *Archive Fever: A Freudian Impression* [1995], trans. Eric Prenowitz (Chicago and London: The University of Chicago Press, 1988).
12. Ibid., pp. 16–17.
13. The relations between light, visibility, and the optics of power are of course seminally discussed in Michel Foucault, *Discipline and Punish: The Birth of the Prison* [1975], trans. Alan Sheridan (New York and Toronto: Random House, 1977).
14. See Jacques Derrida, *Of Grammatology* [1967], trans. Gayatri Chakravorty Spivak (Baltimore: The Johns Hopkins University Press, 1997), pp. 158, 163, for example.
15. Deconstructive engagement with the issue of the future, the to-come (*l'avenir*) can be further pursued through, for example, Jacques Derrida and Maurizio Ferraris, *A Taste for the Secret* [1997], trans. Giacomo Donis (Cambridge, UK: The Polity Press, 2001); and Jacques Derrida, *The Other Heading: Reflections on Today's Europe* [1991], trans. Pascal-Anne Brault and Michael B. Nass (Bloomington: Indiana University Press 1992).
16. Regarding the relationship between repetition and the death drive in Freud's theory of the psyche, see Jacques Derrida, 'Freud and the Scene of Writing' [1966], in *Writing and Difference* [1967], trans. Alan Bass (London: Routledge, 2001); and regarding the suicidal aspect of systems and identities, as an aspect of autoimmunity, see Giovanna Borradori, *Philosophy in a Time of Terror: Dialogues with Jurgen Habermas and Jacques Derrida* (Chicago and London: University of Chicago Press, 2003).
17. Derrida, *Archive Fever*, p. 11. All italics in original.
18. Jacques Derrida, 'Cinema and its Phantoms', trans. Helen Regueiro Elam (unpublished) of 'La cinéma et ses fantômes', *Cahiers du cinema* 556 (2001): 75–85.
19. Jacques Derrida, 'Biodegradables: Seven Diary Fragments', *Critical Enquiry* 15, no. 4 (Summer 1989), p. 865.
20. Published as Jacques Derrida, *Learning to Live Finally: The Last Interview* [2007], trans. Pascal-Anne Brault and Michael Nass (Brooklyn, NY: Melville House Publishing, 2011).
21. The comparatively consistent engagement with photography can be seen from, for example, Jacques Derrida and Marie-François Plissart, *Rights of Inspection*

[1985], trans. David Wills (New York: The Monacelli Press, 1999), to Jacques Derrida, *Copy, Archive, Signature: A Conversation on Photography* [2000], trans. Jeff Fort (Stanford, CA: Stanford University Press, 2010).
22. See, for example, the discussion of survival in Derrida, *Learning to Live Finally*.
23. The term *anthropocene* refers, initially in the work of Paul Krutzen, to a period of history in which humanity's activities on earth are dominant. See, for example, Will Steffen, Paul J. Crutzen, and John R. McNeill, 'The Anthropocene: Are Humans Now Overwhelming the Great Forces of Nature?', *Ambio* 38 (2007).
24. Of course, the irreversible logic of the birds implies a sort of structural *horror*. It is one which renders the implications Kurtz's famous last words in Joseph Conrad's *Heart of Darkness* ('The horror! The horror!')—marking a reversible interface between Enlightenment rhetoric and absolute zones of savagery and dehumanized rapine—historically parochial. The former contemplates the colonial construction of the Western subject in its enduring nineteenth-century cast. The latter probes the construction of visibility, the eye, and eating and is embedded sensorially as a suicidal movement allied to a totalization of twentieth-century horizons in the global era.
25. For a review of the components and theo-archival dustup of this episode, see Gary R. Habermas, '"Gabriel's Vision" and the Resurrection of Jesus', July 2008, www.garyhabermas.com/articles/gabrielsvision1/gabrielsvision.htm; Craig Hazen, 'Gabriel's Vision: an Angelic threat to the Resurrection', *Christian Research Journal* 32, no. 2 (2009); and Patrick Zukeran, 'Gabriel's Vision: An Angelic threat to the Resurrection', 2012, www.probe.org/site/c.fdKEIMNsEoG/b.4426931/k.F448/Gabriels_Vision_An_Angelic_Threat_to_the_Resurrection.htm.
26. For discussion of the relation between neural plasticity and capitalism, see, for example, Catherine Malabou, *What Should We Do with Our Brain?* [2004], trans. Sebastian Rand (New York: Fordham University Press, 2008).
27. David S. Mial, 'The Library versus the Internet: Literary Studies Under Siege', *PMLA* 116, No. 5 (Oct., 2001), p. 1412.

BIBLIOGRAPHY

Walter Benjamin. 'On the Theory of Knowledge, Theory of Progress', in Walter Benjamin, *The Arcades Project*, edited by Rolf Tiedemann and translated by Howard Eiland and Kevin McLaughlin. Cambridge, MA: Harvard University Press, 2002.
Giovanna Borradori. *Philosophy in a Time of Terror: Dialogues with Jurgen Habermas and Jacques Derrida*. Chicago and London, University of Chicago Press, 2003.
Eduardo Cadava. 'Lapsus Imaginis: The Image in Ruins', *October 96* (Spring 2001).
Gilles Deleuze and Fèlix Guattari. *A Thousand Plateaus: Capitalism and Schizophrenia* [1980]. London and New York: Continuum, 2004.
Jacques Derrida, *Archive Fever: A Freudian Impression* [1995], translated by Eric Prenowitz. Chicago and London: The University of Chicago Press, 1988.
Jacques Derrida. 'Biodegradables: Seven Diary Fragments'. *Critical Enquiry* 15, no. 4 (Summer 1989).
Jacques Derrida, 'Cinema and its Phantoms', translation by Helen Regueiro Elam (unpublished) of "La cinéma et ses fantômes"'. *Cahiers du cinema* 556 (2001).
Jacques Derrida. *Copy, Archive, Signature: A Conversation on Photography* [2000], translated by Jeff Fort. Stanford, CA: Stanford University Press, 2010.
Jacques Derrida. 'Freud and the Scene of Writing' [1966], in *Writing and Difference* [1967], translated by Alan Bass. London: Routledge, 2001.

Jacques Derrida. *Of Grammatology* [1967], translated by Gayatri Chakravorty Spivak. Baltimore: The Johns Hopkins University Press, 1997.
Jacques Derrida. *Learning to Live Finally: The Last Interview* [2007], translated by Pascal-Anne Brault and Michael Nass. Brooklyn, NY: Melville House Publishing, 2011.
Jacques Derrida. *On the Name* [1993], edited by Thomas Dutoit and translated by David Wood, Jean P. Leavey, Jnr., and Ian McLeod. Stanford, CA: Stanford University Press, 1995.
Jacques Derrida. *The Other Heading: Reflections on Today's Europe* [1991], translated by Pascal-Anne Brault and Michael B. Nass. Bloomington: Indiana University Press 1992.
Jacques Derrida and Maurizio Ferraris. *A Taste for the Secret* [1997], translated by Giacomo Donis. Cambridge, UK: The Polity Press, 2001.
Jacques Derrida and Marie-François Plissart, *Rights of Inspection* [1985], translated by David Wills. New York: The Monacelli Press, 1999
Michel Foucault. *Discipline and Punish: The Birth of the Prison* [1975], translated by Alan Sheridan. New York and Toronto: Random House, 1977.
Craig Hazen. 'Gabriel's Vision: an Angelic threat to the Resurrection'. *Christian Research Journal* 32, no. 2 (2009).
Catherine Malabou. *What Should We Do with Our Brain?* [2004], translated by Sebastian Rand. New York: Fordham University Press, 2008.
David S. Mial. 'The Library versus the Internet: Literary Studies under Siege'. *PMLA* 116, No. 5 (2001).
J. Hillis Miller, 'The Medium is the Maker: Browning, Freud, Derrida, and the New Telepathic Ecotechnologies'. *The Oxford Literary Review* 30, no. 2 (2008).
Will Steffen, Paul J. Crutzen, and John R. McNeill, 'The Anthropocene: Are Humans Now Overwhelming the Great Forces of Nature?' *Ambio* 38 (2007).

4 Reading in the Library of Catastrophe
W. G. Sebald's *The Rings of Saturn*
Richard Crownshaw

W. G. Sebald's *The Rings of Saturn* (first published as *Die Ringe des Saturn*, in 1995) comprises its narrator's recollection of a walking tour of Suffolk in August 1992, during which he encountered 'the traces of destruction' that contoured the landscape. Those encounters rendered him in a state of 'almost total immobility' and hospitalisation.[1]

The paralysis is a symptom of melancholia (an inability to come to terms with the past), and the belated narratorial act (and the historical memory it entails) the beginnings of a process of mourning what has been destroyed. Both memory and narrative are mapped onto the landscape that has been walked, as the narrator recalls the history of significant places and spaces navigated and the historical and literary associations prompted by such navigations in a manner that is as digressive as the ambulatory route taken. This chapter argues that *The Rings of Saturn*'s orchestration of memory has more in common with the act of reading in the library than with the archivisation of historical knowledge. Indeed, as this chapter argues, the violent and powerful logic of the archive informs the very destruction at the root of the narrator's melancholy state. This chapter, then, posits the library, and memorative reading therein, as a structure for metacommentary on the archive.

A more detailed conception of the library, and archive, is needed. Aby Warburg's concept of the library provides a useful pretext for *The Rings of Saturn*, particularly its orchestration of the traces of the past, and the way those traces (texts of various sorts) construct the subjectivity of the narrator, who might usefully be considered as a librarian of the Warburgian method. Warburg's understanding of cultural history revolves around the 'afterlife' (*Nachleben*) of the past in the present, particularly of antiquity. As Christian Emden puts it:

> Throughout his writings, he seeks to understand the forms of this afterlife: Dürer's representation of the death of Orpheus leads him back to ancient reliefs, in Renaissance medals he detects a union of pagan symbolism and theological humanism; on Flemish tapestries he discovers that medieval clothes *alla franzese* are depicted in ancient Greek style; Hellenistic astral mythology survives in Frescoes in Ferrara; and he

follows the influence of Greek and Neoplatonic astronomy in the writings of Luther and Melancthon.[2]

The afterlife of these images could be described as a form of cultural memory, by which these images and the historical currents they represent are consciously and unconsciously recalled in the present moment and thereby recontextualised. The constellation of past and present is for Warburg a polarisation (energisation) of the latent '*Pathos-Formel*' or emotive nature of the recalled image.[3] The affectiveness of the image is, of course, mediated by and is contingent on the context of its transmission (or remembrance), but the emotive nature of the image is discerned as a trace of the past.

The affective charge of the image competes with the intellectual contemplation of the image: an apprehension of the image that cannot contain its afterlife. In this, the cultural historian attempts to become both subject and object of cultural memory—a conduit for the crystallisations of the past, the embodiment of pictorial memory.[4] Warburg's library, Kulturwissenschaftliche Bibliothek Warburg, was designed to stage this performance of cultural memory. Books in the library were placed according to the 'law of good neighbourliness', according to their correspondent content.[5] Given the oscillation between subject and object that such a performance entails, Philippe-Alain Michaud has described it as an endeavour to abolish the distinctions between knowledge and intuition.[6]

The *Mnemosyne* atlas, created between 1924 and 1929 and housed at Warburg's newly installed library in Hamburg, was the materialisation of Warburg's theory of the history of visual culture, as well as paradigmatic of the principles by which he organised his library. The atlas retraces the fate of images from the history of science, religion, and art to their modern reincarnation (often in mass media form). The atlas's spacing of images had affinities to Eisensteinian montage by which sequencing is a matter of juxtaposition, proximity a matter of the violent collision of representations and their time frames, and in which proximate images bear a relation to each other that is analogous, anachronous, and charged with affect.[7] Warburg has described this spatialisation of images 'an iconology of intervals.' As Warburg puts it,

> The dynamograms of ancient art are handed down in a state of maximal tension but unpolarised with regard to the passive or active energy charge to the responding, imitating or remembering artists. It is only the contact with the new age that results in polarization. This polarization can lead to a radical reversal (inversion) of the meaning they held for classical antiquity.[8]

The display's dynamic, which was not just diachronic but also synchronic, ideally provokes an active form of viewing or intervention. That intervention, much like the performances for which his library was designed, was dependent on receptiveness to the affective charge that was perceived to accompany visual images. The viewer participates in the cultural memory mapped out in *Mnemosyne* and continues that process of 'polarisation': the viewer is the 'receptive surface, a photosensitive plate on which texts and images surging up from the past reveal themselves'.[9]

Christa-Maria Lerm Hayes has suggested (without developing her argument further) that Sebald's narratives are structured in a similar manner to Warburg's act of the visual curation of the past.[10] Rather like Warburg, Sebald, via his narrator, remediates historical texts—in Sebald's case pictorial and written—to produce analogies across time and space between the histories for which those texts stand. In these synchronous, diachronous, and anachronous analogies and their textualisation, the affectiveness of the past is transmitted and amplified. Like Warburg's librarian, Sebald's narrator acts as a conduit for this affective transmission, engorged and disgorged by the temporal flux, both subject and object of cultural memory. The concept of the library allows Sebald's (Warburgian) narrator to participate in cultural memory by way of reading modernity's catastrophes (and their antecedents).

The ethical need for a reading of modernity becomes apparent in light of Rembrandt's *The Anatomy Lesson*. For the narrator, Rembrandt's *The Anatomy Lesson*, housed in the Mauritshuis, represents the violence of early modern discourse. Rembrandt's painting of the Guild of Surgeons depicts the public dissection in January 1632 of the corpse of the petty thief Adriaan Adriaanszoon (alias Aris Kindt), soon after his execution, at the Waaggebouw in Amsterdam, for one of Dr. Nicolaas Tulp's annual anatomy lessons. The 'spectacle' constituted 'a significant date in the agenda of a society that saw itself emerging from the darkness into the light' (12). The significance for that society lies in the Cartesian perspective depicted by the painting:

> Dr. Tulp's colleagues are not looking at Kindt's body [. . . but] the open anatomical atlas in which the appalling physical facts are reduced to a diagram, a schematic plan of a human being, such as envisaged by the enthusiastic amateur anatomist René Descartes, who was also, so it is said, present that January morning [. . .]. In his philosophical investigations, which form one of the principle chapters of the history of subjection, Descartes teaches that one should disregard the flesh, which is beyond our comprehension, and attend to the machine within, to what can be fully understood, be made wholly useful for work, and in the event of any fault, either repaired or disregarded. (13)

Anne Fuchs has commented that Descarte's 'devaluation of the very notion of biological life [. . . which] produces a dangerously utilitarian concept of nature that categorises life according to its usefulness' makes 'a connection between European rationalism and the biopolitics that made Auschwitz possible'.[11] That flesh is made useful, or found at 'fault or disregarded', is prefigured in the body's epistemological subjection and consequent representation: a process captured in Rembrandt's painting by the fact that surgeons look not at the body but at the 'anatomical atlas in which the appalling facts are reduced to a diagram, a schematic plan of the human being'. The flesh or nature is made comprehensible and incomprensible at the same time, subsumed and othered by its very modern representation. As Sebald's narrator puts it, 'Though the body is open to contemplation, it is, in a sense, excluded' (16).

Sebald's positioning of this painting in the text is significant in terms of the way his narrator and we the readers read the artefacts and landscapes of modernity vis-à-vis the epistemological regimes, and the biopolitics they inform, that characterise modernity, the inception of which are emblematised by Rembrandt. Where Fuchs sees a long history of modernity in which the Holocaust is foreshadowed, J. J. Long sees the structures and conditions of modernity not only preceding the Holocaust but also continuing to the present moment of narration, and in fact shaping that narration and how it remembers modernity. For Long, modernity's nexus of the production of knowledge, industrial production, and the production of the subject can be found in the era's archival tendencies and technologies.[12] Long's Foucauldean approach to modernity (often via Foucault's *Discipline and Punish* and *History of Sexuality, Volume One*) sees power imposed not in a top-down fashion and by state prohibition but by the 'concept of the archive that acknowledges the vast plurality of archival practices that emerge in modernity, and an understanding of power that might account for their biological functioning'.[13] Archives came into being to memorialise and solidify monarchical power and then that of the nation state. Under modern epistemic regimes, 'principles of identification, classification and gathering' were able to shape and, indeed, produce modern life and subjectivity. The distribution of bodies in space was, of course, contingent on the uneven development of archival practice across modernity's spheres of activity, the very nature and local purpose of those practices (which took myriad although paradigmatic form), and on those who were disciplined by them.[14]

When exercised through the archive, power is not 'purely repressive' but 'productive'. Bodies are disciplined not just through their 'voluntary submission to explicit regulations' but also through their 'surveillance, observation, registration, and examination'. This additional form of discipline produces correspondent documentary apparatus and methods of information storage. The ever-present possibility of observance and recording leads to the modern subject's internalisation, in a panoptic-like fashion, of regulation. Self-regulation extends to the act of confession (be it in the form of memoir, testimony, diary, or another form of autobiographical expression, the activities of Sebald's narrator's notwithstanding) in which the articulation of one's perceived authentic self in the face of (and in seeking liberation from) power is actually a means by which the self is constituted by that power. The articulation of the self in this manner is not only inspired by the regime of self-surveillance (the internalisation of regulation) but also relates the self to the powerful discourses, practices, and institutions that provide the subject with the authority and interpretive method by which he or she understands him- or herself (the truth of the confession).[15] To understand the extent to which Sebald's narrator and the act of narrative itself are implicated in the power/knowledge nexus that ruins landscapes and bodies, another look at Rembrandt's painting is necessary.

Rembrandt's painting depicts how a power/knowledge nexus lethally produces a disciplined subject and how social control is produced by the archiving of medical knowledge of the body. The painting is also housed in an archival institution, the museum. The legitimating cultural capital amassed in the Mauritshuis has a disciplinary effect on those who visited and visit it—a feeling of belonging to a culturally evolved nation—producing national subjects. This self-regulation or self-surveillance is focused by the spectacular display of art(efacts), and 'spectatorship [. . .] inserts the individual into relations of power, arranging bodies in space and fixing the observer within normative, codified regimes of visual consumption[. . . .] The spectacle disciplines by delimiting what is to be seen and determining how it is to be seen'. The transformation of the exhibits in a museum into spectacle, via their distribution and display, allows the viewer a visual mastery over the spectacular object that is paralleled by the 'workings of the power/knowledge [nexus] that operate through spectacle on the observer himself'.[16]

Within the archive of the museum, Sebald's narrator resists the disciplinary effects of display and finds in Rembrandt's painting resistance to the power/knowledge nexus and biopolitical regime depicted therein. The 'much-admired verisimilitude of Rembrandt's picture proves on closer examination to be more apparent than real'. The dissection shown has begun with the 'offending hand', which is 'grotesquely out of proportion compared with the hand closer to us' and

> anatomically the wrong way round: the exposed tendons, which ought to be those of the left palm given the position of the thumb are in fact those of the right hand. In other words, what we are faced with is a transposition taken from the anatomical atlas, evidently without further reflection, that turns this otherwise true to life painting (if one may so express it) into a crass misrepresentation at the exact centre point of its meaning, where the incisions are made.

This 'deliberate [. . .] flaw in the composition [. . .] signifies the violence that has been done to Aris Kindt. It is with him the victim, and not the guild that gave Rembrandt his commission, that the painter identifies. His gaze alone is free of Cartesian rigidity' (16–17).

Sebald's narrator is acutely aware of the viewer's potential implication in the Cartesian gaze depicted by Rembrandt, despite the visual dissent of the painter's perspective. As the narrator continues, 'If we stand today before the large canvas of Rembrandt's *The Anatomy Lesson* in the Mauritshuis we are standing precisely where those who were present at the dissection at the Waaggebouw stood, and we believe that we see what they saw then' (13). Russel Kilbourn is equally concerned: 'In contemplating the radical reification of an other, the spectator herself, alongside the author ("wir"), is subjected by the painting (reproduced in the book), constrained to view from a site determined by its alignment with the Cartesian coordinates extending outward from the represented visual space'.[17] That those coordinates extend outwards suggests the reader and author (along with painter and spectator) are also perspectivally implicated in a new way of seeing that emerged in the early seventeenth century and which is still apparent in the twenty-first-century novel: 'As Sebald reads it, the beginning of modern medical practice is conflated in Rembrand's painting with the emergence of a new way of seeing. Realism in this context is never separable from the realism of bourgeois capitalist realism, an aesthetic ideology whose progressive phases after the Renaissance extend from the nineteenth century academic painting to the historical and realist novels and finally to twentieth- and twenty-first-century media'.[18] This cultural evolution works from a 'neoplatonic conception' or 'Christian metaphysical dualism' in which representation is predicated on a transcendent and unseen signified towards the 'hard material' and self-referential 'surfaces of commodity culture'.[19] Its progress and conclusion and its various media, argues Kilbourn, are haunted by that unseen shadow, figured as the negative, irrational, and, ultimately, deathly. Under a capitalist economy, the deathly is progressively redeemed as 'productive destruction' and signifies nothing. For Kilbourn, then, *The Rings of Saturn* is a 'multi-faceted memento mori, constructed under the sign of the anti-Cartesian scopic regime' that mourns that which has been redeemed and made fungible, along with memory itself that has been erased from the cultural landscape.[20] In sum, *The Rings of Saturn* mourns modernity's lack of mourning.

According to Kilbourn, painter and author, viewer and reader are implicated in (or, as Long, might have it, disciplined by) an aesthetic in which the deathly can only be glimpsed (lingering 'unseen' in 'plain view in the interstices of dominant culture') depending on, rather like Holbein the Younger's 1533 painting of the two ambassadors, the position from which the text is seen.[21] Where Kilbourn admits a textual haunting, and a stubbornly melancholic subject (Sebald's narrator) at the centre of the text,[22] who cannot mourn the passing of mourning, this chapter suggests a different interpretation of *The Rings of Saturn* in which the possibilities for memory lie in how the text models the act of reading. This is where the concept of the library found in the text might be usefully differentiated from the archive (where critics have often considered the former to be governed by the same logic).[23] Sebald's remediation of the painting transmits, in Warburgian fashion, its affective charge (registered in the narrator's shocked empathy). The intermedial constellation of pasts and presents (painting, museum, novel) loosens the disciplinary hold on author/narrator/reader, allowing modern spectatorship to be transformed into an act of reading the texts, artefacts, and landscapes of modernity. Through an orchestration of historical representations (akin to Warburg's), Sebald intends his reader to be constituted by cultural memory rather than wholly by a power/knowledge nexus. In sum, Sebald's intermediality suggests (pace Kilbourn) that his text is less an archive and more a library in the Warburgian sense—that is, something beyond the traditional idea of a collection of texts. The constellation of texts, with its affective charge, staged by the novel, not only disrupts and exceeds archival logic and intention but also establishes this novel as a meta-commentary on that logic. Not only that: reading archival knowledge in this library, so to speak, illuminates the former's constitutional instability, its internal heterogeneity, and its need to be reread, but in ways that cannot always be prescribed.

John Beck has argued that the emphasis on the act of reading and the narratives that follow makes *The Rings of Saturn* 'a space of and for reading'.[24] The book contains and becomes a space of reading, a library, aligning the narrator's and reader's activities—as before Rembrandt's painting. What, however, does reading entail in Beck's argument? The emphasis on acts and spaces of reading and writing suggests a necessary scrutiny: 'the interrogation of the authority of constructed worlds and how representations shape, influence and legitimate facts and events—how narratives make and unmake worlds' which 'is a direct confrontation with the technology of linguistic power in the modern world'.[25] For example, the narrator recalls the office of a colleague, Janine Dakyns, whose academic work (principally on Flaubert) created an 'amazing profusion of paper' through which 'a virtual landscape had come into being' (85–6). Dakyns claims to find perfect order in this disorder, which has erased the real world and replaced it with a paper one (86). The same might said of Sebald's narrative as a whole—Dakyns's disorderly order writ large—the creation of a 'counter-system, a mirror world that reflects back the [. . .] "truth" of historical experience' that has been 'deformed' by 'Enlightenment rationality [. . . and] the imperial and capitalist projects' that it legitimised. What is to prevent its staging the 'uncanny' return of that deformation?[26] In other words, the digressive nature of the text that records the progress of a body and subjectivity through time and space may in fact reinscribe the very representational order it sets out to critique—a disorderly order (self-)legitimated by the intellectual labour of the narrator and his memorative stance.[27]

As Long argues, Dakyns's study is a failed archive. This 'paper landscape [. . .] constitutes an archive that is completely devoid of systemacity or a publically accessible ordering principle, effectively excluding it from structures of power/knowledge [. . .] The disciplinary archive is thus susceptible to failure from within, to the recalcitrance of embodied materiality, and to local subversion by archival and taxonomic practices that elude the power/knowledge nexus'.[28] Failure then is contingent on the archivist and the archived material, which here is of personal significance rather than of social use. Another such example of useless archival idiosyncrasy would be in Edward FitzGerald's often-incomplete lexical projects (199–200).[29] However, the failure of these archives does not engender an alternative knowledge or historical memory of modernity, no matter how well placed FitzGerald was, for example, to comment on the capitalist reorganisation in the latter part of the nineteenth century of the rural landscape of Suffolk and those labouring classes who tenanted it (202).

A failed archive still retains its potential to function efficiently. For Beck, that failure is ensured by the partiality of reading and writing, foregrounded in *The Rings of Saturn*, which destabilises rather than restabilises the potential tyranny of representation.[30] This chapter argues that reading takes a more detailed turn (or reversal), one that is specific to biopolitical regimes and archival practices. Reading in this sense would offer a qualitatively different hermeneutics than would that of keeping watch over failed archives—a form of literary criticism that risks perpetuating the ideologies materialised by the archive, identifying but not dismantling the archive, and pointing to its need for buttressing in an unintentionally reparative manner.[31] In contradistinction, this suggested reading is informed by Giorgio Agamben's conception of the 'state of exception'.

The state of exception is characterised by the suspension of a code of law through (extra)legal acts that strip subjects of legal recognition in the eyes of the state, engendering noncitizens or 'bare life'. Agamben's examples include Hitler's 28 February 1933 Decree for the Protection of the People and the State, which suspended the Weimar Constitution and declared an (extra)legal civil war against Germany's Jewish citizenry. The legality of such acts under the state of exception is indistinct; the line between what is inside and outside the law is blurred.[32] Those (extra)legal acts have the 'force' but not the 'value' of law.[33] Nevertheless, such acts are only intelligible with reference to the now-suspended body of law, or code, that has been surpassed. In that sense, the legal enunciation works like the relation between langue and parole. Linguistic enunciation (parole) presupposes the existence of a systematised corpus (langue) as the reservoir of possible choices that now recedes behind its materialisation as utterance. Both acts of language and of law claim immanence—to be meaningful in themselves without reference to the structures they have subsumed—enacting a pure relationship with reality.

In the state of exception, the (extra)legal activity, without the (now-suspended) legal grounds, can appear the norm, or normative, because of that suspension. The violent effects of the law appear to be a 'pure violence without logos' and 'claim to realise an enunciation without real reference'.[34] Violence appears to be non-teleological (not the telos of the law), natural, and something which 'purely acts and manifests itself'.[35] A purified violence, emanating from a zone of 'indistinction' (unlocatable) and immanent to itself, is thereby mythologised.[36] It is in the state of exception that law reveals both its correspondence to an enabling context *and* its non-correspondence (to a suspended legal corpus). It is in the state of exception that the structuring of the (extra)legal act—its negative grounds—can be glimpsed and its rhetoric of purity deconstructed.

How, though, to critique the exceptional law (and the exceptional situation) without reinscribing the same logic, without claiming the same immanence of meaning and purity of effect, without paralleling its teleological trajectory, without replacing (extra)legal violence with discursive, representational, or rhetorical violence. For Agamben and Eric Santner, this is a case of studying the law rather than practicing it, thereby establishing a non-relation between law and life.[37] That does not mean the imagination of modern life outside of the law in some pure and natural condition, as this is the very thing that the state of exception has achieved in the production of 'bare life'.[38] Rather, the concept of purity must be appropriated in terms of the 'deactivation' of law in relation to life, 'studied' but no longer 'practiced', establishing not the telos of justice 'but the gate that leads to it' as well and thereby the potential to interrupt mythic violence.[39] In sum, the law must be read—and read, as will be seen, in a fashion after Warburg.

Drawing on Agamben, Eric Santner argues that Walter Benjamin finds the figure of such reading in Kafka's 'The New Advocate' (93–94):[40]

> Reversal is the direction of study which transforms existence into script. Its teacher is Bucephalus, 'the new advocate', who takes the road back without the powerful Alexander—which means, rid of the onrushing conquerer. 'His flanks free and unhampered by the thighs of a rider, under a quiet lamp far from the din of Alexander's battles, he reads and turns the pages of our old books [. . .] But once we have reached this point, we are in danger of missing Kafka by stopping here. Is it really the law which could be thus invoked against myth in the name of justice? No, as a legal scholar Bucephalus remains true to this origin, except that he does not seem to be practicing law—and this is probably something new, in Kafka's sense, for both Bucephalus and the bar. The law which is studied but no longer practiced is the gate to justice.[41]

Santner understands the works of W. G. Sebald as an attempted suspension or deactivation of the law that produces biopolitical or, as Santner has it, 'creaturely life'. This chapter modifies that understanding by focusing on the act of reading. Law and language correspond to each other in their respective enactments. 'Study' found in the nexus of Kafka's, Benjamin's, Agamben's, and Santner's work can be usefully thought of in Sebald's work as reading rather than practising the law. Where Sebald attends to the biopolitical regimes of modernity, the emphasis on reading (and spaces of reading) suggests a means of critiquing the power/knowledge nexus without reproducing its archival logic or the aesthetic implication that so concerns Kilbourn.[42]

Such studious reading is perhaps provoked by and most necessary in what for some critics is *The Rings of Saturn*'s most controversial sequence. On the coastline south of Lowestoft, the narrator ponders the history of herring fishing—a historical memory spatialised by the encounter with the coastal landscape. Put another way, this is walking as reading, as physical progress that drives the narrative because what is encountered generates interpretation.[43] It is the perception of the 'indestructibility of Nature', of which the species, once found in overwhelming numbers, is emblematic, and that catalyses its destruction (53). Herring fishing was 'regarded as a supreme example of mankind's struggle with the power of Nature' (54). Not only overfished but also subject to experimentation, this 'process, inspired by our thirst for knowledge, might be described as the most extreme of sufferings undergone by a species always threatened by disaster' (57). This suffering, it was assumed, given the 'peculiar physiology of the fish left them free of the fear and pains that rack the bodies and souls of higher animals in their death throes. But the truth is that we do not know what the herring feels' (57). Pondering the history of herring, the 'darkening' coastline puts the narrator in mind of 'an article I had clipped from the *Eastern Daily Press* several months before, on the death of Major George Wyndham Le Strange' whose manor house lay nearby (59). The narrator continues: 'During the last War, the report read, Le Strange served in the anti-tank regiment that liberated the camp at Bergen Belsen on the 14th April 1945', after which words the reader turns the page to be confronted by a double-spread photographic image of corpses in thin woodland (59, 60–61). Neither the article nor the narrator mentions Belsen again, and the image is neither captioned nor referred to by the narrator, which is quite typical in Sebald's work. The implication is that this image is of what those liberators found at Belsen. The reproduction of the image without attribution, and so loosened from its provenance and available for its charged juxtaposition with other images to which it finds itself analogous, is, of course, resonant of Warburg's method. Yet, this library of images must be read in the right away to avoid what will become apparent as an archival logic binding these different images and their referents.

The relationship between natural history and the history of genocide is troubling. The Cartesian regime evident in the experimentation on and destructive mastery over nature (as in herring fishing) collapses into the biopolitical regime lethally instituted at Bergen Belsen. Sebald's narrative seems not to have withstood the teleological nature of the Cartesian perspective and of the biopolitical regimes that adopt it. Such a perspective, which rationalises all objects in its path, rendering them fungible and naturalises its own progress. If that is the case, then all social history seems to collapse into natural history, as *The Rings of Saturn* is unable to withstand the representational systems it critically stages. The equation between natural and social history (or the naturalisation of social history) seems apparent in the narration of the gradual destruction of Dunwich, a once great port of the

Middle Ages that succumbed to a series of natural disasters ('catastrophic incursions' of storm, hurricane and coastal erosion). 'Dunwich, with its towers and many thousand souls, has dissolved into water, sand and thin air' (158–159). If natural catastrophes are confused with social ones, it is not surprising that of all the disasters narrated the narrator seems most affected by the damage done to English trees in the hurricane of autumn 1987 (265–267).

Peter Fritzsche takes exception to the comparison of the bodies found at Bergen Belsen and those of herring, to the naturalising terms used to render social history as natural history (as in, for example, the case of Dunwich), to the absorption of historical particularity (most seriously of Bergen Belsen), and to the fact that the Holocaust does not command in this text a form and theory of representation specific and appropriate to the nature of its events.[44] Long argues that the text fails to escape an archival logic that governs its narrative structure. Despite the narrator's attempts to resist modernity's power-knowledge nexus, through a digressive narrative that remembers the 'semantic density' of places navigated (a spatialisation of time) that would otherwise be homogenised (effectively forgotten), the narrative ultimately sets up a series of equivalences between narrative events (times, spaces and places encountered and narrated). In this equivalence, no one event can be privileged over another; and quantative not qualitative differences are registered.[45] (For example, fourteen million trees were destroyed in 1987 [265], sixty billion herring caught [57], and seven hundred thousand murdered at Jasenovac [97].) The narrative does not proceed metonymically (the encounter with place stands in for the encounter with time) but metaphorically (what is encountered is rendered formally similar).[46] A system of similarity, argues Long, is needed to shore up the text's coherence, as narrative digression and dilatoriness threatens to dissolve into incoherence.[47] In sum, the text has installed a 'salient technology of modernity into the very fabric of the narrative', demonstrating an archival mastery of its materials, and the knowledge it generates, from which it cannot escape.[48]

It might be possible that critical commentary has itself succumbed to an archival logic, as the text's similarities can be read differently. The affinities suggested by the text task the reader either with finding a pattern (a natural history that encompasses all things) in which there may be none or with illuminating an arbitrary patterning foregrounded by the narrative. In that sense, the affinities are a strategic means of locating difference.[49] In the example of the natural history given earlier, the history of herring fishing and the history of genocide (or the liberation of the camps) are related by what seems to be a tenuous if nonsensical relational thought (of a 'darkening' coastline), revealing an associative narrative consciousness unfolding peripatetically (articulating the proximity of two spatialised historical memories), more than a structural continuity between the two histories themselves. Having said that, we must remind ourselves that the histories can be related by Cartesian logic unleashed on bodies and nature. Or, as Cosgrove would argue, the history of global capitalism connects vastly differing and devastating industrial processes (such as the processing of humans and animals) that occur unevenly at different times and in different places and which manifest themselves in the shaping of the landscape (be it a body-strewn camp in Germany or a Suffolk coastline).[50] In that sense, the social history of capitalist modernity takes the form of natural history.

It must not be forgotten, however, that the narrativisation of a relation between the bodies of Jews and herring takes place within an intertextual framework. Sebald's narrator is reminded, by the flight of birds over the sea and the cliffs, of Jorge Luis Borges's story 'Tlön, Uqbar, Orbis Tertius', the theme of which is the construction of a fictional world Tlön, its language, and its history, which threaten to subsume its increasingly unverifiable textual origins and to supersede the real world (69–70). Borges's story reminds us of the textual construction of worlds, and the confluence of history and literary narrative, providing a critical distance on the implications of historically relating herring and Jews. The possibility that the reference to Borges's text might institute another tyranny of representation—a deconstruction that deconstructs all but its own terms and its very premise (or an orderly disorder as Beck might put it)—is undermined by the nature of the intertextual reference, which is as digressive as the narrator's own walks. In this sense, Borges provides not an intertext but a paratext and the narrative syntagma unfolds paratactically.

Within the reference to this text lies another: 'The world will be Tlön. But, the narrator concludes, what is that to me? In the peace and quiet of my country villa I continue to hone my tentative translation, schooled on Quevedo, of Thomas Browne's *Urn Burial* (which I do not mean to publish)' (71). The narrator's biographical account of Browne's life and writings bookends his own narrative. The narrator believes that Browne was present at the dissection of Aris Kindt (17), which makes Browne's metaphysics an important philosophical resource in countering the Cartesian perspective enacted there and its modern legacies. Just as that perspective is shadowed by the deathly and irrational, so 'the invisibility and intangibility of that which moves us remained an unfathomable mystery for Thomas Browne too, who saw our world as no more than a shadow image of another one far beyond' (18). In attending to that which haunts the Cartesian gaze, both Sebald (and his narrator) and Browne share the same narrative style and strategy, 'deploying a vast repertoire of quotations and the names of authorities who had gone before, creating complex metaphors and analogies, and constructing labyrinthine sentences that sometimes extend over one or two pages, sentences that resemble processions or a funeral cortège in their sheer ceremonial lavishness' (19). Despite the 'gravitational' pull on his prose, due to the weight of allusion and learning that it bears, it does succeed in gaining a sense of levitation above the objects of its enquiry, providing both transcendent, critical distance and microscopic scrutiny (19). 'And yet, says Browne, all knowledge is enveloped in darkness. What we perceive are no more than isolated lights in the abyss of ignorance, in the shadow-filled edifice of the world. We study the order of things, says Browne, but we cannot grasp their innermost essence' (19). 'Shorthand' for such an order or pattern is the 'quincunx', 'which is composed by using the corners of a regular quadrilateral and the point at which its diagonals intersect. Browne identifies this structure everywhere, in animate and inanimate matter' (19–20). Although 'one might demonstrate *ad infinitum* the elegant geometrical designs of Nature', Nature's continuities produce discontinuity, conformity deformities, seriality 'singular phenomena' (21). As recorded in Browne's *Pseudoxia Epidemica*, the patterns of nature generate the monstrous exception that proves the rule (22). This generative destruction is, Browne finds, universal: in 'every new thing there lies already the shadow of annihilation. For the history of every individual, of every social order, indeed of the whole world, does not describe an ever-widening, more and more wonderful arc, but rather follows a course which, once the meridian is reached, leads without fail into the dark' (24). This inherent destructiveness informs Browne's fascination for the things that survive, as in *Urn Burial* (1658), a 'discourse on sepulchral urns found near Walsingham in Norfolk', which draws on the natural and historical sources for precedent and context in its discussion and cataloguing of the remains of the dead and buried, the things 'unspoiled by the passage of time' (26). The melancholy difficulty in accepting the immanent destruction of things is assuaged by the fact that some things remain: 'Browne scrutinizes that which escaped annihilation for any sign of mysterious capacity for transmigration he has so often observed in caterpillars and moths. That purple piece of silk he refers to, then, in the urn of Patroclus—what does it mean?'

Reference to Browne and the meaning of silk reappears in the final chapter of *The Rings of Saturn*. The detailed history of sericulture is prefaced by an account of Browne's *Musaeum Clausum* or *Bibliotheca Abscondita*, 'a catalogue of remarkable books, listing pictures, antiquities and sundry singular items that may have formed part of a collection put together by Brown but were more likely products of his imagination, the inventory of a treasure house that existed purely in his head and to which there is no access except through the letters on the page' (271). The *Musaeum* includes a reference to the introduction of the secrets of Chinese sericulture to the Western world (273–74). This history of Western sericulture traces its development through the eighteenth century (282–83)—during which the bodies of silk weavers were tortuously harnessed to weaving machines in a manner that could be described as disciplinary in the Foucauldean sense—through its use in the Third Reich's aviation technology and as a symbol of the engineering of racial purity (292–93). The narrative of the final chapter concludes by returning sericulture to Browne, whose father was a silk merchant and who, the narrator recalls but cannot verify, remarked in a passage of the *Pseudoxia Epidemica* that in seventeenth-century Holland when there had been a death, it was the custom to drape, 'all mirrors and all canvasses depicting landscapes or people or the fruits of the field, so that the soul, as it left the body, would not be distracted on its final journey, either by a reflection of itself or by a last glimpse of the land now being lost forever' (296).

Long points out that, after quoting (indirectly but verbatim) from the *Garden of Cyrus* on the quincunx, Sebald adds something not in but sounding like the original: 'we are occupied above all by the abnormalities of creation, be they the deformities produced by the sickness or the grotesqueries with which Nature, with her inventiveness scarcely less diseased, fills every vacant space in her atlas' (21). The term *abnormality* does not enter the German and English lexicons until the nineteenth century. Sebald's addition converts Browne's 'devotional hermeneutics' that 'seeks similitude among diverse singularities that remain irreducibly particular while participating in the oneness of divine creation' into an 'avatar of a distinctly modern episteme'. This modern 'secular negative metaphysics' centres on monstrous abnormality: not the exception that proves the rule but exception as the rule in terms of nature's generative destruction.[51]

If *The Rings of Saturn* generates spaces of and for reading, then the inter- and intratextual use of Browne provides a model of how Sebald's text is structured like a library, facilitating the work of ethical reading (and remembering) by narrator and reader, and therefore commentary on the knowledge/power nexus instituted by archival practice. The compendious narrative style, and it inventory of texts, objects, places, people, and histories, shared by Browne and Sebald's narrator, 'brings the text to a standstill', arresting plot but allowing the 'potentially infinite extension of discourse time'.[52] This arresting narrative style brings reading to a standstill as well. Long argues that the leaps, digressions, convolutions and densities both of and within the narrative can be characterized as a hallmark of modernist difficulty. Such difficulty impedes the reading process or rather reading as consumption and therefore interferes with the text's commodification.[53] More than that, such an uneconomic narrative style also prevents the easy consumption of the text's archival reproduction of the world. Arrested reading affords the opportunity for the kind of study advocated by Agamben. Browne's narratives of destruction may reflect on the irresistible processes of modernity to come later. However, the destructive process leaves something that remains—a materialization of difference and discontinuity that (pace Long and Kilbourn) might disrupt the power/knowledge nexus that naturalises the history of destruction. It all depends how that remnant is read.

That which survives a natural history of destruction (silk) is not posited as an autonomous and stranded remnant of modernity, a prop by which modern experience can be remembered outside of archival logic. As we seen from Sebald's narrator's history of sericulture it is implicated in the disciplining of bodies (e.g., in the industrial production of silk), the power/knowledge nexus (the military and racial technology of the Nazi state), and easing the departure (and forgetting) of the dead. Silk is an artefact, the textual traces (or narrativisation) of which, must be constantly read and reread, or studied (see Agamben), along with the other remains of modernity encountered in this text, in the library that is the text, to prevent the naturalization of a history of destruction, its archivisation. It is, then, all in the reading, which takes place in the library generated by the text, which Browne also generates in his *Musaeum* in order to read Nature's singularities *and* similarities.

NOTES

1. W. G. Sebald, *The Rings of Saturn*, trans. by Michael Hulse (London: The Harvill Press, 1999), p. 3. Further references to this text are made by page number in the main body of the essay.
2. Christian J. Emden, '"*Nachleben*": Cultural Memory in Aby Warburg and Walter Benjamin', in *Cultural Memory: Essays in European Literature and History*, ed. E. Caldicott and Anne Fuchs (Bern, Switzerland: Peter Lang, 2003), p. 214.
3. Ibid., p. 209.
4. Michael Diers, 'Warburg and the Warburgian Tradition of Cultural History', trans. T. Girst and D. von Moltke, *New German Critique* 65 (1995), p. 70.
5. Aby Warburg, quoted in ibid., p. 73.
6. Philippe-Alain Michaud, *Aby Warburg and the Image in Motion*, trans. S. Hawkes (New York: Zone Books, 2004), p. 232.
7. Ibid., pp. 242–44.
8. Quoted in ibid., pp. 281–82.
9. Ibid., pp. 255, 260.
10. Christa-Maria Lerm Hayes, 'Post-war Germany and "Objective Chance": W. G. Sebald, Joseph Beuys, and Tacita Dean', in *Searching for Sebald: Photography after W. G. Sebald*, ed. Lise Patt (Los Angeles: Institute of Cultural Inquiry), pp. 427–30.
11. Anne Fuchs, 'Ein Hauptkapitel der Geschichte der Unterwerfung: Representations of Nature in W. G. Sebald's *Die Ringe des Saturn*', in *W. G. Sebald and the Writing of History*, ed. J.J. Long and Anne Fuchs (Würzburg, Germany: Königshausen & Neumann, 2007), p. 125.
12. J. J. Long, *W. G. Sebald: Image, Archive, Modernity* (Edinburgh, UK: Edinburgh University Press, 2007), p. 10.
13. Ibid., p. 12.
14. Ibid., pp. 12, 30–32.
15. Ibid., pp. 14–17.
16. Ibid., pp. 38–39.
17. Russel J. A. Kilbourn, '"Catastrophe with Spectator": Subjectivity, Intertextuality and the Representation of History in *Die Ringe des Saturn*', in *W. G. Sebald and the Writing of History*, p. 143.
18. Ibid., p. 143.
19. Ibid., pp. 143–44.
20. Ibid., pp. 143–45.
21. Ibid., p. 144.
22. Ibid., p. 145.
23. See Long, *W. G. Sebald*, pp. 7, 10, 12.
24. John Beck, 'Reading Room: Erosion and Sedimentation in Sebald's Suffolk', in *W. G. Sebald – A Critical Companion*, ed. J.J. Long and Anne Whitehead (Seattle: University of Washington Press), p. 77.
25. Ibid., p. 80.

26. Ibid., pp. 77, 81.
27. Ibid., p. 81.
28. Long, *W. G. Sebald*, pp. 85–86.
29. Ibid., 85.
30. Beck, 'Reading Room', pp. 79–80.
31. For a related criticism, see Pierre Macherey and Etienne Balibar, 'Literature as an Ideological Form: Some Marxist Propositions', *Oxford Literary Review* 3, no. 1 (1978), pp. 4–12.
32. Giorgio Agamben, *State of Exception*, trans. Kevin Attell (London and Chicago: University of Chicago Press, 2005), pp. 23–24.
33. Ibid., pp. 38–39.
34. Ibid., p. 40.
35. Ibid., p. 62.
36. Ibid., pp. 51, 59.
37. Ibid., p.64; and Eric Santner, *On Creaturely Life: Rilke, Benjamin, Sebald* (Chicago and London: University of Chicago Press, 2006), p. 94.
38. Agamben, *State of Exception*, pp. 60, 88.
39. Ibid., pp. 64, 88.
40. Santner, *On Creaturely Life*, pp. 93–94.
41. Walter Benjamin, 'Franz Kafka: On the Tenth Anniversary of His Death', in *Illuminations*, ed. by Hannah Arendt, and trans. by Harry Zohn (London: Fontana Press), p. 134.
42. Ibid., pp. 134–35.
43. Beck, 'Reading Room', p. 78.
44. Peter Fritzsche, 'W. G. Sebald's Twentieth-Century Histories', in *W. G. Sebald: History – Memory – Trauma*, ed. Scott Denham and Mark McCulloh (Berlin and New York: Walter de Gruyter, 2006), pp. 292–94.
45. Long, *W. G. Sebald*, p. 143.
46. Ibid., p. 143.
47. Ibid., p. 142.
48. Ibid., p. 144.
49. Sara Friedrichmeyer, 'Sebald's Elective and Other Affinities', in *W. G. Sebald: History – Memory – Trauma*, pp. 80, 82.
50. Mary Cosgrove, 'Sebald for Our Time: The Politics of Melancholy and the Critique of Capitalism in his Work', in *W. G. Sebald and the Writing of History*, p. 103.
51. Long, *W. G. Sebald*, p. 37.
52. Ibid., p. 139.
53. Ibid., p. 140.

BIBLIOGRAPHY

Giorgio Agamben. *State of Exception*, translated by Kevin Attell. London and Chicago: University of Chicago Press, 2005.
John Beck. 'Reading Room: Erosion and Sedimentation in Sebald's Suffolk', in *W. G. Sebald – A Critical Companion*, ed. J.J. Long and Anne Whitehead. Seattle: University of Washington Press.
Walter Benjamin. 'Franz Kafka: On the Tenth Anniversary of His Death', in *Illuminations*, edited by Hannah Arendt and translated by Harry Zohn. London: Fontana Press, 1992.
Mary Cosgrove. 'Sebald for Our Time: The Politics of Melancholy and the Critique of Capitalism in his Work', in *W. G. Sebald and the Writing of History*, edited

by J. J. Long and Anne Fuchs. Würzburg, Germany: Königshausen & Neumann, 2007.
Michael Diers. 'Warburg and the Warburgian Tradition of Cultural History', translated by T. Girst and D. von Moltke. *New German Critique* 65 (1995).
Christian J. Emden. '"*Nachleben*": Cultural Memory in Aby Warburg and Walter Benjamin', in *Cultural Memory: Essays in European Literature and History*, edited E. Caldicott and Anne Fuchs. Bern, Switzerland: Peter Lang.
Sara Friedrichmeyer. 'Sebald's Elective and Other Affinities', in *W. G. Sebald: History – Memory – Trauma*, edited by Scott Denham and Mark McCulloh. Berlin and New York: Walter de Gruyter, 2006.
Peter Fritzsche. 'W. G. Sebald's Twentieth-Century Histories', in *W. G. Sebald: History – Memory – Trauma*, edited by Scott Denham and Mark McCulloh. Berlin and New York: Walter de Gruyter, 2006.
Anne Fuchs. 'Ein Hauptkapitel der Geschichte der Unterwerfung: Representations of Nature in W. G. Sebald's *Die Ringe des Saturn*', in *W. G. Sebald and the Writing of History*, edited by J. J. Long and Anne Fuchs. Würzburg, Germany: Königshausen & Neumann, 2007.
Christa-Maria Lerm Hayes. 'Post-war Germany and "Objective Chance": W. G. Sebald, Joseph Beuys, and Tacita Dean', in *Searching for Sebald: Photography after W. G. Sebald*, edited by Lise Patt. Los Angeles: Institute of Cultural Inquiry.
Russel J. A. Kilbourn. '"Catastrophe with Spectator": Subjectivity, Intertextuality and the Representation of History in *Die Ringe des Saturn*', in *W. G. Sebald and the Writing of History*, edited by J. J. Long and Anne Fuchs. Würzburg, Germany: Königshausen & Neumann, 2007.
J. J. Long. *W. G. Sebald: Image, Archive, Modernity*. Edinburgh, UK: Edinburgh University Press, 2007.
Pierre Macherey and Etienne Balibar. 'Literature as an Ideological Form: Some Marxist Propositions'. *Oxford Literary Review* 3, no. 1 (1978).
Philippe-Alain Michaud. *Aby Warburg and the Image in Motion*, translated by S. Hawkes. New York: Zone Books, 2004.
Eric Santner. *On Creaturely Life: Rilke, Benjamin, Sebald*. Chicago and London: University of Chicago Press, 2006.
W. G. Sebald. *The Rings of Saturn*, translated by Michael Hulse. London: The Harvill Press, 1999.

5 Agendas and Aesthetics in the Transformations of the Codex in Early Modern England

Elizabeth Evenden[1]

INTRODUCTION

Flavius Magnus Aurelius Cassiodorus Senator (ca. 485–ca. 585 CE), the eminent Roman statesman and writer, understood the importance of the written word in the preservation of knowledge. Oral culture could not only maintain but also eradicate information; a written document 'keeps a faithful witness of human deeds; it speaks of the past, and is the enemy of oblivion. For, even if our memory retains the content, it alters the words; but there discourse is stored in safety, to be heard for ever with consistency'.[2] In the sixth century CE, Cassiodorus realised the need to preserve both sacred and secular texts for future generations and wrote a number of treatises on the art of copying text for dissemination and preservation. Similarly, he stressed the importance of the presentation of text, noting that scholarly writing should consider not only the quality of its content but the mise-en-page also.

The codex (from *caudex*, the Latin word for tree bark) originated in the first century CE and was distinct from the roll or tablet in that it was composed of folded sheets sewn along one edge. It was initially a cheap form of production, manufactured with papyrus (Greek πάπυρος, *papyros*, the papyrus plant) or parchment (the skin of a sheep or goat). The term *book* derives from the Greek word βίβλος (Latin *biblos*), which refers to the inner bark of the papyrus plant. The codex was much easier to consult than were its two rival formats, and it was easily portable; such advantages made it popular among the early Christians.[3] With the conversion of the Roman Empire to Christianity in the fourth century, the codex finally became the preferred format for texts in the Christian west.[4] Cassiodorus was especially impressed with the writings of the early Christian fathers, who documented early Church history. He lauded in particular the writings of Eusebius of Caesarea (ca. 263–ca. 399 CE), considering his *Chronicles* to be a true 'image of history'.[5] Content, format, and layout were coming together to produce a lasting history of the early Christian Church.

The documenting of early English Church history sought to preserve its doctrines and practices 'to be heard for ever with consistency' also. The intention of this chapter is not to examine how manuscripts about the

English Church were produced but, rather, how these early English manuscripts were subsequently treated by later collectors and how they kept in codex form and organised into libraries. As Fred Lerner has acknowledged, the methodological approach of Cassiodorus 'emphasised the importance of establishing and preserving the most authoritative of the ancient texts, and [he] was reluctant to discard any potentially useful material'.[6] This chapter considers the preservation of texts from a former age during the early modern period. It also considers the perceived functionality and worth of the codex format for those who interacted with texts about the English Church from their own and previous ages.

More specifically, I examine the way in which one key early modern collector and editor of polemical manuscripts, Archbishop Matthew Parker, chose to turn loose, unbound Anglo-Saxon and medieval manuscripts into codex format and how he saw the codex as a fluid format—one that could be unbound and reassembled, with contents added or removed to suit his needs. Parker admired men such as Cassiodorus and Eusebius for their writing and for their concerns that ecclesiastical history needed to be preserved in books and true doctrine disseminated to avoid both the loss of knowledge and any future corruption of the church.[7] Yet it is ironic that, whilst they all sought to preserve sacred texts for future generations, none of them saw the codices with which they came into contact as sacred artefacts per se; they were merely conveyors of truth (or untruths), storehouses of information.

Like Cassiodorus, Parker sought to preserve the 'most authoritative' texts (implementing his own interpretative value judgements in the process), but whilst Cassiodorus, on the whole, sought not to discard material, Parker sought to retrieve discarded material with one hand while quietly disposing of 'untruths' with the other. Parker's ultimate aim was to re-create a library of texts that proved the lineage of the English Church, and a series of printed texts, based on these recovered codices, which would prove the validity of their doctrine. This chapter therefore explores these motivations behind Parker's actions and his methods when dealing with England's precious codices, with a textual history that had come dangerously close to being lost.

CHRISTIANITY AND THE CODEX: MATTHEW PARKER AND THE QUEST FOR CONTINUITY

In the early modern period, the greatest loss to the nation's libraries came as a result of the dissolution of the monasteries, with the subsequent dispersal of thousands of manuscripts across the country. Some texts made their way into the hands of private collectors, others into the hands of tradesmen in need of wrapping material or binders in need of raw materials, and others were simply thrown away.[8] Many contemporaries were acutely aware that the dispersal of the manuscript holdings of the great religious houses was potentially on the scale of those lost in antiquity and during the embryonic years of Christianity.[9] Whilst the Reformed Church acknowledged that many of the manuscripts dispersed were false doctrines propounded by the papacy, they equally realised that doctrinally sound manuscripts were in danger of becoming lost also. In the doctrinal debates of the mid- to late sixteenth century, it became apparent that the heritage and lineage of the church in England contained in these dispersed manuscripts was in danger of being lost to oblivion.

Much of the recovery of these manuscripts was down to a handful of collectors, such as John Leland (ca. 1503–1552), who acted as agent for the Royal collection, and, under Elizabeth I, Matthew Parker (1504–1575).[10] Parker began his career as a bible clerk; he was a scholar and later a fellow of Corpus Christi College Cambridge, moving on to become dean of Stoke-by-Clare College, Suffolk, only to return to Corpus as its Master. In 1545, he became vice-chancellor of Cambridge University. Under Elizabeth, it was soon apparent that there would be no return to a career in Cambridge. In 1559, he was installed as Archbishop of Canterbury and was quickly involved in defending the Elizabethan Church from its Catholic detractors.

On 14 July 1560, Parker received a forwarded request from a group of German Protestants in Magdeburg, known as the 'Centuriators of Magdeburg'. Their aim was to write a definitive ecclesiastical history, which, ultimately, would be divided into thirteen centuries and cover thirteen hundred years of ecclesiastical history, ending in 1298. Their first volume was published in 1559, with the final tome appearing in 1574.[11] Their leader, Matthias Flacius Illyricus, was asking for information to assist in his writing of this *Ecclesiastica historia*.[12] Parker was specifically asked about the practices of the English Church and of papal usurpation.

Parker's aims for the English Church fell in line with the work of the Lutheran scholars of Magdeberg: all sought to provide a firm answer to the all-important question, 'Where was your church before Luther?' They also all sought to ensure a written testimony of the lineage of their church survived. As Lerner has acknowledged, 'Luther had never intended his words to lead to the destruction of libraries, but his attack on the authority of the Church had unforeseen consequences'.[13] In proving their Reformed Church to be the True Church, their textual heritage, and the proof within those texts, needed to be salvaged. Parker's role was to prove publicly that, although the English Church had previously been polluted with papistical iniquities from the Continent after the Norman Conquest, it was now cleansed of such false dogma and had returned to its original condition. To demonstrate that the English Church was a True Church, with a lineage back to the church fathers, Parker set about collecting numerous early English texts, including Anglo-Saxon chronicles and versions of the Gospels.[14]

Within days, Parker sought the aid of evangelical polemicist John Bale (1495–1563) in this project.[15] Bale duly supplied the archbishop with a list of suitable topics to cover and Parker's Latin secretary, John Joscelyn, helped him by identifying other crucial areas of inquiry.[16] Parker wrote to Sir William Cecil, secretary of state, to say that he was 'spying and searching [for] credible information, among other things, in whose hands the great notable written books [. . .] should remain'.[17]

Parker's team duly set to work seeking out texts across the realm. But this was not so simple a task. The texts that had survived the dissolution were, in many instances, not easy to access—particularly if they had fallen into private hands and collections located far away from London. Manuscripts and their owners needed to be pinpointed when possible. By 1567, John Joscelyn created a further list, identifying the current owners of many of the works sought by Parker; it also highlighted texts for which ownership remained obscure.[18]

On 4 July 1568, Parker wrote to Cecil asking for official backing to access such texts.[19] The Privy Council quickly issued a letter addressed to 'sundry private persons' in possession of 'auncient recordes and monumentes' from the dissolved abbeys, requesting them to allow Parker and his team access to such documents throughout the realm.[20] This request was printed as a broadsheet, indicating the powers given to Parker to make 'a general search after all such records and muniments as related to these Realms, and which upon the dissolution of the monasteries had fallen into private hands; whereby he preserved from perishing some of the most valuable remains of our Church and Nation'.[21]

The preface to Parker's printed edition of Ælfric's *A Testimonie of Antiquitie*, which was most likely written by Parker's Latin secretary and Anglo-Saxon scholar, John Joscelyn, describes the copy-texts chosen by the Archbishop for this revival of Anglo-Saxon scholarship.[22] Parker had examined a number of Old English texts recovered by his team of scouts. For Parker, the prize jewels in his quest to prove the lineage of the English Church were supplied by Worcester and Exeter cathedrals. From Worcester came a Latin/Anglo-Saxon text, which has some crucial points erased. A second copy of the text came from Worcester also, in which the key passages of Anglo-Saxon (removed in the other copy) remained intact. A further copy of the same text came to him from Exeter, which likewise facilitated in the comprehension of what passages had been erased elsewhere. The erased Anglo-Saxon text dealt with the Eucharist, and appeared to refute the Catholic belief in transubstantiation. In Parker's printed edition of the text, in English, Latin, and Anglo-Saxon, the text is restored, with an additional marginal note making its meaning abundantly clear: 'No transubstantiation'.[23]

Similarly, in another text commissioned by Parker, an edition of the *Gospels of the Fower Evangelists*, a parallel Anglo-Saxon English edition of the Gospels, John Foxe declared that Parker was collecting such texts to show that the 'religion [practised] presently [. . .] is no new reformation of things [. . .] but rather a reduction of the Church to the Pristine state of old conformity'.[24] By having such texts circulated in print, Parker was sending a clear message to the

Protestant Church's detractors: the English knew exactly where their church lay before Luther.

Parker's self-imposed remit gave him unprecedented access to a wide range of manuscripts from across the realm. Some he was given as gifts; others were specified to be on loan (although many of these were nonetheless retained by the primate). These manuscripts were gathered together to become, in a sense, his personal collection, and he and his assistants delved through their contents for their required evidence. Evidence for the preserving of these texts as a composite collection comes from how Parker chose to bind these manuscripts into codex format and how he housed them. It should also be noted that, although Parker and his circle were preserving manuscripts that served their needs, this very act was also a process of selection. And selectivity inevitably meant that many texts, because they were not deemed relevant to or, worse still, were believed to be contrary to their remit, were discarded. I now turn to examine this selectivity and how and why these chosen texts were bound into codices.

THE CODEX AND COLLECTIONS—AN ACT OF CONSERVATION?

The Privy Council's broadsheet made it clear that Parker's mission was 'the *conseruation* of such auncienct records and monuments, written of the state and affaires of these her [Elizabeth's] realms of Englande and Irelande'.[25] As such, it highlights the venerable intention to preserve these documents for posterity. By implication, however, it shows this to be an act of selectivity. Those items not deemed worthy or, indeed, suspected to be contrary to Parker's aims were in danger of being lost. Some Anglo-Saxon manuscripts survived in multiple copies, but others remained in a single copy. Some were left with their current guardians, others were removed to Lambeth for inspection by Parker and his team. Of those taken to London, some were selected as useful, and others were deemed irrelevant to him (for whatever reason) and so were discarded. Needless to say, we do not know how many manuscripts—or parts of manuscripts—were lost during this selection process, but it is clear that whilst some books were chosen for subsequent dissemination in print, some were retained by the primate but not reprinted, and some quietly cast aside.

This salvaging aspect of Parker's work was in many ways nothing new. The earliest English printers considered themselves as the saviours of rare manuscripts, pulling a text back from the brink of oblivion. In the prefaces to many English incunabula (books printed before 1500) and early printed texts, printers often claimed as much.[26] Wyknyn de Worde, for example, in his 1530 edition of Chaucer's *The Assemblie of Foules*, informed his readers of how the text had survived in a single manuscript copy. In the preface, he included a poem he had allegedly penned himself, which told the reader how the sole surviving manuscript had 'Layde upon shelfe in leves all to torne' and in danger of being lost for all eternity; his printed edition gave it new life and rescued the contents of the manuscript for future generations. Parker saw himself as doing the same for a number of key Anglo-Saxon texts.[27]

Parker decided to organise his manuscripts; he identified the need to preserve these rare and precious texts and to ensure that the original manuscripts were kept in as robust and pristine a condition as his church. He safeguarded the survival of these manuscripts by having them bound in codex format and organised into a library. He also took the liberty of binding manuscript and printed matter together, if they suited his purpose (which is not always clear, as we shall see). Although the word *codex* is now only applied to manuscript texts, early modern collectors did not see such a distinction. Any text—manuscript or printed—could be bound as a codex and therefore made organisable, identifiable, and classifiable. A codex or book could be many things. As the late librarian of Corpus Christi College, Cambridge, once put it, when discussing how Parker used and created books, it 'depends on what you mean by a book'.[28]

Once a codex came into Parker's hands, it did not necessarily leave them in the state it arrived. If bound, manuscripts were often separated and rebound with different items. One such example is Corpus Christi College Cambridge (hereafter, CCCC) MS 173, known as the *Parker Chronicle and Laws*. This is indeed a copy of an early Anglo-Saxon chronicle, together with a series of laws passed by Alfred and Ine, all of which were compiled by the eleventh century. What is also bound with it, however, is an eighth-century manuscript of the poet Caelius Sedulius's *Carmen Paschale*.[29] These were once two separate codices now bound together by Parker as one, without any clear reason for doing so.[30] When Parker created a catalogue (or 'register') of the texts in his possession, he only made reference to this manuscript as containing the chronicles and the laws.[31] Furthermore, the Sedulius manuscript was a completely different size to its counterparts within the codex, making its inclusion all the more perplexing.

This was not the only codex to conceal disparate texts beneath its boards. CCCC MS 197 is also a composite manuscript. The latter half of this manuscript, referred to as CCCC MS 197B, is an impressive Anglo-Saxon Gospel book. The Gospels are of a much larger size than the other texts with which it is bound. Again, there is no clear connection between the texts that are bound together, and there is no correlation of manuscript size. As a result of trying to fit the Gospels within boards which easily housed the other sundry texts, CCCC MS 197B was severely cropped by the binder, resulting in the loss and damage of both the text and the outer edges of a number of illustrations.[32]

Even printed texts in Parker's collection found themselves at bound in a curious manner. Listed in Parker's catalogue as SP447, this codex is also composite. It includes a seminal tract of the 1540s by Nicholas Bodrugan, which, as Dale Hoak has recently noted, explores the possibility of 'an empire of Great Britain that was also a parliamentary monarchy'.[33] Bound with it is James Pilkington's account of the lightning strike that hit St. Paul's Cathedral on the feast of Corpus Christi in 1561, and *A Proper New Book of Cokerye*, known colloquially at Corpus Christi College Cambridge as 'Margaret Parker's cookbook'.[34] It is hard to find a reason, bibliographically or otherwise, as to why Parker would have chosen to bind such disparate texts together.

Moreover, his description of the codices in his library could be as erratic as his choice of texts to be bound. Indeed, an examination of the title pages of many of these codices reveals that it is not always easy to tell from them what exactly is contained in the volume. SP445, for example, remains in its sixteenth-century binding and is a composite volume of eight printed texts, yet its title page, and its entry in Parker's register, suggests that the volume contains only a single text.[35] In fact, in this instance, the eight texts bound together all deal with the religious and political disputes of the 1530s and 1540s. (In fact, the Bodrugan text would, perhaps, have been better bound here.)

Many of Parker's books, therefore, whether they contain manuscripts, printed matter, or both, can appear something of a minefield of complex and sometimes apparently random contents. It is possible that they were bound with levels of priority; texts identified as crucial to Parker's immediate work were identified and kept safe between boards as soon as possible. Those of less immediate use could be bound between more basic boards, where they would be safe but where they could be later disbound and collected more appropriately; indeed, the more random volumes, with basic binding, may suggest the proximity of their binding to the demise of the archbishop's health and his ultimate death. Better to have the collection bound and have a catalogue of sorts than risk the loss of individual texts. Binding also prevented damage to individual, fragile texts.

Safe storage was not the only consideration. It is interesting to note that, if multiple copies or editions of a manuscript survived, Parker would replace the missing or damaged text by having it added in a counterfeit hand. Parker had in his employ—indeed, in his household—artisans skilled in illustration and different handwriting styles, as well as binders.[36] In effect, he could create a codex that looked authentic, which, in reality, was a composite of more than one manuscript and newly added, counterfeit material. The most prominent of these 'counterfeiters' was identified by Parker as 'Lylye', possibly Peter Lily, the registrar of Parker's consistory court. In 1566, Parker had Lylye replace lost text in a manuscript loaned to the archbishop by Sir William Cecil.[37] (It is worth noting here that Parker's practices extended beyond his own books.) Similarly, CCCC MS 118 includes counterfeit text, copied from another, full manuscript of the same text.[38] So some level of aesthetics clearly did matter to the archbishop.

Parker was not averse to including a new frontispiece or adding material that did not belong to the manuscript in question. On a number of occasions, Parker pulled illustrations from manuscripts or printed texts to acts as frontispieces to other manuscripts he owned. CCCC MS 162, for example, has new flyleaves added to the volume by Parker, at the end of which is a printed illustration of the Crucifixion. On the verso of this image is the manuscript contents list. The illustration is on parchment and is probably Parisian in origin. Similarly, CCCC MS 163 includes a woodcut illustration at the beginning of the book, which has clearly been extracted from another source.[39] Parker appears content to have taken apart incunabula and early printed books (perhaps because their content was at odds with his reformed doctrine) and use their images to make his newly formed codices more aesthetically pleasing.

These aesthetic considerations necessitated the provision of space in which Parker could sit with both the manuscripts and printed matter before him, to make such aesthetic and practical decisions. Because most of his manuscripts were housed at Lambeth Palace, it was easy for Parker to pick and choose what he wished to take and reuse from this wealth of manuscripts at his disposal. From the early 1570s, Parker employed binders at Lambeth, so it became even easier for him to get these new, composite volumes bound exactly to his specifications.[40] As Timothy Graham has noted, 'Almost every manuscript that passed into his hands has undergone some transformation as a result of his ownership'.[41] Lambeth became the centre for many of these transformational acts.

What is worth noting is also the ways in which these texts were bound under Parker's direction. Many of his manuscripts *and* printed books were bound to complement one another aesthetically. Sadly, many of the manuscript bindings have been lost at Corpus Christi College.[42] A number do survive, however, in Cambridge University Library (CUL). Nine volumes survive with sturdy wooden boards covered in leather; three of them also received gold-tooled decoration: an Anglo-Saxon Psalter (CUL, MS Ff.I.23), an Anglo-Saxon translation of the Gospels (CUL, MS Ii.2.II), and a copy of the MacDurnan Gospels (CUL, MS 1370). These were texts not only highly prized but also of great use to the archbishop. The same care and attention was also paid to printed books, the publication of which was backed by Parker. Surviving examples include a copy of the *Gospels of the Fower Evangelists* presented to Elizabeth I by John Foxe (BL shelfmark 675.f.16) and copies of the second edition (1570) of John Foxe's *Acts and Monuments* (popularly known as the 'Book of Martyrs'). The codex format for such important and frequently used texts was sturdy, solid binding, with tooling identifying their special position within Parker's mission and within his library. Other texts worth holding on to, which were, however, of less importance to his activities, received less glamorous adornment. These codices were given nothing more than basic vellum covers and no additional adornment. In the register of books bequeathed after his death, these items are merely listed under the heading of 'Bookes in parchment closures'.[43] The bindings chosen for Parker's codices may have initially been a way of indicating the level of use and authority given to the text enclosed. These may also have been among some of the last to be bound.

It is clear that, by adding tables of contents and indices, Parker's codices were intended for use, rather than being merely acts of conservation per se. Many of his manuscripts are annotated in Parker's own hand (often in his characteristic red crayon). In his printed books, as with his manuscripts, one often sees a flurry of notes by Parker in a particular section, rather than throughout the whole text generally, reflecting Parker's habit of 'hon[ing] in on one point or section rather than digesting the entire text'.[44] Parker's library was a series of codices to move in and out of, in order to collectively to form a response to the issue at hand. As such, Parker's library was for his own personal use and for use by those involved in his project. He was salvaging texts from the brink of oblivion, but he was also quite restrictive as to who could use them while they were in his possession. Unlike later collectors, such as Bodley and Cotton, Parker was preserving texts to use them to serve *his* purpose and to preserve them for the good of *his* church. He was not, as such, preserving them for the purpose of public use. The texts he commissioned to be printed were his way of allowing public access to key texts.

Parker was also restrictive as to who could use his collection after his death.[45] Under the terms of an indenture of January 1574, the archbishop left many of his printed books and most, but not all, of his manuscripts to Corpus Christi College, Cambridge. These bequests were listed in his 'register', although, as noted earlier, the register does not list every text contained in some codices, having been compiled primarily based on the contents pages of these codices (which do not always identify every text found within its boards).[46] The indenture was a complex tripartite agreement among Corpus Christi, Gonville and Caius College, and Trinity Hall. Some books went to Cambridge University Library, and others, not covered by the indenture, passed to his son, John, many of which were subsequently dispersed.[47] Parker took great pains to ensure the preservation of this priceless collection.

In 1572, Parker had a number of copies of his *De antiquitate Britannicae* printed on a private press he had set up in Lambeth Palace. The text details the origins and spread of the Christian Church in England, and its contents are drawn from a number of manuscripts in his possession.[48] Lambeth Palace Library MS 959 is Parker's own copy of the work. On fol. 369^v is a list of books planned for publication at around the same time, all of which projects were overseen by the archbishop.[49] Many texts on the list were indeed published, such as the Anglo-Saxon Gospels and Paris's *Chronica maiora*, as well as works such as Thomas Walsingham's *Historia Breuis* and *Ypodigma Neustriae*.[50] Other texts on the list have not yet been identified, but it is clear by at least their titles that they were all central to Parker's mission to defend the English Church as the True Church, now allegedly returned to its 'pristine state'.

DEFINING THE EARLY MODERN COLLECTION: PURPOSE AND POSTERITY

Parker's encounter with the Magdeberg Centuriators therefore both inspired and aided him in creating a systematic defence of the English Church. Along with his systematic collection of manuscripts, Parker also collected incunabula and early printed books. Moreover, he set about a detailed plan to disseminate in printed format key texts from English ecclesiastical history, contemporary works in defence of the English Church, and a number of works to be purchased by parishes across the realm. Earliest of these was Parker's support for John Jewel's *Apologia Ecclesia Anglicanae*, which was soon translated into English for wider dissemination.[51] He moved on to oversee new books for English parishes, including a new catechism, a new book of Homilies and a new English Bible. Work on the so-called Bishops' Bible (because it was translated by a number of bishops) began in the mid-1560s, in order to replace the bibles in the parish churches of England.[52] (Many parishes were beginning to replace their old bibles with copies of the 'Geneva Bible', which was an accurate translation but which included many marginal glosses and notes of a Calvinist leaning, which were ill favoured by the Elizabethan authorities.) By September 1568, this new edition of the Bible, heavily reliant upon the Henrician 'Great Bible' of 1539, had reached completion. It went on sale that year and was quickly followed by a smaller, quarto edition the following year.[53] Folio bibles were targeted at parishes and wealthy households, whereas the smaller editions were less expensive, given their size, and therefore potentially available to a broader range of purses.

In the preface to the Bishops' Bible, Parker stated that God 'hath preserved these books of the scriptures safe and sounde, and that in their natiue languages they were first written [. . .] and contrary to all other casualties, chaunced upon all other books in mauger of all wordly wittes, who would so fayne haue had them destroyed, and yet he by his mightie hande, would haue them witnesses and interpreters of his will toward mankind'.[54] Parker was doing God's will, and that of Elizabeth and her Privy Council, of course. But while he was conserving some texts, he was also destroying others, acting as both judge and jury over a number of Anglo-Saxon and medieval texts. Ultimately, Parker judged, for a time, what would remain and what would be purged from the canon of literature that passed through his hands.

Those that survived were bound in some format. Those most important to his mission were bound in particularly sturdy binding, indicative of not only the use they would be put to but also the venerated status they enjoyed within his collection. Some received such lavish binding and adornment that they became physical artefacts to be admired in their own right. Aside from their contents, as codices, these works became aesthetically impressive pieces of artistry. Paper, then, could save the writings of history from oblivion; a codex could try to immortalise them.[55]

Parker sponsored—and had bound—a number of works that supported his mission to defend the English Church from its Catholic detractors. These texts ranged in their tactics considerably. Bishop John Jewel's 'apology' was a defence of the English Church from within its ranks; the edition of the Anglo-Saxon Gospels was a reproduction of one of the key works of literature from the English Church, as were the writings of Ælfric, all of which were taken from manuscripts recovered by Parker and his team and deposited within Parker's library for safekeeping. Other works were an amalgamation of the two approaches. Parker's sponsorship of John Foxe's *Acts and Monuments* provides us with just one such example. Parker not only aided Foxe's research and the printing of the book by John Day; he also provided some of the documentation. Foxe's book is, in many ways, a repository in its own right for numerous documents uncovered by dedicated scholars, clergy, statesmen, and antiquaries on Foxe's behalf and, indeed, on behalf of the nation.[56] The fear of evidence being lost to oblivion was very real to Parker and his team.

Parker and his team were aware that libraries were not immune to dispersal, as the Dissolution of the Monasteries testified, but a collected body of data, bound into bulky volumes, stored, and catalogued, was the safest medium they had. Orality—the word of the preacher—was not enough; documentary, supporting evidence was crucial in support of a Reformed doctrine. The emergence of print allowed for greater survival rates of duplicated essential texts. Parker's collection of manuscripts and printed texts, under his auspices as primate of the English Church, afforded some security for the body of evidence mounted in its defence. His complex arrangements to safeguard these texts after his death reflect something of his continued concerns for the survival of this evidence. His commissioning of printed texts reflects both his desire to create and disseminate multiple copies of key texts and his desire for his flock to gain wider knowledge of the 'Truth'—a Truth not simply to be accepted but to be studied by an increasingly literate society, who could see the supporting evidence for themselves. By salvaging texts and storing them first in codex format and then within a library, Parker and his fellow confessionalists were therefore transforming the social meaning of books, one that stressed the importance of maintaining and safeguarding a body of historical evidence.[57] To that end, Parker and his team were not just creating manuscript and printed codices; they were creating the history of a nation, at the heart of which was a library.

Such an image of unity and truth was nevertheless subsisted by heterogeneity and doubt at the level of the book. Many of Parker's books, whether they contain manuscripts, printed matter or both, and as I have shown in detail, can appear something of a minefield of complex and sometimes apparently random contents. Nevertheless, we must remember that this was a period in which printed books, like manuscripts, were usually purchased unbound. If you purchased small tracts, it would make sense to bind a number of them together to protect them. But the binding of texts together was very much an esoteric, personal choice. Today we expect our printed books to be bound and can still reveal our preferences for them (soft back or hard back), but we have no choice on how our texts are bound together between boards. So we must remember that Parker's notion of a 'printed book' was not what we perceive one as today. Our perception of manuscripts as loose manuscripts is likewise frequently inaccurate. Surveying the contents of Parker's library, we must also discard our traditional perceptions of what constitutes a book. The world of the printed book has been our safety zone from Gutenberg to the present day, if it is now subject to some displacement from forms of digital writing and collecting. Indeed, although some digital texts are based on print conventions, such as the unity of the single-authored monograph, others pertain to greater collaging of potentially heterogeneous writings. Thus, there might be some comparability between our contemporary world of knowledge and Parker's sixteenth-century codicological practices.

NOTES

1. I would like to thank Gill Cannell at the Parker Library, Corpus Christi College Cambridge, and Gabriel Sewel at Lambeth Palace Library for their assistance and advice during the writing of this chapter.
2. Cassiodorus, *Variae of Magnus Aurelius Cassiodorus Senator, the Right Honourable and Illustrious Ex-quaestor of the Palace, Ex-ordinary Consul, Ex-master of the Offices . . .*, trans. S. J. B. Barnish, (Liverpool, UK: Liverpool University Press, 1992), XI.383–6, p. 160.
3. On Martial's commendation of the *pugillaribus membraneis* (a codex made of parchment), see Colin H. Roberts and T.C. Skeat, *The Birth of the Codex*, (London and Oxford, UK: Oxford University Press, 1983), pp. 24–29. Martial's comments, in a poem introducing a revised edition of the *Apophoreta*, are the first known references to the codex as a literary form.
4. See chapters 9 ('Why Did Christians Adopt the Codex? Inadequacy and Practical Considerations'), 10 ('The Christian Adoption of the Codex: Two Hypotheses') and 11 ('The Christian Codex and the Canon of Scripture') in Roberts and Skeat, *The Birth of the Codex*, pp. 45–54, 55–61, and 62–66, respectively. Also see David Diringer, *The Book before Printing: Ancient, Medieval and Oriental* (New York: Dover Publications, 1982); and L. W. Hurtado, *The Earliest Christian Artefacts: Manuscript and Christian Origins* (Oxford, UK: Oxford University Press, 1987).
5. Cassiodorus, *Institutiones*, I.17.2. See Anthony Grafton and Megan Williams, *Christianity and the Transformation of the Book: Origen, Eusebius, and the Library of Caesarea* (Cambridge, MA: Harvard University Press, 2006), p. 142.
6. Fred Lerner, *The Story of Libraries: From the Invention of Writing to the Computer Age* (New York and London: Continuum, 2010), p. 26.
7. Parker owned a number of works by Cassiodorus, including his *Institutiones*. (CCCC MS 68, fos. 1^r–12^r. In true Parkerian style, his manuscripts of Cassiodorus are in composite codices, rather than individually bound items. MS 68, for example, also contains two other works (a *Gelasian decree de libris recipiendis*, fo.1^r and Theodulf of Orleans's *De ordine baptismatis*, fos.12^v–15^r).

8. See C. E. Wright, 'The Dispersal of the Libraries in the Sixteenth Century' in *The English library before 1700*, ed. F. Wormald and C. E. Wright (London: University of London, Athlone Press, 1958), pp. 148–75.
9. C.E. Wright, 'The Dispersal of the Monastic Libraries and the Beginning of Anglo-Saxon Studies', *Transactions of the Cambridge Bibliographical Society* 1 (1951), pp. 208–37.
10. Parker is the main focus for this chapter, but for a detailed discussion of the life and career of John Leland, see the extensive researches of James P. Carley, including his entry on Leland in the *Oxford Dictionary of National Biography* (Oxford, UK: Oxford University Press, 2004) and 'John Leland and the Foundation of the Royal Library: The Westminster Inventory of 1542', *Bulletin of the Society for Renaissance Studies* 7 (1989), pp. 13–22.
11. Gregory B. Lyon, 'Baudouin, Flacius, and the Plan for the Magdeburg Centuries', *Journal of the History of Ideas* 64 (2003), pp. 253–72.
12. *Ecclesiastica historia, integram ecclesiae Christi ideam . . ., secundum singulas centurias perspicuo ordine complectens,*13 vols. (Basle, 1559–74).
13. Lerner, *The Story of Libraries*, p. 93.
14. A number of scholars have worked on the foundation and contents of Parker's library but they focus on his collecting of manuscripts *or* his ownership of printed texts *or* on specific manuscripts. (The aim of this chapter, rather, is to examine specifically the practice of placing both manuscripts and printed texts in codex format and the motivation for doing so.) See, by way of example, Nancy Basler Bjorklund, 'Parker's Purpose for his Manuscripts: Matthew Parker in the Context of his Early Career and Sixteenth-Century Church Reform' in *Old English Literature in its Manuscript Context*, Medieval European Studies 5 (Morgantown: West Virginia University Press, 2004), pp. 217–41; Bruce Dickins, 'The Making of the Parker Library', *Transactions of the Cambridge Bibliographical Society* 6 (1972): 19–34; and Timothy Graham, 'Matthew Parker and the Conservation of Manuscripts: The Case of CUL MS Ii.2.4', *Transactions of the Cambridge Bibliographical Society* 10 (1995), pp. 630–41.
15. Norman L. Jones, 'Matthew Parker, John Bale, and the Magdeburg Centuriators'. *Sixteenth Century Journal*, 12 (1981), pp. 35–49. On Bale and his use of and search for manuscripts, see, by way of example, Leslie P. Fairfield, *John Bale: Mythmaking for the English Reformation* (Lafayette, IN: Purdue University Press, 1976); Ernst Gerhardt, '"No quyckar merchaundynce than library bokes": John Bale's Commodification of Manuscript Culture', *Renaissance Quarterly* 60 (2007), pp. 408–33; and Yoko Wada, 'Bale to Parker on British historical texts in Cambridge college libraries', *Transactions of the Cambridge Bibliographical Society* 4 (1994), pp. 511–19. Also see note 16.
16. Bale responded to Parker on 30 July 1560 (Cambridge University Library, MS. Add. 7489.) On Bale and Joscelyn's work with Parker, see their respective entries in the *Oxford Dictionary of National Biography* and Timothy Graham and Andrew G. Watson, *The Recovery of the Past in Early Elizabethan England: Documents by John Bale and John Joscelyn from the Circle of Matthew Parker* (Cambridge, UK: Cambridge Bibliographical Society, 1998).
17. John Bruce and Thomas Perowne, *Correspondence of Matthew Parker* (Cambridge: Cambridge University Press, 1853), p. 186.
18. British Library, MS Cotton Nero C. iii., fos. 209–12. Texts sought for whom ownership was not identified but a copy was later acquired include Richard of Devizes's *De rebus gestis Ricardi primi*, which is now CCCC MS 339. (See Timothy Graham, 'Matthew Parker's Manuscripts: An Elizabethan Library and its Use' in *The Cambridge History of Libraries in Britain and Ireland, Vol.1: to 1640*, ed. Elisabeth Leedham Green and Teresa Webber [Cambridge: Cambridge University Press, 2006], pp. 322–41.)

19. Bruce and Perowne, *Correspondence*, p. 327.
20. CCCC MS 114, fo.49ʳ.
21. Privy Council broadsheet (STC 7754.6), dated 7 July 1568.
22. Ælfric, *A testimonie of antiquitie shewing the auncient faith in the Church of England touching the sacrament of the body and bloude of the Lord here publikely preached, and also receaued in the Saxons tyme, aboue 600. yeares agoe* (London, 1566?). On the exact dating of this text, which survives in two states, see Erick Keleman, 'More Evidence for the Date of *A Testimonie of Antiquitie*', *The Library*, 7th series, 7 (2006), pp. 361–76.
23. For a discussion of this text, see Benedict Scott Robinson, 'John Foxe and the Anglo-Saxons' in *John Foxe and his World*, ed. Christopher Highley and John N. King (Basingstoke, UK: Ashgate Press, 2002), pp. 54–72.
24. John Foxe and John Joseclyn (eds.), *The Gospel of the fower Ebangelistes translated into vulgare toung of the Saxons, newly collected out of auncient Monuments of the sayd Saxons, and now published for testimonie of the same* (London, 1571) STC 2961. See R.M. Liuzza, ed., *The Old English Version of the Gospels, Volume 1: Text and Introduction*, Early English Text Society (Oxford, UK: Oxford University Press, 1994).
25. Privy Council broadsheet (STC 7754.6). My italics.
26. See Elizabeth Evenden, 'The Impact of Print: The Perceived Worth of the Printed Book in England, 1476–1575' in the *Oxford Medieval Handbook*, ed. Elaine Treharne and Greg Walker (Oxford, UK: Oxford University Press, 2009).
27. See Peter Lucas, 'Parker, Lambarde and the Provision of Special Sorts for Printing Anglo-Saxon in the Sixteenth Century', *Journal of the Printing Historical Society* 28 (1999), pp. 41–69.
28. Raymond I. Page, *Matthew Parker and his Books: Sandars Lectures in Bibliography Delivered on 14, 16, and 18 May 1990 at the University of Cambridge* (Kalamazoo: Western Michigan University, 1993), p. 11.
29. See Carl P.E. Springer, *The Gospel as Epic in Late Antiquity: 'Paschale Carmen' of Sedulius* (Leiden, the Netherlands, and Boston, MA: Brill, 1988).
30. On this compiling and scribes of this composite manuscript, see Carl P.E. Springer, *The Manuscripts of Sedulius: A Provisional Handlist*, Transactions of the American Philosophical Society, (Philadelphia, MA: Amer Philosophical Society, 1995), p. 42; and M.B. Parkes, 'The Palaeography of the Parker Manuscript of the Chronicle, Laws and Sedulius, and Historiography at Winchester in the Late Ninth and Tenth Centuries', *Anglo-Saxon England* 5 (1976), pp. 149–171.
31. The entry for this manuscript in Parker's register states only 'Annales Saxonixi ecclesie Cantuariensis / Leges Aluredi regis } willelm cyng'. (CCCC, MS 575, fo. 62.)
32. Page did not mix his words in his assessment of the treatment of this manuscript copy of the Anglo-Saxon Gospels, referring to this cropping by the binder as 'a wanton act for which Parker must be held responsible'. See Page, *Matthew Parker and his Books*, p. 49.
33. Nicholas Bodrugan, *An Epitome of the Title that the Kynges Maiestie of Englande, hath to the Souereigntie of Scotlande Continued vpon the Auncient Writers of both Nacions, from the Beginning* (London, 1548) STC 3196. See Dale Hoak, 'William Cecil, Sir Thomas Smith, and the Monarchical Republic of Tudor England' in *The Monarchical Republic of Early Modern England: Essays in Response to Patrick Collinson*, ed. John McDiarmid (Aldershot, UK: Ashgate Press, 2007), p. 48.
34. James Pilkington, *The True Report of the Burnyng of the Steple and Church of Poules in London* (London, 1561) STC 19930. On the speculation surrounding

the actual authorship of this account and on its discussion of the providential nature of this event, see Alexandra Walsham, *Providence in Early Modern England* (New York: Oxford University Press, 1999), p. 232. *A Proper Newe Booke of Cokerye* (London, 1557?) STC 3366. See also Anne Ahmed, ed., *A Proper New Booke of Cokerye: Margaret Parker's Cookery Book* (Cambridge, UK: Corpus Christi College Cambridge, 2002).
35. Page, *Matthew Parker and his Books*, pp. 11–12. On the practice of producing manuscript titles pages in late-fifteenth- and early-sixteenth-century codices, see Margaret M. Smith, *The Title-Page: its early development 1460–1510* (London and New Castle, DE: The British Library and Oak Knoll Press), pp. 47–74.
36. See Elizabeth Evenden, *Patents, Pictures and Patronage: John Day and the Tudor Book Trade* (Aldershot, UK: Ashgate Press, 2008), pp. 109–111.
37. See Bruce and Perowne, *Correspondence*, p. 426.
38. Page, *Matthew Parker and his Books*, pp. 51–52. Other examples include Parker's copy of Ælfric's grammar (CCCC MS 449), which had a number of quires missing, which were replaced with counterfeited text copied from another manuscript (British Library, MS 15 B. xxii).
39. See Page, *Matthew Parker and his Books,* pp. 50–51.
40. See Evenden, *Patents, Pictures and Patronage*, pp.109–113; and H.M. Nixon and Mirjam M. Foot, *The History of Decorated Bookbinding in England* (Oxford, UK: Clarendon Press, 1992), pp. 36, 38–40.
41. Graham, 'Matthew Parker's Manuscripts', p. 328.
42. Many volumes in Corpus Christi were rebound in the mid-eighteenth century and their original bindings discarded. See Page, *Matthew Parker and his Books,* pp. 8–9.
43. See Graham, 'Matthew Parker's manuscripts: an Elizabethan library and its use', p. 329.
44. Sherman, *Used Books*, p. 20.
45. Page, *Matthew Parker and his Books*, p. 45.
46. M.R. James, *The Sources of Archbishop Parker's Collection of MSS at Corpus Christi College, Cambridge, with a Reprint of the Catalogue of Thomas Markaunt's Library*, Cambridge Antiquarian Society Octavo Publications 32 (Cambridge, 1899), M.R. James, *A Descriptive Catalogue of the Manuscripts in the Library of Corpus Christi College Cambridge,* 2 vols. (Cambridge, 1912); Raymond I. Page, 'The Parker Register and Matthew Parker's Anglo-Saxon MSS', *Transactions of the Cambridge Bibliographical Society* 8 (1981), pp. 1–17.
47. For a detailed discussion of Parker's bequests see Graham, 'Matthew Parker's Manuscripts', pp. 336–41.
48. Matthew Parker, *De antiquitate Britannicae ecclesiae & priuilegiis ecclesiae Cantuariensis cum Archiepiscopis eiusdem 70.* (London, 1572) STC 19292. On this press and on the printing of *De Antiquitate Brittanicae* at Lambeth see Evenden, *Patents, Pictures and Patronage*, pp. 108–109. The text opens with a woodcut borrowed from the quarto edition of the Bishops' Bible (1568), overseen by Parker (see the following discussion). His practice of taking images from one text and using them in another therefore extended to printed books also.
49. This list is discussed in detail by Page, *Matthew Parker and his Books*, pp. 56–59.
50. Thomas Walsingham (1360–1420), *Historia breuis Thomae VValsingham, ab Edwardo primo, ad Henricum quantum* (London, 1574) STC 25004; and *Ypodigma Neustriae vel Normanniae: per Thomam de Walsingham: ab irruptione Normannorum vsq[ue] ad annum. 6. regni Henrici quinti* (London, 1574) STC 25005.

51. John Jewel, *Apologia ecclesiae anglicanae* (London, 1562) STC 14581.
52. *The Bible in English that Is to Say, the Content of the Holy Scriptures, Both of the Olde and New Testament, according to the Translation that is Appointed to be Read in Churches* (London, 1568) STC 2102.
53. STC 2103. A second folio edition was printed in 1572 (STC 2107).
54. Matthew Parker, 'A Preface into the Byble', *Bible in English* (1568), sig.2^r.
55. Many of the texts bound by Parker for his own collection and as presentation copies for the great and the good of Elizabethan England have certainly been preserved by later generations as much for their value as an aesthetic commodity as for their contents. For a discussion of such examples, see Evenden, *Patents, Pictures and Patronage,* pp. 105–117.
56. This is an enormous topic in its own right, and beyond the scope of this essay, but the sources and composition of Foxe's mammoth text is discussed in detail in Elizabeth Evenden and Thomas Freeman, *Religion and the Book in Early Modern England: the Making of John Foxe's 'Book of Martyrs'* (Cambridge: Cambridge University Press, 2011).
57. On the 'social meaning' of books and libraries, see Jennifer Summit, *Memory's Library: Medieval Books in Early Modern England* (Chicago: University of Chicago Press, 2008), p. 12.

BIBLIOGRAPHY

Anne Ahmed, ed. *A Proper New Booke of Cokerye: Margaret Parker's Cookery Book*. Cambridge, UK: Corpus Christi College Cambridge, 2002.

Nancy Basler Bjorklund, 'Parker's Purpose for his Manuscripts: Matthew Parker in the Context of his Early Career and Sixteenth-Century Church Reform', in *Old English Literature in its Manuscript Context*, Medieval European Studies 5. Morgantown: West Virginia University Press, 2004.

John Bruce and Thomas Perowne. *Correspondence of Matthew Parker*. Cambridge: Cambridge University Press, 1853.

James P. Carley. 'John Leland and the Foundation of the Royal Library: The Westminster Inventory of 1542'. *Bulletin of the Society for Renaissance Studies* 7 (1989).

Cassiodorus. *Variae of Magnus Aurelius Cassiodorus Senator, the Right Honourable and Illustrious Ex-quaestor of the Palace, Ex-ordinary Consul, Ex-master of the Offices . . .*, translated by S. J. B. Barnish. Liverpool, UK: Liverpool University Press, 1992.

Bruce Dickins. 'The Making of the Parker Library'. *Transactions of the Cambridge Bibliographical Society* 6 (1972).

David Diringer. *The Book before Printing: Ancient, Medieval and Oriental*. New York: Dover Publications, 1982.

Elizabeth Evenden. 'The Impact of Print: The Perceived Worth of the Printed Book in England, 1476–1575', in the *Oxford Medieval Handbook*, edited by Elaine Treharne and Greg Walker. Oxford, UK: Oxford University Press, 2009.

Elizabeth Evenden. *Patents, Pictures and Patronage: John Day and the Tudor Book Trade*. Aldershot, UK: Ashgate Press, 2008.

Elizabeth Evenden and Thomas Freeman. *Religion and the Book in Early Modern England: the Making of John Foxe's 'Book of Martyrs'*. Cambridge: Cambridge University Press, 2011.

Leslie P. Fairfield. *John Bale: Mythmaking for the English Reformation*. Lafayette, IN: Purdue University Press, 1976.

Ernst Gerhardt. '"No quyckar merchaundynce than library bokes": John Bale's Commodification of Manuscript Culture'. *Renaissance Quarterly* 60 (2007).

Lawrence Goldman, ed. *Oxford Dictionary of National Biography*. Oxford, UK: Oxford University Press, 2013.
Anthony Grafton and Megan Williams. *Christianity and the Transformation of the Book: Origen, Eusebius, and the Library of Caesara*. Cambridge, MA: Harvard University Press, 2006.
Timothy Graham. 'Matthew Parker and the Conservation of Manuscripts: The Case of CUL MS Ii.2.4'. *Transactions of the Cambridge Bibliographical Society* 10 (1995).
Timothy Graham. 'Matthew Parker's Manuscripts: An Elizabethan Library and its Use', in *The Cambridge History of Libraries in Britain and Ireland, Vol.1: to 1640*, edited by Elisabeth Leedham Green and Teresa Webber. Cambridge: Cambridge University Press, 2006.
Timothy Graham and Andrew G. Watson. *The Recovery of the Past in Early Elizabethan England: Documents by John Bale and John Joscelyn from the Circle of Matthew Parker*. Cambridge, UK: Cambridge Bibliographical Society, 1998.
Dale Hoak. 'William Cecil, Sir Thomas Smith, and the Monarchical Republic of Tudor England', in *The Monarchical Republic of Early Modern England: Essays in Response to Patrick Collinson*, edited by John McDiarmid. Aldershot, UK: Ashgate Press, 2007.
L. W. Hurtado. *The Earliest Christian Artefacts: Manuscript and Christian Origins*. Oxford, UK: Oxford University Press, 1987.
M. R. James. *A Descriptive Catalogue of the Manuscripts in the Library of Corpus Christi College Cambridge*, 2 vols. Cambridge, 1912.
M. R. James. *The Sources of Archbishop Parker's Collection of MSS at Corpus Christi College, Cambridge, with a Reprint of the Catalogue of Thomas Markaunt's Library*, Cambridge Antiquarian Society Octavo Publications 32. Cambridge, 1899.
Norman L. Jones. 'Matthew Parker, John Bale, and the Magdeburg Centuriators'. *Sixteenth Century Journal* 12 (1981).
Erick Keleman. 'More Evidence for the Date of *A Testimonie of Antiquitie*'. *The Library*, 7th series, 7 (2006).
Fred Lerner. *The Story of Libraries: From the Invention of Writing to the Computer Age*. New York and London: Continuum, 2010.
R. M. Liuzza, ed. *The Old English Version of the Gospels, Volume 1: Text and Introduction,* Early English Text Society. Oxford, UK: Oxford University Press, 1994.
Peter Lucas. 'Parker, Lambarde and the Provision of Special Sorts for Printing Anglo-Saxon in the Sixteenth Century'. *Journal of the Printing Historical Society* 28 (1999).
Gregory B. Lyon. 'Baudouin, Flacius, and the Plan for the Magdeburg Centuries'. *Journal of the History of Ideas* 64 (2003).
H. C. G. Matthew and Brian Harrison, eds. *Oxford Dictionary of National Biography*. Oxford, UK: Oxford University Press, 2004.
H. M. Nixon and Mirjam M. Foot. *The History of Decorated Bookbinding in England*. Oxford, UK: Clarendon Press, 1992.
Raymond I. Page. *Matthew Parker and his Books: Sandars lectures in bibliography delivered on 14, 16, and 18 May 1990 at the University of Cambridge*. Kalamazoo: Western Michigan University, 1993.
Raymond I. Page. 'The Parker Register and Matthew Parker's Anglo-Saxon MSS'. *Transactions of the Cambridge Bibliographical* Society 8 (1981).
M. B. Parkes. 'The Palaeography of the Parker Manuscript of the Chronicle, Laws and Sedulius, and Historiography at Winchester in the Late Ninth and Tenth Centuries'. *Anglo-Saxon England* 5 (1976).
Colin H. Roberts and T. C. Skeat. *The Birth of the Codex*. London and Oxford, UK: Oxford University Press, 1983.

Benedict Scott Robinson. 'John Foxe and the Anglo-Saxons', in *John Foxe and his World*, edited by Christopher Highley and John N. King. Basingstoke, UK: Ashgate Press, 2002.

Margaret M. Smith, *The Title-Page: Its Early Development 1460–1510*. London and New Castle, DE: The British Library and Oak Knoll Press, 2001.

Carl P. E. Springer. *The Gospel as Epic in Late Antiquity: 'Paschale Carmen' of Sedulius*. Leiden, the Netherlands, and Boston, MA: Brill, 1988.

Carl P. E. Springer. *The Manuscripts of Sedulius: A Provisional Handlist*, Transactions of the American Philosophical Society. Philadelphia, MA: Amer Philosophical Society, 1995.

Jennifer Summit. *Memory's Library: Medieval Books in Early Modern England*. Chicago: University of Chicago Press, 2008.

Yoko Wada. 'Bale to Parker on British Historical Texts in Cambridge College Libraries'. *Transactions of the Cambridge Bibliographical Society* 4 (1994).

Alexandra Walsham. *Providence in Early Modern England*. New York: Oxford University Press, 1999.

C. E. Wright. 'The Dispersal of the Libraries in the Sixteenth Century', in *The English Library before 1700*, edited by F. Wormald and C. E. Wright. London: University of London, Athlone Press, 1958.

C. E. Wright. 'The Dispersal of the Monastic Libraries and the Beginning of Anglo-Saxon Studies'. *Transactions of the Cambridge Bibliographical Society* 1 (1951).

6 Magical Values in Recent Romances of the Archive

Suzanne Keen

> 'All literary manuscripts have two kinds of value: what might be called the magical value and the meaningful value' (Philip Larkin, 'A Neglected Responsibility').[1]

The recent conversations about manuscript collecting represented by events such as the October 2006 British Library colloquium, 'Manuscripts Matter,' emphasize the meaningful value of authors' working papers. Meaningful value, that which enlarges scholarly understanding of a writer's life and work, not only matters to the international scholarly community but also contributes to the national heritage. In both Larkin's essay and in the most well-known fictional treatment of the problem, A. S. Byatt's 1990 novel *Possession*, U.S. acquisitiveness threatens to deplete a British natural resource, English literary manuscripts, before their value can be recognized and resources gathered to keep them at home. Arguments, real and fictionalized, about the ultimate deposition of writers' papers in libraries in Britain or abroad pit wealth, acquisitiveness, and the greed of the private collector (or rich American university) against penury, neglected obligations, and the threatened public interest. Thus, the call to responsibility for proper acquisition and stewardship of manuscripts in English archives tacitly (sometimes explicitly) regards Americans warily and competitively.

In this context, I argue, recent archival romances by young American novelists Jenny Davidson, Elizabeth Kostova, and Leslie Silbert give the American research quester an altruistic makeover. If, according to convention, American collectors, amateur researchers, and scholars appear as unscrupulous rogues such as Byatt's Mortimer Cropper (whose activities extend to attempted grave robbery), then the young American protagonists of novels by Davidson, Kostova, and Silbert must more than make up for the criminal predation of their elder compatriots. Their success is explained not only by their appreciation for the meaningful value of the literary archive but also by their amazing ability to activate its magical value. This in turn depends on a corporeal connection with the past that overwrites the usual sympathetic, imaginative connection with exchange of body fluids or their symbolic surrogates. Whereas research questers inevitably sift through the archive for evidence that can be translated into knowledge, the shift towards the magical value of the archival emphasizes facts of the body: blood, sweat, tears, spit, paint, and ink.

The quest for the truth enacted in contemporary British romances of the archive, a subgenre I name and examine in *Romances of the Archive in Contemporary British Fiction* (2001), typically restores both knowledge and manuscripts to their rightful owners, judged in heritage terms. The novels can be easily recognized, for they consistently include the following features:

- Character-researchers, endowed with the corporeality and 'round' psychology of the realistic novel
- Romance adventure stories, in which 'research' features as a kernel plot action, resulting in strong closure, with climactic discoveries and rewards
- Discomforts and inconveniences suffered in the service of knowledge (actually part of the romance plot, but so played up as to deserve separate emphasis)
- Sex and physical pleasure gained as a result of questing (these stories about 'brains' are always also stories about bodies)
- Settings and locations (such as libraries and country houses) that contain archives of actual papers
- Material traces of the past revealing the truth
- Evocation of history, looking back from a postimperial context[2]

A revision of this list of key traits to account for the recent American contributions requires one alteration and one shift of emphasis. The alteration consists of the caveat that a *post*imperial perspective does not obviously pertain to a group of American writers. The fact that since 2003, young American citizens have 'gone abroad' in two quite distinct fashions, as part of an invading and occupying army, on one hand, and as visiting students in the universities of the Old World, on the other, suggests at least two major categories of socioeconomic advantage—race and gender—and concomitant attitudes towards the past, on the part of those travelers. Indeed, the Americanness of the research questers places greater emphasis on their traveling, for even when the document-driven mystery starts in the New World, it propels these protagonists to the Old World. Although acknowledging the researcher-characters' access to world-class libraries, electronic collections, experts, databases, and interlibrary loans (for they are postmodern navigators of the information stream), these narratives insist on movement back to sources located in Europe. The location of libraries holding literary archives derives part of its uncanny attraction from a simple fact: so few material traces of a writing life remain situated, just the birthplace, the writers' houses, the resonant settings, the grave, and the archive. When everything else associated with a writer belongs to a country of the imagination, equally accessible from Dhaka and North Dakota, the papers that reside in Dorset possess a special status.

Archives draw scholars. The meaningful value of literary archives contributes directly to the economy, through tourism and the spending of visiting scholars, and to the nation's sense of pride in its great export—in cultural capital terms—the language, its literature, and the iconic brands of its writers. As Sarah Brouillette writes, postindustrial Britain is deliberately cultivating a 'brand-based visitor economy,' designed to cultivate the tastes of international consumers: 'Brand UK is meant to strengthen diplomatic ties, encourage corporate investment, and win the loyalty of global citizen-consumers whose appreciation for artistic freedom should guarantee their love for the products, services, and ideals that originate in the UK'.[3] Whether living writers still struggling to eke out existences benefit from this effort remains to be seen, for, as Brouillette argues, 'writers tend to work against—by self-consciously highlighting—instrumental uses of their texts and of their cultural cachet'.[4] The dead authors of canonical literature put up no such fuss: They can safely be exhumed,[5] their desks rifled, their reputations ruined or restored,[6] their literary remains put to use,[7] their DNA sequenced,[8] and their fictional characters redeployed in plot lines of others' devising.[9] Conventionally, physical travels to the loci associated with famous writers and their fictional characters make possible imaginative uses of the past. In romances of the archive, the chronotope of the road combines with an archeological impulse to dig into the buried past. To accomplish even the first tasks of the archival romance, then, questers have to be willing to embark on travels that may look a lot like tourism until they reveal what no guidebook records and what no traditional homebody scholar has been able to see. Thus, paradoxically, the scholarly questers of romances of the archive participate in the enrichment of cultural capital by coming back to the site of 'Brand UK' and discovering the lost treasures of meaning that have been misplaced by the custodians of the truth.

A salient part of Larkin's warning to his fellow archivists concerned their neglect of contemporary writers' manuscripts, which could at that time be collected for the asking by Americans who then made off with them to found the great collections of modern manuscripts in the United States.[10] Contemporary British romances of the archive fantasize about a correction of that problem, as I have earlier argued. Crimes solved, answers found, mysteries resolved, and reputations restored: romances of the archive vouch for the existence of an attainable truth that can be located and restored to an English archive by the right scholar-adventurer. In these generic circumstances, how can a successful archival quester ever be an American? In Greimasian terms, can an American actant be budged from its conventional position as an antagonistic 'opposer,' the cowboy in a black hat, as A. S. Byatt has it, all the way to the questing subject?[11] Some contemporary British archival romances have allowed a modest number of American characters to supply assistance in a 'helper' role, but overall, these fictions have mimicked the attitude of their antecedent spy thrillers to cast even well meaning Americans as competitors rather than fellow travelers in their intellectual quests.[12] After Dan Brown, however, the generic possibilities have shifted and expanded.

First, tales of intellectual quests dosing readers with scholarly content and arcane lore have become a truly popular form, a prominent mode for international best sellers. A transition from the highbrow postmodern archival romances of the early 1980s to the more numerous and accessible middlebrow scholarly thrillers of the twenty-first century has occurred. Since the publication and runaway success of *The Da Vinci Code* (2003), the popular subgenre I name 'romances of the archive' has become even more appealing to publishers of mass-market fiction and their reading public. This despite the fact that romances of the archive inevitably involve an element of the crash course—on academic subjects such as art history, architecture, archaeology, chess, or craft lore such as poisoning, bookbinding, cracking secret codes, and the devious use of library catalogs. As novelist Louis Bayard observes, it seems that *The Da Vinci Code* 'has made thrillers safe for ceaseless pedagogy'.[13] If the first wave of English archival romances follow on the English translation of Umberto Eco's *The Name of the Rose* (translated 1983), expressing both the nationalistic fervor of the Falklands period and the anxieties of the postimperial condition, as I argue in *Romances of the Archive*, the current popular form romps through English and Continental libraries with a tourist's avid pleasure, consuming a juicy European past. The archive as midden of Euro-trash scandal comes into its own in these decidedly un-musty tales of murder, sexual adventuring, and slippery identity. Even in the most staid of the recent research narratives, such as Australian novelist Kate Grenville's *Searching for the Secret River* (2006), historiographical concerns cede prominence to identity quests and empathetic fusion with distant relatives or soul mates.

Second, in addition to the altered national identity of protagonists (Americans allowed to romance the archive), conventional gender stereotypes have also undergone revision as the subgenre has entered the popular reading market, in which, after all, most of the readers and book purchasers are female. In *Romances of the Archive*, I asked why so few fictional archival questers, and authors of archival quests, were female. This seemed an odd phenomenon given the demographics of literary studies since the 1980s.[14] Katherine Neville's popular novels *The Eight* (1988) and *The Magic Circle* (1998) were exceptions to the rule of a hypermasculine character type, represented in popular film by Indiana Jones and in fiction by countless romance-questing Rolands, all the way to Byatt's Roland Michell. My tentative explanation for the dearth of female romance authors and questers in a genre that, after all, includes exemplary precursors such as Lady Mary Wroth and Edmund Spenser's Britomart, has been challenged as inadequate by Jackie Buxton:

> Keen muses on the relative paucity of romances of the archive authored by women. The question is a good one, and it is inadequately answered

by reference to the exigencies of the publishing industry (women writers are well-represented in detective fiction circles), or to the anxiety of influence generated by Byatt's *Possession* (197). Keen chooses not to pursue her observation that 'male writers are responsible for by far the majority of recent British adventurous fictions of archival quests [. . .], and this tantalizing question is left dangling'.[15]

Although I still have no better insight as to why female authors steered clear of a new subgenre that was flourishing throughout the 1980s and 1990s, preferring detective fiction, fantasy, science fiction, and emergent chick lit among the popular kinds, I do observe that the situation has changed. Since *The Da Vinci Code*, archival romances written by women with female protagonists have proliferated, moving female researchers from sidekick position to central protagonist. Adventurer Alice Tanner of Kate Mosse's *Labyrinth* (2005) is almost certainly the best known of the new generation of female intellectual sleuths. Others appearing in novels of the last three years include Atlanta museum curator Deborah Miller, art history student and archaeologist Finn Ryan, rare-book expert and manuscript restorer Hanna Heath, literary detective Cotton Stone, and Vatican paleographer Sister Ottavia Salina, in novels by A. J. Hartley, Paul Christopher, Geraldine Brooks, Lynn Sholes, and Matilde Asensi, respectively.[16] The newly won normativity of the female research quester belatedly reflects women's scholarly accomplishments and adds to the traditional attainments of the female detective (Harriet Vane and Miss Marple) an action-adventure skill set. It is perhaps not irrelevant that Patricia Cornwell's forensic detective Kay Scarpetta has provided since 1990, when she was introduced in *Postmortem*, a compelling model of an athletic and mentally tough female protagonist. The life experiences of younger authors, coming of age in an academy that welcomes female scholars, certainly contributes to their characterization of female research questers.

This essay examines novels by three young female Ivy League graduates. Jenny Davidson's *Heredity* (2003), Leslie Silbert's *The Intelligencer* (2004), and Elizabeth Kostova's international best-seller *The Historian* (2005) bring an element of erudition derived from scholarly experience to formula fiction dedicated to imagined adventures. Davidson, born in London in 1971 but transplanted to Philadelphia, where she grew up, has degrees from both Harvard (BA, 1993) and Yale (PhD, 1999). A scholar of eighteenth-century literature and culture, Davidson is an associate professor of English and Comparative Literature at Columbia University. As a Guggenheim Fellow and the author of distinguished scholarly works, Davidson possesses direct experience of research conducted in the great libraries of the British Isles; she gives her protagonist Elizabeth Mann a travel-guide researcher's excuse to visit funky places such as the Hunterian Museum at the Royal College of Surgeons, and she endows her character with a high school summer job in a forensics lab, completing her contemporary research credentials. Although novelist Leslie Silbert has chosen a different (investigative) career path, she has similar educational credentials to Davidson; with a 1998 bachelor's degree in History of Science from Harvard, and Renaissance literary studies conducted at both Oxford and Cambridge Universities, she knows her way around a manuscript collection. However, Silbert's work as a private investigator provides the basis not only for her splashy publicity but also for her fictional protagonist Kate Morgan's job as private contractor for a covert Central Intelligence Agency (CIA) operation. With a professor father and a librarian mother, Elizabeth Kostova was primed to appreciate the historical and archival. An early travel experience in Europe was enlivened by her father's retelling of Dracula stories (which in Bram Stoker's original is also constituted by an archival collection of narrative fragments).[17] Kostova put a later significant travel experience to work in the decade-long composition process of *The Historian*. After graduating from Yale and entering her MFA program, Kostova went for a year to Bulgaria to record folk music. There she met her husband and gained firsthand knowledge of many of the places she would subsequently employ as settings.[18] A young woman's travel experiences receive Kostova's foregrounding, on a trip that bounces from archive to archive. About libraries, vividly and recognizably depicted in her novel, Kostova singles out Oxford's for praise: 'Those libraries are so beautiful, and not only are they full of treasures, but they're such a pleasure to sit in. And smell—they smell so good'.[19]

For these books to succeed as popular thrillers, the scholarly credentials and insider knowledge of academic settings cannot overwhelm the bodily romance plots, so each of the writers treated here places strong emphasis on sensual experiences, detailing smells, tastes, the texture of stage-makeup, and sexual feelings. In this, they cleave to their generic antecedents, where the physicality of books, papers, and manuscripts is met and matched by the sensitive instruments of researchers' corporeal selves. Yet if romances of the archive insistently repeat vocational plot lines, in which a sole special individual is called to the quest for truth, the historiography of these tales points towards conspiracy as an attractive form of causal explanation: secret groups, dispersed across continents and perpetuated down the generations, perpetrate, obfuscate, and guard. Professional status is shown to rely on craft lore and its ruthless protection. The historical interests of the novels by Davidson, Kostova and Silbert reveal conspiratorial premises, in an efflorescence of paranoid style, in Richard Hofstadter's term. The material conditions of late capital suggest that conspiracy is diffused throughout the global system, and the circulation of texts, money, and blood interpenetrate one another. If the truth can be located, as romances of the archive conventionally insist, these texts invest in the embodied, physical discoveries of their sexy, brainy protagonists. That is, these texts owe as much to Jeanette Winterson's *Written on the Body* (1992) and *Sexing the Cherry* (1989) as they do to their immediate literary-historical sources: Christopher Marlowe's tragedies (1580s–90s) and his erotic narrative poem *Hero and Leander* (1598) for *The Intelligencer*, Henry Fielding's *Jonathan Wild* (1743) and Defoe's *Moll Flanders* (1722) for *Heredity*, and Bram Stoker's *Dracula* (1897) and Emily Brontë's *Wuthering Heights* (1847) for *The Historian*. As this essay necessarily turns towards cloning, in *Heredity*, and vampirism, a central preoccupation of *The Historian*, it should be acknowledged that romances of the archive also characteristically scrape or siphon off a great deal of material from source texts, borrowing the juicy stuff from classics in order to reanimate dead letters.

Elizabeth Mann of Jenny Davidson's novel *Heredity* relates in hard-boiled first-person, present-tense narration the unfolding tale of her research into the practices of eighteenth-century anatomists, her adulterous affair with a fertility doctor, her discovery of a manuscript written by the notorious thief-taker Jonathan Wild's last wife, and her obsession with bearing Jonathan Wild's clone, implanted by her lover along with several eggs fertilized in vitro with his own sperm. The victim of an unethical tubal ligation carried out by her vengeful father (also a doctor) when she becomes pregnant at age sixteen, Elizabeth has a serious case of mixed motives, but her defiance of historical determinism looms large in her wish to bring Jonathan Wild back to life: 'It's not like the Jonathan Wild clone's going to pop out speaking in eighteenth-century thieves' cant and selling stolen rattles back to the other babies in the nursery', she objects to her lover Gideon, who has carried out the experimental implantation of eggs. 'In the twenty-first century, Jonathan Wild could do anything: He could be an investment banker, or the director of a big research lab, or a movie producer. He could enter any one out of hundred of cool and disreputable professions,' she argues.[20] In her personal life, Elizabeth wishes to thwart the deterministic plot lines of heredity. She discovers in the course of the novel that her lover Gideon fails as a musician because his musician father is infertile; he is really the son of his mother's physician—doctor begets doctor. She resists her friend's and lover's insistence that she should become a physician herself; disgusted by doctors' ethical lapses from the eighteenth century right through the twenty-first, she defiantly works as a poorly paid researcher for a *Let's Go*–like series of travel guides rather than pursue medical studies. Yet by the end of the novel, following in her father's footsteps and perpetuating his genetic line, she has been admitted to Columbia Medical School and appears to be on her way to fulfill her genetically programmed destiny to bear a child and study medicine. The child she bears has to be Gideon's and her own, conceived through assisted reproduction but not clone of the eighteenth-century Wild. Those embryo clones have all died in the dish, making way for a continuation of Gideon's Holocaust-surviving genes.

If the mad-science plot, inspired by *Jurassic Park* and the cloning of Dolly the sheep, comes to a dead end, the research plot cleaves to archival romance conventions by enacting a fantasy of easy access to lost historical truths. Early in the narrative, Elizabeth acquires a manuscript that she rapidly authenticates and contextualizes through research at the British

Library. The odd lot of water-damaged papers from the country-house auction, 'a dud [. . .] nothing but papers [. . .] devoid of interest', turns out to be the autobiographical account of Wild's wife Mary, pastiched in competent eighteenth-century style by Davidson.[21] Because the pages of the found manuscript are stuck together, Mann seeks assistance from a conservator at the British Museum, and Dr. Menzies doles out the photographs of the restored pages in batches throughout the novel. Thus, Davidson creates a logical premise for Mann's installment reading of the last years of Wild's life in intervals. Although the present day Mann comments on the 'coincidence' of her having the same name as Jonathan Wild's first wife, other near rhymes in character names (Mendez/Mendoza/Menzies) operate more uncannily, so eighteenth- and twenty-first-century plots cleave even before the bone scrapings from Jonathan Wild's skeleton get into the hands of the genetic manipulators. Davidson blends contemporary genetic science and gothic conventions of uncanny repetition to affect the time collapse typical of romances of the archive. Rightly named Elizabeth Mann, the twenty-first century researcher becomes the love rival of her eighteenth-century subject Mary Wild. Whereas Mary attempts to seduce the diseased Wild into unprotected sex before his execution, twenty-first-century Elizabeth schemes to bear his clone. Both defy the expressed wish of Wild, who (unsuccessfully) attempts to avoid the sex and to dodge the anatomists who seize his corpse. Elizabeth's avowed sympathy for Wild's horror of postmortem dissection does not prevent her from scraping his bones under false pretenses to get his genetic material.

The obsessional drive of the cloning plot flirts with the possibility of the ultimate time-collapse. Reanimating an eighteenth-century person three centuries later, whereas the underlying question (would Wild be the same Wild or a different man altogether?) defies genetic determinism. Yet the story of biological drives that contains Davidson's research plot insists that impulsive humans are scarcely in control of their own destinies. With the genes in control, it is no wonder that this story about intellectual elites, with its highly credentialed and brainy characters, first and foremost documents a series of sex acts. The conspiracy theory that Davidson unfolds in *Heredity* is announced by her title; the genes conspire to fling their copies down through the centuries. What else would drive a woman to goad her syphilitic husband into unprotected sex or would compel modern women to undergo fertility treatments? The only alternative, one offered in graphic detail by Davidson's description of her character's cutting behavior, is the drive to self-destruction. In *Heredity*, however, Eros beats Thanatos every time, even extending to incestuous resolutions. Mann's affair with Gideon reenacts with self-hatred her passion for her abusive father; to even the score, inside the historical story, Mary Wild seduces her stepson, and Mann imagines them 'traveling together as a married couple' in Maryland, picturing 'their descendents spread out all over the country, running used-car dealerships and protection rackets, prisons and police departments, body shops and a constellation of other rackets'.²² The seeds of eighteenth-century criminality are not all exterminated by executioners after all; they survive today in the American South. It matters not that the cloning attempt fails because America already possesses Jonathan Wild's genes, like it or not, and their expression constitutes core elements of U.S. national character, not so unrelated to Englishness. Like the doubled characters who link the eighteenth and twentieth centuries, and the incestuous couplings of characters, the nations appear in Davidson's novel as kissing cousins, bound by both attraction and repulsion. They cannot choose to dissociate themselves.

A degree of cultural anxiety persists, however, in texts in which American researchers discover what the English have forgotten or chosen not to know about their past. One token of this anxious desire to be taken seriously, even when writing in the pulpiest types of formula fiction, shows in the 'bibliographic essays' documenting the authors' scholarly labors and the rosters of eminent scholars who have lent a hand to the young writers. Jenny Davidson lists the British Library, Widener Library at Harvard, Sterling Library at Yale, Butler Library at Columbia, and the Hunterian Museum, adopting a convention of scholarly writing in which archivists, librarians, and curators are thanked for their guidance. Even in scholarly work, such a list carries a credentialing claim, but when appended to a fictional work, it operates as a paratext of authenticity, verifying both the author and his or her inventions. Better yet, conjuring the names of foremost authorities in eighteenth-century literary and cultural studies says that these are the author's fantasies, but they have been vetted by a pantheon of great scholars and writers: Bromwich, Rawson, and Coetzee! Leslie Silbert's thriller *The Intelligencer* boasts the commercially important appendix of a 'Readers Club Guide', with cozy question-and-answer sessions with the author and discussion questions for use in book groups, but Silbert also includes an interpretive 'Author's Note', defending her speculations about Christopher Marlowe, *Hero and Leander*, and the playwright's spying activities. There she tips her hat to a 'former Renaissance literature professor' whose theory about the ending of Marlowe's posthumously published poem influenced the story she tells about his faked death.²³ Coyness gives way to fulsomeness several pages later, in the acknowledgements, in which 'the brilliant Stephen Greenblatt,'—'author of [Silbert's] favorite Marlowe essay of all time, for sharing his theory about Marlowe's *Hero and Leander* and inspiring the end of this novel'—receives his obeisance. Both *Heredity* and *The Intelligencer* enact versions of the archetypal father–daughter drama, with intrepid daughters breaking away from controlling dads, but their acknowledgements tell another story. These authors are good students, deferential to authority even as they play fast and loose with the materials of English (literary) history.

Silbert's spy thriller, like Davidson's *Heredity*, interweaves chapters set in the present day with scenes from the last episodes of Christopher Marlowe's life. The archival element takes the form of a bound volume of encrypted intelligence reports, culled from Elizabethan spymaster Walsingham's files, and set up by the manipulative villain Cidro in a staged robbery to involve CIA-connected private eye Kate Morgan in the decryption. With expertise in reading Renaissance secretary hand, revealing invisible ink, decrypting numerical codes, and using Cardan grilles and computers, Kate possesses the skill-set that makes her the perfect operative for a scholarly assignment, conveniently for the international master criminals intent on using her to exact revenge on her U.S. senator father. The work on the manuscripts is carried out with the spectacular ease that typify scholarly labor in romances of the archive, needing only brief consultations with experts in old paper or assists from genealogical researchers to complete the picture of an old book of intel that still urgently matters to one hopeful treasure-hunter.

To paint with a broad brush interpretively, *The Intelligencer* solves a literary mystery about the ending of Marlowe's *Hero and Leander* by inventing an escape plot for Christopher Marlowe and his androgynous lover, '*Lee Ander*son', in her disguise as a boy. The death of Marlowe in a quarrel over the bar bill in a Deptford inn that Silbert writes as a setup, with stage makeup and a body double, demonstrates the apparent death by stab wound. As in *Heredity* and in many earlier archival romances, a dual-time scheme alternates scenes in the historical past with the contemporary spy thriller (in a plot involving the rescue of a captured CIA operative who has been tortured in an Iranian prison). There's nothing new under the sun when it comes to torture, betrayal, conspiracy, and revenge announcing Silbert's juxtapositions of past and present day.

The author explains that she took her formal cue from Tom Stoppard's play *Arcadia* (1993). Silbert explains, 'When I first saw *Arcadia* in 1997, I was captivated and awed at how Stoppard deftly interwove stories separated by centuries. Years later, as a prepared to start writing my first novel, remembering Stoppard's play convinced me to try a similar structure'.[24] *The Intelligencer* strains at the seams where it attempts to do more than juxtapose past and present, and the genealogical explanation for the villain Cidro's link to a smuggling Sir Robert Cecil owes more to Arthur Conan Doyle's 'Adventure of the Musgrave Ritual' than to the artful interrelationships of *Arcadia*. That Kate Morgan and her creator Leslie Silbert are no callow treasure hunters, however, the novel avows in its final scene, when the priceless jade dragon makes its way to the private collection at Buckingham Palace. In Silbert's vision, a baron may be a master thief, a descendent of an Elizabethan aristocrat may be a scamming, bankrupt trader, but a Queen Elizabeth is still a Queen Elizabeth, interchangeably deserving of homage and treasure. The fate of the recovered intelligence reports, obviously of immense interest to historians and literary critics, is entirely occluded by the recovery of the jade dragon and, in the parallel present-day plot, of the lost CIA operative (Morgan's presumed-dead fiancé). Because he has lost his memory, Kate Morgan must let him go, so she leaves her research adventure empty-handed, an altruistic laborer in the pursuit of truth, or a protagonist in search of a sequel.

In virtually every way, Elizabeth Kostova's whopping vampire story *The Historian* outdoes the slighter archival romances discussed thus far. An international best seller with a 2008 Amazon sales rank of 8,719 (in contrast to *The Intelligencer*'s 179,385 ranking and *Heredity*'s 1,468,188 ranking), Kostova's *Historian* rewarded the author for her ten years of labor on the novel with a huge two-million-dollar advance and instantaneous worldwide sales.[25] A physically imposing text at 642 pages, *The Historian* also boasts the greatest narrative complexity of the three texts under discussion, with a Russian-doll set of embedded narrative levels, interpolated collections of letters and documents, and alternating plot lines following several present-day characters. Kostova credits *Wuthering Heights* for inspiring the formal qualities and narrative situation[26] of *The Historian*, but aside from the generational repetitions, the structure of the novel seems more a cross of Italo Calvino's *If on a Winter Night a Traveler* (1981) and Wilkie Collins's sensation fiction. True to its gothic generic inheritance, *The Historian* is an easy book to follow, despite its superficial enigmas (Kostova conceals her female protagonist's name), and it delivers a huge amount of history, book lore, and travelogue without straining a popular readership's attention.

Piggybacking on the vampire legends popularized by Bram Stoker in *Dracula* and elaborated for decades by Anne Rice, *The Historian* re-centers this lore in its historical sources and actual locations, in a romance of the archive emphasizing travel as research. *The Historian* stages a research quest that takes as its goal rescue of the kidnapped, restoration of family, and cure for the sins of the fathers, altruistic goals, carried out with the cooperation of an international coalition of scholars and vampire hunters. Their craft expertise ranges from bibliographic knowledge to the vampire assassin's lore, and along the way, Kostova's main characters collect the toolkit and instructions they will require to exterminate their quarry. They do so by gaining access to key collections of documents recording prior generations' steps along the same process of search and destruction. Each library, special collection, archive, or private stash consulted by the pair of questers is described with near-erotic intensity, so it comes as no surprise that when they finally corner the immortal vampire, the climactic event occurs after the discovery of his own diabolical library, the count's own archive of books and manuscripts, '*a storehouse beyond compare*' and '*a treasure house*' built over centuries of collecting.[27] Throughout romances of the archive, emphasis falls on the physical container of the library, not just the archive it holds. Gaining access to the library's catalogs and shelves at once promises the researcher the chance to track the next document and provides a dramatically fitted stage for confrontations in the stacks.

Kostova's Dracula, seducer of historians and bibliophiles, begins as a book collector to gather occult knowledge, but continues as a connoisseur of violence, heresy, genocide, and especially torture. He relishes the twentieth century; his collection includes a copy of *Mein Kampf*. Dracula's library not only neatly demonstrates the premise of this collection of essays, that the library itself, through its reassuring architecture of containment, may promise to preserve memory and secure knowledge, but it also instantiates through its lost, stolen, hidden, and mis-shelved holdings the traces of trauma and obscurity. In the vampire's library tales of suffering document the perfectibility of evil and the futility of attempting to safeguard loved ones and future generations against its expression. The contaminant runs back through the centuries, and true to gothic form, cannot be eliminated. Curiosity itself invites Dracula to re-embody himself whenever a historian reopens the case. Researching Dracula through his textual remains reanimates the monster and infects the researcher. Epic adventurers of citation tracing bring the questers nearer to the truth and source without closing in on a cure. The conspiracy of Dracula hunters turns out to be inextricably intertwined with his vampire minions; one cannot trust the librarians when they turn out to be in league with Dracula, justifying American mistrust of Old World cultural heritage and its protectors. Thus, Kostova blends the attractions of the archival romance, with its blandishments about an accessible truth, with a parable about original sin, figured as curiosity and as epidemic disease. In Kostova's circular gothic plot, each unfortunate reader perpetuates the infection by succumbing to a narrative that cannot be stopped from repeating itself. Although the time period of the most recent level of her story is deliberately set before the information age made so many documents instantly accessible through the World Wide Web, Kostova's parable reflects on the proliferation and repetition of information in our popular conception of the internet—never really gone once it has been posted, always available for resuscitation, and never fully private even when encrypted. Kostova uncannily evokes the way information harms its seeker in her tale of de-crypt.

Twenty-first-century adaptations of the archival-romance formula show, in these three novelists' first books, consciousness of the promises and limitations of digital archives and electronic communication. Yet these contemporary fictions insist on the materiality of texts, manuscripts, and their physical containers. Each of these novels respond to the earlier characterization of Americans as oafish despoilers of national treasures with tales of deft researchers (young women with top-notch American educations) creatively decoding mysteries that have baffled European custodians of texts for centuries. They demand of these attractive protagonists questing in the traditional sense of travel, in order to bring them into physical contact with source material. They show a great interest in what Larkin characterizes as the more universal response to literary manuscripts, appreciation of the magical value: 'This is the paper he wrote on, these are the words as he wrote them, emerging for the first time in this particular miraculous combination'.[28] In all three novels treated in this chapter, the archived texts themselves possess seductive powers. Davidson's Mann lusts after Jonathan Wild as she reads; Silbert's Morgan is sucked into Cidro's criminal conspiracy through her feeling for Renaissance ciphers; generations of historians succumb to Dracula when they find a little dragon-bearing book on their desks. The unleashed magical value of the archival romances turns out to be considerably more promiscuous than the cultural capital inhering in the books' or papers' meaningful value. The younger generation of archival quester, far from abandoning reading and living in blissful ignorance of the past, demonstrates a libidinal ability to bring it back to life. This scenario extends a central fantasy of the heritage industry, in which costumed interpreters invite ticket-bearing visitors into sanitized reconstructions of a lost habitus. Contemporary archival romances by young women writers go beyond dress-up and pastiche, all the way to an embodied reclamation of heritage.

NOTES

1. Philip Larkin, 'A Neglected Responsibility: Contemporary Literary Manuscripts', in *Required Writing: Miscellaneous Pieces 1955–1982* (New York: Farrar, Straus & Giroux, 1984), pp. 98–108.
2. Suzanne Keen, *Romances of the Archive in Contemporary British Fiction* (Toronto: University of Toronto Press, 2001), p. 35.
3. Sarah Brouillette, 'Contemporary Literature, Post-Industrial Capital, and the UK Creative Industries', *Literature Compass* 5, no. 1 (2008), p. 122.
4. Brouillette, 'Contemporary Literature', p. 122.
5. Among the writers who have been dug up after burial, Edgar Allen Poe and Percy Bysshe Shelley are the most well known. The locus classicus for disinterment in search of a manuscript is Dante Gabriel Rossetti's retrieval of a manuscript he placed in the grave of his wife, Elizabeth Siddal Rossetti.
6. See, for instance, the suggestion that Thomas Hardy gave his first wife Emma syphilis in Robert Alan Frizzell, 'Emma Lavinia Hardy: A Retrospective Diagnosis', *TLS*, 6 December 2006.
7. A comprehensive list here would be long. See, for example, D. M. Thomas, *Charlotte: The Final Journey of Jane Eyre* (London: Duckworth, 2000).
8. For the most notorious attempt to harness physical evidence to solve a historical mystery, see Patricia Cornwell's nonfiction research quest *Portrait of a Killer: Jack the Ripper Case Closed* (New York: G. P. Putnam, 2002).
9. Jasper Fforde's Tuesday Next novels serve as exhibit A of such playfully postmodern appropriations. See Jasper Fforde's *The Eyre Affair* (London: Hodder and Stoughton, 2001) and its sequels. See also Valerie Martin, *Mary Reilly* (New York: Doubleday, 1990).
10. See Larkin, 'A Neglected Responsibility', pp. 101–06.
11. On Greimasian actants, see Suzanne Keen, *Narrative Form* (Houndmills, UK: Palgrave Macmillan, 2003), pp. 84–85.
12. See, for instance, Josephine Tey's *Daughter of Time* (New York: Macmillan, 1952). In *Possession*, Byatt gives a generous helping role to her American feminist theorist, Leonora Stern, but the discovered papers get to stay in England to be edited by the author's lineal descendent, English feminist Maud Bailey. See A. S. Byatt, *Possession: A Romance* (London: Chatto and Windus, 1989).
13. See Louis Bayard, 'A Stab in the Dark: A Lovely Spy Sets out to Crack a Code that's Four Centuries Old,' a review of Leslie Silbert's *The Intelligencer*, in *Washington Post Book World*, 28 March 2004.
14. Keen, *Romances of the Archive*, pp. 196–98.

128 Suzanne Keen

15. Jackie Buxton, 'Casaubon Revamped: Contemporary Adventures in the Archive', a review of Keen's *Romances of the Archive in Contemporary British Fiction*, *Contemporary Literature* 44, no. 2 (2003), p. 350.
16. See A. J. Hartley, *The Mask of Atreus* (New York: Berkeley Books, 2006); Paul Christopher, *Michelangelo's Notebook* (New York: Onyx, 2005); Geraldine Brooks, *People of the Book* (New York: Viking, 2008); Lynn Sholes, *The Last Secret* (Woodbury, MN: Midnight Ink, 2006); and Matilde Asensi, *The Last Cato*, trans. Pamela Carmell (New York: Rayo/Harper Collins, 2006).
17. Elizabeth Kostova, Author Profile, Amazon.com, accessed 25 October 2011, www.amazon.com/Elizabeth-Kostova/e/B001ILMACG/ref=sr_tc_ep?qid=1319547312.
18. Elizabeth Kostova, Author Profile (accessed 25 October 2011).
19. Dave Weich, 'In Elizabeth Kostova's Carrel', interview with Elizabeth Kostova, Powell's Books Author Interviews, accessed 25 October 2011, www.powells.com/blog/interviews/in-elizabeth-kostovas-carrel-by-dave/.
20. Jenny Davidson, *Heredity* (New York: Soft Skull Press, 2003), pp. 219–20.
21. Ibid., p. 27.
22. Ibid., p. 217.
23. Leslie Silbert, *The Intelligencer* (New York: Washington Square Press, 2004), p. 331.
24. Ibid., appended 'Readers Club Guide', unnumbered fifth page.
25. Upon publication in June 2005, '*The Historian* sold more copies than *The Da Vinci Code* on its first day, and went straight to the top of the *New York Times* Bestsellers list', according to Gary Younge, in 'Bigger than Dan Brown', *The Guardian*, 18 July 2005, p. 4.
26. Weich, interview with Elizabeth Kostova.
27. Elizabeth Kostova, *The Historian* (New York: Little, Brown and Company, 2005), p. 573.
28. Larkin, 'A Neglected Responsibility', p. 99.

BIBLIOGRAPHY

Matilde Asensi. *The Last Cato*, translated by Pamela Carmell. New York: Rayo/Harper Collins, 2006.
Geraldine Brooks. *People of the Book*. New York: Viking, 2008.
Sarah Brouillette. 'Contemporary Literature, Post-Industrial Capital, and the UK Creative Industries'. *Literature Compass* 5, no. 1 (2008).
Jackie Buxton. 'Casaubon Revamped: Contemporary Adventures in the Archive', a review of Keen's *Romances of the Archive in Contemporary British Fiction*. *Contemporary Literature* 44, no. 2 (2003).
A. S. Byatt. *Possession: A Romance*. London: Chatto and Windus, 1989.
Paul Christopher. *Michelangelo's Notebook*. New York: Onyx, 2005.
Patricia Cornwell. *Portrait of a Killer: Jack the Ripper Case Closed*. New York: G. P. Putnam, 2002.
Jenny Davidson. *Heredity*. New York: Soft Skull Press, 2003.
Jasper Fforde. *The Eyre Affair*. London: Hodder and Stoughton, 2001.
Robert Alan Frizzell. 'Emma Lavinia Hardy: A Retrospective Diagnosis'. *TLS*, 6 December 2006.
A. J. Hartley. *The Mask of Atreus*. New York: Berkeley Books, 2006.
Suzanne Keen. *Narrative Form*. Houndmills, UK: Palgrave Macmillan, 2003.
Suzanne Keen. *Romances of the Archive in Contemporary British Fiction*. Toronto: University of Toronto Press, 2001.

Elizabeth Kostova. *The Historian*. New York: Little, Brown and Company, 2005.
Philip Larkin. 'A Neglected Responsibility: Contemporary Literary Manuscripts', in *Required Writing: Miscellaneous Pieces 1955–1982*. New York: Farrar, Straus & Giroux, 1984.
Valerie Martin. *Mary Reilly*. New York: Doubleday, 1990.
Lynn Sholes. *The Last Secret*. Woodbury, MN: Midnight Ink, 2006.
Leslie Silbert. *The Intelligencer*. New York: Washington Square Press, 2004.
Josephine Tey. *Daughter of Time*. New York: Macmillan, 1952.
D. M. Thomas. *Charlotte: The Final Journey of Jane Eyre*. London: Duckworth, 2000.
Dave Weich. 'In Elizabeth Kostova's Carrel', interview with Elizabeth Kostova, Powell's Books Author Interviews. Accessed 25 October 2011. www.powells.com/blog/interviews/in-elizabeth-kostovas-carrel-by-dave/.

7   Classifying Fictions
Libraries and Information Sciences and the Practice of Complete Reading
Michelle Kelly

INTRODUCTION

It has been argued that 'literature has no taxonomic system [. . .] only a confused aggregate of overlapping classifications from different points of view'.[1] This, too, is the case for fiction holdings in libraries, which are subject to a range of diversified and decentralised systems, approaches, and procedures. No method of classifying fiction has achieved the level of satisfaction necessary to produce a standard practice. Indeed, librarian Gregg Sapp identified fiction as 'the most misunderstood of all library materials'. He argued that 'the apparent impossibility of conceptually classifying fiction has led librarians to establish more objective criteria for providing for its retrieval, such as the author's name, nationality, or period of activity. By doing this, librarians do not so much *classify* fiction as *organize* it'.[2] The distinction between classification and organisation may seem slight, but recourse to an expedient is necessarily significant: organisation is a surrogate, introduced in reaction to a specific kind of book material too intractable to be handled in any other way. Fiction classification is not only an instrumental operation undertaken by libraries on behalf of their patrons; it is also, as Sapp suggests, an encounter with the particularly problematic character of fiction books. The impasse is revealing: it indicates the singularity of fiction as a book work among others.[3]

'Librarians', it has been remarked, 'are among the foremost mediators of fiction within the literary world'.[4] I would contend that the profession's substantial experience with prose fiction is both under-recognised and neglected by those involved in literary scholarship and literary pedagogy. Fiction has been historically significant within public library collections, and there is much evidence to suggest that the predominance of fiction has been a consistent feature of their circulation records.[5] Focusing broadly on public libraries and on adult fiction (as distinct from juvenile or young adult fiction and novels as opposed to short stories or other prose formats), this chapter looks to librarians' involvement with fiction, not to inform practice in the area, but to mobilise library and information science (LIS) as an underutilised resource to reflect on the material and characteristics of fiction anew. At the outset,

Classifying Fictions   131

it must be acknowledged that *classification* is a shorthand term referring to an area of significantly various professional and intellectual practices and commitments: classification is a form, a process, and a function all at once; it takes place in language, in physical spaces, and online, through an array of material and digital instantiations.[6] In this chapter, then, classification is invoked first of all as the activity of putting book objects into a meaningful arrangement or the schedules designed to conduct this activity, that is, shelf classification or 'classification in space'.[7] I focus on shelf classification in order to explore the material conditions of fiction at a particularly charged moment for paper information products.

In developing a sense of literary taxonomy as a 'confused aggregate' with which I began this introduction, I might turn here to Ernest Cushing Richardson's 1901 articulation of the distinction between *shelf classification* and *card classification*, the two modes of book classification then extant. The difference, Richardson suggested, 'is like the difference between big rough lumps of mixed ores and smaller purer specimens which can be arranged with greater exactness'.[8] For Richardson, books 'are real petrifications, or rather planets in an advanced stage of evolution, where the mass of ideas has passed out of the fluid into a solid unchanging state', and he counsels that books 'must, as a rule, be handled as a whole just as the physiographer handles his conglomerate mass, not as the chemist who resolves his into the individual atoms'.[9] Richardson was referring to all kinds of books, and not only fiction, but these early metaphors will emerge as particularly compelling descriptions for the treatment of fiction books. Their opposition indicates two broad attitudes toward the treatment of fiction: those that classify according to the totality of a work and those that classify according to its particular elements.

This attention to classification may seem antique in the twenty-first century. 'Is Classification Necessary after Google?' is the title of a recent *Journal of Documentation* essay, in which Birger Hjørland asks, 'Can information retrieval (IR) theoretically be carried out perfectly without any kind of "classification"?'[10] Observing that two major Danish libraries have 'almost entirely ceased using their own classification systems as well as classifying their books themselves', Hjørland speculates on some of the reasons why the professional practice of classification may be languishing, including the centralised production of classification data, 'large scanning projects' (such as Google Books) which can facilitate full text searching, a new reliance on user tagging, and a low level of use of libraries' online public access catalogues (OPACs) to identify relevant works.[11] Moreover, reflection on the shelf classification of printed fictional material may seem especially inconsequential after digitisation, which has occasioned an era in which 'readers are not restricted to selecting only the books to which they have immediate physical access' but can obtain them from a range of online retailers such as The Book Depository and Amazon, and library patrons can access fiction through enhanced interlibrary loan services and digital content providers such as OverDrive, and an era in which fiction is not only reproduced but *produced* in an array of nonprint formats, giving rise to hypertext and cell phone fiction, to online fan and erotic fiction, to interactive locative narrative.[12]

There are two observations which can be made to mediate between such objections and my objectives in this chapter. The first specifically responds to the multiplication of ways that readers may source and choose their fiction. Although book selection is a critical textual practice and an important area of research with a growing literature of its own, it has an entirely different series of implications for classification, whether classification is conducted physically or digitally.[13] Classification has a distinct mode of intent: its systems are designed to accommodate any work produced, construing printed fiction as a total and interconnected field of practice in a way that the user-centric field of book selection cannot. The second observation is a broader response for print in the new information landscape. It is an impoverished interpretation that takes the present digital moment in terms of challenge alone: such a moment must also be critically rendered in response to the immense opportunity it presents for reflection upon the specific work that print books do. The digital not only alters, imperils, enhances, and degrades a number of facets of textual order; it also operates as a foil that allows printed books—those objects irredeemably 'conditioned by [...] paper and binding'—to be substantively distinguished in a way which has never before been possible.[14]

In addressing these issues, I start my investigation by plotting a chronology of librarians' and library researchers' statements on the classification of fiction books. From these statements emerges a common lament for the general disregard of fiction classification and the lack of achievement in its practice. Ultimately, the chronology shows that fiction classification is an activity which has been locked in a stalemate throughout its history. In the following section, I move to develop this professional commentary with an account of professional activity, outlining the predominant methods and approaches of contemporary fiction classification. The difficulties that librarians have encountered in developing these methods lead them to formulate significant instrumental descriptions of fiction. I consider some of these descriptions in the next section of this essay, looking to librarians' and library writers' articulations of the singularities of fictional material—an intriguing series of statements of fictional reflexivities which originate from outside of literary studies but which nevertheless intersect constructively with its discourses. Of particular interest here is the proposal from the library sector for an interpretive technique of reading designed to facilitate classification: a complete and thoroughgoing reading which will be familiar to practitioners of literary study. In classificatory practice, fiction appears as a distinguished kind of printed matter which resists casual encounter, and in my concluding remarks, I question whether this might illuminate the unique and interdependent roles of the format of the printed book and a technique of complete reading for fictional forms of expression.

FICTION CLASSIFICATION: A PERPETUAL PREHISTORY

In *Primitive Classification* (1903), Émile Durkheim and Marcel Mauss observed that 'not only has our present notion of classification a history, but this history itself implies a considerable prehistory'.[15] Nevertheless, if modern, rational classification aims for comprehension and uniformity, fiction has historically resisted such totalisation: as I argue, it forestalls an exit from the indeterminacies of the past. Yet to remark on the lack of a standard method of fiction classification is not a condemnation of the library as a practicing institution: more than one hundred years of professional testimony accumulates to suggest that the concept of fiction classification is, in a fundamental sense, unexcogitable. Durkheim and Mauss characterise the prehistory of classification as a 'state of indistinction' which is 'impossible to exaggerate'.[16] Indeed, the following indicative list of references and citations demonstrates how the fiction practices of public libraries have long existed in a state of ambivalence.

In an 1899 article, E. A. Baker contended that 'our artificial arrangements of books, skilfully constructed catalogs, open-access systems, and other methods of alluring and improving the reader [. . .] stop short at fiction'.[17] In 1958, R. S. Walker suggested that 'there is no doubt that much of the disinterest in, if not active opposition to, the classification of fiction, is due to the absence of any accredited and efficient scheme'.[18] In 1985, Gail Harrell described 'a clear indication of a lack of consensus on a best, or even a very good, means to categorize fiction'. 'Because no one classification scheme has been adopted as standard or universal', she observed, 'each library or library system decides individually on a method or methods for classifying its adult fiction. Methods vary from librarian to librarian and even from branch to branch within a system'.[19] In 1992, Susan Hayes argued that 'access to works of imaginative literature in academic and, especially, public libraries is clearly inadequate in comparison to the detailed access provided for works of non-fiction'.[20] Similarly, in 1994, Clare Beghtol suggested that 'the potential value of basic research' into content access for fiction 'lies in its attempt to bring modern classificatory thought and techniques to bear on a segment of the world of documents that has not received detailed attention in classification theory and practice'.[21] Likewise, in 1995, Liangzhi Yu and Ann O'Brien remarked that 'the arrangement of the fiction collection has remained a perplexing issue for decades'.[22] It is the case that there has been a greater level of optimism about fiction in libraries recently. In 2000, Jarmo Saarti observed that

> Fiction retrieval has become one of the interesting special issues within information science during the past few years. This is a consequence of several facts. The most important of them is the need for fiction retrieval and secondly, the possibilities for creating retrieval systems for fiction have increased, due to the development of computerised environments for information retrieval.[23]

However, these developments pertain to selection and retrieval more than classification and arrangement, and as late as 2005, Rune Eriksson was able to contend that the efforts of various specialist fiction classifiers and classification researchers have 'turned out to have little effect in the real world' and that 'the classification of imaginative literature has not changed very much since the days of Dewey'.[24]

Writers who have concerned themselves with libraries' organisation of fiction are united in their clear identification of an insufficient and impolitic practice, composed of makeshifts and compensations. Fictional material has proved persistently recalcitrant to the imperatives of classification: its placing on shelves and within schemes. From 1899 to the twenty-first century, the exhortations which have regretted the deficiencies of fiction classification form a series which is very long-standing indeed. The 125-year-long discourse around an institution's experience of organising fiction has a weight and a traction of its own: it makes a history—or, rather, a perpetual prehistory—of the disoperation of classification for the arrangement of fiction, a disoperation which isolates fiction classification from modern precepts of rationality, preventing its escape from its own prehistorical conditions. Durkheim and Mauss's early-twentieth-century sociological account of classification powerfully characterises the 'indistinction' of fiction classification, as demonstrated throughout the duration of its history as a library procedure.

CONTEMPORARY FICTION CLASSIFICATION

When practitioners and researchers of library classification investigate fiction classification's disoperation, their analysis often settles on one criterion in particular: fiction has proved specially and consistently resistant to the incursion of information science's concept of *subject*. Subject is the source and spring of fiction's distinction amongst other printed materials the library acquires and administers. 'Classifying a work of fiction according to any subject criteria is extremely difficult', writes Sapp. 'The very nature of fiction makes the task so'.[25] Fictional works 'do not seem to be "about" a "subject" in the commonly recognized sense', argues Beghtol, and she goes on to suggest that 'there seems to be no satisfactory way of determining "representativeness" for fiction'.[26] Eriksson contends that 'class marks as well as subject headings are not very suitable devices for reflecting some of the most important features of fiction'.[27] He explains:

> normally fiction does not deal with a particular subject matter, but stages a world with a lot of topics [. . .] an essential part of fiction is the narrative; and [. . .] in general subjects are not treated as isolated units, but as something fictitious characters relate to and respond to, intellectually and emotionally.[28]

So what are the classification practices which have been implemented simultaneously to (and in spite of) the enduring frustration around the inadequacy and irregularity of extant procedures, and the recognition of the constitutional intractabilities of fictional material to classification by subject? It is extremely difficult to make conclusive observations about common approaches to placing fiction books on library shelves, because there is a dearth of empirical and statistical research on the topic. Citing the two-page 1985 article 'The Classification and Organization of Adult Fiction in Large American Public Libraries' in 1987, Sharon L. Baker and Gay W. Shepherd identify its author, Gail Harrell, as 'the only author to describe practices followed in a large number of libraries'.[29] Harrell conducted a survey which elicited responses from forty-nine U.S. library systems serving a population of one hundred thousand or more readers. She found that 94 per cent of these library systems enlists genres such as 'Science fiction and/or fantasy', 'Westerns', 'Detective and/or mystery and/or suspense', 'Love and/or romance', 'Espionage and/or spy', 'Gothics', 'Horror and/or ghost stories', 'Adventure', and 'Humour and/or satire' in order to 'arrange and organize a part of their fiction collections'.[30] However, her results also showed that there was little correspondence between the different types of genre categories used by different libraries. Nor did Harrell's results specify the proportions of the fiction collections which were separated out into genre for the 94 per cent of large American library systems that implemented a genre separation or how fiction undifferentiated by genre was treated. There was also evidence of a significant level of use of what Harrell called 'special categories', most notably large print and new books.[31] Harrell updated her findings with a 1993 questionnaire, which similarly found that the use of genre categorisation for adult fiction was predominant among a large number of libraries, that of these libraries a majority used more than one category, and that format and special category influences continued to play a role in the arrangement of fiction.[32]

Since Harrell's survey, substantial relevant literature reviews have been conducted, including Yu and O'Brien's work on adult fiction librarianship in 1996 and Jessica E. Moyer's work on adult fiction, reader advisory services, and libraries in 2005.[33] Nevertheless, neither of these describes research which examines library fiction arrangement practices in a survey mode akin to Harrell's work. Nor does the bibliography of Rune Eriksson's 2010 thesis 'The Classification and Indexing of Fiction—A Theoretical and Historical Perspective' offer any English-language titles which appear promising.[34] Andrej Pogorelec and Alenka Šauperl write that 'Slovenian public libraries have traditionally used [the Universal Decimal Classification] as the only subject information on belles-lettres'.[35] Mirja Iivonen explains that the language of a work is the only device enlisted to subdivide fiction in the Finnish context, and so 'the practice adhered to in most public libraries in Finland [is] to treat fiction collections as a block mainly organized in alphabetic order'.[36] Neither of these articles offers statistical information to substantiate their assertions about the common practices of their country. Amy J. Richard reports on a study which found that 94.1 percent of surveyed public libraries in North Carolina 'used some sort of genre fiction classification'; however, the study she refers to is unpublished.[37] Beyond Harrell's work on U.S. libraries, there appears to be no recent, comprehensive, large-scale investigation which authoritatively represents public library practices in relation to fictional works.

A schematic approach is thus required to start to develop a sense of the range of fiction classification practices in libraries. Yu and O'Brien suggest that outside major classification systems such as the Dewey Decimal Classification (DDC) and the Library of Congress Classification (LCC), fiction is generally handled in one of two ways. The first involves 'distinguishing types of fiction with spine labels or separate shelves, which is usually referred to as categorization'.[38] This encompasses the predominant practices recorded by Harrell; in particular, I would venture, the predominance of genre as an organising device. Another important facet which can be incorporated here is a division of the type serious/recreational fiction.[39] The second approach described by Yu and O'Brien involves 'applying [an] A–Z order according to authors' names'.[40] They suggest that alphabetisation 'used to be seen as almost the only method [. . .] and it is still applied in most libraries to the so-called general fiction [section]'.[41]

In order to consider the DDC's and the LCC's approach to classifying fiction, it is necessary to look at their treatment of the wider category of literature, encompassing other literary forms such as poetry and drama, as well as secondary materials such as literary criticism, biography, and reference works. In the DDC's literature class, 'the subject or topical aspect is secondary to language, literary form, and period, which are the main facets of literature'.[42] The DDC 'in general' uses only the primary facets of language, literary form, and period when a book is written by a single individual (the category which surely accounts for the largest proportion of fiction in libraries); it is multiply authored works ('collections and criticism') which might involve other facets such as 'style, mood, themes, and subjects'.[43] The LCC is similarly objective: in this system, the 'classification of literature differs from classification in other subjects in that languages and forms take precedence over topic'.[44] Sapp has remarked on the fact that neither the LCC nor the DDC—'the two major universal classification schemes'—facilitate 'primary subject access to fictional works'.[45] It is perhaps the approaches of these two principal classifications which most definitively illustrate the troubles of subject for fiction.

In addition to fiction as it is treated by these major systems (as well as others including the Universal Decimal Classification, Colon Classification, Bliss Bibliographic Classification, and Cutter Expansive Classification), specialised fiction classification schemes have emerged from library work and research.[46] Two highly developed examples of such schemes are Annelise Mark Pejtersen's Analysis and Mediation of Publications (AMP) and Clare

Beghtol's Experimental Fiction Analysis System (EFAS).[47] The AMP system is based on what it identifies as four 'dimensions' of fiction: subject matter (including 'psychological development and description' and 'social relations'); frame ('the setting in time and place chosen by the author as the scenario of his [sic] work'); author's intention ('the author's attitude towards the subject'); and accessibility (including 'readability' and 'physical characteristics').[48] As noted earlier, Eriksson has suggested that specialised fiction classifications have not had a great deal of impact. 'Usually', he writes, 'these more or less skilfully developed systems were put into practise at the same library that employed the creator but apparently they were very seldom used anywhere else'.[49] Moyer substantiates this position when she refers to Harrell's research to argue that 'classification schemes like Pejtersen's have been adopted in only a very few libraries and most are still in the theoretical stage'.[50] Moreover, both the AMP and the EFAS are indexing systems, and thus do not address the placing of books on shelves in any extensive way.[51] The introduction of the concept of fiction indexing at this point is significant. Saarti has observed that 'studies on the classification of fiction can be divided into two categories—those that discuss the shelf classification of fiction and those that see the classification as a means for the content description of fiction'.[52] Indexing is overwhelmingly associated with the latter. The distinction between the two approaches is vital, as its articulation helps to clarify how the more 'dedicated' the endeavour of fiction classification becomes, the more the process seems to be inexorably drawn towards content description.

Thus, the evidently diversified practices of libraries arranging their fiction stocks could with justification be described as inconsistent. The empirical, statistical, and anecdotal evidence available bears out Sapp's observation that fiction books on shelves are more often organised than classified. The predominance of genre and categorisation treatments represents the obtuse but ongoing endeavour of libraries to achieve some form of topical arrangement for fiction books. The specialised fiction systems constitute an acknowledgement of the non-topical orientation of these common practices, and an attempt to ameliorate them, but they are systems which seem to never gain purchase. As an activity, fiction classification, indeed, remains indistinct, persistently half-formed, and essentially unresolved.

THE SINGULARITIES OF FICTION

In the LIS examples given here, it is the concept of subject which is the criterion distinguishing fiction as a kind of book work that is singular amongst all others.[53] The unique status of fiction in libraries has led some writers in the LIS field to develop unique descriptions of fiction's singularity, expressed instrumentally. Beghtol, for example, does not endorse, but does recognise, the validity of treating fictional works as 'entities', that is, 'classes with one and only one possible member'.⁵⁴ While the librarian may deal with substitutes of works from artistic mediums such as visual art, music, and theatre in the form of prints, scores, and recordings, the proximity of 'the work' and the physical object has led to D. W. Langridge's observation that literature is unique in that 'the librarian is expected to handle the actual products of the artist'.⁵⁵ Indeed, the singularity of fiction in the library has been recognised in several intriguing ways. Librarians have identified formal and procedural differences between fiction and nonfiction, and commented on the ramifications of these for readers and for their own practice. So, for instance, fiction has been found to be distinguished by its lack of certain bibliographic features which are often characteristic of nonfictional work, and which in fact facilitate classificatory processes. Sapp has quantified some of these differences: 'fiction does not have abstracts; fiction does not follow scientific methodologies; fiction does not employ highlighting devices to emphasize major concepts'.⁵⁶ Saarti has recognised that one manifestation of fiction's difficult relationship with subject is that 'free text search cannot be used efficiently when searching fictional material. This becomes apparent if we compare it [. . .] with the search and retrieval of natural sciences literature, where the text is usually very topical and unambiguous'.⁵⁷

Library science demonstrates one particular instrumental response to fiction's singularity that is especially significant. It consists in the proposition that the nature of fiction could or should compel a classifier to read a piece of fiction *in its entirety*. It is apparent that such a process would be no less than essential for specialised fiction classification schemes which must identify elements of fiction such as 'social relations' and 'readability'. Beghtol explains that although her study of the classification of fiction does not focus 'on whether implementation of [a fiction] system would be an economically sound choice for a particular information agency', she asserts that 'it seems clear from the study of previous fiction analysis systems that analysis of a work of fiction would require a classifier to read the work'.⁵⁸ She continues, arguing, 'Reading complete works of fiction is not an intellectual impediment to detailed fiction analysis, although it might prove an economic barrier to an information agency', concluding with the recommendation that 'so little is known about fiction as a document type [. . .] shortcuts are, at present, inadvisable'.⁵⁹

The proposal to undertake an extended engagement with the whole of a text, however, has not been made in relation to dedicated fiction systems exclusively. Following on from his list of formal bibliographic features which distinguish fiction from nonfiction, Sapp writes that 'for these and many other reasons, it [almost seems] the indexer would have to read an entire novel in order to represent its content'.⁶⁰ Sapp's tone suggests that any proposition or injunction to read an entire work has the potential to induce incredulity; nevertheless, comprehensive reading—a standard approach in literary studies—appears to be a defensible method in LIS writing. Of course, library science offers counterinstances to those writers who would explicitly or implicitly urge close, complete reading. Christine DeZelar-Tiedman, for example, conducted an investigation to determine whether 'dust jacket copy, or back-of-book copy on paperbacks, provides enough information to apply subject headings to fictional works', concluding that these 'usually provided sufficient information'.[61] Indeed, such paratextual classification would seem to offer a more expedient and executable method. Although it defies belief that fiction classification will ever proceed on a large scale with classifiers reading complete works of fiction—nor is this a pressing item on LIS agendas, nor is this essay an attempt to solve the problems presented by fiction classification—the recommendation of this technique of long reading is of note. Fiction classification is a practice which can perceptibly confound relations between the roles of classifier and reader and between the processes of classification and interpretation, it opens a rich shared space of activity between literary studies and LIS, and it might also be understood to endorse the edge of space occupied by the material it handles—the paper fiction book—as a natural border.

CONCLUDING REFLECTIONS

I stated in the Introduction that I wanted to consider shelf classification first, partly because the meaningful arrangement of fiction on shelves cannot neglect the imbrications of fiction with the codex. Shelf arrangement of fiction may be conducted inconsistently, but the condition of its activity is that it brings the book-object with it. I have noted and described the two ways that LIS practices treat these objects: through shelf classifications which prioritise handling fiction books as 'classes with one and only one possible member' and through systems of content description which aim to account for facets of fictional expression with increasing nuance. I have come to the view that in addition to identifying and demarcating these methods in terms of technique, much may be gained by conceiving of them in terms of *manner* as well.

The first manner—associated with frustrated endeavours of meaningful shelf classification—sees fiction books as highly resolved instances of Richardson's description of all books as 'planets in an advanced stage of evolution'; heeds his associated injunction that 'books must, as a rule, be handled whole'; and encompasses all of the difficulties and travails that have been expressed by librarians and library writers mired in the enterprise of handling fiction as a hard material. This manner responds to fiction by implicitly heralding its self-sufficiency and self-containedness: just as fiction books can be 'viewed as creating their own individual worlds', the figure or metaphor of this first manner might be nothing less than the world.[62] This is in accord with Walter J. Ong's analysis of the various relationships of orality, writing (script), and print with narrative, wherein print 'can convey the impression [. . .] that the material the text deals with is [. . .] complete or self-consistent', and the book is 'a complete unit, self-contained in its silent inner logic'.[63] The metaphor of the second manner—associated with the obscurer systems of fiction content description touched on in this essay—might be performance, as in Hayes's incisive phrase 'performing subject analysis on fiction', invoking both the medical practice of dissection as well as a theatrical practice of simulation.[64] The second manner is indicated by librarians and library writers advocating the labour of a thoroughgoing reading in order to unpick a fictional work and to apply a classificatory apparatus that acts as a simulacrum for the work, representing as many fictional facets as can conceived. In spite of the wide space of operation between these metaphors—the world and the performance—the field of fiction classification has found highly intricate ways of steering many diverse paths between the guiding light of classification and the pole of organisation. It is possible that it is because of the wide space of operation between its metaphors that the field has remained so spectacularly irresolute. Although the two manners are mobilised to significantly different practical effect—as evidenced by their respective techniques—there cannot be a statement of priority between them in terms of integrity. Both flounder because of it: the first because it attempts to sustain its integrity in the face of intractable material and the second because it persists in designing and producing convoluted and resource-heavy systems in spite of the fact that these are not generally adopted.

The technique of the second manner for treating fiction—thoroughgoing reading—has already worked to introduce a third: the practices of literary studies. In fiction librarianship, there is a significant level of interest in literary studies and literary theory, and Anat Vernitski and Pauline Rafferty have outlined some of the reasons for this:

> Fiction retrieval asks questions about the nature of fictional documents; the relationships between fiction and knowledge organization; the status of the fictional entity as individual entity and as part of a putative class; the 'aboutness' of the fictional document; and the challenge of the polysemic nature of fiction for information retrieval design. Many of these questions overlap with the kinds of questions asked by literary theorists about the nature of text and textuality, about genres and intertextuality, about separateness and interconnections.[65]

I have touched on several of these points of convergence in this chapter, but the one I have focused on is the shared technique of long reading. That library science has worked to produce the recommendation of a total, comprehensive reading for printed fiction does not only operate to verify the efficacy of the same technique for literary studies: it might be thought to reveal a codependence of technique and material, or a way in which prose fiction taking up whole books solicits or even *demands* complete reading. Emanating from the distinct professions and practices of library science and literary study, the clarification of the facility of complete reading is a serviceable resource at a time when fictional forms are being reconfigured in a digital environment, and the issue of digital reading is coming to the fore.

In calling for a pedagogy that conceives of literacy as including the multiple competencies of close reading, hyper-reading, and machine reading, N. Katherine Hayles employs a criterion of locality to distinguish textual context. In Hayles's terminology, monolocality denotes a 'single text' with the extremely rich context of the surrounding work and other works linked to it through intertextuality; multilocality is typically associated with 'screen-based' media, where 'many textual fragments are juxtaposed [and] context is truncated'.[66] Hayles makes no neat correspondence between the different kinds of reading and print or digital text, indeed noting that close reading can interact 'synergistically' with web reading, and that hyper-reading was not unknown in the Renaissance, where an apparatus called a 'book wheel' was able to simultaneously display several open books on a rotating device.[67] The investigation of fiction classification perhaps functions to clarify complete reading as a practice that is strongly associated with (and yet distinct from) close reading, in relation to the differential contexts of reading environments.

As a technique, complete reading does not necessarily require close reading's linguistic and rhetorical scrutiny, but it does thrive in a monolocal context and certainly entails monolocality's rich meaning environment.[68] Complete reading can be undertaken in a digital environment, but the definition of what 'complete' reading might mean in this context is inherently more flexible, fluid, contestable, and unstable than in the monolocal context of a printed book. The critical differential for fiction as a printed book is the long history of also viably treating them as a 'conglomerate mass', as in genre and alphabetical arrangements. Material which is to be validly treated in the manner of a petrification *or* a performance—when practice *delivers every line*—is material that is implicated in the production of a space of substantial autonomy: fiction's famous performance of a world. The LIS philosophies and practices which have—with equal integrity—resulted in two radically different methods of treating material *completely* invite us to consider whether fiction can perform in the same way when presented in or produced for multilocal reading environments, whether this is a capacity that should be properly granted to print fiction, and, if so, how it might be further explored as a formal quality of print fiction within an emerging literacy that incorporates multiple modes of human and nonhuman reading of print and digital text.

NOTES

1. David Perkins, 'Literary Classifications: How Have They Been Made?', in *Theoretical Issues in Literary History*, ed. David Perkins (Cambridge, MA: Harvard University Press, 1991), pp. 253–54.

2. Gregg Sapp, 'The Levels of Access: Subject Approaches to Fiction', *Reference Quarterly* [*RQ*] 25, no. 4 (1986), p. 488. At Sapp's first observation, relating to the uncertainty that surrounds fiction in libraries, he cites A. W. McClellan, *The Logistics of a Public Library Bookstock* (London: Association of Assistant Librarians/Library Association, 1978). Italics in the original.
3. I use this phrasing with a nod to Garrett Stewart's euphonic 'bookwork'—his name for the work done by a genre of art which uses books as its material and thus 'studies the book by generalizing it'. 'Book-works'—the installation pieces and sculptures which comprise the genre—'are *texts by other means*, not to be read *in* as discourse but rather—as denatured things, alienated, dysfunctional—to be read whole'. Garrett Stewart, 'Bookwork as Demediation', *Critical Inquiry* 36, no. 3 (2010), pp. 456, 435. Italics in the original.
4. Liz Greenhalgh and Ken Worpole, with Charles Landry, *Libraries in a World of Cultural Change* [1995] (Abingdon, UK: Routledge/Taylor & Francis, 2004), p. 132.
5. In the period between 1850 and 1900, Nick Moore has suggested that 'over 50 per cent of loans were fiction' in many British public libraries; a proportion which increased 'to over 80 per cent in some cases'. Today the Public Lending Right (PLR) uses data collected from sample library authorities to generate an estimate of the proportion of all British public library book loans by category, and its findings attest to the ongoing popularity of fiction. In 2010–11, the PLR calculated that adult fiction accounted for 42 per cent of all loans, followed by the category 'Children's, Teenage and Educational' (which includes fiction and nonfiction) with 35.9 per cent. The adult nonfiction category 'Lifestyle, Sport and Leisure' was the next-highest ranking category with 7.2 percent. Nick Moore, 'Public Library Trends', *Cultural Trends* 13, no. 1 (2004), p. 30; PLR, 'Loans by Category', accessed June 24, 2012, www.plr.uk.com/mediaCentre/loansByCategory/loansByCategory.htm; and PLR, 'Loans of Books by Category (%s): 2009/10—2010/11', accessed June 24, 2012, www.plr.uk.com/mediaCentre/loansByCategory/2010-2011ByCategory.pdf.
6. Francis Miksa has observed that the period from 1950 onwards has seen library cataloging and classification transform 'into a strikingly complex matter based on extraordinary amounts of technical detail'. There are, moreover, a great many other library tools and practices which are closely related to or involved in classification, including metadata, cataloguing rules, indexing, subject headings, and authority records. Digitisation has seen the development of new forms for information organisation, including tagging and folksonomies. Francis Miksa, 'A Review Article: Chan, Taylor, and the Future of Cataloging Texts', review of *Cataloging and Classification: An Introduction*, by Lois Mai Chan, with the assistance of Theodora L. Hodges, and *Introduction to Cataloging and Classification*, by Arlene G. Taylor, with the assistance of David P. Miller, *Library Quarterly* 79, no. 1 (2009), pp. 132–33, 138.
7. Ernest Cushing Richardson, *Classification: Theoretical and Practical* (New York: Scribner's, 1901), p. 48.
8. Ibid, p. 52.
9. Ibid., pp. 47–48, 84.
10. Birger Hjørland, 'Is Classification Necessary after Google?', *Journal of Documentation* 68, no. 3 (2012), p. 301.
11. Ibid., pp. 299–300, 300.
12. Denice Adkins and Jenny E. Bossaller, 'Fiction Access Points across Computer-Mediated Book Information Sources: A Comparison of Online Bookstores, Reader Advisory Databases, and Public Library Catalogs', *Library and Information Science Research* 29, no. 3 (2007), p. 355.

13. For a recent example of book selection research, see Kamy Ooi and Chern Li Liew, 'Selecting Fiction as Part of Everyday Life Information Seeking', *Journal of Documentation* 67, no. 5 (2011), pp. 748–72.
14. Richardson, *Classification*, p. 52.
15. Émile Durkheim and Marcel Mauss, *Primitive Classification* [1903], trans. Rodney Needham [1963] (Chicago: University of Chicago Press, 1969), p. 5.
16. Durkheim and Mauss, *Primitive Classification*, p. 5.
17. E. A. Baker, 'The Classification of Fiction', *Library World* 1, no. 10 (1899), p. 198.
18. R. S. Walker, 'Problem Child: Some Observations on Fiction, with a Sketch of a New System of Classification', *Librarian and Book World* 47, no. 2 (1958), p. 22. Capitalisation in this quotation has been altered.
19. Gail Harrell, 'The Classification and Organization of Adult Fiction in Large American Public Libraries', *Public Libraries* 24, no. 1 (1985), pp. 14, 13.
20. Susan Hayes, 'Enhanced Catalog Access to Fiction: A Preliminary Study', *Library Resources and Technical Services* 36, no. 4 (1992), p. 441. Similarly Clare Beghtol observed that 'classification theorists have not concentrated on the problems of creating bibliographic classification systems for the fine arts and humanities [. . .] science and technology have virtually monopolized the attention of classificationists both in theory and practice'. Clare Beghtol, *The Classification of Fiction: The Development of a System Based on Theoretical Principles* (Metuchen, NJ: Scarecrow, 1994), p. 14.
21. Beghtol, *Classification of Fiction*, pp. 12–13.
22. Liangzhi Yu and Ann O'Brien, 'Domain of Adult Fiction Librarianship', in *Advances in Librarianship*, vol. 20, ed. Irene P. Godden (San Diego: Academic Press, 1996), p. 179.
23. Jarmo Saarti, *Kaunokirjallisuuden sisällönkuvailun aspektit. Kirjastoammattilaisten ja kirjastonkäyttäjien tekemien romaanien tiivistelmien ja asiasanoitusten yhdenmukaisuus* [Aspects of fictional literature content description: Consistency of the abstracts and subject indexing of novels by public library professionals and clients] (Oulu, Finland: Oulu University Library/Oulun Yliopisto, 2000), p. 183. *Kaunokirjallisuuden sisällönkuvailun aspektit* is written in Finnish but includes an English abstract and summary, from which all quotations are sourced.
24. Rune Eriksson, 'The Classification and Indexing of Imaginative Literature' (paper presented at the American Society for Information Science and Technology's 16th Workshop for the Special Interest Group on Classification Research, Charlotte, NC, October 29, 2005), p. 1.
25. Sapp, 'Levels of Access', p. 495. In this article, Sapp also suggests that 'the subject of any novel is much more likely to be expressed collectively, rather than singularly' (p. 495). Similarly, Saarti writes that fiction 'consists of several meaningful facets, and indexing or classification schemes become thus multifaceted'. Saarti, *Kaunokirjallisuuden sisällönkuvailun aspektit*, p. 184.
26. Beghtol, *Classification of Fiction*, pp. 22, 266.
27. Rune Eriksson, 'Klassifikation og indeksering af skønlitteratur—et teoretisk og historisk perspektiv' [The classification and indexing of fiction—a theoretical and historical perspective] (PhD diss., Danmarks Biblioteksskole, 2010), p. viii.
28. Ibid.
29. Sharon L. Baker and Gay W. Shepherd, 'Fiction Classification Schemes: The Principles behind Them and Their Success', *Reference Quarterly* [*RQ*] 27, no. 2 (1987), p. 249.
30. Harrell, 'Classification and Organization of Adult Fiction', pp. 14, 13. Capitalisation in the original.

31. Ibid., p. 14.
32. Gail Harrell, 'Use of Fiction Categories in Major American Public Libraries', in *Guiding the Reader to the Next Book*, ed. Kenneth D. Shearer (New York: Neal-Schuman, 1996), pp. 149–57. Genre coincides with subject more than any other criterion enlisted to order fiction: Annelise Mark Pejtersen and Jutta Austin, for instance, recognise that genre classification 'represents an attempt to group fiction by content rather than by formal aspects'. Nevertheless, genre does not, for this attempt, constitute a subject: the authors criticise it for categorising by overly 'general or selective criteria'. Nor does it constitute a satisfactory basis for classification, because 'it invariably leads to the division of a library's fiction stock into two parts: genre systems are generally so crude that the majority of novels cannot be classified by them but have to remain in alphabetical arrangement by author'. The alphabetisation method of fiction classification is considered in greater detail at a later point in this chapter. Annelise Mark Pejtersen and Jutta Austin, 'Fiction Retrieval: Experimental Design and Evaluation of a Search System Based on Users' Value Criteria', pt. 1, *Journal of Documentation* 39, no. 4 (1983), pp. 231, 232.
33. Jessica E. Moyer, 'Adult Fiction Reading: A Literature Review of Readers' Advisory Services, Adult Fiction Librarianship, and Fiction Readers', *Reference and User Services Quarterly* 44, no. 3 (2005), pp. 220–31.
34. One of the challenges of fiction classification research for English language speakers is the amount of compelling material on the subject that is untranslated, particularly from Scandinavian countries.
35. Andrej Pogorelec and Alenka Šauperl, 'The Alternative Model of Classification of Belles-Lettres in Libraries', *Knowledge Organization* 33, no. 4 (2006), p. 204. Pogorelec and Šauperl infer some of the other countries which employ the Universal Decimal Classification when they write that the alternative fiction classification system they devised 'could be used in Slovenian libraries and libraries with a similar tradition, e.g., the states of the former socialist Yugoslavia or the Austrian Empire' (p. 205).
36. Mirja Iivonen, 'On the Library Classification of Fiction', *Scandinavian Public Library Quarterly* 21, no. 1 (1988), p. 12.
37. David W. Singleton, 'Genre Fiction Classification in North Carolina Public Libraries' (Master's paper, University of North Carolina at Chapel Hill, 1992), p. 20; quoted in Amy J. Richard, 'Genre Fiction Classification: A Study of the Durham County Library' (Master's paper, University of North Carolina at Chapel Hill, 1999), n.p.
38. Yu and O'Brien, 'Domain of Adult Fiction Librarianship', p. 180.
39. Describing a shelf classification experiment for fiction in the town of Kajaani, Finland, Jarmo Saarti reports that 'traditional genres—e.g., detective novels, thrillers—were [easy] to classify', whereas 'serious fiction was most difficult to classify'. He identifies two factors involved in the particular challenge of placing 'serious' fiction on the shelves: 'it is in the nature of serious fiction not to open easily for classification', and 'serious fiction readers tend to avoid the situation where serious fiction is classified according to genres—or according to any other basis'. Jarmo Saarti, 'Feeding with the Spoon, or the Effects of Shelf Classification of Fiction on the Loaning of Fiction', *Information Services and Use* 17, nos. 2–3 (1997), p. 168.
40. Yu and O'Brien, 'Domain of Adult Fiction Librarianship', p. 180. Beghtol suggests that an A–Z arrangement by author is not merely a convenient approach to deal with obstinate material, but that it can in fact be interpreted as a kind of classification: 'classification-by-creator'. Beghtol here presents a stimulating idea that has significant facility to reconfigure what otherwise presents as a dry organisational practice; simultaneously, however, she recognises that

'while the practice of classification-by-creator is widespread, little theoretical attention has been given to it'. Beghtol, *Classification of Fiction*, pp. 21, 22.
41. Yu and O'Brien, 'Domain of Adult Fiction Librarianship', p. 180. At their observation that an A–Z order 'used to be seen as almost the only method', Yu and O'Brien cite John Dixon, ed., *Fiction in Libraries* (London: Library Association, 1986).
42. Lois Mai Chan, *Cataloging and Classification: An Introduction*, with the assistance of Theodora L. Hodges, 3rd ed. (Lanham, MD: Scarecrow/Rowman Rowman & Littlefield, 2007), p. 346. In the Dewey Decimal Classification, 'Literature' is one of ten main classes, occupying the 800–899 range, and fiction can be classified within this array. Nevertheless, in her chapter on the DDC Chan explicitly notes that 'in many libraries, fiction in English is not classified [. . .] it is assigned the letter *F* and subarranged alphabetically by order' (p. 350, italics in the original).
43. Ibid., p. 346.
44. Lois Mai Chan, *A Guide to the Library of Congress Classification*, 5th ed. (Englewood, CO: Libraries Unlimited, 1999), p. 353. Although the Library of Congress Classification includes a subclass titled 'PZ Fiction and juvenile belles lettres', this name is somewhat misleading. Chan notes that until 1980, 'the Library of Congress classed all works of fiction in English, including translations into English, in subclass PZ', but a 1980 change in policy means that 'since then, American fiction has been classed in PS, English fiction in PR, and translations into English with the original national literatures' (p. 362).
45. Sapp, 'Levels of Access', p. 489.
46. Special classification schemes might also be developed from the basis of these more established systems. In 2003, Monika Szunejko gave an account of two special literature classifications implemented at the libraries of Murdoch University and the University of Western Australia, each a different revision of the DDC. Monika Szunejko, 'Literature Classification Schemes at Two West Australian University Libraries: Murdoch University and the University of Western Australia', *Cataloging and Classification Quarterly* 36, no. 2 (2003), pp. 45–57.
47. Pejtersen has written about her fiction classification system in several publications. For an introduction to AMP, see Pejtersen and Austin, 'Fiction Retrieval'. EFAS is described in Beghtol, *The Classification of Fiction*. Specialist genre fiction classifications have also been developed; see Alastair Cameron, *Fantasy Classification System* (St. Vital, MB: Canadian Science Fiction Association, 1952); and Antony Croghan, *Science Fiction and the Universe of Knowledge: The Structure of an Aesthetic Form* (London: Coburgh, 1981).
48. Pejtersen and Austin, 'Fiction Retrieval', pt. 1, p. 234.
49. Eriksson, 'Classification and Indexing of Imaginative Literature', p. 1.
50. Moyer, 'Adult Fiction Reading', p. 221. Harrell has also observed that 'although [the AMP] scheme has been implemented in Denmark, there is no evidence in the literature that suggests this system is being employed anywhere in the United States'. Harrell, 'Classification and Organization of Adult Fiction', p. 13.
51. Anat Vernitski has proposed an intriguing intertextual fiction classification scheme that would relate different fictional texts based on the categories quotation, allusion, variation, sequel, and prequel, but as with the AMP and the EFAS, Vernitski's classification is ultimately an indexing scheme. Anat Vernitski, 'Developing an Intertextuality-Oriented Fiction Classification', *Journal of Librarianship and Information Science* 39, no. 1 (2007), pp. 47–48.
52. Saarti, *Kaunokirjallisuuden sisällönkuvailun aspektit*, p. 184. Fiction indexing is a critical element in those electronic databases which facilitate fiction

organisation and retrieval, but which are not predicated on the presence of the physical book. These include online fiction resources from the library sector such as EBSCO's NoveList, OCLC's FictionFinder, and WorldCat Genres, as well as Kirjasampo in Finland and Litteratursiden in Denmark. User tagging of fictional works is a variant of fiction indexing that has emerged with the digital epoch: Alenka Šauperl, for instance, investigates tags submitted by users to Amazon and online reader advisory service LibraryThing. Alenka Šauperl, 'Pinning down a Novel: Characteristics of Literary Works as Perceived by Readers', *Library Review* 61, no. 4 (2012), pp. 292–94.

53. There is one provocative exception to the understanding of fiction's singularity in this regard. Richard Davies advocates that works of philosophy should be 'treated as fiction', that is, arranged in a single alphabetic sequence by author. 'The positive good that such an arrangement seeks is philosophical neutrality', Davies writes, 'given the highly controversial and fissiparous nature of the activities that are embraced under the rubric "philosophy"'. Richard Davies, 'Should Philosophy Books Be Treated as Fiction?', *Knowledge Organization* 36, nos. 2–3 (2009), p. 121.
54. Beghtol, *Classification of Fiction*, p. 33.
55. D. W. Langridge, *Classification and Indexing in the Humanities* (London: Butterworths, 1976), p. 83.
56. Sapp, 'Levels of Access', p. 495.
57. Saarti, *Kaunokirjallisuuden sisällönkuvailun aspektit*, p. 183.
58. Beghtol, *Classification of Fiction*, p. 11. Hayes investigates another facet of the professional issues around the implementation of a more complete reading of fiction, conducting an empirical investigation which measured the time it took cataloguers to provide increased subject access to fictional works. Hayes, 'Enhanced Catalog Access to Fiction', p. 453.
59. Beghtol, *Classification of Fiction*, p. 11. The value of Beghtol's prudence is convincingly supported by David Lonergan's account of the classification of Michael Crichton's 1976 novel *Eaters of the Dead*. This work, a retelling of *Beowulf*, was misclassified as nonfiction by the Library of Congress and assigned the LCC number DL31.I2613, for Viking History. Lonergan's contention is that 'the misclassification of *Eaters of the Dead* [. . .] might have been prevented', and he makes four recommendations for reducing the chance of such an error in the future: one of these is that cataloguers should 'read [. . .] books thoroughly in cases of ambiguity or confusion'. David Lonergan, 'Fooling LC: Michael Crichton and *Eaters of the Dead*', *Behavioral and Social Sciences Librarian* 16, no. 2 (1998), p. 70.
60. Sapp, 'Levels of Access', p. 495.
61. Christine DeZelar-Tiedman, 'Subject Access to Fiction: An Application of the *Guidelines*', *Library Resources and Technical Services* 40, no. 3 (1996), pp. 205, 208. DeZelar-Tiedman writes that 'few libraries have the resources to pay cataloguers to read and interpret fiction; perhaps they will find book jacket copy an effective summarizing tool for providing a reasonable level of access to these valuable library materials' (p. 210).
62. Adkins and Bossaller, 'Fiction Access Points', p. 365.
63. Walter J. Ong, *Orality and Literacy: The Technologizing of the Word* [1982] (London: Routledge, 1995), pp. 133, 150. This first manner of treating fiction books is also clearly related to Ong's observation that 'in a writing or print culture, the text physically bonds whatever it contains and makes it possible to retrieve any kind of organization of thought as a whole' (p. 141).
64. Susan Hayes, 'Use of Popular and Literary Criticism in Providing Subject Access to Imaginative Literature', *Cataloging and Classification Quarterly* 32, no. 4 (2001), p. 72.

65. Anat Vernitski and Pauline Rafferty, 'Approaches to Fiction Retrieval Research: From Theory to Practice?', in *Innovations in Information Retrieval: Perspectives for Theory and Practice*, ed. Allen Foster and Pauline Rafferty (London: Facet Publishing, 2011), p. 50. At their observation about the status of fiction as an entity and as part of a class, Vernitski and Rafferty refer to Beghtol's *The Classification of Fiction* as an example; at their observation on the 'aboutness' of fiction, they cite Beghtol's book as well as Pauline Rafferty and Rob Hidderley, *Indexing Multimedia and Creative Works: The Problem of Meaning and Interpretation* (Aldershot, UK: Ashgate, 2005). There are many other examples of writings in library science which investigate the potential of literary scholarship for its practice. As previously discussed, Vernitski's work on intertextual classification of fiction operates in the intersection between the two fields, as does work by Susan Hayes. See also Judith A. Ranta, 'The New Literary Scholarship and a Basis for Increased Subject Catalog Access to Imaginative Literature', *Cataloging and Classification Quarterly* 14, no. 1 (1991), pp. 3–26.
66. N. Katherine Hayles, *How We Think: Digital Media and Contemporary Technogenesis* (Chicago: University of Chicago Press, 2012), pp. 74, 61, 74. The algorithms brought into being by machine reading have an eliminated or impoverished context—perhaps extending to a 'word-frequency list' (p. 74)—but because I am concentrating on human readers, I do not consider the question of machine reading in detail here. Hayles attributes the concept of hyper-reading to James Sosnoski, 'Hyper-Readings and Their Reading Engines', in *Passions, Pedagogies, and Twenty-First Century Technologies*, ed. Gail E. Hawisher and Cynthia L. Selfe (Logan, UT: Utah State University Press; and Urbana, IL: National Council of Teachers of English, 1999), pp. 161–77. In the quotation from Hayles, 'screen-based' is a direct quotation from Sosnoski's work (p. 167).
67. Hayles, *How We Think*, pp. 69, 61–62. Hayles acknowledges John Guillory as her source for the description of the book wheel. John Guillory, 'How Scholars Read', *ADE Bulletin* 146 (2008), pp. 8–17.
68. Hayles earlier paraphrased John Guillory's description of close reading: 'detailed and precise attention to rhetoric, style, language choice, and so forth through a word-by-word analysis of a text's linguistic techniques'. John Guillory, 'Close Reading: Prologue and Epilogue', *ADE Bulletin* 149 (2010), pp. 8–14.

BIBLIOGRAPHY

Denice Adkins and Jenny E. Bossaller. 'Fiction Access Points across Computer-Mediated Book Information Sources: A Comparison of Online Bookstores, Reader Advisory Databases, and Public Library Catalogs'. *Library and Information Science Research* 29, no. 3 (2007).
E. A. Baker. 'The Classification of Fiction'. *Library World* 1, no. 10 (1899).
Sharon L. Baker and Gay W. Shepherd. 'Fiction Classification Schemes: The Principles behind Them and Their Success'. *Reference Quarterly [RQ]* 27, no. 2 (1987).
Clare Beghtol. *The Classification of Fiction: The Development of a System Based on Theoretical Principles*. Metuchen, NJ: Scarecrow, 1994.
Alastair Cameron. *Fantasy Classification System*. St. Vital, Manitoba: Canadian Science Fiction Association, 1952.
Lois Mai Chan. *Cataloging and Classification: An Introduction*, with the assistance of Theodora L. Hodges, 3rd ed. Lanham, MD: Scarecrow/Rowman & Littlefield, 2007.
Lois Mai Chan. *A Guide to the Library of Congress Classification*, 5th ed. Englewood, CO: Libraries Unlimited, 1999.

Antony Croghan. *Science Fiction and the Universe of Knowledge: The Structure of an Aesthetic Form*. London: Coburgh, 1981.
Richard Davies. 'Should Philosophy Books Be Treated as Fiction?'. *Knowledge Organization* 36, nos. 2–3 (2009).
Christine DeZelar-Tiedman. 'Subject Access to Fiction: An Application of the *Guidelines*'. *Library Resources and Technical Services* 40, no. 3 (1996).
Émile Durkheim and Marcel Mauss. *Primitive Classification* [1903], translated by Rodney Needham [1963]. Chicago: University of Chicago Press, 1969.
Rune Eriksson. 'The Classification and Indexing of Imaginative Literature'. Paper presented at the American Society for Information Science and Technology's 16th Workshop for the Special Interest Group on Classification Research, Charlotte, NC, 29 October 2005.
Rune Eriksson. 'Klassifikation og indeksering af skønlitteratur—et teoretisk og historisk perspektiv' [The classification and indexing of fiction—a theoretical and historical perspective]. PhD diss., Danmarks Biblioteksskole, 2010.
Liz Greenhalgh and Ken Worpole, with Charles Landry. *Libraries in a World of Cultural Change*, [1995]. Abingdon, UK: Routledge/Taylor & Francis, 2004.
John Guillory. 'Close Reading: Prologue and Epilogue'. *ADE Bulletin* 149 (2010).
John Guillory. 'How Scholars Read'. *ADE Bulletin* 146 (2008).
Gail Harrell. 'The Classification and Organization of Adult Fiction in Large American Public Libraries'. *Public Libraries* 24, no. 1 (1985).
Gail Harrell. 'Use of Fiction Categories in Major American Public Libraries', in *Guiding the Reader to the Next Book*, edited by Kenneth D. Shearer. New York: Neal-Schuman, 1996.
Susan Hayes. 'Enhanced Catalog Access to Fiction: A Preliminary Study'. *Library Resources and Technical Services* 36, no. 4 (1992).
Susan Hayes. 'Use of Popular and Literary Criticism in Providing Subject Access to Imaginative Literature'. *Cataloging and Classification Quarterly* 32, no. 4 (2001).
N. Katherine Hayles. *How We Think: Digital Media and Contemporary Technogenesis*. Chicago: University of Chicago Press, 2012.
Birger Hjørland. 'Is Classification Necessary after Google?'. *Journal of Documentation* 68, no. 3 (2012).
Mirja Iivonen. 'On the Library Classification of Fiction'. *Scandinavian Public Library Quarterly* 21, no. 1 (1988).
D.W. Langridge. *Classification and Indexing in the Humanities*. London: Butterworths, 1976.
David Lonergan. 'Fooling LC: Michael Crichton and *Eaters of the Dead*'. *Behavioral and Social Sciences Librarian* 16, no. 2 (1998).
Francis Miksa. 'A Review Article: Chan, Taylor, and the Future of Cataloging Texts', review of *Cataloging and Classification: An Introduction*, by Lois Mai Chan, with the assistance of Theodora L. Hodges, and *Introduction to Cataloging and Classification*, by Arlene G. Taylor, with the assistance of David P. Miller. *Library Quarterly* 79, no. 1 (2009).
Nick Moore. 'Public Library Trends'. *Cultural Trends* 13, no. 1 (2004).
Jessica E. Moyer. 'Adult Fiction Reading: A Literature Review of Readers' Advisory Services, Adult Fiction Librarianship, and Fiction Readers'. *Reference and User Services Quarterly* 44, no. 3 (2005).
Kamy Ooi and Chern Li Liew. 'Selecting Fiction as Part of Everyday Life Information Seeking', *Journal of Documentation* 67, no. 5 (2011).
Walter J. Ong. *Orality and Literacy: The Technologizing of the Word* [1982]. London: Routledge, 1995.
Annelise Mark Pejtersen and Jutta Austin. 'Fiction Retrieval: Experimental Design and Evaluation of a Search System Based on Users' Value Criteria', pt. 1. *Journal of Documentation* 39, no. 4 (1983).

David Perkins. 'Literary Classifications: How Have They Been Made?', in *Theoretical Issues in Literary History*, edited by David Perkins. Cambridge, MA: Harvard University Press, 1991.
Andrej Pogorelec and Alenka Šauperl. 'The Alternative Model of Classification of Belles-Lettres in Libraries'. *Knowledge Organization* 33, no. 4 (2006).
Pauline Rafferty and Rob Hidderley. *Indexing Multimedia and Creative Works: The Problem of Meaning and Interpretation*. Aldershot, UK: Ashgate, 2005.
Judith A. Ranta. 'The New Literary Scholarship and a Basis for Increased Subject Catalog Access to Imaginative Literature'. *Cataloging and Classification Quarterly* 14, no. 1 (1991).
Ernest Cushing Richardson. *Classification: Theoretical and Practical*. New York: Scribner's, 1901.
Jarmo Saarti. *Kaunokirjallisuuden sisällönkuvailun aspektit. Kirjastoammattilaisten ja kirjastonkäyttäjien tekemien romaanien tiivistelmien ja asiasanoitusten yhdenmukaisuus* [Aspects of fictional literature content description: Consistency of the abstracts and subject indexing of novels by public library professionals and clients]. Oulu, Finland: Oulu University Library/Oulun Yliopisto, 2000.
Jarmo Saarti. 'Feeding with the Spoon, or the Effects of Shelf Classification of Fiction on the Loaning of Fiction'. *Information Services and Use* 17, nos. 2–3 (1997).
Gregg Sapp. 'The Levels of Access: Subject Approaches to Fiction', *Reference Quarterly [RQ]* 25, no. 4 (1986).
Alenka Šauperl. 'Pinning down a Novel: Characteristics of Literary Works as Perceived by Readers'. *Library Review* 61, no. 4 (2012).
James Sosnoski. 'Hyper-Readings and Their Reading Engines', in *Passions, Pedagogies, and Twenty-First Century Technologies*, edited by Gail E. Hawisher and Cynthia L. Selfe. Logan, UT: Utah State University Press; and Urbana, IL: National Council of Teachers of English, 1999.
Garrett Stewart. 'Bookwork as Demediation'. *Critical Inquiry* 36, no. 3 (2010).
Monika Szunejko. 'Literature Classification Schemes at Two West Australian University Libraries: Murdoch University and the University of Western Australia'. *Cataloging and Classification Quarterly* 36, no. 2 (2003).
Anat Vernitski. 'Developing an Intertextuality-Oriented Fiction Classification'. *Journal of Librarianship and Information Science* 39, no. 1 (2007).
Anat Vernitski and Pauline Rafferty. 'Approaches to Fiction Retrieval Research: From Theory to Practice?', in *Innovations in Information Retrieval: Perspectives for Theory and Practice*, edited by Allen Foster and Pauline Rafferty. London: Facet Publishing, 2011.
R. S. Walker. 'Problem Child: Some Observations on Fiction, with a Sketch of a New System of Classification'. *Librarian and Book World* 47, no. 2 (1958).
Liangzhi Yu and Ann O'Brien. 'Domain of Adult Fiction Librarianship', in *Advances in Librarianship*, vol. 20, edited by Irene P. Godden. San Diego: Academic Press, 1996.

8 Autobiobibliographies
For Lovers of Libraries
Martin McQuillan

> *I hereby undertake . . . not to bring into the Library or kindle therein any fire or flame . . . and I promise to obey all rules of the Library.*[1]

DERRIDA IN THE LIBRARY

In the early stages of the 'Envois' section of Jacques Derrida's *La Carte Postale*, the narrator is led through the streets of Oxford by his guides, 'Jonathan and Cynthia', towards the Bodleian library where he will encounter for the first time the postcard of Socrates and Plato from the manuscript by Matthew Paris.[2] The narrator, let us not call him or imagine him to be Derrida, is concerned that he is being set up as the subject of a spectacle, staged in order to witness the effect the image has on him: 'I suspect them of having had a plan. They themselves knew the *carte*'.[3] It is only one instance of the paranoia he exhibits in this tale of clandestine love and secret letters that is presented in full as a work that is both and neither philosophy and literature. 'Do you think there are listening devices? That our letters are opened? I don't know if this hypothesis terrifies me or if I need it', he comments just before describing his first experience of the postcard:

> Jonathan and Cynthia were standing near me next to the glass case, the table rather, where laid out, under glass, in a transparent coffin [*cerceuil*], among hundreds of displayed reproductions, this card had to jump out at me [*devait me sauter aux yeux*]. I saw nothing else, but that did not prevent me from feeling that right near me Jonathan and Cynthia were observing me obliquely, watching me look. As if they were spying on me [*s'ils guettaient*] in order to finish the effects of a spectacle they have staged (they have just married more or less).[4]

The translation seems to add a scopophilic layer to the scene, with the newlyweds on the lookout for or lying in wait for [*s'ils guettaient*] the coup de théâtre and the coup de grâce of their scheme: *un coup d'envois*, to use a football term—when it all kicks off. Here the library, or more accurately the threshold of the library, not at a bookshelf but at a display case, perhaps outside the library proper, is figured as a space for distrust, obsession, deception, and entrapment. The image of Socrates and Plato is merely an invitation to the narrator to enter the library to discover its secrets. The postcard is bait for the philosopher, a McGuffin in this Hitchcockian scene; what lies behind it is the vault of the library and the trap of writing.

On one hand, the narrator is taken by the image because for him it disproves a certain encyclopaedic logic of the library. The library as depository of all knowledge, an archive that takes its authority from its comprehensive sweep and genealogy of legitimation:

> Be aware that everything in our bildopedic culture, in our politics of the encyclopaedic, in our telecommunications of all genres, in our telematicometaphysical archives, in our library, for example the marvellous Bodleian, everything is constructed on the protocolary character of an axiom, that could be demonstrated, displayed on a large *carte,* a post card of course, since it is so simple, elementary, a brief, fearful stereotyping (above all say or think nothing, that jams telecom). The charter is the contract for the following, which quite stupidly one has to believe: Socrates comes *before* Plato, there is between them—and in general—an order of generations, an irreversible sequence of inheritance.[5]

The encyclopaedic principle and the culture of legitimation it predicates through the value of presence granted by every image depend on this protocol of inheritance. This is also why the great libraries are attached to the oldest and most prestigious universities. It is through the sedimentation of generations that they derive their authority and confer it on those who study there. The idea of the university and the authority of the library are inseparable in this respect. One might go so far as to say that no universities without the library and no library without the universal encyclopaedic principle, or the filial principle of inheritance—'Socrates comes *before* Plato'. Yet in depicting Socrates's writing being dictated *by* Plato, the historical and filial inversion of the Matthew Paris image puts all of this at risk. It challenges the received wisdom of the ages, of every library, and every university, of the entire metaphysical tradition. Brazenly on display, rather than buried, in a transparent coffin [*cerceuil*] or casket in the portico before the pillars of the library it bears testimony to something that deconstruction has previously suspected: that the authority of every received tradition, including that of the university and the encyclopaedic principle itself, depends on a foreclosure of alterity, whereby metaphysics or the encyclopaedic becomes the very principle by which they justify themselves, as wellspring and effect of their own operation. Rather than being the result of an established inheritance of authoritative generations, they are the outcome of their own textual performance. As the narrator puts it, 'all of this is not without [. . .] political consequences. They are still difficult to calculate'.[6]

The narrator is drawn to the image in the fortune-telling book almost as if it were his destiny to discover it. He is not guided there by accident. However, as the Envois well knows, destination is as much a trap as inheritance. The search for Socrates and Plato lures him into the library and slowly infects him with the sort of archive fever that deconstruction ought to be inoculated against. But the *mal d'archive* is an autoimmunity, something that eats away the narrator's resistance from within. The narrative arc of the Envois takes him back to Oxford to read the manuscript and so answer certain questions accrued through the course of his writing. His destination is the Duke Humfrey's Library, the oldest reading room in the Bodleian, where the Paris manuscript was held in the late 1970s. The Duke Humpfrey's library holds, amongst other things, the archive of the Conservative Party of the United Kingdom. The narrator describes arriving in Oxford from the nominative determinative town of Reading, and is impatient for its oak-panelled splendour:

> I went right over, in the morning, one hour after my arrival, to the Bodleian. The librarian seemed to know me (I didn't understand very well, she alluded to the difficulty that my book [the Paris manuscript] seems to have given her), but this did not get me out of the oath [*serment*]. She asked me to *read* it (it is a question of engaging oneself to respect the rules of the library, the treasures to be protected are priceless). Therefore I read it and handed her back the cardboard covered with transparent paper that she had tendered me. At this point she starts to insist, I had not understood: no you have to read it out loud [*à haute voix!*]. I did so, with the accent you make fun of all the time, you can see the scene. We were alone in her office. I understood better the marriage ceremony and the profound presuppositions of Oxonian performativism. What would an oath that you did not say out loud be worth, an oath that you would only read, or that while writing you would only read? Or that you would telephone? Or whose tape you would send?[7]

The Paris manuscript presents the cataloguing system of the library with problems, but it is not beyond its parameters. The narrator is distracted by his own desire and does not fully understand what he is being asked to do. The rules of the library must be obeyed, and one must affirm this by oath; with one hand on the written word and speaking aloud, one must swear in front of an officer of the archive. The library requires the reader to present and correct, no telephoning in of a performance or sending a show reel. Reading in the library requires a public commitment, like matrimony or collegiate life. One reads in silence and swears aloud:

> Did I tell you, the oath that I had to swear out loud (and without which I would never have been permitted to enter) stipulated, among other things, that I introduce neither fire nor flame into the premises: '*I hereby*

undertake . . . not to bring into the Library or kindle therein any fire or flame . . . and I promise to obey all rules of the Library'.[8]

The narrator must promise to submit himself to the authority of the encyclopaedic principle and not to burn the metaphysical house of index cards to the ground. However, as de Man tells us, only a God can promise: only the absolute and indivisible can avoid the inaugural perjury of the oath. The narrator, who as a narrator, is already divided and a ruin of himself, has no hope of keeping the promise he does not fully understand that he is making. Equally, the library, jealous to guard its treasures, does not know what it is allowing to cross its threshold: a postmodern Prometheus kindling the flame of deconstruction, a harbinger of a new Enlightenment that risks the seemingly irreversible protocols of the reading room.

However, our narrator is also bound by the promise he makes. He will persist with it just as his reading undoes those bonds. He is looking for answers in the manuscript known in the Bodleian as 'Ashmole 304', bequeathed to the library as part of the collection of Elias Ashmole, dedicated and ruthless antiquarian, founder of the Ashmolean museum who on one occasion failed to visit the constituency of which he was standing as a member of Parliament because his horoscope predicted he would lose.[9] When presented with the manuscript the narrator is thrilled by its unexpected colour and by the intricacies of the fortune-telling procedure. His fate is sealed, and he is drawn further into the book. Giddy as a schoolboy, he is overwhelmed and must leave the library for air but he cannot resist returning to the book. The temptation to add his own encryption is too great:

> One day I will be dead, you will come all by yourself into the Duke Humphrey Room, you will look for the answer in this book. And you will find a sign that I am leaving in it now (after others, for there has been no lack of barbarians, nor of perjurers, before me) [*après d'autres car les barbares n'ont pas manqué, ni avant moi les perjures*].[10]

The narrator can only repeat the encyclopaedic gesture of burying a secret deep within the archive. He will be true to the archive and obey all the rules of the library, for despite appearances all the readers of the manuscript who have come before him have also been breakers of oaths, perjurers and bigamists, barbarians at the gates ready to overturn the protocols of inheritance. The narrator will be faithful to the library in his own fashion. He will burn the correspondence of the Envois but not the manuscript and not the 'bildopedic culture' or the 'politics of the encyclopaedic'. These remain intact as the architectonic principle through which the beloved reader are guided in order to find this hidden message: an answer to be found in a book.

However, this is a postcard, and it is open on both sides for all of us to read. He leaves a trail of breadcrumbs for anyone with a research grant and a rudimentary knowledge of Latin to find the message. The fortune-telling

154 *Martin McQuillan*

book works in the manner of those flow charts found in children's magazines or 'pick your own adventure' books today. From a series of choices made, the reader is guided towards a number of possible outcomes, the logarithmic combination of turns creating the possibility of different destinies. However, like a roll of the dice, the 'Pronostics of King Socrates' can never abolish chance, there can only ever be a finite number of outcomes written down, and ultimately a set number of routes through to them.[11] The narrator goes on to detail a particular path through the pages of the book, one that can be retraced with a little care. The route is complicated and involves the introduction of an initial limited randomness by the spinning of a wheel, subsequently lost from the manuscript. This takes us from instructions on how to use the book at fol. 31r, '*Documentum subsequentis consideracionis quae socratica dicitur*', followed by the famous miniature of Plato and Socrates at fol. 31v, to

> On the next page [fol. 32v] a double entry chart, a small computer if you will (*Tabula inscripta 'Computentur capita epigrammatum'*) gives you, in AE 4, *Spera fructuum* [AE 4 actually reads 'Ficus fruct(us).'— MMcQ], referring you thereby to one of a series of circles, each divided into 12 sections and 12 names. The circles are six, it seems to me (Spera, specierum, Sp. Florum, Sp. Bestiarum, Sp. Volatilium, Sp. Civitatum, Sp. Fructuum finally, in which you have just fallen, in AE 4, then, and in the section 'ficus'). Are you following? You take yourself off then to the circle of fruits [fol. 34r], you look for the slice 'fig', as on a menu or a pie [*sur une carte ou sur une tarte*], and you read, under the heading 'Ficus', our question, An erit [fol. 34r reads 'e(ss)et' though it is 'erit' elsewhere] bonum ire extra domum vel non [whether it is good to go out of the house?]. This is indeed the question, not so? Underneath, you are referred elsewhere. To whom? But to the King . . . And the king of Spain, *Ite ad Regem Hispanie*. There are, it seems to me, 16 kings [fols. 39r-40r, with the King of Spain at fol. 39r col. I], and each one proposes 4 answers, 4 sentences, 4 'verses or Judgements'. Since your figure is 4, your sentence is the fourth one. Guess, what it says . . .[12]

The destiny is not the result of pure chance but a calculation based on a number of set outcomes. In this sense, the fortune is programmed, the result of a computational logic. It is in other words, an effect of a certain encyclopaedic principle. There is no deconstruction of the possibility of destination, only the illusion of destinerrance here, only an arrival at a place to which the author will have guided us. It will have been our destiny as readers to obey all the rules of the library; rules of the 'telematicometaphysical archive' that we can in principle never escape but only ruin by our own perjured commitment to it.

Before we reveal the final score (what the fourth sentence says) in our own gesture of obedience to the encyclopaedic rules of the library, it might be worth noting that the Paris manuscript (Ashmole 304) is not an original text. It would seem to be a copy of a previous version of the 'Pronostics of King Socrates', which would have been in circulation. Ashmole 304 is in fact a composite volume, which contains other fortune-telling texts and is constructed from what would appear to be scraps and remnants of parchment used for more significant or sacred books. The inscription and the illumination are of a much higher quality than a later edition of the King Socrates text also held in the Bodleian collection, but nevertheless the conclusion that an antiquarian would derive from the manuscript is that it was intended for private use amongst the monks of St Albans rather than as a work of knowledge to be held in a library. The medieval mind was quite capable of holding the divine, the secular and even the profane together in a single field of vision, and it is in no way surprising that Paris and his fellow monks should read for pleasure this pagan almanac. However, it is, one might say, a reprint. 'I confide to you this solemn and sententious aphorism: did not everything between us begin with a reproduction?' (9) the narrator of the Envois writes to his love from Oxford. The Paris manuscript is a copy, the postcard is a facsimile, the oath in the library is the repetition of words printed on a laminated card, and the promise is the reiteration of a performance ruined at its origin by the possibility of its own perjury. The love affair, like the commitment to the rules of the library, may obey certain laws and follow a certain logic, but it is a form of mimesis: it copies an inherited model. The Envois obeys all of the conventions of the literary loves and epistolary fictions that come before it. No doubt it subverts these conventions and opens them up to new possibilities, but it is always obliged to stay in touch with a model that it at once disavows or betrays and whose laws it is obliged to respect. Everything in the library begins with a reproduction even if it is the repetition of an original perjury or betrayal, and the reader is always 'after others, for there has been no lack of barbarians, nor of perjurers, before me'. Quite literally, the library, any library, is a collection of reproductions: a warehouse of books, reprints, and copies. This is true of even those great libraries like the Bodleian rightly famed for their 'original manuscripts', for here we will always find the most decisive logic of reproduction. Sitting in his room at Baliol College, the narrator dreams of writing:

> first to reassemble an enormous library on the *courrier,* the postal institutions, the techniques and mores of telecommunication, the networks and epochs of telecommunication throughout history—but the 'library' and the 'history' themselves are precisely but 'posts', sites of passage or of relay among others, stases, moments or effects of *restance,* and also particular representations, narrower and narrower, shorter and shorter sequences, proportionally, of the Great Telematic Network, the *worldwide connection* [in English in original]'.[13]

This is a curious encyclopaedic fantasy. The Postal Principle, as Derrida outlines it, may be the very thing that opens up the closed logic of the encyclopaedic protocol. Here the narrator desires to assemble 'une énorme bibliothèque' of the 'courrier', both post person and correspondence, an entire archive that would run [*courir*] away with itself, circumnavigating the entire globe.[14] However, such a library or written history could only ever be part of the history of the Post itself, one relay among many, one more reproduction, representation, and exchange. The bibliopedic culture of representation must necessarily be a Platonism. A library that would contain the entire history of the Post must be as big as the world itself. Like the only true map in Borges's famous story 'On Exactitude in Science', it must be an exact copy of the thing it describes. Any other library could only ever be an edited collection of selected or representative works. This selection or editing would remain, says Derrida, as an effect of '*restance*', which as Alan Bass notes in footnote 5 to his translation of 'To Speculate—On "Freud"' means 'that which remains because it cannot be judged, the undecidable excess'.[15] There can never be a protocol adequate to the laws of the encyclopaedia; no ultimate justification for selection and inclusion would be possible. Nevertheless, selection occurs, and the edition, undecideable and unreadable, remains to be read. This is the ruin, the perjury, at the heart of the library: the myth of comprehension, of the comprehensive, the definitive, and the authoritative. The encyclopaedic principle will do everything in its considerable power to cover its tracks here. It will obscure this logic and set up powerful, inertial borders to police who or what may enter into the library. It will require ticket checks, letters of introduction and accreditation, the taking of signatures, and the swearing of oaths. However, as a room full of paper it is essentially a tinderbox in which any Prometheus might kindle a flame.

It is educative to note how many libraries refuse or limit reproduction, as the narrator notes of the ironic performative on the reverse of each postcard: 'reproduction prohibited'.[16] Derrida's own bequest of papers to the University of California, Irvine (UCI) explicitly forbids digital reproduction in order to put the archive 'online'. Although a limited amount of reprographics is possible with the due permissions, the scholar of Derrida must first make a pilgrimage to the library and bear witness to the aura of the work of philosophy. The Bodleian has made a selection of images from Ashmole 304 available online but jealously guards the 'image-rights' of its treasures. The library is at once selective and enclosed: these after all are 'special collections'. There can be no access to them with prior approval or supervision. The narrator of the Envois writes, '"Reproduction prohibited", which can be translated otherwise: no child, inheritance prohibited, filiation interrupted, and sterile midwives [*accouchers*, literally one who is present at the bedside]'.[17] For those who know a little of the autobiographical allusions of the Envois, the prohibition against reproduction is intriguing. For those who read in libraries, the prohibition is the basis of the encyclopaedic principle, one that both predicates the possibility of the library as such and is undone by it at every turn, on every shelf, in every corner, by every reader who gives birth to future generations of thought through their own labour. Socrates's mother, Phaenarete, was also a midwife.

The fourth sentence of the king of Spain in Ashmole 304 [fol. 39r, col. I, 'Rex yspanie', line 4] reads, 'Si iueris, cum lucro redibis', which with the tenses literally translated means, 'If you shall have gone, you shall return with profit'. We should perhaps not be surprised by this paranoid narrator's capacity for sentimentality as the love affair draws to its conclusion. Equally, we should be happy to take this as our own destiny. Whether it is good to go out of the house, to visit the library perhaps, if we go we shall return with profit. This is what happens when we agree to invest in or speculate on a love for the Encyclopaedic.

EDITING DE MAN EDITING

Lovers of libraries will know well the experience of destinerrance within the archive: the *dérive* from one book to another that leads us farther into the labyrinth of reference in pursuit of an unknown telos, reading without a map or guide. Events of reading in this way lead us to unforeseen and unrecognisable destinations. My own work on the Paul de Man papers held in the Archives and Special Collections of the University of California, Irvine, has led to some unexpected outcomes. It was while editing for publication de Man's 1973 manuscript on Rousseau, *Textual Allegories*, that my attention was drawn to another of de Man's projects on Rousseau that demanded to be edited.[18]

In line with Viking Press's long-standing series, *The Portable Rousseau* was commissioned from de Man in 1972. The volume was intended as a pedagogical guide collating significant texts by Rousseau and would respond to the interest in Rousseau created by the work of Derrida, Althusser, and de Man himself. The collection was to contain original English-language translations of texts by Paul and Patricia de Man as well as reproductions of certain standard translations of Rousseau. The book was never completed during his lifetime, but the papers in the UCI archive suggested that a significant amount of material had already been completed. Whereas the later *The Essential Rousseau*, edited and translated by Lowell Blair for Meridian in 1983, went some way towards filling the pedagogical need of a collection of primary texts by Rousseau, it lacks the intellectual ambition and scholarly sweep of the proposed book by de Man. Indeed, *The Essential Rousseau* is really only a lightly edited collection of four complete texts (first and second discourses, 'The Social Contract', and the *Profession*). De Man envisioned something much more comprehensive and encyclopaedic. This was the essential problem of *The Portable Rousseau*, despite the capacious nature of the Viking series: de Man's edition was far too big to ever be published as a single volume; its portability would have been minimal. De Man as an editor needed to be a little more selective. It was immediately obvious to me that the length of the proposed volume made it quite unsuitable for publication in book form today but would make an ideal subject for online publication. There is nothing more suited to the virtually comprehensive ambitions of the encyclopaedic than the Internet. *The Portable Rousseau* is now available online, alongside *Textual Allegories*, through the UCI library portal.[19]

The work presented online includes de Man's editorial corrigenda, drafts of planned introductions to the volume, and original translations by Paul and Patricia de Man. The translations and editorial texts were written over the decade between 1972 and 1983; the revisions and transcriptions were done in the period after his death from 1983 to 2006 by, amongst others, Ellen Burt, Cynthia Chase, Patricia de Man, and the de Mans's daughter Patsy. The editorial material includes an agreed 'Table of Contents' and 'Principle of Selection' that reveal the entire edition itself to be a critical reading of Rousseau. De Man proposes to demonstrate the link between the political Rousseau of 'The Social Contract' and the literary Rousseau of *Julie* and the *Confessions* through the inclusion of the 'Essay on the Origins of Language' (a full English-language translation of the essay is available online). This constituted a significant move in Rousseau studies, which at this time persisted in separating out Rousseau's generic writing, often viewing them as contradictory. De Man's gesture here, and in *Textual Allegories* (which became the second half of *Allegories of Reading*), is to show that the literary and political texts of Rousseau should all be considered as figurative texts, characterized by different tropes but all essentially operating according to the same figurative principles. The importance de Man places on the 'Essay on the Origins of Language' is then a significant opening of Rousseau scholarship at this time: this editing is not innocent or unknowing; it is a critical commentary on how Rousseau had been read hitherto.[20]

As it became clear that this 'Table of Contents' would prove to be both too long for the commissioned series and too expensive to realize through reproduction rights (on the request of his editor at Viking), de Man produced a later table of contents (included online as 'Optimal Table of Contents'). This is accompanied by a text on the 'Status of Translations' that outlines available possible translations of standard texts by Rousseau and their relation to copyright. Two introductory texts are also available. The first, transcribed by Ellen Burt, is a draft of de Man's proposed introduction to the volume. The second, a twelve-page text titled 'Rousseau', comes from the manuscript of *Textual Allegories* which was retained by Patricia de Man at the time of the bequest to UCI to use as a possible introduction to *The Portable Rousseau* as she sought to complete the original Viking commission after the death of her husband. It was the pursuit of these missing pages that caused the swerve from editing *Textual Allegories* to *The Portable Rousseau*. The translations by Paul and Patricia de Man then follow according to the proposed order of the original 'Table of Contents'. However, some deviations should be noted. The translations from the *Nouvelle Héloise* by Patricia de Man are taken from a continuously numbered manuscript prepared for final copy. It includes a small number of letters not listed in the 'Table of Contents'. An extant translation by Patricia de Man of Part I, Letter V of the *Nouvelle Héloise* is also included as an appendix to the online publication although it is not part of the continuous manuscript of translations from this Rousseau text. Given the potentially infinite resource of online publication, it seemed to me unhelpful to scholarship not to attempt my own encyclopaedic gesture of comprehensiveness by reproducing all of the available material. It ought to be possible now to assemble *The Portable Rousseau* as originally conceived as a series of links to the translations by Paul and Patricia de Man as well as the proposed standard translations that would have been included in Viking publication. However, for copyright reasons this final act of reconstruction has not yet been realised.

It should be noted that the six available pages of de Man's planned introduction, transcribed by Ellen Burt, are themselves an admirable essay on the topic of the encyclopaedic principles of the library. De Man is interested in treating the whole of Rousseau's work, refusing the fundamental gesture of division and separation that to his mind clouded contemporary Rousseau scholarship. For de Man, the very thing that is striking about Rousseau is the diversity of the genres that his writing ranges over and simultaneously masters. Although this was not uncommon for eighteenth-century authors, it seems to have become a trait now lost because of professionalization and specialization. We no longer expect our poets to be novelists and our philosophers to be librettists. Rousseau's oeuvre demonstrates an un–self-conscious universal ambition, whereas the protocols of the telematicometaphysical archive requires not only comprehension but within it taxonomy and specialist expertise also. Yet Rousseau's writing defies such classification. As de Man writes of the relative lack of critical interest in Rousseau at the time, 'this hesitation in [invoking] him as part of the monumental gallery of the canonical masterworks of all times, is due to an excess, rather than a lack of influence'. Thus, Rousseau's place in the library has hitherto not been secured. De Man points out that while the *Julie* was one of the most popular novels of its day there had not been a new English-language translation since the 1780s. However, argues de Man, the spirit of Rousseau is larger than the entire library that would seek to contain him: 'we don't read Rousseau in the works of Rousseau [anymore] because we constantly encounter him under the signature of so many other writers. Rousseau's influence is so all-encompassing, so all-powering that it has become impossible to observe it in its own right'. The fragment of the introduction then goes on to map out a prospectus for the all-encompassing effects of Rousseau: from his fellow *philosophes* Voltaire and Diderot to English romanticism, Kant, Hegel, Hölderlin, Goethe, nineteenth-century French literature (all of it), Victorian criticism, the American Revolution, Marx, Leo Strauss, Althusser, Hannah Arendt, and Derrida. Not unlike the narrator of the 'Envois', it is an extraordinary dream of 'une énorme bibliothèque', a vast library and history of the Great Telematic Network and worldwide connection of Rousseau. It is not surprising that de Man never completed this introduction. Oversized as the edited translations were, this introduction outlines a project far bigger than the book designed to hold it. De Man offers us notes towards a taxonomy of Rousseau criticism and lists of those relays and stases through which the thought of Rousseau runs, but he was unable to undertake the encyclopaedic work required to complete the task he set himself. It may have been the case that de Man found his other projects on Rousseau and later aesthetic ideology much more compelling than the editing of this volume, but equally one can see that even de Man may have been daunted by the vastness of the work he was proposing here. The problem with publication, length aside, was never the completion of the translations; it was in truth the completion of the introduction. Perhaps de Man's mind rebelled against the encyclopaedic principle, this arch debunker of totalizations could not bring himself to obey the rules of the library and complete this inventory of Rousseau's influence. However, the correspondence with his editor held in the UCI papers, shows that even up until his death he still planned to complete the book. Unlike Kafka, he left no order to take fire into the library and burn everything after his death. The siren call of the encyclopaedic principle is an irresistible lure for the scholar even if our whispered perjured promises to it are the ruins of our own funeral pyre.

A LOVER OF LIBRARIES

In the 'Dictionary of Received Ideas' that accompanies his *Bouvard and Pécuchet*, Flaubert says of libraries 'always have one at home, especially if you live in the country'. Although this would invalidate the need to seek an answer to 'Whether it is good to go out of the house?' in the 'King Socrates', it would presuppose the existence of substantial property as well as an expert principle of selection on the part of the home owner. The joke is that the would-be scholars Bouvard and Pécuchet deem it necessary to advise others that a library is an essential requirement for their work. The dictionary itself is another example of the encyclopaedic principle that puts in play a mastery that can never realize itself. In the *Philosophical Dictionary*, Voltaire says of libraries that the 'astounding multitude of books should not scare [. . .] Paris contains about seven hundred thousand men [and] one cannot live with them all [. . .] one chooses three or four friends. Thus must one no more complain of the multitude of books than of the multitude of citizens'.[21] Choosing your friends carefully in a library would be a good editing principle, the selectivity that sits at the heart of the comprehensive ambition of the library. Curiously, the section on libraries has been edited out of the English-language Penguin edition of the dictionary. Voltaire himself was no stranger to making enemies. He quarrelled with Casanova when he told him that his translation of *l'Ecossaise* was a bad one. The Scottish play may have brought misfortune to Casanova, but by way of riposte, he reserved some choice words for Voltaire in the memoirs he wrote while working in the library at Dux (living in the country, as it were). One of the most striking features about the memoirs is the amount of time Casanova spends in libraries. He is in a library almost as often as he is in a boudoir. It is not, as is commonly supposed, that the library at Dux represented a retreat for Casanova from the exertions of his extraordinary life; libraries are completely central to those adventures. Casanova's seemingly boundless appetites are surely informed by the encyclopaedic principle of cataloguing the taxonomy of women and human experience. He often manages to combine the bedroom and the library in select episodes:

> As soon as it was time, I repaired to the temple, and while I was waiting for the idol I amused myself in examining the books of a small library in the boudoir. They were not numerous, but they were well chosen and worthy of the place. I found there everything that has been written against religion, and all the works of the most voluptuous writers on pleasure; attractive books, the incendiary style of which compels the reader to seek the reality of the image they represent. Several folios, richly bound, contained nothing but erotic engravings. Their principal merit consisted much more in the beauty of the designs, in the finish of the work, than in the lubricity of the positions. I found amongst them the prints of the Portier des Chartreux, published in England; the engravings of Meursius, of Aloysia Sigea Toletana, and others, all very beautifully done. A great many small pictures covered the walls of the boudoir, and they were all masterpieces in the same style as the engravings.[22]

The library is a prelude to 'delightful ecstasy' on the sofa with his mistress dressed as a nun. In this auto-bio-bildo-libido-bibliographical scene Casanova is struck by the editorial principles of selection in the library, the books are not numerous, but 'they were well chosen'. The editorial predicate and the encyclopaedic principle cannot be separated: no libraries without editors and no editors without libraries. Just as no library can ever be complete, no edition can ever be definitive. Casanova's own commitment to the library takes the form of his fourteen-year cataloguing of Dux as well as the cataloguing of his life. However, with the latter, he was a librarian who was careless of his own manuscripts, emerging as they did in Leipzig twenty-two years after his death. Another example of the excess of writing, the *restance* that cannot be judged or edited, the profit that returns within an economy that overspills the walls of the library both defeating and initiating the encyclopaedic protocol whether it is Jacques Casanova, Jacques Derrida, memoirs for Paul de Man, or memoirs of lovemaking on sofas in Venice. In the dictionary, Voltaire notes that whilst Rome had twenty-nine great public libraries, 'there are now more than four thousand important libraries in Europe. Choose which suits you, and try not to be bored'.[23] Life is never boring for a lover of libraries whether he or she owns a Kindle or kindles a flame.

NOTES

1. Jacques Derrida, *The Post Card: from Socrates to Freud and Beyond*, trans. Alan Bass (Chicago: Chicago University Press, 1987), p. 216.
2. Ibid., p. 16.
3. Ibid., p. 16.
4. Ibid., p. 16.
5. Ibid., p. 20.
6. Ibid., p. 21.
7. Ibid., p. 208.
8. Ibid., p. 216.
9. C. H. Josten, ed., *Elias Ashmole (1617–1692). His Autobiographical and Historical Notes, his Correspondence, and Other Contemporary Sources Relating to his Life and Work*, vol. I (Oxford, UK: Clarendon Press, 1966), pp. 220–25.
10. Derrida, *The Post Card*, p. 217.
11. On the question of chance and delimitation see my reading of Mallarmé's 'Un Coups de Dés' in the introduction to Paul de Man, *The Post-Romantic Predicament*, ed. M. McQuillan (Edinburgh, UK: Edinburgh University Press, 2012).
12. Derrida, *The Post Card*, p. 217. For the purpose of brevity I have edited out the start of the trail which goes over two pages of the Envois; however, this is a journey the reader might want to make for him- or herself. I have inserted in square brackets the pages of Ashmole 304 referred to by Derrida and offered the occasional translation from the Latin. I am extremely grateful to Dr Bruce Barker-Benfield, senior assistant librarian in the Department of Special Collections at the Bodleain Library for guiding me through the manuscript to this destination.
13. Ibid., p. 27.
14. Ibid., p. 32.
15. Ibid., p. 261.
16. Ibid., p. 37.
17. Derrida, *The Post Card*, pp. 39, 44–45.
18. Paul de Man, *Textual Allegories*, http://ucispace.lib.uci.edu/handle/10575/1091.
19. Paul de Man, ed., *The Portable Rousseau*, http://ucispace.lib.uci.edu/handle/10575/1093.
20. I have discussed elsewhere the tradition of reading Rousseau in America that comes from Leo Strauss. See my 'De Man and the Neo-Cons', *Derrida Today*, Vol. 5, 2012.
21. Voltaire, *Philosophical Dictionary*, Project Gutenberg html edition, ww.gutenberg.org/files/18569/18569-h/18569-h.htm, p. 192.
22. Ibid.
23. Ibid., p. 193.

BIBLIOGRAPHY

Jacques Derrida. *The Post Card: From Socrates to Freud and Beyond*, translated by Alan Bass. Chicago: Chicago University Press, 1987.

Paul de Man. *The Post-Romantic Predicament*, ed. M. McQuillan. Edinburgh, UK: Edinburgh University Press, 2012.
Paul de Man, ed. *The Portable Rousseau*. http://ucispace.lib.uci.edu/handle/10575/1093.
Paul de Man. *Textual Allegories*. http://ucispace.lib.uci.edu/handle/10575/1091.
C. H. Josten, ed. *Elias Ashmole (1617–1692). His Autobiographical and Historical Notes, his Correspondence, and Other Contemporary Sources Relating to his Life and Work*, vol. I. Oxford, UK: Clarendon Press, 1966.
Martin McQuillan, 'De Man and the Neo-Cons', *Derrida Today*, Vol. 5, 2012.
Voltaire. *Philosophical Dictionary*. Project Gutenberg html edition, www.gutenberg.org/files/18569/18569-h/18569-h.htm.

9 'That Library of Uncatalogued Pleasure'

Queerness, Desire, and the Archive in Contemporary Gay Fiction

Kaye Mitchell

INTRODUCTION: QUEER ARCHIVES

Discussions of the purpose and value of lesbian and gay archives, and more abstract speculations on the meanings of the 'queer archive' emerge in the shadow of those influential musings on the archive conducted by Foucault (in, for example, *The Order of Things*) and Derrida (in, for example, *Archive Fever*). The archive has become, consequently, less a place, more 'a way of seeing, or a way of knowing; [. . . .] a symbol or form of power'.[1] Whether this makes the idea of the archive ripe for queer appropriation or irrevocably tainted by its association with authority, institutionalisation, and regulation is the question underlying what follows. Can we so easily dismiss the archive's etymological echoes of, in Derrida's words, 'the *commencement* and the *commandment*' of the law in our formulation of a queer archive?[2] For Foucault, the archive does not merely memorise events or practices but determines what can be said and thought.[3] The consequent realisation of the ambiguous and contradictory nature and effects of the queer archive are evident in representations of archives and libraries found in several contemporary gay and lesbian fictions. Such fictions evince a more ambivalent attitude towards the archiving of material relating to sexuality, towards recordkeeping and public cultures organised around sexuality, and towards the very idea of the 'archive' and its connotations than much recent queer theoretical writing. In the literary instances that follow, I adduce the knowledge that the archive protects and produces is both enlightening and—to some extent—restrictive, regulative, and even coercive.

Yet Derrida also claimed, in *Archive Fever*, that 'There is no political power without control of the archive, if not of memory. Effective democratization can always be measured by this essential criterion: the participation in and the access to the archive, its constitution, and its interpretation'.[4] Lesbian, Gay, Bisexual and Transsexual (LGBT) archives have thus, rightly, been seen as part of the 'democratization' of gay and lesbian identities, an indication of their accession to some version of political power and public visibility, and part of a vital commitment 'to rediscover our past, control our present, and speak to our future', in the words of the founders of the Lesbian

Herstory Archives (LHA) in New York, for example.[5] Moreover, the power in question is generally represented as distinct from the forms of state power, even running counter to them.

It is hardly surprising, then, that the very notion of the 'queer archive' has, for the most part, been greeted as a positive development by queer theorists. Such an archive is held to be countercultural, generally not state run or funded, part of the creation of community/activist spaces and/or 'safe' spaces, part of a long-overdue assertion of visibility, and an aid in the construction of individual and collective identities. The queer archive is composed of 'ephemera' and guided by emotion and thus is at odds with traditional archive holdings (asserting, thereby, the very democratization of *evidence* and the expansion of what counts as knowledge and history).[6] In their insistence on ephemera, claims Ann Cvetkovich, 'the collectors of gay and lesbian archives propose that affects—associated with nostalgia, personal memory, fantasy, and trauma—make a document significant'.[7] This emphasis on affect seeks to confer on the holdings of queer archives a value unrelated to their material worth, to contest their exclusion from 'official histories'—and to initiate new models of archivization and historical analysis. In fact, Foucault touches on this interlinking of affective response and historical selection as early as 1979, in 'The Life of Infamous Men'. Stressing that his collection of these 'lives' is 'in no way a history book', he avers that

> [t]he selection that shall be found in it has conformed to nothing more important than my taste, my pleasure, an emotion, laughter, surprise, a certain fright or some other feeling, whose intensity perhaps I would have difficulty in justifying now that the first flush of discovery is past.[8]

Although not 'important', the brief lives that he collects have produced in him a set of 'physical' impressions—'as if it would be possible to have others'—and his archival encounters bequeath him 'that vibration which I feel even today'.[9] The affective archival encounter thereby becomes central to the experience and practice of queer history. In what follows, I want to highlight both the 'sensible relation to the past' in, and the affective *dissonance* of, the archival encounters represented in my chosen literary texts, and consider the ramifications of this dissonance for any queer embrace of the archive as concept, signifier, or motif.[10]

Queer archives have been concerned both with the (defiant) creation of a public culture and with the safeguarding and validation of private cultures and lives; they have also crucially been involved in the work of memorializing the lives lost to AIDS. Such archives can be virtual and are allegedly noncanonical—propounding alternative values and valences.[11] According to this positive reading of them, queer archives, in their very existence and operation, bring about the *queering* of the concept of the archive— and the queering of history, truth, evidence, and authority, traditionally understood—in which 'queering' involves a destabilisation that is conceived as necessarily subversive, and practically deconstructive. Thus,

> Queer archives can be viewed as the material instantiation of Derrida's deconstructed archive; they are composed of material practices that challenge traditional conceptions of history and understand the quest for history as a psychic need rather than a science.[12]

Cvetkovich is not the only theorist to champion (rightly) the existence of the queer archive. Elsewhere, Judith Halberstam has proposed an 'archive of queer subcultures' that would include 'ethnographic interviews with performers and fans', 'queer zines, posters, guerrilla art, and other temporary artifacts', and 'descriptions of shows along with the self-understandings of cultural producers'.[13] The archive becomes, on this view, a *route to* 'self-understanding', not merely a *record of* it. Charles E. Morris III is more hesitant in his embrace of the queer archive, warning that 'archives are [. . .] rhetorical sites and resources', part of the 'usable past' that 'functions ideologically and politically, often insidiously'.[14] Yet he too adheres to the maxim that 'silence = death'.[15] As Alexandra Juhasz avers, 'It is not our suffering that is compelling but *our willingness to name and record it,* and in so doing, make it communal and move it into the present'.[16] This could stand as a summary of the affirmative view of queer archives.

However, as Judith Halberstam recognises, the queer archive is more than a collection of material objects. Indeed, 'the notion of an archive has to extend beyond the image of a place to collect material or hold documents, and it has to become a floating signifier' for certain 'kinds of lives'.[17] It is this wider understanding of the archive as 'floating signifier' that I consider here. In any discussion of 'the archive', we are faced with the very plurality of locations, collections, and historiographical and political practices to which this term might refer, as well as the myriad effects that such 'archives' might produce. This very malleability of 'the archive' suggests both its uses and its limitations for us, and the preceding examples reinforce its affective power, its crucial role in the construction of identities, its conceptual capaciousness, its indeterminate locus, its historical reach, and its semantic slipperiness and productivity. I ask, then, 'How does "the archive" signify in a queer context and what are its effects for the lives that it seeks to describe?' If its meanings are myriad then they are not always positive, nor do archival encounters produce only positive feelings. Complicating, rather than contesting, the affirmative view, I suggest that the 'queering of the archive' is not a straightforward process and that the very notion of the archive is apt to be treated with scepticism within queer culture. The 'psychic need' for history, identity, community, and visibility that Cvetkovich adduces is real enough, but the 'instantiations' that archives involve threaten the kind of reification of identity and of certain types of knowledge that seems decidedly un-queer.

Halberstam's 'floating signifier' conception of the archive might seem to move it away from the specificity of place and the limitations of a mere 'repository' of information, yet those associations cannot be so easily dismissed. Moreover, they provoke further, more troubling associations in their turn. Antoinette Burton warns that 'if the official archive is a workplace, it is also a panopticon whose claim to total knowledge is matched by its capacity for total surveillance.'[18] These ideas of 'total knowledge' and 'total surveillance' are central to the emergence of modern conceptions of sexuality, particularly homosexuality. Indeed, it is possible to argue that the notion of the queer archive is fatally bound up with what Foucault termed the 'will to knowledge', that 'has persisted in constituting [. . .] a science of sexuality'.[19] He writes of

> the multiplication of discourses concerning sex in the field of exercise of power itself: an institutional incitement to speak about it, and to do so more and more; a determination on the part of the agencies of power to hear it spoken about, and to cause *it* to speak through explicit articulation and endlessly accumulated detail.[20]

Is not the queer archive, whatever form it takes, part of this 'endlessly accumulated detail', part of the 'multiplication of discourses' around sex, part of the turning of sex into signification? Is it not, by definition, institutional? How can it resist incorporation by, or imitation of, 'the agencies of power'? The very 'ephemera' of the queer archive allows for anything and everything to be re-characterised as somehow, in some form, to do with sexuality. This appears to confirm Foucault's characterisation of 'the nineteenth-century homosexual' as 'a personage, a past, a case history, and a childhood' and his claim that 'nothing that went into his total composition was unaffected by his sexuality'.[21] Sexuality thus extends into all areas of life, all parts of history. If the queer archive is always incomplete, it is also all-consuming. The question is whether this signals its subversion, its threat to the non-queer (parts of which it seeks to colonise), or its compliance with dominant regimes of knowledge and dominant ideologies of identity, or its vapidity, hinting at more troubling effects of the expansion of 'queerness' as a category.

THE ARCHIVE AND/IN QUEER FICTION

Suzanne Keen has noted the high incidence of contemporary novels featuring archives and archival research. She defines these 'romances of the archive' as follows:

> They have scenes taking place in libraries or in other structures housing collections of papers and books; they feature the plot action of 'doing

research' in documents. They designate a character or characters at least temporarily as archival researchers, as questers in the archives. They unabashedly interpret the past through its material traces; they build on a foundation of 'documentarism', answering the postmodern critique of history with invented records full of hard facts.[22]

I want to suggest that the archive inhabits a more equivocal and troublesome place within contemporary gay and lesbian fiction in particular, where the histories that it unearths and the identities that it serves to construct, make visible and consolidate, are both more nebulous and more fraught than the 'hard facts' of which Keen writes.[23] In the novels I discuss, the processes of selection and interpretation that the building and consulting of archives necessarily involves are highlighted. Desire is shown to be central to our encounters with archives, not desire that is contained by 'documentarism'— indeed, my broader topic here is the centrality of desire to any consideration of the archive.[24]

Before looking at some recent gay and lesbian fiction, it would be instructive to consider a crucial scene in Radclyffe Hall's 1928 novel *The Well of Loneliness*. Following the death of her father, the heroine Stephen Gordon discovers in a locked cabinet in his study a hidden library of sexological works by writers such as Richard Von Krafft-Ebing. This secret library lures her as if with a mystical power:

> She had never examined this special book-case, and she could not have told why she suddenly did so. As she slipped the key into the lock and turned it, the action seemed curiously automatic.
> For a long time she read; then went back to the book-case and got out another of those volumes, and another . . .
> Then suddenly she had got to her feet and was talking aloud—she was talking to her father: 'You knew! All the time you knew this thing, but because of your pity you wouldn't tell me. O, Father—and there are so many of us—thousands of miserable, unwanted people, who have no right to love, no right to compassion because they're maimed, hideously maimed and ugly—God's cruel; He let us get flawed in the making.'[25]

In discovering these works she discovers herself, her identity, and her (nominal) community; she finds an explanation for her strangeness; she 'knows' herself (and knows herself recorded, analysed, and catalogued), but the knowledge is not comforting. She learns that there are others like her, but the pathologizing model of inversion that the sexological works propose is never questioned. Indeed, Jay Prosser cites this discovery of the secret library as one of two key episodes in *The Well* which demonstrate that the novel 'is thoroughly enmeshed in the sexological discourse of inversion', suggesting that, at this moment, 'Stephen finds the key to her own identity', and her unlocking of the bookcase constitutes an 'unlocking of the truth'.[26] The bookcase, then, stands in for the whole archive of sexological discourse, providing Stephen with a 'master narrative' of her sexual selfhood but simultaneously denying her a voice of her own.[27] It is notable how, in the passage cited previously, Stephen is denied both agency and genuine self-knowledge: she 'could not have told' what had drawn her to the bookcase; rather, she succumbs to its inexorable allure. The 'action' of unlocking it is 'curiously automatic', rather than an act of will, decision, or determination. The action of reading is strangely repetitive and hypnotically enthralling ('another [. . .] and another'), and, as the ellipses indicate, it is not clear how much time passes or what Stephen is thinking as she reads. When she does, finally, speak, it is in a voice of anguish and incomprehension—and of hopefulness—which expresses what Heather Love has described, in her reading of the novel, as a 'dynamic of identification and disidentification' with the wider queer community.[28] When, subsequently, Stephen leaves Morton, she takes away with her only her father's secret library, nothing else; it is described as 'hers by some intolerable birthright'.[29]

Stephen's discovery of the secret library indicates the fraught connections between homosexual identity and official informational resources, between private lives and public documents. The very secrecy of the library indicates the segregation of material pertaining to homosexual lives from other collectible documents; it suggests also its embedment in institutionalised discourses (medical, scientific), whose aim is often to regulate and legislate. This episode, consequently, raises the question of whether the very idea of a public library or archive of works pertaining to homosexuality can be divorced from the pseudo-scientific study of sexuality (predominantly so-called deviant sexuality) that emerged in the late nineteenth century, in the form of sexology.

This question can be taken a little further by analogy with a query that Derrida makes, in relation to the 'archive' of psychoanalysis. He asks, 'In what way has the whole of this field [of psychoanalysis] been determined by a state of the technology of communication and of archivization?' and goes on to explain:

> The archive, as printing, writing, prosthesis, or hypomnesic technique in general is not only the place for stocking and for conserving an archivable content *of the past* which would exist in any case, such as, without the archive, one still believes it was or will have been. No, the technical structure of the *archiving* archive also determines the structure of the *archivable* content even in its very coming into existence and in its relationship to the future. The archivization produces as much as it records the event.[30]

It is pertinent to consider, therefore, the extent to which the functioning of the archive of sexology—'its very coming into existence', 'its relationship to the future'—serves to structure, to order, and even to produce its 'content': homosexual identity and experience from the late nineteenth century onwards. For the origins (*commencement*) of homosexual identity and the social controls (*commandment*) first exercised on homosexuality (as an identity) are located in a sexology that, in its urge to taxonomise and record, is itself a kind of archival practice. An awareness of the *productive* and the *constructive* nature of the archive, in this quite sceptical sense, informs the representation of archives, libraries, private and public collections of documents, and even literary canons, within certain contemporary gay novels.[31] These fictions are able to eschew and yet comment on the taxonomic practices of sexology; to demonstrate the emotive and identificatory potential of histories, archives, records, and documents; and, in turn, to move towards alternative forms of classification and recording of gay lives, new 'libraries'. These fictional representations of archives are not necessarily representations of *queer archives*, yet they provoke anxiety and indecision around *archives more generally*, and around the possibility of a truly queer archive. This is precisely an anxiety that the processes of 'archivization' might serve to produce (limit, contain, co-opt) the events and experiences of queer lives, such that those events and experiences cannot either speak for themselves or work to unsettle, reimagine, and renew the processes of archivization.

THE 'LIBRARY OF UNCATALOGUED PLEASURE': *THE SWIMMING-POOL LIBRARY* (1988)

In Alan Hollinghurst's *The Swimming-Pool Library*, the leisured protagonist Will Beckwith is a decidedly unwilling investigator and archivist of gay history, as he reads the octogenarian Charles Nantwich's diaries, discovers pornographic photographs, and inspects the partially revealed Roman mosaic in Nantwich's basement. Throughout the book, the revelation of secret histories, identities and connections is tied to the revelation of personal/private *documents* (this is really a novel about historical documentation and evidence)—or, more pertinently, documents which have a kind of liminal existence at the threshold of the public/private world. To this extent, the novel certainly qualifies as a 'romance of the archive'.

In her discussion of *The Swimming-Pool Library*, Keen asserts that archive research here creates 'felt connections' and 'brings into uncanny proximity the questers and the historical subjects they pursue'.[32] Categorising Hollinghurst's novel as a '[romance] of the archive in the social-problem mode', she proceeds to describe such novels as aiming 'to defeat bafflement, identify villains, and restore responsibility for judging to fiction', to participate in the 'moral training of the sympathetic imagination', and to put an 'emphasis on achieving empathy with human subjects'.[33] Yet *The Swimming-Pool Library* might also be read as withholding judgement, disrupting and troubling processes of empathy and identification (on the part of the protagonist and the reader), and resisting moral certainties and definite conclusions. Will is troubled by the past injustices and complicities that he uncovers—but not unduly so, and the novel ends with him apparently continuing his life of self-gratification and solipsistic leisure.

In fact, his mixed feelings about the worth of the archival quest and its interest for him are evident from the outset. The invitation to write Nantwich's memoirs seems 'at first a monstrous request'. He feels that 'the prospect of the Nantwich book, which was alluring, was also oppressive', and wishes 'to keep my life clear of interference from the demands and misery of other people', which such a project appears to entail.[34] The Nantwich book here represents an 'archive' both personal and supra-personal; its assorted documents not only relate the events of Charles Nantwich's life, but also stand in for queer history (or at least the history of queerness in the twentieth century—Nantwich is as old as the century). If, as Cvetkovich argues, 'affects [. . .] make a document significant', then what are we to make of Will's affective response to the memoir project as both 'alluring' *and* 'oppressive'?[35] Despite his reservations, Will takes home a bag of material from Charles to peruse. This 'archive' (as he refers to it) comprises 'a set of quarto notebooks, bound in brown boards, rubbed and worn at the edges—most of them with a clear ink inscription on the front cover'.[36] (Here, and elsewhere in the novel, there is a notable attention to the materiality of the documentation.) He also finds 'tucked between the pages' of the notebooks 'postcards, letters, drawings, even hotel bills and visiting cards', material whose seeming randomness thus demands organisation, interpretation, the making of vital and meaningful connections. An accompanying diary similarly has letters and documents between its pages, and there is 'a large buff envelope bulky with photographs'. Will turns to the photographs first, believing that 'they would be, although enigmatic, the keys or charms to open the whole case to me'.[37]

As it transpires, however, the photos are only intermittently and erratically revealing ('they did little to enlighten me'), and the 'case' is very far from being 'open' to him.[38] His reaction to the notebooks is even more ambivalent:

> I flipped through the notebooks, picking on odd sentences, getting caught for a paragraph, but feeling irritated, almost piqued by the way the life in them went parochially on. [. . .] It was the awful sense of another life having gone on and on, and the self-importance it courted by being written down and enduring years later, that made me think frigidly that I wasn't the man for it.[39]

Here, there is little sense, as in Keen's reading, of joy in the archival quest, or even of an understanding of its value, nor is there (recalling Foucault and Dinshaw) an excitement at the 'vibration', the queer 'touches across time' that such a quest facilitates. Indeed, the use of *frigidly* precisely repels touch, denies desire. It is the present (Charles's 'incoherent' current life, his dramas with his servant) that interests Will, not history, and if the archive of gay history permits him to make connections between his own life in the present and 'the many lives of Charles Nantwich', these connections are rarely, if ever, productive of either consolation or certainty.[40]

Elsewhere in the novel, we see how compromised the archive is in its association with privilege and in the meanings that it imposes. As Will looks at his grandfather's photo album with his young nephew, Rupert, it is described in the following terms:

> It had the generous proportions of an Edwardian album, many, many broad dark grey pages, tied in with thick silk cords which knotted at the edge outside, the whole protected with weighty boards covered with green leather, tooled with flowers around the border, and with a pompous but impressive 'B' beneath a coronet in the centre.[41]

This particular historical 'archive' is literally bound in wealth and entitlement; its very design (its sumptuousness) lends gravitas and meaning to the histories that it contains and displays. But there is also something rather forbidding and stifling about it. Recalling a previous occasion on which they had looked at the album together, Will thinks, 'I had had the impression that [Rupert] was committing it to memory, working out the connections. It was a sort of book of life to him, and I was the authoritative expounder of its text'.[42] The irony of this is clear: Will is far from authoritative in his reading of historical documentation, as will later become evident when he finally apprehends his own grandfather's role in the imprisonment of gay men (including Nantwich) in the 1950s, a fact of which he was—unlike his family and friends—utterly ignorant. His reading of other incidents and people (past and present) is likewise shown to be partial and misguided. Nevertheless, the comments on the album here gesture towards the processes of history making: the imperative of memory, the search for 'connections', and the belief that history are contained in such documents, that it is readable. Looking at one of his own school photographs, Will notes 'the already period-looking photograph, in which the faces took on a greater clarity as time went by'.[43] However, rather than offering the reassurance that Keen suggests, the novel continually questions in what this 'clarity' might reside, drawing attention to the simplifying processes at work when we read the past through its fragmentary and possibly duplicitous traces.

Given such conditions, desire and sexual identity may be the *most* difficult and duplicitous of historical subjects. On this occasion, the discussion of the photographs turns into a game of spot-the-homosexual: Rupert asks of each of the men in successive images, 'Was *he* a homosexual?' before declaring 'almost everyone is homosexual, aren't they?'[44] The images are read for their sexual clues, but at the same time, it is acknowledged how misleading some of the images might be:

'That Library of Uncatalogued Pleasure' 173

I was saved from the sexual analysis of the next set of pictures, the Oscar Wilde Society Ball, by the doorbell ringing. (The dress-note that year had been 'Slave Trade', and the spectacle of predominantly straight boys camping it up to the eyeballs would have been confusing to the child's budding sense of role-play.) [45]

Ultimately the novel affects an ambivalent relationship to the archive and—by extension—to certain stable and unitary conceptions of gay history and gay identity. This ambivalence is evident in Will's description of the 'swimming-pool library' of the title, whilst describing his hedonistically homosexual schooldays. The 'library' here refers to the swimming pool and its changing room, and the 'librarian' is a prefect. The prefects/librarians are 'chosen on grounds of aptitude for particular tasks', and Will is the 'Swimming-Pool Librarian' due in no small part to his 'aptitude [. . .] for playing with myself and others'. The swimming pool is the scene of his 'earliest excesses', it represents sexual discovery, pleasure.[46]

> I still dream, once a month or so, of that changing-room, its slatted floor and benches. In our retrogressive slang it was known as the Swimming-Pool Library and then simply as the Library, a notion fitting to the double lives we led. 'I shall be in the library', I would announce, a prodigy of study. Sometimes I think that shadowy, doorless little shelter—which is all it was really, an empty, empty place—is where at heart I want to be. [. . .] Nipping into that library of uncatalogued pleasure was to step into the dark and halt. Then held breath was released, a cigarette glowed, its smoke was smelled, the substantial blackness moved, glimmered and touched. Friendly hands felt for the flies. There was never, or rarely, any kissing—no cloying adult impurity in the lubricious innocence of what we did.[47]

The swimming-pool library is a protected, idealised place, but it is, importantly, 'empty', and its pleasures are 'uncatalogued'. Rather than being a rebuke, this implies nostalgia for an era pre-categorisation when homosexual behaviour did not imply relationship, community, or identity but was purely pleasurable and, in various senses, both unrecorded and *unproductive*.[48] There is, too, a pleasure here in *secrecy*, even invisibility, and a pleasure in the *moment*—a moment unencumbered by any awareness of, or debt to, either past or future. This decisive scene in the novel has two echoes elsewhere in the text. On the opening page, Will muses on the 'inverted lives' of the tube workers, thinking, 'Such lonely, invisible work must bring on strange thoughts; the men who walked through every tunnel of the labyrinth, tapping the rails, must feel such reassurance seeing the lights of others at last approaching, voices calling out their friendly, technical patter'.[49] Later on, Charles Nantwich reminisces fondly about the homosexual era *before* decriminalisation, saying that 'it was unbelievably sexy'; 'it was still kind of underground, we operated on a constantly shifting code, and it was so extraordinarily moving and exciting when that spurt of recognition came, like the flare of a match!'[50] All three descriptions elucidate the thrill of the 'underground' homosexual life, the frisson of 'recognition' (so closely allied to the frisson of desire itself). But the tentative and transient visibility signified by the glow of a cigarette end, the dimly approaching lights, the 'flare of a match' should be distinguished from the well-lit surveillance that cataloguing and archivisation bring about. If the archive banishes gloom, it also, by implication, threatens a desire that flourishes most abundantly in the darkness.

The archive does also, of course, stimulate desire. As Will looks at old photographs belonging to the seedy photographer Staines, the experience is clearly eroticised: 'There was something wanton about the way he let us rummage, and about the muddle of the system. I felt each picture encourage a question, or hint at some urgent, tawdry secret'.[51] Yet Will expresses an anxiety that the work of putting together the memoir will interfere with his erotic activities, almost as if he has to choose between these two options.[52] And his use of the word *frigidly*, to describe the way in which the notebooks initially repel him is telling. In this way, *The Swimming-Pool Library* holds out the possibility of a documentary archive of gay male history in the twentieth century. It hints at the 'alternative modes of knowledge' that Cvetkovich attributes to the queer archive, anoints (certain select) gay men as the keepers of their own archives. It also situates the archive in the intimate spaces of private homes and concealed documents, envisaging that archive as a route to 'self-understanding' (as Halberstam advocates), and it asks the reader to make connections both historico-political and affective between the lives of Charles Nantwich and Will Beckwith. However, Will's own affective ambivalence towards the recording and cataloguing of gay history and his apparent refusal of the 'self-understanding' that such a project might offer, imply, finally, an erotic liberation in the *rejection* of this particular queer archive and a delight in the *transience* of both memory and desire, suggesting that these are 'psychic needs' as compelling as (and fatally at odds with) the 'psychic need for history' that Cvetkovich identifies.

'THE BOOKS, THE TERRIBLE BOOKS!': *FINGERSMITH* (2002)

In her scholarly writing, Sarah Waters has argued for the value of continuing to construct 'lesbian romance in the interstices of historical narrative'.[53] In *Fingersmith*, lesbian desire is discovered 'in the interstices' of a library of pornographic narratives and images which, by its very operation and arrangement, seems to deny or suppress the existence of such a desire. In the novel, Maud Lilly assists her tyrannical uncle, Christopher Lilly (modelled on Henry Spencer Ashbee), in cataloguing his ever-expanding library of Victorian pornography, before her life is disrupted by the arrival of the 'fingersmith' (thief) of the title, Sue. The archive is here associated with darkness, obscurity, shadows, and secrecy—and with masculine authority and masculine desire. It undergoes a shift during the course of the narrative, however, so that it is ultimately revealed to the light, and reappropriated as a locus of female desire and, significantly, female creative agency. Offering a subtext to the main romantic narrative, then, the novel documents the transformation of a definitively un-queer patriarchal archive into an incipiently queer archive of lesbian desire and can therefore be read as speculating on the malleability of 'the archive' as a floating signifier for certain types of lives, and assessing the archive's latent potential for transformation and reappropriation.

At the outset, however, Briar, where Maud lives and where the archive is located, is repeatedly described as dark, dull, and black. As Maud tells Sue, 'the sun never shines here. My uncle has forbidden it. Strong light, you see, fades print'.[54] The library in which Christopher Lilly works tirelessly to compile his *Universal Bibliography of Priapus and Venus* is, Sue discovers, 'dark and dim and shabby', its door guarded by 'some creature's head with one glass eye'.[55] When Sue enters the library, she sees Maud, her hands uncharacteristically bare: 'All about her, over all the walls of the room, were shelves; and the shelves had books on—you never saw so many. A stunning amount. How many stories does one man need? I looked at them and shuddered'.[56] Her physical response to this space is one of intense revulsion. The windows are painted over and the lamps are shaded, reinforcing the impression of gloom; inset in the floor is an ominous brass hand, 'with a pointing finger'.[57] When she is a child, and first at Briar, Maud's uncle explains the brass finger in the floor to her:

> These are uncommon books, Miss Maud, and not for ordinary gazes. Let me see you step once past that pointing finger, and I shall use you as I would a servant of the house, caught doing the same—I shall whip your eyes until they bleed.[58]

This library is not to be looked on. It contains forbidden knowledge, conceals forbidden desires (desires which Mr. Lilly attempts to marshal into a kind of taxonomy, as if this will protect him and others from them). To look on the secret library is to make your eyes bleed—an image as sexualised as it is violent. Maud will lose her innocence when she is permitted, finally, to approach the archive and know its secrets. The library is thus clearly marked out as a masculine zone of privilege, of restriction (clearly bounded and subject to surveillance), its contents secret and—it is implied—fragile.

Her uncle's impulse to collect and index this material is represented by Maud as a 'mania', and she says, 'Should I struggle, it will draw me deep into itself, and I will drown'.[59] So the archive threatens to engulf all around it and comes to stand for Maud's oppression, her violated childhood and continued imprisonment. In the library, the lamp's smell 'of smouldering dust' is 'the smell of the parching of my own youth', as Maud performs her childhood exercises of copying pages of text into a book, then erasing them and beginning again in an endless process. The futility of the endeavour underlines the extent to which she is merely an instrument of the archive (as when, later, she is forced to read aloud foreign texts that she cannot understand to gentlemen visitors).[60] This palimpsest image, however, also hints at the ways in which the documents of the archive might be overwritten, overlaid with her own desires, her own meanings, or might be read for the more subversive possibilities underlying their heterosexual and patriarchal surface. This is not yet evident to Maud, however; as a child, she fears 'the spectres of past lessons, imperfectly erased'.[61]

Maud's imprisonment by the archive—literal and symbolic—is consolidated in the image that gradually emerges of her as a book herself, part of her uncle's collection. Thus, she opines, 'He has made me like a book. I am not meant to be taken, and touched, and liked. I am meant to keep here, in a dim light, for ever.'[62] Later, she says while showing the visiting Mr. Rivers her uncle's emblem on a plate pasted into the front of a book, 'Sometimes [. . .] I suppose such a plate must be pasted upon my own flesh—that I have been ticketed, and noted and shelved—so nearly do I resemble one of my uncle's books'.[63] This expresses, perhaps, the extent to which lesbian desire has been stymied by its very inclusion within patriarchal, homophobic archives. It hints also at a more general horror of cataloguing, which might stand in the way of any kind of lesbian archive, however innovative, however benignly motivated. Whilst gay and lesbian archives do indeed 'assert the role of memory and affect in compensating for institutional neglect', Waters's novel suggests that it is not only institutional *neglect* that is the problem but also the sheer weight of institutional *attention* to lesbianism.[64] If queer archives are to counter this attention with more attention, it must be the kind of attention that will serve to 'express our sinister wisdom' (in the words of Joan Nestle), and for this to occur, a wholesale transformation of the archive is required.[65]

Where is desire, in this archive-in-progress of Maud's uncle, an archive that attempts to document all possible manifestations and expressions of desire? The urge to be comprehensive is an urge to identify and anatomise sexual predilections but the result, as is clearly demonstrated here, can only be to stifle desire. For Christopher Lilly, the passion is purely that of the bibliophile—'the lust of the bookworm'—and this, it is suggested, is the sign of his particular perversity.[66] His is an archive fever expressed through a mania for order, a desire stimulated only by the 'marbling' of pages and the 'morocco' of a spine.[67] Meanwhile, Maud's exposure to the pornographic material initially stimulates her burgeoning adolescent sexuality, but her attitude towards the material changes as she gets older: 'I understand my uncle's books to be filled with falsehoods, and I despise myself for having supposed them truths. My hot cheek cools, my colour dies, the heat quite fades from my limbs'.[68] If this is the end of her embarrassment, it also seems

'That Library of Uncatalogued Pleasure' 177

to represent the death of her desire—for the present, at least. If she knows 'everything', if she is 'as worldly as the grossest rakes of fiction', she also knows 'nothing'—knows herself and her own desires least of all.[69] When Sue later asks her, 'Don't you feel your passion, when Mr Rivers gazes at you?' Maud thinks, 'I never do feel it. [. . .] I don't want to feel it. I should hate myself, if I did! For I know it, from my uncle's books, for too squalid a thing—an itch, like the itch of inflamed flesh, to be satisfied hectically, wetly, in closets and behind screens'.[70] The 'knowledge' of desire that the collection gives her is a corrupted knowledge, which distorts her perception of her own feelings.

Later, when she discovers her desire for Sue, it takes her by surprise: 'Is this desire? How queer that I, of all people, should not know!'[71] More shockingly, this changes Maud's relationship with the archive of pornographic works where she labours every day: 'Even my uncle's books are changed to me; and this is worse, this is worst of all. I have supposed them dead. Now the words [. . .] start up, are filled with meaning'.[72] It is her desire that animates the archive, not the other way around, yet she doubts this at first. After reading aloud a work on 'all the means a woman may employ to pleasure another, when in want of a man', she fears not only that her illicit desire is writ upon her for all to see, but she is also 'ashamed to think that what I have supposed the secret book of my heart may be stamped, after all, with no more miserable matter than this' and thus may 'have its place in my uncle's collection'.[73] The tangible inscription of Maud's desire and its inclusion in her uncle's collection, works to delegitimate her desires and undermine the intensity of her feelings. Maud must struggle to not become a book in her uncle's tawdry collection, a product of it, but rather a producer herself, a wellspring of desire whose life and excess cannot be so easily catalogued and contained: lesbian desire must be freed from this constricting archival history if it is ever to live and breathe.

It is therefore unsurprising that, before fleeing Briar with Rivers, Maud exacts her revenge on the archive itself, taking a razor to the pages of the books in a carefully calculated act that is both malicious and erotic: 'it is terribly hard, I almost cannot do it—to put the metal for the first time to the neat and naked paper. I am almost afraid the book will shriek, and so discover me. But it does not shriek. Rather, it *sighs*, as if in longing for its own laceration'.[74] Much later, after her uncle's death, Maud moves back into the library, transforming it from prison to refuge. She removes the brass hand in the floor; the door, when Susan arrives in search of her, is left open; she scrapes the paint from the windows to let in the light; and, notes Sue, 'the shelves were almost bare of books'.[75] Maud explains that now she makes her living by writing such works, and when Sue takes the paper she has dropped and asks, 'What does it say?' Maud replies, 'It is filled with all the words for how I want you . . . Look'.[76] This text becomes, in the closing paragraph, part of an implied seduction, part of their romantic denouement, and the pornography collection is, then, imaginatively resignified as a hidden history of female pleasure and desire—rather than as a means of the objectification, imprisonment, and abuse of women. However, this imaginative resignification can only happen when the original archive has been effectively violated, dismantled, stripped of its regulatory potential, and emptied of its former contents and their associations.

In this way, Waters's novel seems to confirm Martha Vicinus's invocation to 'look to the margins, to the ruptures and breaks' in order to 'piece together a history of women speaking to each other'.[77] Maud and Sue find queer desire at the heart of an oppressively heterosexual archive of Victorian pornography, they find ways to formulate their own illicit and otherwise unspeakable desires in new terms. The 'knowledge' that Maud gains from her engagement with the archive of pornography to some extent allows her to understand her feelings for Sue—she is not 'innocent'. But that knowledge is also dangerous in the way that it threatens to distort and smother her desire, so the symbolic destruction of the library must occur before she can become the author of her own desires. In dismantling and then re-inhabiting the library, however, she does not simply replace it in kind. What she creates through the medium of her own writings in fact reveals the very tenuousness and precariousness of the archive of lesbian desire (and these writings are not communicated, so the reader must imagine them for herself). As Kate Chedgzoy writes, the lesbian archive's 'lack of a visible material and spatial foundation may, from one point of view, testify to its fragility and marginality as a manifestation of public culture', but, 'from another point of view, [its] dispersed and decentered nature [. . .] tells a story about the ubiquity of lesbianism and about its thorough imbrication in the forms and practices of more obviously archived literary cultures'.[78] This accords with Vicinus's claim that 'lesbian desire is everywhere, even as it may be nowhere' (a point borne out by nearly all of Waters's novels).[79] Yet it is difficult to conceive of the archival practices that will do justice to this 'ubiquity' and that will be able to represent this 'imbrication', especially when the institutional traces of lesbianism are to be found in archives of the most patriarchal, heteronormative kind (at worst), or hidden in allusions to female companionship and friendship (at best). Lesbian history, even more than the history of male homosexuality, is made up of 'fragmentary evidence and ghostly immanences' and thus requires 'multiple interpretative strategies'.[80] Does the archive facilitate such 'interpretative strategies' or hinder them? Does it sustain such 'ghostly immanences' or seek to exorcise them? That these questions remain unanswered—necessarily—accounts for the double-edged nature of the archive as figured in *Fingersmith*.

CONCLUSION: DUST AND DESIRE

The preceding analyses raise the question of how 'queer' the archive might be, by revealing the moments at which the very (anti)logic of 'queerness' and the slipperiness of desire militate against the reifying, authoritarian impulses of the archive. As I hope I have shown, the knowledge and histories that archives contain are often difficult and troubling from a queer perspective. For Stephen, in *The Well of Loneliness*, the sexological archive offers the possibility of an identity and the solace of a nominal community of 'inverts', but leaves her troublingly bound by pathological analyses. For Will Beckwith, in *The Swimming-Pool Library*, the encounter with the archive brings with it an injunction to responsibility and collectivity that is not wholly desired—that in fact seems to run counter to desire—and an unlooked-for awareness of a history that is, in different ways, shaming and contradictory. For Maud and Sue, in *Fingersmith*, the archive is a prison and, whilst Waters does gesture towards the reappropriation of archival discourses of sexuality in the service of queer desires, the eroticisation of the wrecking of the library (the pages *sighing* masochistically under the knife) suggests that queer desire is only truly liberated at that moment of symbolic destruction.

The archives and the libraries I have considered here are very different in their nature and content, yet each novel reflects, implicitly or otherwise, on the significance of recordkeeping and cataloguing for our understanding of queer lives, histories and identities, and on the sensible (palpable, present, material) nature of the past as it is traced in documentary evidence. Each finds queer desire in documents whose significatory and political potential remains open to debate, analysis and (re)interpretation. Each, too, highlights the affective power of archives and libraries (queer or otherwise) whilst suggesting that feelings of delight and consolatory experiences of connection across time will always be tempered by feelings of shame, terror, or even, more crushingly, indifference. The fundamental ambivalence of the archival encounter for queer subjects is what I have sought to bring to light in my readings of these texts, and I maintain that the negative taint of surveillance, pathologization, and restriction remains to haunt our more affirmative aspirations for queer archives.

In each of these novels, we see the difficulty of deciding what might count as the 'evidence' or 'documentation' of a queer life—of deciding 'what kinds of objects might stand in, metonymically, for the queerness of desire itself'[81]—and the difficulty, in the archival process, of resisting 'the coherence of narrative', in favour of the 'fragmentary and ostensibly arbitrary'.[82] As Robert Mills argues, we need to look for new 'ways of interpreting objects queerly without at the same time monumentalizing gay identity, or treating it as a universal given'.[83] This queering of the archive will involve, he claims: the abandonment of 'linear-progress narratives [. . .] in favour of stories that take as their point of departure sexual intensities, tastes and roles, gender dissonances, dispositions and styles, queer feelings, emotions and desires'. It will also involve the adoption of 'a style of presentation partly modelled on scrapbooks and collage', and the use of 'fragments, snippets of gossip, speculations, irreverent half-truths' instead of 'the representative "object"'. And it will be motivated not by 'a desire for a petrified "history as it really was" but by the recognition that interpretations change and that our encounters with archives are saturated with desire'.[84]

To this, I would add that the queering of the archive must also involve a contestation of the archive's original connection with the home. As Derrida avers, the archive 'has the force of law, of a law which is the law of the house (*oikos*), of the house as place, domicile, family, lineage, or institution'.[85] Such homes are ones from which lesbian and gay people may have been expelled, as with the family histories from which they may have been expunged. The heteronormativity of home, family, and lineage, so figured, is such that queer archives (and in some cases the homes which house them) must seek to resignify the very concepts of 'home' and 'history' in the search for new understandings of lineage, new genealogies. This re-signification has arguably begun, in the creation of grass-roots and 'community-based archive[s]' such as the LHA, which offer 'a "safe space," a nourishing home',[86] or which represent 'safe havens for history',[87] but the heteronormativity of home has not yet been comprehensively exorcised.

If the archive is home, it is also dust. Returning from her onerous work in the library, Maud exclaims, 'But here is dust [. . .] from my uncle's shelves! Oh! The books, the terrible books!'[88] Later, she describes the act of denying Sue her birthright, and bringing her up in Mrs. Sucksby's house of thieves, as 'like taking a jewel, and hiding it in dust', and yet—'that dust falls away'.[89] Maud, too, is a jewel (a 'pearl') who is revealed only when the dust falls away, yet the real jewel in the archival dust here—and in all these texts—is desire, waiting to be uncovered and threatening to disrupt the most staid of histories. For Steedman, dust is not only 'the immutable, obdurate set of beliefs about the material world, past and present, inherited from the nineteenth century', but it is also, more optimistically, 'about circularity, the impossibility of things disappearing, or going away, or being gone'.[90] As she says, 'nothing *can be* destroyed', and she notes the 'ceaseless making and unmaking, the movement and transmutation of one thing into another'.[91] The obduracy of the archive can thus be re-thought through a notion of 'transmutation' which captures the force of desire, its mutability—its essentially deviant, peripatetic nature; its aptitude for sublimation; its insistence; and its interstitial existence. In responding to the 'queerness of desire itself',[92] any queer archive must weigh intransigence with evanescence, must temper the demands of ordering and recording with the quite different demands of desire.

NOTES

1. Carolyn Steedman, *Dust* (Manchester, UK: Manchester University Press, 2001), p. 2.
2. Jacques Derrida, *Archive Fever* (Chicago: Chicago University Press, 1996), p. 1.
3. Michel Foucault, *The Archaeology of Knowledge* [1969], trans. A.M. Sheridan Smith (London: Routledge, 2002), p. 146.

4. Derrida, *Archive Fever*, p. 4n1.
5. *Lesbian Herstory Archives News*, April 1975, 1, quoted in Polly J. Thistlethwaite, 'Building "A Home of Our Own": The Construction of the Lesbian Herstory Archives', in *Daring to Find Our Names*, ed. James V. Carmichael (Westport, CT: Greenwood Press, 1998), p. 153.
6. It is not only 'queer' archives that are comprised of ephemera. Community archives and personal collections frequently contain items that might be deemed ephemeral and ephemera may even find their way into official, public/state archives. I'm grateful to Jerome de Groot for a discussion of this point, and for his useful reminder that, 'scholars have recently begun to work on the ephemerality of the archive in an attempt to rewrite those lost among the patriarchal cracks—the working classes, women—by for instance looking at texts which imply biography, or at materials long unconsidered like account books, parish registers, marginalia' (e-mail message to author).
7. Ann Cvetkovich, *An Archive of Feelings* (Durham, NC: Duke University Press, 2003), pp. 243–44.
8. Michel Foucault, 'The Life of Infamous Men', in *Michel Foucault: Power, Truth, Strategy*, ed. Paul Fuss and Meaghan Morris (Sydney: Feral Publications, 1979), p. 76.
9. Foucault, 'Infamous Men', p. 77.
10. Carolyn Dinshaw, *Getting Medieval* (Durham, NC: Duke University Press, 1999), p. 142.
11. Cultural historians are beginning to take notice of the effects of digitisation on our participation in and with history. In *Consuming History*, Jerome de Groot comments that, 'The information revolution fundamentally changes the paradigms for understanding, engaging with, and owning the past', and notes the 'dislocation of authority models or hierarchies of meaning' in the accessing of history via the internet (Jerome de Groot, *Consuming History* [London: Routledge, 2008], p. 91). For these reasons, queer archives frequently stress their virtuality.
12. Cvetkovich, *Archive of Feelings*, p. 268.
13. Judith Halberstam, *In a Queer Time and Place* (New York: NYU Press, 2005), p. 169.
14. Charles E. Morris III, 'Archive Queer', *Rhetoric and Public Affairs* 9, no. 1 (2006), p. 146.
15. Morris, 'Archive Queer', p. 148.
16. Alexandra Juhasz, 'Video Remains: Nostalgia, Technology, and Queer Archive Activism', *GLQ* 12, no. 2 (2006), p. 328, my emphasis.
17. Halberstam, *In a Queer Time*, pp. 169–70.
18. Antoinette Burton, 'Introduction: Archive Fever, Archive Stories', in *Archive Stories: Facts, Fictions, and the Writing of History*, edited by Antoinette Burton (Durham, NC: Duke University Press, 2005), p. 9.
19. Michel Foucault, *History of Sexuality Vol 1: The Will to Knowledge* [1976] (Harmondsworth, UK: Penguin, 1998), pp. 12–13.
20. Ibid., p. 18.
21. Ibid., p. 43.
22. Suzanne Keen, *Romances of the Archive in Contemporary British Fiction* (Toronto: University of Toronto Press, 2001), p. 3.
23. In fact, I think this is also the case for the non-queer fictions that make up the majority of Keen's source material in *Romances of the Archive,* including the text to which she devotes most attention, A. S. Byatt's *Possession* (1990). The troubling of truth and understanding is not, then, unique to queer archive fictions.
24. Burton asserts that desire is 'a crucial component of the archive experience', but that this has been 'obscured' by 'discourses of rationalization' since the nineteenth century. Burton, 'Introduction', p. 11.

25. Radclyffe Hall, *The Well of Loneliness* [1928] (London: Virago, 1982), p. 207.
26. Jay Prosser, "'Some Primitive Thing Conceived in a Turbulent Age of Transition": The Transsexual Emerging from *The Well*', in *Palatable Poison*, ed. Laura Doan and Jay Prosser (New York: Columbia University Press, 2001), pp. 130, 131.
27. Prosser, "'Some Primitive Thing'", p. 131.
28. Heather Love, *Feeling Backward* (Cambridge, MA: Harvard University Press, 2007), p. 102.
29. Hall, *The Well*, p. 235.
30. Derrida, *Archive Fever*, pp. 16–17.
31. I can only discuss two texts in detail here, but I would also direct the interested reader to Patricia Duncker's *Hallucinating Foucault* (1996), in which the archive sets up a dangerous erotic encounter between reader and author, which culminates in the death of the latter, and Adam Mars-Jones's *The Waters of Thirst* (1993), in which a private pornography collection takes on the status of a memorialising archive for a porn star possibly suffering from AIDS whilst also standing for the narrator's own anxieties about impending death. In both cases, death, desire, and the archive meet in a manner that is not as consolatory as Keen implies in her characterisation of 'romances of the archive'. It is also interesting to compare the protagonist's intense, physical encounter with archival documents in *Hallucinating Foucault*—'I sat staring at the pages, stupid and shaking, my skin tingling [. . .]'—with Foucault's own account of an archival encounter in 'The Life of Infamous Men'. See Patricia Duncker, *Hallucinating Foucault* (London: Picador, 1996), p. 75.
32. Keen, *Romances*, pp. 181–82.
33. Ibid., pp. 182, 183.
34. Alan Hollinghurst, *The Swimming-Pool Library* [1988] (London: Vintage, 1998), pp. 81, 85, 86.
35. Cvetkovich, *Archive of Feelings*, pp. 243–44.
36. Hollinghurst, *Swimming-Pool*, p. 95.
37. Ibid.
38. Ibid., p. 96.
39. Ibid., pp. 96–97.
40. Ibid., p. 129.
41. Ibid., p. 59.
42. Ibid.
43. Ibid., p. 60.
44. Ibid., pp. 60, 61.
45. Ibid., p. 61.
46. Ibid., p. 140.
47. Ibid., p. 141.
48. This is an idea picked up in recent contributions to queer theory, such as Lee Edelman's *No Future: Queer Theory & the Death Drive* (Durham, NC: Duke University Press, 2004), which figures 'queerness' as wilfully non-redemptive, unproductive, and refusing any investment in some posited future. 'Queerness' is thus aligned with the death drive. If the archive is about the past, it is also, crucially, about the future—about the preservation of that history for posterity, and therefore represents an investment in a possible, collective, future.
49. Hollinghurst, *Swimming-Pool*, p. 1.
50. Ibid., p. 247.
51. Ibid., p. 160.
52. Ibid., p. 88.
53. Sarah Waters, 'Wolfskins and Togas: Maude Meagher's *The Green Scamander* and the Lesbian Historical Novel', *Women: A Cultural Review* 7, no. 2 (1996), p. 177.

'That Library of Uncatalogued Pleasure' 183

54. Sarah Waters, *Fingersmith* [2002], (London, UK: Virago, 2003), p. 68.
55. Waters, *Fingersmith*, pp. 201, 74.
56. Ibid., p. 75.
57. Ibid., p. 76.
58. Ibid., p. 188.
59. Ibid., p. 194.
60. Ibid., p. 195.
61. Ibid.
62. Ibid., pp. 123–24.
63. Ibid., p. 218.
64. Cvetkovich, *Archive of Feelings*, p. 241.
65. Joan Nestle, 'Notes on Radical Archiving from a Lesbian Feminist Standpoint', *Gay Insurgent* 4/5 (1979), pp. 10–11. Full text available at www.outhistory.org, at http://209.200.244.13/wiki/An_Early_Conversation_about_Gay_and_Lesbian_Archives:_From_the_Pages_of_The_Gay_Insurgent,_1978.
66. Waters, *Fingersmith*, p. 199.
67. Ibid.
68. Ibid., p. 201.
69. Ibid., p. 203.
70. Ibid., p. 237.
71. Ibid., p. 277.
72. Ibid., p. 279.
73. Ibid., pp. 279, 280.
74. Ibid., p. 290.
75. Ibid., p. 541.
76. Ibid., p. 547.
77. Martha Vicinus, '"They Wonder to Which Sex I Belong": The Historical Roots of the Modern Lesbian Identity', in *The Gay and Lesbian Studies Reader*, ed. Henry Abelove et al. (London: Routledge, 1993), p. 434.
78. Kate Chedgzoy, 'In the Lesbian Archive', *GLQ* 11, no. 3 (2005), p. 461.
79. Vicinus, 'They Wonder', p. 433.
80. Ibid., p. 436.
81. Robert Mills, 'Queer Is Here? Lesbian, Gay, Bisexual and Transgender Histories and Public Culture', *History Workshop Journal* 62 (2006), p. 260.
82. Cvetkovich, *Archive of Feelings*, p. 242.
83. Ibid.
84. Mills, 'Queer is Here?', p. 262.
85. Derrida, *Archive Fever*, p. 7.
86. Thistlethwaite, 'Building "A Home of Our Own"', p. 157.
87. Cvetkovich, *Archive of Feelings*, p. 244.
88. Waters, *Fingersmith*, p. 103.
89. Ibid., p. 543.
90. Steedman, *Dust,* p. ix, p. 164.
91. Ibid., p. 164.
92. Mills, 'Queer is Here?', p. 260.

BIBLIOGRAPHY

Antoinette Burton. 'Introduction: Archive Fever, Archive Stories', in *Archive Stories: Facts, Fictions, and the Writing of History*, edited by Antoinette Burton. Durham, NC: Duke University Press, 2005.
Kate Chedgzoy. 'In the Lesbian Archive'. *GLQ* 11, no. 3 (2005).

Ann Cvetkovich. *An Archive of Feelings*. Durham, NC: Duke University Press, 2003.
Jacques Derrida. *Archive Fever*. Chicago: Chicago University Press, 1996.
Carolyn Dinshaw. *Getting Medieval*. Durham, NC: Duke University Press, 1999.
Patricia Duncker. *Hallucinating Foucault*. London: Picador, 1996.
Lee Edelman. *No Future: Queer Theory & the Death Drive*. Durham, NC: Duke University Press, 2004.
Michel Foucault. *The Archaeology of Knowledge* [1969], translated by A. M. Sheridan Smith. London: Routledge, 2002.
Michel Foucault. *History of Sexuality Vol 1: The Will to Knowledge* [1976]. Harmondsworth, UK: Penguin, 1998.
Michel Foucault. 'The Life of Infamous Men', in *Michel Foucault: Power, Truth, Strategy*, edited by Paul Fuss and Meaghan Morris. Sydney: Feral Publications, 1979.
Jerome de Groot. *Consuming History*. London: Routledge, 2008.
Judith Halberstam. *In a Queer Time and Place*. New York: NYU Press, 2005.
Radclyffe Hall. *The Well of Loneliness* [1928]. London: Virago, 1982.
Alan Hollinghurst. *The Swimming-Pool Library* [1988]. London: Vintage, 1998.
Alexandra Juhasz. 'Video Remains: Nostalgia, Technology, and Queer Archive Activism', *GLQ* 12, no. 2 (2006).
Suzanne Keen. *Romances of the Archive in Contemporary British Fiction*. Toronto: University of Toronto Press, 2001.
Heather Love. *Feeling Backward*. Cambridge, MA: Harvard University Press, 2007.
Robert Mills. 'Queer Is Here? Lesbian, Gay, Bisexual and Transgender Histories and Public Culture'. *History Workshop Journal* 62 (2006).
Charles E. Morris III. 'Archive Queer'. *Rhetoric and Public Affairs* 9, no. 1 (2006).
Joan Nestle. 'Notes on Radical Archiving from a Lesbian Feminist Standpoint'. *Gay Insurgent* 4/5 (1979).
Jay Prosser. '"Some Primitive Thing Conceived in a Turbulent Age of Transition": The Transsexual Emerging from *The Well*', in *Palatable Poison*, edited by Laura Doan and Jay Prosser. New York: Columbia University Press, 2001.
Carolyn Steedman. *Dust*. Manchester, UK: Manchester University Press, 2001.
Polly J. Thistlethwaite. 'Building "A Home of Our Own": The Construction of the Lesbian Herstory Archives', in *Daring to Find Our Names*, edited by James V. Carmichael. Westport, CT: Greenwood Press, 1998.
Martha Vicinus. '"They Wonder to Which Sex I Belong": The Historical Roots of the Modern Lesbian Identity', in *The Gay and Lesbian Studies Reader*, edited by Henry Abelove et al. London: Routledge, 1993.
Sarah Waters. *Fingersmith* [2002]. London, UK: Virago, 2003.
Sarah Waters. 'Wolfskins and Togas: Maude Meagher's *The Green Scamander* and the Lesbian Historical Novel'. *Women: A Cultural Review* 7, no. 2 (1996).

10 The Archive, the Event, and the Impression

Simon Morgan Wortham

ARCHIVE-ABILITY

In Derrida's *Paper Machine*, the archivable deposit—the book, for instance—takes its place, or its *slot,* only by dint of a metonymic series which runs from thesis or book, to library and institution, to law and statute, to state deposit and nation-state.[1] Yet this metonymic chain, which represents a powerful system that ties together knowledge, the academy, and legal, political, and social structures, is the site of constitutive slippage as much as stable linkage. For Derrida, the place or slot of the archive opens on the strength of a margin of difference which is also an uncloseable opening to the other. In one sense, the archive takes place in a situation of '*domiciliation*' or 'house arrest' (2), abiding in a more or less permanent dwelling which, however, marks the 'institutional passage' or movement from the private to the public, though not necessarily from the secret to the non-secret. This is because, for Derrida, the archived text may—indeed, cannot but—always keep in reserve what in its attestation can never be reduced or exposed to mere 'evidence' or 'proof'. The archive is formed through acts of consignation which therefore entail not only 'assigning residence or [. . .] entrusting so as to put into reserve (to consign, to deposit), in a place and on a substrate', but also 'the act of *con*signing through *gathering together signs*' (3), about which more will be said later. Although it is undoubtedly the aim of consignation to 'coordinate a single corpus, in a system of synchrony in which all elements articulate the unity of an ideal configuration' (3), nevertheless, this very same feature of the archive renders it '*eco-nomic*' in a 'double sense': 'it keeps, it puts in reserve, it saves, but in an unnatural fashion'. Thus, every archive is at once '*conservative*' and '*institutive*', at once highly traditional and, in making its own form and law, radically inventive or revolutionary (7). The archive is not merely the passive receptacle and, thus, external substrate or support of what comes to be archived. Rather, it constructs its own law in a situation which is neither simply autonomous or auto-foundational (for how can law found itself in a lawful fashion?) nor crudely heteronomous (the archive can never *simply* found its own law, to be sure, yet nonetheless, Derrida ask us to think of the archive as not merely the inactive recipient of another's desires, strategies, or interests).

Paper Machine invites us to be highly cautious about thinking that the rise of new technology and media imply simply the irreversible destruction of a paper-centric (concept of the) archive—a paper-centricity that, as far as such thinking is concerned, might therefore be consigned, once and for all, to the archives. Hence, instead of just tracing the more or less dramatic impact of new mediatic and technological forms and practices on the very possibility of the archive, it might be possible to argue that the archive of the humanities—indeed, the humanities *as* archive—in fact guards or, as Derrida elsewhere puts it, *double-keeps* a legacy whose event is nevertheless still to come and whose configuration is still under way. Far from presenting the humanities as simply the residue of an intellectual or cultural past (as so often happens nowadays), one might thereby rethink the humanities in terms of what we might call an indispensable *archive-ability* going beyond the archive 'itself', one which, as Derrida might say, perhaps grants the possibility of a future as such.

And yet, such *archive-ability* as irreducible potentiality may perhaps alter irredeemably what is meant by and done in the name of the humanities. As Samuel Weber has pointed out, the use of the suffix *–ability* in the writings of Walter Benjamin (where it is found in recurring terms such as *translatability*, *reproducability*, *citability*, and so on), and in the work of Jacques Derrida (iterability receives most attention from Weber), always 'entails a virtuality that is never fully actualizable and therefore involves an "experience" of movement and alteration rather than a reproduction of the same—or of the self'.[2] As Weber puts it, such *–abilities* do not emerge 'merely as an anticipation of a possible realization', or in other words as the prospect of a fully possible possibility, but instead become '*immediately* effective qua possibility itself' (45). (For Weber, 'im-mediate' suggests the idea that such possibility does not emerge as simply a means to an end, although neither should such possibility be construed as a simple 'end' in itself, but rather a way of thinking difference as, precisely, constitutive.) What is involved in *–ability* words in both Benjamin and Derrida, then, is a possibility, a potentiality, or a transformativity which, much less than a simple add-on, in fact turns out to inhabit from the outset the very structure of the term that it modifies. For instance, iterability for Derrida names the necessary possibility of the inscriptive mark's repeatability—and not, as Weber points out, 'the manifest fact of repetition' (58)—which therefore supplements the mark at its very origin, so that différance or divisibility is in fact *constitutive* of its (therefore non-self-identical) 'presence'. Moreover, because such 'impossible-possibility'—in contrast to a fully possible potentiality—by definition exceeds the given or supposed capacities of the subject construed as rational agent or sovereign presence (or, in other words, since this 'possibility' goes beyond the 'masterable-possible'), Benjamin's or Derrida's *–abilities* elude containment by any conception of the 'human', the 'humanistic' or the humanities. Such *–abilities*, in other words, are always on their way to becoming 'other' by dint of a more original potentiality or virtuality than that which is found in the traditional conception of the human being.

ARCHIVE AND EVENT

In his interview with Giovanna Borradori conducted just a few weeks after the attacks in the United States on the World Trade Center and the Pentagon, Derrida dwells on Borradori's opening suggestion that 'September 11 (*le 11 septembre*) gave us the impression of a *major event*'.[3] Now, Derrida's thinking of the event—that is, the event that might indeed be worthy of its name—implies an irreplaceable and unmasterable singularity, a pure idiomaticity (strictly speaking, beyond even the idiom) that evades its own appropriation by any given language, discourse or context and that therefore dislocates the interpretative horizon on which it is hoped or expected to appear. Yet this 'absolute surprise' and 'unanticipatable novelty' (91) does not simply place the event forever outside the 'world', in some simple sense. Instead, it is precisely what is non-appropriable in the event (for instance, the irresolvable and uncontainable aporia which marks the event and advent of the 'demos': that is, the non-disentangleable rift between freedom and equality) which in fact charges it with world-opening force. This is one reason why 9/11 leaves the *impression* of a major event. As Derrida points out, if in the aftermath of the attacks the Americans, and indeed the entire world, could have been reassured beyond all doubt that the destruction of the Twin Towers constituted an absolutely unrepeatable violence, an outermost horizon of evil that would never again be crossed, the 'work of mourning' might have been both a smoother and more short-lived process. Yet 9/11 remains an event to the extent that it cannot be consigned to the past, but continues to inflict on us the traumatism of the 'to come'. Thus, 9/11 may be 'an ineffaceable event in the shared archive of a universal calendar', but the archiving of the event does not so much store, deposit, consign, or contain it, as tremble with its very *impression* (even if the date or datedness of 9/11 seeks to fix, stabilise, memorialise, or amortize the event, at the same time this designation harbours the prospect of a terrifying, intensifying, radically transforming repeatability). And this impression is *itself* an event, as Derrida insists (88). (At one point in the interview, he notes that 'the real "terror"' of 9/11 came not so much from the actual attacks but rather from the exploitation of their 'image' in the media 'by the target itself' (108), so that the event was produced as much by the target—the U.S.—as by the Islamist hijackers.) It is not just, as Derrida writes of the archive in *Archive Fever*, that there is 'accumulation and capitalization of memory on some substrate and in an exterior place'—an extrinsic support, a detachable prosthetic which the event in its irreplaceable singularity threatens to absolutely exceed and thus incinerate—because the archiving of the event *in precisely its impossible transaction with the event* is *itself* something of an event.[4]

What we are thinking of here, between the *impression* and the *event*, recalls, in Derrida's *Paper Machine*, the impossibility of thinking of paper—until recently, and perhaps still today, the means we privilege for recording our impression of events—as simply passive and secondary in relation to the act or event of writing. Here, paper is not so much a historically circumscribed technological convenience, an extrinsic support for the psychic or imaginative process which joins itself to bodies and materials only in order that, through writing, evanescent thoughts (events of thinking) may be concretised or 'stored'. Instead, for Derrida, paper itself provides the very figure for considering the paradoxical divisibility of a series of traits, *feuilles* or folds. In particular, Derrida regards paper's supposed function as a *subjectile* or bodily support for the traces or marks 'that may come along and affect it from the outside' to be part of a 'discourse' that is 'heavy with [. . .] assumptions' (42–43). This discourse becomes problematic at the point when we ask whether, when we say 'paper', we mean 'the empirical *body* that *bears* this conventional name' (my italics) or whether we are 'already resorting to a rhetorical figure' (52). The problem is apparent, in other words, when we come to understand that the notion of 'an empirical *body* that *bears*' the name of paper already gives itself over to a figure of speech, so that the reference to the 'empirical' here is not in fact supported merely 'empirically'. How could 'paper' *support* the figure of itself as (a) *body*? The advent of paper is therefore an event to the extent that the *impression* it bears is also in some way unbearable (it cannot itself bear it), and this transaction between the bearable and unbearable, like the aporia of the demos, leaves open a future. Thus, there is a future *for paper,* says Derrida, whatever we may come to mean by that term beyond a 'discourse [. . .] heavy with assumptions', and perhaps beyond the apparent waning of a paper-centric era.

In the interview with Borradori, Derrida grapples more than once with this thought of the event and its impression:

> The 'impression' cannot be dissociated from all the affects, interpretations, and rhetoric that have at once reflected, communicated and 'globalized' it, from everything that also and first of all formed, produced, and made it possible. The 'impression' thus resembles 'the very thing' that produced it. Even if the so-called 'thing' cannot be reduced to it. Even if, therefore, the *event* itself cannot be reduced to it. The event is made up of the 'thing' itself (that which happens or comes) and the impression (itself at once 'spontaneous' and 'controlled') that is given, left, or made by the so-called 'thing'. We could say that the impression is 'informed', in both sense of the word: a predominant system gave it form, and this form then gets run through an organized information machine (language, communication, rhetoric, image, media, and so on). This informational apparatus is from the very outset political, technical, economic. But we can and, I believe, must (and this duty is at once philosophical and political) distinguish between the supposedly brute fact, the 'impression', and the interpretation. It is of course just about impossible, I realize, to distinguish the 'brute' fact from the system that produces the 'information' about it. But it is necessary to push the analysis as far as possible. (88–89)

In this passage, the event and the impression are brought into a highly complicated relation of antagonistic, unstable intimacy. Although we should always seek to distinguish the 'brute fact' of the event from the 'impression' that is produced of it by the 'organized information machine', nevertheless, this impression is itself, in another sense, *part of the event*, as much indissociable and 'spontaneous' as 'controlled' and 'informed', Derrida tells us. In other words, its apparent spontaneity is always to some extent 'controlled', for sure, yet, for all that, such spontaneity is not merely, or not totally, controlled. Indeed, the impression thus carries within itself a divisible trait that redoubles the inextricable divisibility of impression and event. If to distinguish the 'supposedly brute fact' from the system that produces the '"information" about it' requires us to assume our philosophical and political duties, nonetheless presumably the word *duty* is chosen carefully by Derrida here, as a term which everywhere in his own thought would come to be associated with the conditional rather than the unconditional. Much less than directing us towards a 'pure' and unmediated experience of the event, then, this dutiful undertaking once more calls for a complex transaction, in fact an always irreconcilable yet necessary negotiation, between the conditional and unconditional, between the unappropriable and the call for a 'movement of appropriation' which must nevertheless always *falter* somewhat at the 'border' or 'frontier', calling up a sense or impression of incomprehension that is itself, first of all, an event (90) or, rather, producing itself as event—one that gives rise to a new impression, perhaps, transacting riskily between acknowledged or 'produced' incomprehension, on one hand, and the profound call for another intelligibility, on the other.

ARCHIVE AND IMPRESSION

'But what is an impression in this case?' (88). It is in a 'seemingly "empiricist" style', Derrida tells us, 'though aiming beyond empiricism', that he deploys the term *impression* (and one might begin by disputing whether 'empiricism' has its origins in the empirical):

> as an empiricist of the eighteenth century would quite literally say [. . .] there was an 'impression' there, and the impression of what you call in English—and this is not fortuitous—a '*major event*' (88).

Of course, *impression* is a term that comes to Derrida, several years before the 'Autoimmunity' interview in *Philosophy in a Time of Terror*, somewhat unexpectedly as he responds to a call from Elisabeth Roudinesco, to participate in an international colloquium: 'Memory: The Question of Archives'. Derrida thus speaks of how this term comes to inhabit the title of a lecture that was to be revised and published as *Archive Fever*:

> I undoubtedly owe you, at the beginning of this preamble, a first explication concerning the word *impression,* which risks, in my title, being somewhat enigmatic. I became aware of this afterward: when Elisabeth Roudinesco asked me on the telephone for a provisional title, so as indeed to send the program of this conference to press, almost a year before inscribing and printing on my computer the first word of what I am saying to you here, the response I then improvised ended up in effect imposing the word *impression.* (25)

Now, according to a certain transaction 'between two orders or, rather, between order and its beyond', as Derrida put it in the 'Autoimmunity' interview (133), the production or *event* of psychoanalysis, for instance, is not indifferent to the conditions of its archivization and archivable *impression.* Writing in *Archive Fever* of 'the geo-techno-logical shocks which would have made the landscape of the psychoanalytic archive unrecognizable', such as 'MCI or AT&T telephonic credit cards, portable tape recorders, computers, printers, faxes, televisions, teleconferences, and above all E-mail', Derrida says,

> I will limit myself to a mechanical remark: this archival earthquake would not have limited its effects to the *secondary recording,* to the printing and to the conservation of the history of psychoanalysis. It would have transformed this history from top to bottom and in the most initial inside of its production, in its very *events.* This is another way of saying that the archive, as printing, writing, prosthesis, or hypomnesic technique in general is not only the place for stocking and for conserving an archivable content *of the past* which would exist in any case, such as, without the archive, one still believes it was or will have been. No, the technical structure of the *archiving* archive also determines the structure of the *archivable* content even in its very coming into existence and in its relationship to the future. The archivization produces as much as it records the event. (16)

Although, as Derrida tells us in 'Autoimmunity', the event is to be thought of as irreducible to its impression, nevertheless, the conditions of archivization transact with the very event or advent of psychoanalysis in order to produce its event. A few pages later, Derrida goes on:

> [we] should not close our eyes to the unlimited upheaval under way in archival technology. It should above all remind us that the said archival technology no longer determines, will never have determined, merely the moment of the conservational recording, but rather the very institution of the archivable event. It conditions not only the form or the structure that prints, but the printed content of the printing: the *pressure* of the *printing,* the *impression,* before the division between the printed and the printer. (18)

Here, once more, the impression, in the sense of the very *pressure* of *printing*, names an intimate friction, a dynamic transaction (hostile *and* hospitable) between the printer and the printed, between the event (of psychoanalysis) and its impression 'in print'. This pressure of the impression is at once singular in its occurrence, finding or making 'its trace in the unique *instant*' (99) when momentarily one cannot be separated from the other, yet this apparent synchronicity which might otherwise translate the archive's dream of a 'single corpus' or 'unity of an ideal configuration' is disrupted at the origin, because the impression is always divisible, repeatable, and iterable: 'The possibility of the archiving trace, this simple *possibility*, can only divide the uniqueness. Separating the impression from the imprint' (100). The impression, in other words, 'would have been possible [. . .] only insofar as its iterability, that is to say, its immanent divisibility, the possibility of its fission, haunted it from the origin' (100).

If I am here citing copiously from Derrida, in order perhaps to fashion a text that archives the traces of his thought according to a law which must be both conservative and institutive, but which also seeks to conjure an impression of the *event* of his thinking, then a just few more quotations from *Archive Fever* may be called for:

> Unlike what a classical philosopher or scholar would be tempted to do, I do not consider this impression, or the notion of this impression, to be a subconcept, the feebleness of a blurred and subjective preknowledge, destined for I know not what sin of nominalism, but to the contrary, as I will explain later, I consider it to be the possibility and the very future of the concept, to be the very concept of the future, if there is such a thing and if, as I believe, the idea of the archive depends on it (29).
>
> It is not the question of a concept dealing with the past that might *already* be at our disposal or not at our disposal, *an archivable concept of the archive*. It is the question of the future, the question of the future itself, the question of a response, of a promise and of a responsibility for tomorrow. The archive: if we want to know what that will have meant, we will only know in times to come. Perhaps. (36)

For Derrida, the notion of the impression of an event as being at once distinct and indistinct from the event, a part of which, in other senses, it is not a part, itself may be considered by some to amount to a weak concept or subconcept, yet the complex logic of the impression as it unfolds painstakingly in the texts we are reading here is in fact crucial to a thinking which, instead of consigning the event to an irreplaceable and irretrievable past, or indeed to an indivisible instant or unique present, entails perhaps the very possibility of a concept of the future—that is, a future for the event as the 'to come', insofar as it remains restlessly worked or bound into a complex relationship with its impression. Here, as we have already said, the archive of the event is not thinkable merely as a stable and exterior site of consignation or depositing, not least because the very idea of the archive calls for new forms of thinking which resist the notion that we might call upon '*an archivable concept of the archive*'. Thus, the archive and the concept of the archive do not find their origin or foundation—or indeed their future—in what is, simply, archivable. For Derrida, one might even say, this makes the archive, for us, today and tomorrow, an event, perhaps. And, as such, Derrida once more moves us away from the idea that an archive simply accommodates, violates, monumentalises, and amortizes the event. Certainly in *Archive Fever*, the question of the psychoanalytic archive is bound to a thinking of the psychoanalytic event to come, an event which not only marks 'in advance' the entire landscape of our intellectual, disciplinary, historical, and cultural 'archive', but which is still destined to transform it:

> I wish to speak of the *impression left* by Freud, by the event which carries his family name, the nearly unforgettable and incontestable, undeniable *impression* (even and above all for those who deny it) that Sigmund Freud will have *made* on anyone, after him, who speaks *of him* or speaks *to him,* and who must then, accepting it or not, knowing it or not, be thus marked: in his or her culture and discipline, whatever it may be, in particular philosophy, medicine, psychiatry, and more precisely here, because we are speaking of memory and of archive, the history of texts and discourses, political history, legal history, the history of ideas or of culture, the history of religion and religion itself, the history of institutions and of sciences, in particular the history of this institutional and scientific project called psychoanalysis. Not to mention the history of history, the history of historiography. In any given discipline, on can no longer, one should no longer be able to, thus one no longer has the right or the means to claim to speak of this without having been marked in advance, in one way or another, by this Freudian *impression*. (31)

Thus, as *Archive Fever* turns its attention to an extended reading of Yosef Hayim Yerushalmi's *Freud's Moses: Judaism Terminable and Interminable*, the very event of Yerushalmi's book is viewed by Derrida in terms of 'dramatic turn' and 'stroke of theater' (37) which, in a rather sudden and surprising way, threatens to unravel a painstaking work of scholarship fit for the archive itself. This comes at the point when Yerushalmi departs from the classical norms and conventions of scholarly writing in order to apostrophize inventively according to a complex fiction which hails Freud's spectre: 'Professor Freud, at this point I find it futile to ask whether, genetically or structurally, psychoanalysis is really a Jewish science; that we shall know, *if it is at all knowable*, only when much future work has been done. Much will depend, of course, on how the very terms *Jewish* and *science* are to be defined' (cited in *Archive Fever*, 37, with italics added by Derrida). This question of psychoanalysis as perhaps a Jewish science (because, as Yerushalmi points out, it can only be decided in the future) radically transforms 'the relationship of such a science to its own archive', transforming in turn the meaning of the terms or concepts being used here, and, for that matter, their (conceptual) relationship to one another: 'science', 'archive' ('Jewish', too; 45). This orients them—even and especially according to their 'rich and complex history'—towards an unprogrammable future, or, rather, opens them to it. Thus, the archive, the very 'structure of the archive', is 'spectral' (84) in the sense that, like the ghost of Hamlet's father in *Specters of Marx*, it begins by coming from the future.[5]

SINGULARITY AND EVENT

This laboriously worked body of citations from Derrida has been crafted in order to contribute to a certain line of debate that in fact crosses and divides the entire humanities. One way to capture a sense of the controversy in question is to turn our attention to Timothy Clark's *The Poetics of Singularity*.[6] For Clark, the concept or quasi-concept of singularity— a term which involves us in a reading of Derrida, Heidegger, Blanchot, Gadamer, and, more recently, contemporary critics such as J. Hillis Miller and Derek Attridge—has provided the means for those within a broadly deconstructive tradition to oppose or resist the 'cultural politics paradigm' which today seems largely to dominate the entire field of interpretation. For Clark, this paradigm may be understood in terms of acts of interpretation where the chosen object of study—the literary text, for example—is in the last analysis referred and reduced to its cultural or historical 'context', or located it in terms of a 'politics of identity' which gives texts meaning in terms of 'ethnicity, nationality, religious affiliation, class or gender' (1). Such a paradigm, suggests Clark, might be judged to stealthily reintroduce 'intellectual dogmatism' in its very manner of proceeding, as well as provide a cover for 'the premature good conscience of much politically engaged criticism' (2). 'Singularity', meanwhile, has established the means to 'affirm an understanding of the "literary"' in terms that refuse 'to be conceptualisable or mastered' (i.e., merely 'archived') by the paradigmatic framework of 'culture' itself (1): 'Singularity names the specific being of a text or work, inflected so as to underline its resistance to being described in general categories or concepts' (2). Singularity, therefore, may be allied in certain of its key features to that dimension of Derrida's thinking about the event which emphasises what is 'unforeseeable and irruptive', the 'absolute surprise' and 'unanticipatable novelty' that makes an event worthy of its name. And yet, Clark notes, the argument 'that literature should finally be valued rather because it is inassimilable to fixed stances or cultural programmes' than because it might be understood in terms of its cultural significance is 'now becoming rather shop-soiled' (1). Although singularity has 'borne the main weight of the argument' in books such as Hillis Miller's *Black Holes* (1999) or Derek

Attridge's *The Singularity of Literature* (2004), Clark worries that the argument is sometimes made 'with a rather vaguely self-justifying force' (2).⁷ Singularity is 'good' because it evades or disrupts paradigmatic mastery, but for this very reason, the analysis of singularity must be brought up short if one is to avoid repeating the paradigmatic approach of describing the object according to 'categories or concepts' which become more 'general'. The singularity of singularity, in other words, can tend to encourage a rather sterile opposition in which the impasse between 'culturalist' and 'deconstructive' approaches sediments into mutually self-justifying hostility. And according to which deconstructive thought may be perceived as running the risk of giving way or giving ground on the still-crucial question of the 'historical', the 'political', and so on. Now, it is certainly not my interest here to reappropriate these terms *in their classical meanings* for the deconstructive tradition or, for that matter, to broker a deal between two very different modes of enquiry. Rather, through close attention to some relevant texts by Derrida, I simply want to demonstrate that the thinking of singularity, the singularity of the event for example, certainly need not come at the price of a poorly thought-out antagonism towards all that might fall outside the 'pure' event construed as unique, unrepeatable, or a-paradigmatic. What we have learnt from *Archive Fever*, and the 'Autoimmunity' interview, about the impression and the event, or the event and the archive, does not so much (if at all) reconcile the event of a text with the question of the context that receives and interprets it, as reformulate the very question of the 'event' so that the impression and the archive form an inextricable part of its thinking. This, in turn, equips us—indeed, requires us—to carry a deconstructive thinking of the event into the very 'archive' of all of our 'culture' and 'disciplines' whatever they may be. Such would have to include, as Derrida puts it in *Archive Fever*, 'the history of texts and discourses, political history, legal history, the history of ideas or of culture, the history of religion and religion itself, the history of institutions and of sciences [. . .]. Not to mention the history of history, the history of historiography' (30). My, how 'history' is repeated here!—but it is a repetition which, as it opens onto new horizons, indeed horizons without horizon, transforms the meaning of term it repeats, as something of an event, perhaps.

METONYMIES OF THE ARCHIVE

> I mentioned the Greek word *biblion* not to sound scholarly, or even—it's too easy—to explain the word *bibliothèque*. I spoke Greek to observe in passing that *biblion* has not always meant 'book' or even 'work' [. . .]. But does any oeuvre, be it literal or literary, have as its destiny only a 'bookish' incorporation? This must be one of the very many questions that await us.⁸

In 'The Book to Come', Derrida notes that *biblion* 'didn't initially or always mean "book", still less "oeuvre",' but could instead 'designate a support for writing'—paper, bark, and tablets (6). Thus, *biblion* itself gathers and extends a series of 'metonymies', metonymies which, perhaps in the very nature of their metonymic relations, do not so much harmonize particular instances by dint of an overarching generality, referring varied examples to a single point of origin, as indicate a series of uneven shifts and potentially unstable movements, as much historical as they are linguistic. If in Greek *bibliotheke* means 'the slot for a book', its 'place of *deposit*'—linking our sense of the library to a more original notion of storage, *putting*, or depositing—one should nevertheless not forget that this supposed 'act of immobilizing, of giving something over to a stabilizing immobility', as Derrida puts it, in fact only take places under the banner or in the wake of a word that itself *gathers* without exactly just 'setting down, laying down, depositing, storing' (6–7). 'The idea of gathering together, as much as that of the immobility of the statutory and even state deposit, seems as essential to the idea of the book as to that of the library', he writes, adding that 'there will be no surprise in rediscovering these motifs of the *thetic* position and the collection: of the gathering together that is statutory, legitimate, institutional, and even state or national' (7). Here, no doubt quite rightly, an entire ensemble is gathered up—thesis, book, library, institution, law, statute, state deposit, and nation-state—although also laid down somewhere between a metonymic series and a thetic order. However, if, as Derrida contests, 'all these motifs are themselves collected together in the question of the *title*' (7)—that which allows orderly depositing (classification, cataloguing, and so forth)—then what function is *biblion* to assume, and what limits does it assign, as the very term which gathers?

In 'Paper or Me, You Know', Derrida observes that the 'norms and figures of paper [. . .] are imposed on the screen: lines, "sheets", pages, paragraphs, margins, and so on' (46), whereas a paper-centric language still pervades the discourse of computer programmes ('cut', 'paste', 'clip', etc.).[9] Nevertheless, here he allows himself to wonder about the future of the *bibliothèque* in view of 'texts, documents, and archives that are further and further away from both the support that is paper and the *book* form'. '"What about the book to come?" Will we continue for long to use the word *library* for a place that essentially no longer collects together a store of books?' What happens when, sooner or later, libraries become spaces that are dominated by 'electronic texts with no paper support, texts not corpus or opus—not finite and separable oeuvres; groupings no longer forming texts, even, but open textual processes offered on boundless national and international networks, for the active or interactive intervention of readers turned coauthors, and so on' (7–8).

'The Book to Come' was presented to introduce a discussion with Roger Chartier and Bernard Stiegler at the Bibliothèque nationale de France (BNF) in March 1997. In May 2003, Derrida returned to the BNF in order to celebrate the donation to the Library by Hélène Cixous of an archive of letters, notebooks, and dream journals. Just as any testimony worthy of its name must keep a secret at precisely the point it is weighed as reliable attestation, keeping in reserve that which is radically heterogenous in relation to 'evidence' or 'proof', so this encrypted writing 'smuggles in that which is and remains unavowable, even as it is being avowed, brings it in clandestinely, as contraband', as Derrida writes in *Geneses, Genealogies, Genres and Genius: The Secret of the Archive*.[10] The library is thus transformed through the encryption of this address, the unavowable–avowed, hence, the readable–unreadable. Speaking thus, speaking secretly, beyond its own depositing, storage, or potential immobilization, the Cixous archive inhabits the theatricalised space of the psyche, engages or disturbs the other, its scenography becoming that of the 'unconscious'. Cixous's texts engage the memory, and pervade the dreams, of the true guardian of the archive. As Derrida tells us in 'The Principle of Reason', faithful guardianship (of knowledge, tradition, the archive, the institution) paradoxically entails keeping what one does not have and 'what is not yet': the possibility of the *to come*—because to keep without a certain 'double keeping', to merely defend, encircle or enclose, is to risk the greatest infidelity. Those who blindly assert the principle of reason badly negotiate a tautological circle on the one side (reason's grounds or justification *is* reason) and what is abyssal on the other (if reason cannot ground itself in reason without risking irrationalism or question begging, what *is* its foundation?). The faithful guardian must therefore observe a certain 'strategic rhythm' of the 'blink', neither keeping a hard-eyed watch over reason's transparent good sense nor falling into blind dogmatism, but opening and closing the eye in (viewless) view of a certain barrier and a certain abyss.[11] Such a 'double keeping' demands of the faithful guardian that he or she gather in a certain way of non-gathering, a gathering of what *cannot* be gathered, a winking eye cast over what cannot be brought to light. And because, in Derrida's *Geneses, Genealogies, Genres and Genius*, Cixous's archive addresses 'the library's unconscious' as much as its double-keeping guardian who must avow the unavowable, keep beyond keeping, its gift implies a certain transformation of the BNF itself, intruding on or prizing open that metonymic series (thesis, book, library, institution, law, statute, state deposit, nation-state) in order to expose and commit the Library to the 'unconditional', beyond or in spite of the 'national' (33). As Martin McQuillan, in his foreword to Derrida's text, puts it,

> The donation of the Cixous archive to the BNF is a dangerous gift because it compels the library to avow what it cannot comprehend, to guard what it cannot have, to house what it cannot master. Rather, the donation of Cixous's letters, notebooks and, above for Derrida, her dream journals [. . .] represents an abyssal opening beyond the eyes of the library (xi).

The Archive, the Event, and the Impression 197

The Cixous archive thus remains unmasterable by any form of sovereignty: 'she has handed over to the BNF an all-powerful, powerless other', as McQuillan puts it (xi). As McQuillan notes, Derrida insists that 'the corpus remains immeasurably vaster than the library supposed to hold it' (72). This strange relation between the part and the whole not only exposes the BNF to its supposed 'outside', to the 'unconditional': it also recalls, in Derrida's *Glas*, the very question of the anthological. Digging into the roots of this word, we find something like its original meaning in the gathering of flowers. In *Glas*, the flower is a part, a figure, or an example of the whole of rhetoric or poetics. Yet as 'the poetic object par excellence', or as the very 'figure of figures', the flower simultaneously partitions, sets apart, distinguishes, determines, delimits these fields in general. The flower is both—and seemingly impossibly—gatherer and gathered. As Derrida therefore observes, the flower comes to 'dominate all the fields to which it nonetheless belongs'. At which point, of course, it simultaneously stops 'belonging to the series of bodies or objects of which it forms a part'.[12] Not unlike Cixous's archive, therefore, the flower is only to be comprehended, only to be gathered, as an 'all-powerful, powerless other'. This aporia, which Derrida names as that of a 'transcendental excrescence', is also perhaps that of philosophy, whose asymmetrical contract with the university consists in the fact that, in one sense, philosophy belongs to the university which, in another, it itself partitions or allots. And the same aporia concerns the relation of literature to its institution, or, here, to the library.

On the other hand, in *Archive Fever*, the death drive is to be discovered at or as the foundation of the Freudian archive. The death drive is the 'original proposition' which stops psychoanalysis from becoming 'a lot of ink and paper for nothing' (8–9). But the death drive, as Derrida calls us to remember, 'not only incites forgetfulness, amnesia, the annihilation of memory, as *mneme* or to *anamnesis*, but also commands the radical effacement, in truth the eradication, of that which can never be reduced to *mneme* or *anamnesis*, that is the archive, consignation, the documentary or monumental apparatus as *hypomnema*, *mnemotechnical* supplement or representative, auxiliary or memorandum' (11). If the death drive is indeed invoked as the principle reason for conserving psychoanalysis' paper(s), no wonder that the 'archive always works, and *a priori*, against itself' (12). The 'silent vocation' of what psychoanalysis archives is therefore to 'burn the archive', 'incite amnesia', and thereby refute 'the economic principle' of the archive as 'accumulation and capitalization of memory on some substrate and in an exterior place' (12). In *The Post Card*, Derrida recounts his own promise not to '*bring into the Library or kindle therein any fire or flame*'.[13] Derrida is required to take this oath before he is permitted entry to Oxford's Bodleian in order to view the original illustration by Matthew Paris of Socrates and Plato, the image at the 'centre' of the book. Yet Derrida recites (re-cites) his promise with certain omissions:

> Did I tell you, the oath that I had to swear out loud (and without which I would have never been permitted to enter) stipulated, among other

things, that I introduce neither fire nor flame into the premises: '*I hereby undertake . . . not to bring into the Library or kindle therein any fire or flame . . . and I promise to obey all the rules of the Library* (211, 216).

What do these ellipses suggest? At the first time of asking, their insertion means that Derrida's promise is not recited in full, it is not recited as *the* or *a* full promise. At the second, they imply that something other, some other than the fire or flame just mentioned, has suddenly been incinerated by dint of an elliptical gap. But what exactly incinerates, here, what burns, if not the fire and the flame that Derrida openly states and refutes in the cited part of the promise? Although Derrida, by the more dutiful insertion of ellipses, would seem to observe (indeed *guard*) the 'proper' rules of quotation, in contrast perhaps to *The Post Card*'s wholly errant and insupportable general convention of 'the blank of 52 signs' that constantly interrupt the text, the recited promise nevertheless burns with elliptical omissions, omissions however which are not of 'fire' and 'flame'. Does Derrida's recitation, his *text*, break or keep its promise? Does something or nothing burn; or is it *both,* impossibly, undecidably, beyond memory or forgetting, economy or aneconomy? In order to approach this question, let me cite from the first section of *The Post Card*, which is composed of letters to an unnamed lover: 5 June 1997: 'I am sending you Socrates and Plato again [. . .] my small library apocalypse' (11, the blank of 52 spaces replaced by my own ellipses); 7 September 1977:

> the one that I call Esther. You know, I confided to you one day, why I love her. Her or her name, go figure it out, and each letter of her name, of her syngram or her anagram. The quest for the syngram Esther, my whole life. One day I will divulge, I do not yet accept them enough to tell them. Only this, for you, today. Estér is the queen, the second one, the one who replaces Vashti for Ahasheuros. What she saves her people from, a holocaust without fire or flame. (71)

Here, once more, Derrida's guardianship is of the unavowable–avowed, whereas the one he loves *saves*, just as, in *Geneses, Genealogies, Genres and Genius*, the BNF must 'Save in its unconscious' nothing other than the unsaveable–saving Cixous's dream archive. Her 'people' saved from 'a holocaust without fire and flame'—but, then, if from this flameless, fireless holocaust, from fire and flame itself? Does nothing or something burn?

Like the question itself, the Cixous archive should remain open, without condition (an open secret). Derrida ventures that, if the archive 'is to be meaningful, that is, if it is to have a future, [it] should be at the heart of an active research centre, of a new kind, open to scholars from all parts of the world' (83). This, of course, was Derrida's dream for an International College of Philosophy. McQuillan, in his forward to *Geneses, Genealogies, Genres and Genius,* wonders about what possible 'architecture' might 'link the Cixous collection at the Bibliothèque Nationale to the Derrida archive at the University of California, Irvine and to any future deposit of Derrida letters and manuscripts'. Indeed, he wonders how the archive might 'stay open 24 hours a day, 7 days a week, 365 days a year, to accommodate all the researchers of the world linked by the thread of Cixous-Derrida? What would be the paces, virtual or imagined, material and concrete, of such a Centre without centre?' (xiii). The 'enormous problematic of the archive and the other', as McQuillan puts it, into which we are thrown by *Geneses, Genealogies, Genres and Genius* reintroduces the question of computerization and electronic media, one that Derrida tackles with the utmost rigour in *Paper Machine*. Will the technological developments associated with Derrida's own generation keep the archive endlessly open while causing paper to be burnt up by something like a death drive? As Derrida observes, Cixous 'always writes by hand, no matter what, she writes using a tool—pencil or pen—that is, without a machine or machine-tool; without a typewriter or a word processor. Something which is fairly unusual and of critical importance for the archives of which we speak' (39). For Derrida, such a notion of the traditional archive's demise is perhaps not altogether in keeping with his thought of what the archive double keeps:

> For what we are dealing with is never replacements that put an end to what they replace but rather, if I might use this word today, restructurations in which the oldest form survives, and even survives endlessly, coexisting with the new form and even coming to terms with a new economy (9).

Here, once more, for Derrida, the archive archives itself as remarkable event, the resources of which—singular, inventive, unarchivable as such—thus remain always still to come. Each archive is, in its very archivization, an archive of the future, even—and perhaps especially—where the 'oldest' survives. For Derrida, indeed, the very question of the future remains inseparable from this thinking of the archive, even—and perhaps especially—if the archive turns out to outlive those able to 'read' or reconstruct it. For the humanities, as I suggested at the beginning, the futural dimension of such archive-thinking—the very notion of *archive-ability* in the sense I have tried to develop here—may be its foremost challenge as well as its most promising resource.

NOTES

1. Jacques Derrida, *Paper Machine* (Stanford, CA: Stanford University Press, 2005). Further references are given in the body of the text.
2. See Samuel Weber, *Benjamin's-abilities* (Cambridge, MA, and London: Harvard University Press, 2008), p. 15. Further references are given in the body of the text.

3. Jacques Derrida, 'Autoimmunity: Real and Symbolic Suicides: A Dialogue with Jacques Derrida', in *Philosophy in a Time of Terror: Dialogues with Jürgen Habermas and Jacques Derrida*, ed. Giovanni Borradori (Chicago: Chicago University Press, 2003), p. 85. Further references are given in the body of the text.
4. Jacques Derrida, *Archive Fever: A Freudian Impression* [1995], trans. Eric Prenowitz (Chicago and London, University of Chicago Press, 1996), p. 12. Further references are given in the body of the text.
5. See Jacques Derrida, *Specters of Marx: The State of the Debt, the Work of Mourning, and the New International*, trans. Peggy Kamuf (New York: Routledge, 1994).
6. Timothy Clark, *The Poetics of Singularity: The Counter-Culturalist Turn in Heidegger, Derrida, Blanchot and the Later Gadamer* (Edinburgh, UK: Edinburgh University Press, 2005). Further references are given in the body of the text.
7. J. Hillis Miller, 'Black Holes', in J. Hillis Miller and Manuel Asensi, *Black Holes / J. Hillis Miller; or, Boustrophedonic Reading* (Stanford: Stanford University Press, 1999); Derek Attridge, *The Singularity of Literature* (London: Routledge, 2004).
8. Jacques Derrida, 'The Book to Come', in *Paper Machine* (Stanford, CA: Stanford University Press, 2005), pp. 4–18, 5–6. Further references are given in the body of the text.
9. Jacques Derrida, 'Paper or Me, You Know . . . (New Speculations on a Luxury of the Poor), in *Paper Machine*, p. 46. Further references are given in the body of the text. See also, in the same book, 'Machines and the "Undocumented Person"', pp. 1–3; and 'The Word Processor', pp. 19–32.
10. Jacques Derrida, *Geneses, Genealogies, Genres and Genius: The Secrets of the Archive* (Edinburgh, UK: Edinburgh University Press, 2006), p. 31. Further references are given in the body of the text.
11. Jacques Derrida, 'The Principle of Reason: The University in the Eyes of its Pupils', *Diacritics* 13, no. 3 (1983), pp. 3–20, reprinted in Jacques Derrida, *Eyes of the University: Right to Philosophy 2* (Stanford, CA: Stanford University Press, 2004), pp. 154–55.
12. Jacques Derrida, *Glas* (Lincoln: University of Nebraska Press, 1990), p. 14. Further references are given in the body of the text.
13. Jacques Derrida, *The Post Card: From Socrates to Freud and Beyond* (Chicago: University of Chicago Press, 1987), p. 216. Further references are given in the body of the text.

BIBLIOGRAPHY

Derek Attridge. *The Singularity of Literature*. London: Routledge, 2004.
Timothy Clark. *The Poetics of Singularity: The Counter-Culturalist Turn in Heidegger, Derrida, Blanchot and the Later Gadamer* Edinburgh, UK: Edinburgh University Press, 2005.
Jacques Derrida. *Archive Fever: A Freudian Impression* [1995], translated by Eric Prenowitz. Chicago and London: University of Chicago Press, 1996.
Jacques Derrida. 'Autoimmunity: Real and Symbolic Suicides: A Dialogue with Jacques Derrida', in *Philosophy in a Time of Terror: Dialogues with Jürgen Habermas and Jacques Derrida*, edited by Giovanni Borradori. Chicago: Chicago University Press, 2003.
Jacques Derrida. 'The Book to Come', in *Paper Machine*. Stanford, CA: Stanford University Press, 2005.

Jacques Derrida. *Geneses, Genealogies, Genres and Genius: The Secrets of the Archive*. Edinburgh, UK: Edinburgh University Press, 2006.
Jacques Derrida. *Glas*. Lincoln: University of Nebraska Press, 1990.
Jacques Derrida. *Paper Machine*. Stanford, CA: Stanford University Press, 2005.
Jacques Derrida. 'The Principle of Reason: The University in the Eyes of its Pupils' [1983], in Jacques Derrida, *Eyes of the University: Right to Philosophy 2*. Stanford, CA: Stanford University Press, 2004.
Jacques Derrida. *The Post Card: From Socrates to Freud and Beyond*. Chicago: University of Chicago Press, 1987.
Jacques Derrida. *Specters of Marx: The State of the Debt, the Work of Mourning, and the New International*, translated by Peggy Kamuf. New York: Routledge, 1994.
J. Hillis Miller. 'Black Holes', in J. Hillis Miller and Manuel Asensi, *Black Holes/ J. Hillis Miller; or, Boustrophedonic Reading*. Stanford, CA: Stanford University Press, 1999.
Samuel Weber. *Benjamin's-abilities*. Cambridge, MA, and London: Harvard University Press, 2008.

11 Cataloguing Architecture
The Library of the Architect
Andrew Peckham

INTRODUCTION

This chapter sets out, in a series of six episodes (paired between buildings and books), an expanded conception of what constitutes *the library of the architect*. The thematic content moves, as if evolving a library, from initial consideration of the spatial and intentional logic of an architect accumulating and housing a collection of books or publishing a 'complete works', to subsequently focus on two separate readings that address a pair of library buildings and an architectural treatise. It concludes with a retrospective examination of contrasting chronologies: the evolution of a library which seeks to reconstruct a 'history' of its site and a book that presents a 'natural history' of an architectural practice's work.

If architects design libraries they may also collect books and publish their work, self-conscious in hindsight about publicity and their reputation. This latter metalinguistic aspect to architecture, in which the publication of the architectural treatise, monograph, or catalogue interfaces with a broader concept of the library, conditioned the reception of the German rationalist architect O. M. Ungers at the culmination of his career. In parallel, the work of the Swiss architect firm Herzog & de Meuron is viewed in the context of its documentation in a periodically published *The Complete Works*, displaced momentarily in 2002 by the substantive book (exhibition catalogue as artefact) titled *Natural History*.[1] The relationship between the library designed *by* the architect, and the library *of* the architect (whether a private collection of books or, more vicariously, the publications that come to represent a practice's work), elides the status of the library as an institution with a more personal architectural connotation. This touches on how an understanding of form, and of an architectural oeuvre, or indeed the psyche and self-regard of the individual architect, may all be understood to condition a conception of the architect's library.

The library as a building type may subsequently have acted out Victor Hugo's nineteenth-century contention that the invention of printing displaced architecture's symbolic role, reducing the library to a *machine à lire* of book stacks and an index set within a 'functional' space. Yet if the public library was also reinvented as an avatar of a social democratic modernism, it suffered a distinct malaise in the later twentieth century. Digitisation has affected the 'image' of library buildings (as they are transformed by new media technologies) without changing their spatiality much. The culture and occupation of the library interior, where a multitasking sociability now *incorporates* the activity of reading, has nonetheless changed radically; however, one can question its conceptualization as a 'datascape' or information landscape.[2] The individual architect may conceive his or her design strategies within such a context, eliding 'landscape' and 'archive' (of form, data or information); indeed, O. M. Ungers's 'morphological' preoccupations and recurrent collagist strategies were associated with both models.

Herzog & de Meuron's CCA exhibition *Archaeology of the Mind* (2002) and Andres Lepik's 'Acropolis of the Mind', the penultimate chapter in *OMU: Cosmos of Architecture* (2006), share an allusion to a 'retrospective' design mentality. John Elsner argues of John Soane (whose house-museum is one precedent for Ungers's *studiolo*) that his collection of models 'not only form a direct link' between his profession 'as an architect and his persona as a collector' but that his search for an appropriate place for them (his 'Model Room') reflects a 'constant discomfort with the finality towards which his collection was moving'.[3] It is with the relationship between accumulation and conclusiveness that the first chapter opens three paired episodes that are symmetrical about the activity of reading: 'Accumulation and Completion', 'Reading Texture / Reading Architecture', and 'Building and Rhetoric: Natural History?'

ACCUMULATION AND COMPLETION

> I am unpacking my library. Yes, I am. The books are not yet on the shelves, not yet touched by the mild boredom of order.[4]

The development of O. M. Ungers's own library (as a collection and an interior space) follows the construction, alteration and extension of his Cologne Belvederestrasse studio house of 1958. This is documented in three photographs illustrating Jasper Cepl's essay 'Ungers and His Books', published in the book catalogue accompanying the architect's final Berlin 'retrospective'.[5] They follow the stages that Walter Benjamin describes in the transcript of his talk 'Unpacking My Library', in which initially 'my library consisted of no more than two or three shelves which increased only by inches each year'. 'This was', he argues, 'its militant age, when no book was allowed to enter it without the certification that I had not read it'.[6]

A monochrome photograph, taken circa 1959 shows Ungers's unoccupied living room (a library by default). To one side a variety of loosely stacked books are supported on partially occupied open wooden shelves (obscured by three framed pictures). The atmosphere is domestic, cultured, and ascetic

(Bauhaus chair, contemporary desk, paintings, books, and harpsichord), and although the sense of occupation does not appear overdetermined, the exact location of the furniture is as set out in plans published of the building.

Benjamin discusses a qualitative change when the scale of his collection grows beyond immediate necessity and his 'books acquired real value, or, at any rate, were difficult to obtain', which compels him to issue his 'first major book orders [. . .] to secure [. . .] irreplaceable items'.[7] The inference is that the books have become commodities in their scarcity, their market condition, and the rationale for acquisition. The second photograph of 1985 serves as a portrait of Ungers and his wife Liselotte, presenting a corner of the library formed by altering (opening up) two rooms in their studio house. Full height encased bookshelves in dark timber constitute a conspicuously full reentrant wall of books (and leather bindings) encroaching on the space but fitted into the perimeter of a square ceiling grid (as if setting out prospective coffering). There is a contrasting, if studied, casualness about the owners' stance and the papers spread across the surfaces of a substantive inlaid desk and adjoining table.

Beyond the acquisition of value lies the practice of collecting, as Benjamin notes in a military analogy:

> Collectors are people with tactical instinct; their experience teaches them that when they capture a strange city, the smallest antique shop can be a fortress, the most remote stationary store a key position.[8]

The third and conclusive photograph, by Candida Höfer, was taken immediately behind Unger's seat at his desk in the library, or *studiolo*, located within the so-called Kubushaus extension (1989). As shown in Figure 11.1, an assertive white concrete frame delineates the double height interior. Set back in shadow, bookshelves line the perimeter, whereas at the ground level, two vertical openings reveal the glare of illumination outside, where brick piers stand dematerialised in graphic outline. The first floor level appears open, but closer inspection reveals a simple balustrade subsumed by similar dark, timber-lined shelving immediately beyond. A continuous frieze of white squares forms a cornice above the gallery whereas immediately below dark niches are occupied by iconic objects. Two white busts inhabit half-height pedestals subdividing each of the upper structural bays (another stands empty). The view, synonymous with that of the architect at his desk, is not quite symmetrical. Books lie variously open, half-closed, or face-up on the tabletop.[9] There is a predominant surfacial whiteness undisturbed by shadow highlights illumination from roof-lights above and beyond the frame of the image. The ambience is 'reflective' but subject to scrutiny from the figures inhabiting the balcony.

How, Benjamin asks, 'do books cross the threshold of a collection and become the property of a collector?'[10] Three partial images of the room, library, and *studiolo* not only reveal shifting modes of occupation and

Figure 11.1 O.M. Ungers's desk in his *Studiolo*. © Candida Höfer/VG Bild-Kunst, Bonn 2008. Original in colour.

the display of books, but they also trace a formal trajectory progressively associating the identity of the collection with a particular conception of a rationalist architecture. The prerogative of the architect, but equally where does the transformation of the studio house cross the threshold of propriety to manifest or represent qualities of the collection that lie beyond its ownership?

We move from a focus on the living room 'library', unpretentious in the shelving of books nonetheless placed within the culture of fine art and music, to a later regard for their status as a collection. In the altered room, the architect's square ceiling grid, lit at intervals by globe light fittings, is modified to correlate with the width of the long rectangular window. Ungers poses hand on hip leaning against a drawing board supported on a plan chest—the props of the professional architect, chairman of Cornell School of Architecture for ten years. The diagonal inflection towards his wife Liselotte, fronting what was now an extensive collection of books, appears opportune. The foreword to Ungers' first major publication available in English *Architecture as Theme*, carried more than an obligatory reference to his family.[11] He notes his wife's editorial contribution to his writing jotted down 'with so little effort', and indebted 'to her critical vision'. In an anecdote, Cepl reveals Ungers's decision back in the 1950s not to read novels, only architectural books.[12] Yet his key text, 'Architecture of Collective Memory' (1979), refers extensively to Italo Calvino's *Invisible Cities*. Liselotte Ungers's presence, set against the shelved books, is speculatively collaborative.

The altered library space and its contents prefigure the rational order of the later *studiolo* cube, with its representative structural grid and walled enclosure of books. Earlier, the elements accumulate, but beneath the studied casualness, a certain proprietorial poise has yet to acquire architectural form and hierarchy. Inside the completed Kubushaus, the resolutely dark timber lining, bookshelves, and furniture are set within a less-than-absolute Cartesian frame. Its integral balcony slab reads from below as projected outwards through the surrounding lining of bookcases (to engage the layered-brick construction beyond—distinct from the abstract order cultivated inside). From below, the plane of the ceiling contrasts with the deep, centrally located reveals of skylights reflecting subdued daylight into the space. This sense of detachment correlates with the estranged quality of the volumetric frame set away from the enclosure and within the ceiling and floor surfaces.

Benjamin concludes 'Unpacking My Library' by enacting his observation that the 'real collector' lives in his objects: 'So I have erected one of his dwellings, with books as the building stones, before you, and now he is going to disappear inside, as is only fitting'.[13] At Belvederestrasse, rather than delving into a critic's philosophical narrative we arrive inside Ungers's *studiolo*, a paradigmatic space secured by a monolithic stone exterior. Furnished with neoclassical desks and tables, this is both a workplace and a cerebral ideal (thematically associated with Benjamin's 'antique shop as fortress'), but although the catalogue of elements is pictorially complete, the interior remains spatially ambiguous. This instability is manifest precisely where the striving for order is strongest (an attribute of the original house as it turned the street corner). Incorporating the upper balcony, the structural frame reads anecdotally as a set of pillars supporting the ceiling and Ian Hamilton Findlay's duplicate heads of Apollo. The gridded surfaces of the ceiling and floor oscillate in the visitor's perception, reflecting a vertical axis of symmetry. The relationship between architecture and books, between what is built and read, however didactic, contrary, or compensatory, is also necessarily incomplete and subject to fluctuation. In the mind of the architect, disowning the role of collector, it remained part of wider 'work in progress', however conclusive the geometric formality of the Kubushaus—a paradox shared by serial architectural monographs.

Herzog & de Meuron's *The Complete Works* were representative in this respect, published initially in three consistently designed volumes tracing the chronological evolution of their work from 1978 to 1996 (the fourth following in 2009 had similar covers but a reformatted content).[14] This had the limitation of suppressing distinctions between individual projects, but the virtue of providing a coherent register against which change could be viewed.

All was not quite what it seems however, because volume 2 was published first in 1996 and was followed a year later by volume 1 and subsequently by volume 3 in 2005. The latter two were both published nine years retrospectively, so that, although including a brief list of ongoing projects, they remained out of key with the immediate currency of the work. Artfully published in monochromatic cloth covers of a minimalist character, azure blue, earth brown, and bright orange, respectively, only the name of the practice is printed in capitals across the centre line of each cover (the project period listed immediately below).[15] Consolidating Herzog and de Meuron's practice of the late 1980s, the initial publication covered only three years (1989–91) but already affected the status of a definitive oeuvre, one marked with aesthetic intent.

Herzog & de Meuron's equivalent material procedure was to 'pack up' and store their redundant 'working models' in crates, to be subsequently 'excavated', prematurely aged, by the curators of the CCA (Montréal) exhibition *Archaeology of the Mind* (2002) and to be documented in their book catalogue. The architects' own photo portraits in the successive volumes of the *The Complete Works* age more predictably, looking back to a youthful 1980s from the vantage point of the expanding practice of the early 1990s, and forward in 1996 to their current prestigious status.[16]

With this trajectory in mind, the design of Eberswalde Technical College Library, begun in 1994, belongs firmly to the third volume. In contrast, the 'library' at Cottbus is transitional in its development from library to media centre. Instigated a year earlier in 1993, and consequently only listed in the third volume, the building was not completed until 2004. Beyond the auspices of that publication, the Media Centre becomes associated with subsequent work. Had the graphic design and content of *The Complete Works* at this stage outlived its usefulness? Its overall format registered a rational *inventory*, but in contrast the *catalogue* associated with the architects' CCA exhibition incorporated a more diverse and accumulative thematic content.

The three volumes of *The Complete Works* are each, in turn, introduced by Gerhard Mack. His view becomes increasingly authoritative but largely rehearses the architects' own thinking. Each volume includes short texts by Jacques Herzog (or with de Meuron) followed by an interview transcript where a conversation cultivates the flavour of theoretical discourse. The primary content, however, of images, drawings, diagrams, working details, and models is presented in a consistent format only broken, occasionally, where more significant projects gain a double-page spread. It is notable that exhibitions of the practice's work are presented in an identical manner to the buildings and projects, although the architects have emphasised their reflective or discursive intent.

Representing the collaborative 1995 Paris exhibition at the Pompidou Centre, curated by Rémy Zaugg, a set of eight large photographs occupy doubled pages in volume 3. These highlight the particular character of the adjustable tables on which the exhibition was mounted. Mack suggests they 'are reminiscent of the reading halls of libraries', idiosyncratically putting forward the concept of 'the study room as a model of a museum'. Redolent of the institutional character of postwar library provision in which furniture occupied flexible space, an interrogatory character to the layout prevailed as if the fictive 'reading room' served an archive identified with a traumatic event. All sense of nostalgia for the past life of projects was seemingly eliminated in a distanced and objective stance towards the documentation of their work. 'Serialization doesn't know a hierarchy', Mack concluded, but what the initial volumes of *The Complete Works* suggest, and the exhibition manifests in an extreme form, is an aspiration to a form of consistency complete in itself.[17]

Herzog & de Meuron's two academic libraries derive from a less consistent sensibility, one conceived at a threshold between mediated representation and functional imperatives. Although the rationalist totality of Ungers's conception of a 'library of form' appears out of key with such disjunctive procedures, comparison between these buildings and his treatise *cataloguing* drawings provides a divergent insight into contradictions more readily reconciled on paper than in built form.

READING TEXTURE/READING ARCHITECTURE

Conceived immediately following the inception of what was much later to become Herzog de Meuron's Cottbus Media Centre, the library for the Fachhochschule (Technical College) at Eberswalde set an important precedent. As shown in Figure 11.2, its simple boxlike form presented a radical split between the iconographic character of the external facades (conceived with photographer Thomas Ruff) and the neutral functional layout of the interior to what is a modest three-storey college library extension.[18] The building attracted critical publicity for the application of a homogeneous pattern of photographic images to its precast concrete cladding and strips of glazing.[19]

Attempts to explain the representational aspect of the facades have tended to overlook any direct relationship between the materiality of their panels and the library programme.[20] It is through the medium of the images themselves that this emblematic surface has been referred to the collective political and cultural 'memory' of the town, institution, and library.[21] The

Cataloguing Architecture 209

Figure 11.2 Fachhochschule Library, Eberswalde, corner detail. © The Author. Original in colour.

character of the building as a gift-wrapped memory box was contentious to ex-citizens of the German Democratic Republic (GDR), but its iconography is an index of a provocative quality where a cultural (or polemical) surface 'skin' overlays the prosaic 'body' of the building. Any direct association with the precast concrete building systems of the GDR has generally been set aside; nonetheless, the building *is* made of concrete panels.[22] The library still primarily contains written texts; however, the applied imagery is a sign of the contemporary shift from a verbal to a predominantly visual digital culture.

The archaic origins of the library Lionel Casson claims for when a group of clay tablets first came to form 'a collection of works [. . .] for consultation'. Tablets were apparently stored on their sides, not unlike panels.[23] If one addresses the panels as material artefacts rather than at face value, then it is their association with clay tablets and the process of inscription, the incision or engraving of a tactile text, which is the subtext of the 'memories' evocatively traced in Ruff's images. Gottfried Semper's contention was that 'annihilation' of material reality produces a conscious expression of monumentality. Yet here it is the very stolidity and the erosion of the surface of these crafted precast concrete panels, which reminds us of antiquity, of the written record and the archaic form of the library as a collection of tablets.

In complete contrast to the building at Eberswalde, the much larger Media Centre (ICMC) at Bradenburg Technical University was completed later in 2005. Originally conceived as a library in the 1993 competition brief for the strategic reorganisation of the university campus, it was later revised to incorporate university-wide provision and administration of information technology and information services. Distinct in character from that in Herzog & de Meuron's earlier competition entry a smaller freestanding nine-storey building was subsequently developed, set in a landscaped terrain of picturesque curved paths. According to the architects, it constituted a *solitaire* derived from a 'purposeful configuration of many flows of movement' (however, this is open to question). In a wider context, however, the flattened concavity of the building's return curve suggests the presence of a facade towards the main road, whereas on its shorter sides, it takes on a more singular character (as if it were a tower).

Experientially the external appearance of the library is ambivalent, vacillating between the weight of a monolith and the delicacy of a veiled screen.[24] Viewed up close, the flat surface of the individual glazed rain-screen panels predominates, whereas at a distance, the building's overall monumental aspect is viewed against the skyline positioned on a slight rise of greensward. But this duality is simplistic because it can equally appear set against a darkening sky and illuminated by a low sun, as a hardened carapace or armature whose glinting surface reflects and refracts.[25] In brighter light, the sinuous form, alternately illuminated and in shadow, appears as a field of facetted calligraphy, its further extent reading obliquely in contrast as if an intricate fretwork (see Figure 11.3).[26]

Figure 11.3 Bradenburg Technical University Information, Communication and Media Centre, Cottbus, façade (late afternoon). © The Author. Original in colour.

The building may also be conceived as a casket whose delicate decorative appliqué epitomises the *value* of the collection of books and digital technologies inside. Externally, the building's surface curves as if the unwinding of a scroll. The illegible calligraphy printed onto the component sheets of glass was formed by superimposing a series of handwritten texts in different languages, but the visitor's perception, initially subsumed by the overall texture of the façade, settles on the individual hieroglyph. Each arbitrary figure forms part of an overlay on the component pieces of glass. Set out in angular faceted curves, the continuity of the textual field veils open gaps between the individual panels of the rain-screen construction. The move from readable 'texts' incorporated into previous projects to this form of indecipherable *texture* is reinforced by a parallel preoccupation with texture inside the building (the metal mesh ceilings and partitions and the surface quality of the reading tables).

Commonplace descriptions of the building naturalise its form as an amoeba, a cloverleaf, or a 'clamshell', but only in plan does the building deserve this natural connotation. The biological inference however is suggestive since an enigmatic object surfaced in an overlapping and fragmentary script forms a visual parallel with a DNA 'library' (and its cloned overlapping fragments of DNA). The process of unravelling the genome and sequencing DNA constitute a rational paradigm for a contemporary library represented in the form of an unreadable code.

In their earlier work, Herzog & de Meuron affected the media fetish for writing (or 'imaging') on the face of buildings (such as Koolhaas or Nouvel), a general trait that surfaced in the contemporary architecture of the late twentieth century (becoming a normative cliché in library design).[27] The initial orthogonal proposal for the Cottbus Library seemingly concluded this phase which the visuality inscribed at Eberswalde sought to transcend. The reworking of the project prompted the displacement of a typographical aesthetic into the flux of illegible hieroglyphs that finally constituted the external surface of the Media Centre. The tactile implication of inscription is overlaid by the abstract surface of a surrogate scroll; an archaic monumentality in the form of an armature slurs with an otherwise weightless, and primarily visual, digital culture.

In complete contrast, O.M. Ungers's resolutely solid, traditional, non-digital 'visual treatise', *10 Kapitel Über Architektur* (*Architecture in 10 Chapters*), was published in 1999 as a discursive inventory of his work, presented in a modest square format. The four inset squares inscribed on the cover are overwritten with a bold, full-height letter *U*. An alphabetical intent is registered, and individual letters on each of the succeeding pages spell out the architects' surname. The book's thickness is substantial and conducive to being held and flipped through, so ironically our first impression of its content tends to be fleeting and at odds with the separate content of each of its ten chapters.[28] As both a treatise and an exhibition catalogue, it does not fully represent the architect's intellectual credentials being primarily a collection of drawings, rather than of texts, from all periods of his career.[29]

The title page for each chapter is typically followed by historical drawings taken from Ungers's own collection of architectural treatises, and each section is concluded with a short quotation from his writings. Viewed in sequence, the chapters primarily emphasise geometry, the cube, and the column. Both Ungers's realized libraries, the Baden State Library in Karlsruhe and his own library, are included, and their treatment may be taken as representative.

The State Library building is illustrated at the end of chapter 9, 'Von dem elementaren Aufbau einfacher Konstruktionssysteme' ('Of Elementary Forms of Construction') and is identified in a definitive axonometric drawing of the realised scheme. A working conceptual sketch of the initial design for the reading room returns us to the original competition, followed by a tentative outline of the revised reading room dome (eventually built). We flip from its model, a section through the Pantheon, to its layout in the arrangement of structural ribs. Ungers's aphorism defers the necessity for invention in architecture, whereas illustrations from Filarete and Laugier attest to the 'natural' origins of the structural frame in the primitive hut. Finally, the concluding image is of 'nature transformed' in the courtyard at Karlsruhe, where the primary focus remains the dome as archetype but the subtext is the nature of tectonic reconfiguration.

There is, necessarily perhaps, a certain distance in each chapter between the principle to be elucidated and its demonstration. The Belvederestrasse house and its library (or *Kubushaus*) are documented in chapter 4, 'Von den menschlichen Maßstäben' ('Of Human Scale'), but the implication of anthropomorphic geometry can only be assumed in the projects for houses that follow. Ungers speaks of the architect as a craftsperson, 'an artisan whose craft mutates into art' in striving for 'perfection and flawlessness', yet notes how permanence disregards imperfection.[30] The sectional drawing together of the articulated brick house and of its singular library delineates something of this, whereas a loosely sketched elevation of old and new concludes earlier improvisations. The pencil line, tracing the familiar form of the house, integrated with its boundary wall, seems out of key where a provisional version of the library stands out above the perimeter. Four subsequent pages of small sketches are revealing, and unexpected, because they experiment with quite different versions of the library interior, caught between the centrality of the volume and the quadrilateral nature of its subdivision. The dilemma of a central, or offset, stair remains unresolved in a room surrounded by books.

When one leafs through his treatise reveals that the overall consistency of Ungers's oeuvre was indebted to an evolving conceptual methodology—less a collector's architecture than an operative archive of form.[31] The solidity of the book is deceptive because, inside, occasional wilfulness defers a rational trajectory. Herzog & de Meuron's two libraries invert this condition, wilful externally, perhaps, but typologically exact behind the façade. We experience Ungers's *oeuvre* leafing through the thickness of his treatise rather as we 'read' texture at Cottbus, subliminally, but beneath the incipient idealism of his aphorisms lies contrary evidence. Its co-ordinates are less certain but might be filed under *inventories*.[32]

BUILDING AND RHETORIC: NATURAL HISTORY?

Ole Bouman and Roemer van Torn's ready assimilation of the library metaphor, in conversation with O. M. Ungers, represents (and parodies) Ungers's own library and his architecture as a rational catalogue. They rhetorically question what 'the library itself [is] asking', situating his work at odds with the logic of postmodernism and confined to a 'Platonic' cul-de-sac (accumulating 'silent archetypes of eternity').[33]

Within Ungers's wider oeuvre, however, the Baden State Library in Karlsruhe, developed from a competition in 1979 and not to be realised until 1991, marked a fault line in his architectural development.[34] The institution of the public library was accommodated in a building conceived as a process of 'mining the past' but realised under the auspices of generic 'space planning'.[35] The archaeological theme parallels the rhetoric surrounding Herzog & de Meuron's working practice presented in the exhibition book/catalogue *Natural History* (2002), which I will discuss in due course.

Ungers sought contextual justification for an austerely abstract architecture (later described as 'without adjectives'), characterized as 'found' or 'site-specific' with reference to neoclassical Karlsruhe.[36] The six-storey transversely orientated cruciform body of the library was aligned with the primary axis of Weinbrenner's St. Stephan's Church adjacent to the site.[37] The stolid entrance to the building presented a trussed and split gable wall towards the public garden cut through the urban block.[38] The curiosity of this composition lies in its formulation: 'the idea of designing a building that anticipates its own history', 'that looks as if it has always been there'— something belied by its subsequent transformation.[39]

On the upper floors, the book stacks overlapped with, and surrounded, a centrally located public reading room. Square in plan this stepped down from the second floor in a series of internal terraces towards an enclosed garden court. Enigmatically represented in a surreal perspective, an artificial landscape of archetypal rocks and distorted trees provided a plateau, below which the buildings appeared to slip into the ground in a palimpsest-like conception of 'rewriting' the site.[40] Set out over the reading room, a skeletal ring beam inscribed a circular geometry from which a series of arched steel girders followed the line of the pyramidal roof above.[41] Perspective drawings representing the interior of the library were populated by ambiguous figures, alternately characterised in nineteenth- or twentieth-century dress. A similar temporal ambiguity adhered to the structure of the reading room: the stepped configuration and arched profiles are redolent of Boulée's vaulted Royal Library project, whereas the arched girders and inset columns resemble those of Labrouste's *Biblioteque Nationale* (*National Library*) in Paris.

The Baden library service, however, evidently required an increased floor area identified with the provision of flexible generic space and instigated a thickening of the bulk of the library. Compositionally the building was reduced to a symmetrical distribution of service cores, together with two four-storey cross-axial slots acting as internal light wells, complemented by the provision of a single central 'volume' (see Figure 11.4). This notional reading room open to the surrounding stacks retained the centrality of its elaborate precursor.[42] Capped by a dome and lit from an augmented central skylight, it is an accessible but also spatially detached volume. If *bibliotheke* (the slot for a book) emphasises functional space, and the etymology of 'volume' links the book to the scroll, then perhaps it is this space, rather than its dome, which retains (in existential terms) an emblematic purchase on antiquity.[43]

Ungers, faced with the contemporary spatial limitations of classical types, sought to moderate generic space with a rationalist sensibility. Vestiges of classicism adhere to typological fragments (dome, cruciform, and vestibule) and the albeit deracinated centrality of an evacuated axial arrangement. From the inception of the project, his explanation conflated claims to a decomposition of Weinbrenner's architecture with its antithesis, a literal 'contextualism'. Where the building claimed to embody a fictional preexisting state, a reverse chronology applied: the genesis of the existing buildings on the site was somehow to be 'discovered' in the form of the library that

Figure 11.4 Baden State Library, Karlsruhe, Reading Room © Dieter Leistner. Original in colour.

postdated them.[44] This conceptual mining of the past claimed archetypal authenticity in a form of archaeology, a theme also employed by the curators of *Herzon & de Meuron: Archaeology of the Mind* (CAA 2006) to record the associative qualities of the models intrinsic to the architects' design practice. In Ungers's case, the imperatives of contemporary functionality threatened to erase his attempt to retrieve the history of the site, a problem circumvented in the conceptual separation of a cultural façade and an empirical plan in Herzog & de Meuron's libraries.

The substantive Canadian Centre for Architecture exhibition book/catalogue, *Herzog & de Meuron: Natural History* (2002), similarly breaks with the measured tone of the previously inventoried *The Complete Works*. It parallels aspects of the book catalogue published with O. M. Ungers's Berlin retrospective *Cosmos of Architecture* (2006). Both contain a variety of essays several of which focus on the architectural models fundamental to their exhibitions, but are characteristically different in their design.[45] *Natural History* presents a facetted and tactile matt black cover: an aesthetic artefact, one imbued in the metallic, copper-coloured print and title (alternately picked out in shale grey) with a geological mineral association. The book is structured in relation to six themes, several of which overlap with Ungers's *10 Kapitel Über Architektur*.[46] It moves from compressed visual documentation of exhibits, developmental models and associated objects and drawings—all itemised, numbered and coded by the architects—to extended discursive essays. Each section is introduced by double pages exhibiting the grain of textured felt as a dark background to the minimal white lettering of the title. In turning the page, this is juxtaposed with the identity of a subsequent iconic image. The content then typically reverts to graphically inverted text—a fragment of the editor and architect(s) in conversation. These transcriptions are interspersed, at extended intervals, within densely arranged visual material picturing investigative models and associated sources. Placed on a black ground they are succeeded by illustrated essays in which critics and artists address discursive topics correlating with the architects' preoccupations. *Natural History* is divided in format between two realms: one characterised by visual association and the other offering a more cerebral discussion.[47]

The concept for the exhibition intended to highlight the design development of Herzog & de Meuron's buildings, predominantly with reference to their working models. 'In the cellar of their office, hundreds of chests and boxes are piled high—fragments, rejects', Philip Ursprung, the curator, explained, providing a 'material' record of design development.[48] The curators' active imaginations conceived the 'unpacking' of this archive as if an excavation: 'For the purposes of the exhibition we imagined that we were archaeologists of the future who came across hundreds of models [. . .] without knowing what they meant', thus, self-consciously distancing themselves from Benjamin's 'mild boredom of order'.

Models identified with the duration of a particular project acquire the fictional status of allusive antiquities, signs of a previous life perhaps, but instrumentally blunted objects. In the architects preferred view, they are 'just waste' (the product of a process we know to be the procedural aspect of design).[49] But waste to an archaeologist may be more significant than valued artefacts may be: the manuscripts cast into a synagogue's inaccessible *geniza* provided a unique cross section through the historical record.[50] To intersperse art objects and everyday things with so-called waste from the design process is to endow the latter with a particular status.[51] Herzog's recourse to the metaphor of waste, or the geological 'sedimentation of bones and fossils', parallels Ungers's claim that his objects are accumulated not collected.

Double pages in *Natural History* show Herzog & de Meuron's crates being unpacked (see Figure 11.5).[52] On one side, the 'Eberwalde Panels' lie open, and on the other, a diminutive model of Cottbus library, subject to close scrutiny, has emerged from its box. At a glance, the packing cases look to be employed in transporting the objects to be exhibited but are for their permanent storage. The event observed is the expression of a curatorial archaeology felt more forcefully here, perhaps, than in the static form of the exhibition (their two libraries, the 'tablets' at Eberswalde preceding Cottbus's enveloping 'scroll', constitute their own temporal reversal).

The Eberswalde panels are recurrently illustrated in *Natural History*; the modishly imprecise colour photograph fronting the section on 'Imprints and Moulds' is also presented smaller and sharper before the introduction to the book. Redolent of a sculptor's studio, it represents less the technical process of manufacture than the interface between conceptual intent and physical

Figure 11.5 'Model crates 2002' (*Herzog & de Meuron: Natural History*, 330–31). © Centre Canadien d'Architecture/Canadian Centre for Architecture Montréal and Lars Muller Publishers. Photo Michel Boulet. Original in colour.

realisation, which is the primary focus of the exhibition (and its book).[53] For Ungers at Karlsruhe, this involved the protracted gestation, revision, and eventual construction of the new State Library, presenting a micro-history of the rift between a historical order of things and the imperatives of the present.

CONCLUSION

John Elsner identifies three modes of the architect John Soane's acquisitive sensibility inherent in his attitudes to, and models of, antiquity: antiquity as it *was* in the present (ruins), antiquity in an *imagined* perfection, and antiquity as a *source* of objects (to be collected).[54] Ungers's practice, through the different libraries discussed here, present a more ambivalent relation to 'history' (whether understood as ancient history, as an intentionally 'distressed' record of the more recent past, or as the duration of their own process of realisation). The contemporary site of the Baden State Library was viewed archaeologically as *imaginatively* perfected in the form of Ungers's competition entry (latterly perhaps 'ruined' by the requirements of 'generic space'), just as his own brick house in a sense constituted a *ruin* of its end of terrace condition, ultimately deferred by its other: the *imagined* typological perfection of the Kubushaus. Conversely, a dissonance surfaces between the classical order and format of his visual treatise and the content of its recurrent speculative sketches seeking out an *imagined* perfection whose rational form, whether in its graphic depiction or ultimate construction, bears traces of their speculative ambiguities. In contrast *Herzog & de Meuron: Natural History* created a fictive archaeology at odds with the consistent stasis of the first three volumes of their *The Complete Works*. The emblematic façades of the architects' two academic libraries materialize a 'present' antiquity (not to be found in the archive). This intimates the parameters of their subsequent mediated practice, so seductively rearranged inside the vivid green covers of the fourth volume of *The Complete Works*.

Herzog & de Meuron's archive of form was crated up in the basement of their office and embodied for posterity in the disparate content of the book *Natural History* (and its associated exhibition). Ungers's valedictory studio library housed his books but not the archive of form that resided in the conceptual strategies projected and built in his early work. Both identify to some degree with the collector's concern for consistency and completion, undone perhaps in Herzog & de Meuron's altered *The Complete Works* and in the traces of instability inherent within Ungers's own library. *Natural History* served to consolidate a point of departure, framed by the conceptual experimentation of Herzog & de Meuron's two academic libraries. Simply planned, their interiors submit to the pragmatic demands of library services, whereas their externally sophisticated forms of representation suggest that the anachronistic scroll and tablet remain allusive in an age of digitisation, the scrolling of narrative, and the handheld virtual interface.

NOTES

1. Philip Ursprung, ed., *Herzog & de Meuron: Natural History* (Baden, Germany: Lars Muller, 2002).
2. Anna Klingmann, 'Datascapes: Libraries as Information Landscapes', in *Building for Books: Traditions and Visions*, ed. Susanne Bieri and Walter Fuchs (Basel, Switzerland: Birkhauser, 2001), pp. 410–13.
3. John Elsner, 'A Collector's Model of Desire', in *The Cultures of Collecting*, ed. John Elsner and Roger Cardinal (London: Reaktion, 1994), p. 160.
4. Walter Benjamin, 'Unpacking My Library', in Walter Benjamin, *Illuminations*, ed. Hannah Arendt (New York: Schocken, 1969), p. 59.
5. Jasper Cepl, 'Ungers and his Books', in *OMU: Cosmos of Architecture*, ed. Andres Lepik (Ostfildern, Germany: Hatje Cantz, 2006), pp. 30–35.
6. Benjamin, 'Unpacking My Library', p. 62.
7. Ibid.
8. Ibid., p. 63.
9. Presenting an oblique reference to neoclassicism.
10. Benjamin, 'Unpacking My Library', p. 61.
11. Oswald Matthias Ungers, *Architecture as Theme* (New York: Rizzoli, 1982), p. 7.
12. Cepl, 'Ungers and his Books', p. 31.
13. Benjamin, 'Unpacking My Library', p. 67.
14. Gerhard Mack, ed., *Herzog & de Meuron 1978–1981*, vol. 1 of *The Complete Works* (Basel, Switzerland: Birkhäuser, 1997); *Herzog & de Meuron 1989–1991*, vol. 2 of *The Complete Works* (Basel, Switzerland: Birkhäuser, 1996); *1992–1996*, vol. 3 of *The Complete Works* (Basel, Switzerland: Birkhäuser, 2000); and *Herzog & de Meuron 1997–2001*, vol. 4 of *The Complete Works* (Basel, Switzerland: Birkhäuser, 2009).
15. The words, coloured light pink, lime green, and light blue in chronological sequence, alternately coincide with, stand out from, and finally oscillate against, their respective colour fields.
16. At this latter date, all four partners were photographed, as if for a group portrait, in the objective forensic idiom favoured by contemporary German photographers.
17. Two moves transformed the neutral space of the building: rows of fluorescent tubes were set across service conduits running below the ceiling slab, and a grid of tables set out on which drawings, photographs and documents were displayed beneath transparent sheets. See Mack, *Herzog & de Meuron: 1992–1996*, pp. 126–29.
18. Originally designed by the architects and lined in timber, the interior fit-out was finally chosen by the client from 'off-the-peg' catalogues. This was both a logical consequence of the concept for the building and a symptom of a longstanding historical trend. Battles notes that in Melvil Dewey's nineteenth-century rationalisation of library services, the relation between the library, its readers, and shopping was not simply a metaphor. See Mathew Battles, *Library: An Unquiet History* (New York: Norton, 2003), p. 144.
19. Viewing the library as a tattooed body, the architects refer to *sgraffito* decoration in Swiss vernacular building. Parallel attributions focus on film (strips or loops of negatives, animation sequences, and newsreels) and the propaganda associated with the poster 'wall'. The storage theme informing the cladding of an earlier warehouse for Riccola at Laufen (rhetorically manipulated in Thomas Ruff's representative image) has also encouraged overinterpretation of the 'serial' elevations, as if they were bookshelves, denoting the stacking of books. Only Forster has convincingly identified specific associations with the

layout and embellishment of historic manuscripts. A vertical reading of the images as a series of Chinese scrolls is belied by their horizontal emphasis and serial repetition, alternately seen to constitute a series of friezes. See Gerhard Mack, 'Building with Images', in *Herzog & de Meuron: Eberswalde Library*, ed. Pamela Johnson (London: Architectural Association, 2000); Valeria Lieberman, '"Reflections on a Photographic Medium", "Memorial to the Unknown Photographer", or "Visual Diary?": Thomas Ruff's Newspaper Photos', in *Herzog & de Meuron: Eberswalde Library*; and Kurt Forster, 'Pieces of Four and More Hands', in Ursprung, *Herzog & de Meuron: Natural History*, pp. 55–58.

20. One image does however show students working in a library. Only a reading of the panels as analogous to a set of printing plates has connected them materially to the production of books. See Lieberman, 'Reflections', p. 56.
21. Mack, 'Building with Images', p. 27.
22. The photographic techniques and hand crafted nature of their production, employing a retardant which enabled the images to be 'washed' from the concrete panels after their main body had cured, has been likened to the 'natural' process of erosion which reveals fossils. A raw brutalism has been displaced in exposing both the 'grain' of history and of the process of making.
23. Lionel Casson, *Libraries in the Ancient World*, New Haven/London: Yale, 2001, pp. 3–7.
24. Its character fluctuates depending on distance and relative light conditions. Gottfried Semper's categorisation of textile hangings as the conceptual foundation of 'enclosure' resonates with this diaphanous façade. Concomitant associations with weaving or tapestry also apply to literary texts metaphorically (or literally in embroidered form). Chartier discusses 'the proximity of text and fabric' in the eighteenth century. See Roger Chartier, *Inscription and Erasure: Literature and Written Culture from the Eleventh to the Eighteenth Century* (Philadelphia: University of Pennsylvania Press, 2007), pp. 101, 102. Here the move from readable text to an illegible texture seeks to 'represent' language. Carrie Asman's close reading of Semper's categorisation of 'directional ornament' aptly describes the qualities that characterise the Media Centre's enclosure, evoking the 'fleeting phenomena' of a digital age. This lends a certain irony to the billowing sun blinds caught unintentionally by wind penetrating the rain-screen façade. Carrie Asman, 'Ornament and Motion: Science and Art in Gottfried Semper's Theory of Adornment', in *Herzog & de Meuron: Natural History*, p. 385.
25. Less an armoured object than one voided in which detached moments of transparency are read against its surface. The building is static, but the perception remains in a state of flux.
26. As if laser cut from a thickness of material, these fictive perforations present an image at odds with the constructive reality of the assembly of glass panels.
27. This was first heralded in a literally typographic context: the graphic notation of chunks of explanatory text visualised as the arrangement of proposed extensions to the cruciform headquarters of the *Helvetia Versicherung* competition (1989).
28. These identify Geometry; Orthogonal Multiplicity; The Order of the Column; Human Scale; Morphological Transformation; Mathematical Laws of Proportion; The Proportioning of Facades; The Logic of Spatial Organisation; Elementary Construction, and finally Figural Composition, as the key aspects of architecture. See Oswald Matthias Ungers, *10 Kapitel über Architektur*, ed. Anja Sieber-Albers with Jutta Voerhoeve (Köln: Dumont, 1999).
29. In sampling representative projects, individual drawings are (typically) printed on a single page. The rough-and-ready nature of the sketches coexists with

Cataloguing Architecture 221

exquisitely detailed, definitive drawings of each project or building, set in generous white space.
30. Ungers may have identified his earlier self as the Brutalist craftsman working to acquire the status of the humanist artist (attuned to rational perfection), but equally the Brutalist artist acquires the conceptual and tectonic craft of a rational architecture.
31. The preoccupation is related to Ungers's teaching practice in his early days at the TU in Berlin. See Erika Mühlthaler, ed., *Lernen von O M Ungers* (Berlin/Aachen: Arch+, 2006).
32. This is no more than a litmus test of his thinking. The notion of a design as an archive of form was first made explicit in the formal notation developed for the 1964 Enschede student housing project. McIsaac's exemplary study employs the term *inventoried consciousness* to describe a salient characteristic of the literary culture of German modernity. He is wary of overdetermined archival affiliations but the concept is pertinent to aspects of Ungers's and of Herzog & de Meuron's practices. See Peter McIsaac, *Museums of the Mind: German Modernity and the Dynamics of Collecting* (Philadelphia: University of Pennsylvania Press, 2007).
33. Ole Bouman and Roemer van Toorn, eds., *The Invisible in Architecture* (London: Academy Editions, 1994), p. 52.
34. Oswald Matthias Ungers, *Architektur 1991–1998* (Stuttgart: DVA, 1998), pp. 152–56; Oswald Matthias Ungers, *Die Badische Landesbibliothek Karlsruhe* (Stuttgart: Verlag Gerd Hatje, 1992); and Martin Kieran, *Oswald Mathias Ungers* (Zurich: Artemis, 1994), pp. 128–33.
35. A long-standing priority in the provision of flexible library services.
36. See Benedetto Gravagnuolo, *Oswald Mathias Ungers: Four Works* (Naples: Clear, 1992), p. 12. In German, the term *eigenschaften* elides 'adjective' and 'quality', pointing to what becomes definitive in Ungers's late work (where he described his final *Haus III* as 'The House Without Qualities').
37. See Kenneth Frampton and Silvia Kolbowski, eds., *O M Ungers: Works in Progress* (New York: Rizzoli, 1981), pp. 12–14, 62–71; and Ungers, *Architecture as Theme*, pp. 88–95.
38. One of several alluding to the church.
39. This nonetheless still complemented the typological arrangement of the old State Library building nearby.
40. See Ungers, *10 Kapitel über Architektur*, p. 763.
41. Internally outlining the residual presence of a fictive dome.
42. Glazed in on the two floors above, it reads more like a void created in the overall Cartesian grid. Separated out from the open book storage below, blind openings are concluded with a 'pictorial' frieze of squares, complementing the ornate wooden floor below.
43. Ian Hamilton Findlay's sculptural *Library Fragments* (1991) line the pillars, evoking a lost culture of classicism.
44. This was more plausibly acted out in the duration of the project itself. The engineered structure of the reading room originally proposed was displaced by a substantive rotunda, implied in the competition project but now modelled directly on the Pantheon.
45. In *Natural History*, the models are not primarily descriptive or directly related to drawings and photographs of realised projects. Instead, they document procedural development and loosely associative material.
46. Namely, 'Transformation and Alienation', 'Appropriation and Modification', 'Stacking and Compression', 'Imprints and Moulds', 'Interlocking Spaces', and 'Beauty and Atmosphere'.
47. Though the architects and their critics habitually elide the two in philosophising materially and thinking associatively.

48. Ursprung, 'Exhibiting Herzog & de Meuron', in Ursprung, *Herzog & de Meuron: Natural History*, pp. 35, 36.
49. "These archived objects are therefore nothing more than waste-products": "we have never been interested in producing objects invested with an aura [. . .] of an artwork" (ibid., pp. 74, 75). Is Herzog realistic about the models as no more than a means to an end or disingenuous given the artifice of the book and the cultural context of the exhibition? Deyan Sudjic's perceptively critical review noted how iconic art works were 'held hostage on the walls of the museum, binding them into the display of Herzog & de Meuron's architectural projects.
50. Matthew Battles proposes the *geniza* as the library's 'other', the uselessness of its contents at odds with 'vested interests' lurking behind the transparent 'enlightenment' of the library. See Battles, *Library*, pp. 194, 195.
51. Just as Ungers' 'collections', setting aside the architects' view that they represented no more than the acquisition of knowledge, provided cultural validation, or compensation, for the relative achievement of his architecture.
52. Ursprung, *Herzog & de Meuron*, pp. 330, 331.
53. In a second double page of small black-and-white images (ibid., pp. 254, 255), we see the production of the panels: the technicians, the moulding process, the stencils that imprint the retardant onto the concrete surface, and the washing out of the still soft mix. The previous colour photographs, devoid of people, display the panels, close-up inclined on pallets and raised off the floor as technical products.
54. Elsner, 'A Collector's Model', p. 165.

BIBLIOGRAPHY

Carrie Asman. 'Ornament and Motion: Science and Art in Gottfried Semper's Theory of Adornment', in *Herzog & de Meuron: Natural History*, edited by Philip Ursprung. Baden, Germany: Lars Muller, 2002.
Mathew Battles. *Library: An Unquiet History*. New York: Norton, 2003.
Walter Benjamin. 'Unpacking My Library', in Walter Benjamin, *Illuminations*, edited by Hannah Arendt. New York: Schocken, 1969.
Ole Bouman and Roemer van Toorn, eds. *The Invisible in Architecture*. London: Academy Editions, 1994.
Lionel Casson. *Libraries in the Ancient World*. New Haven, CT, and London: Yale, 2001.
Jasper Cepl. 'Ungers and his Books', in *OMU: Cosmos of Architecture*, edited by Andres Lepik. Ostfildern, Germany: Hatje Cantz, 2006.
Roger Chartier. *Inscription and Erasure: Literature and Written Culture from the Eleventh to the Eighteenth Century*. Philadelphia: University of Pennsylvania Press, 2007.
John Elsner. 'A Collector's Model of Desire', in *The Cultures of Collecting*, edited by John Elsner and Roger Cardinal. London: Reaktion, 1994.
Kurt Forster. 'Pieces of Four and More Hands', in *Herzog & de Meuron: Natural History*, edited by Philip Ursprung. Baden, Germany: Lars Muller, 2002.
Kenneth Frampton and Silvia Kolbowski, eds. *O M Ungers: Works in Progress*. New York: Rizzoli, 1981.
Benedetto Gravagnuolo. *Oswald Mathias Ungers: Four Works*. Naples: Clear, 1992.
Pamela Johnson, ed. *Herzog & de Meuron: Eberswalde Library*. London: Architectural Association, 2000.
Martin Kieran. *Oswald Mathias Ungers*. Zurich, Switzerland: Artemis, 1994.

Anna Klingmann. 'Datascapes: Libraries as Information Landscapes', in *Building for Books: Traditions and Visions*, edited by Susanne Bieri and Walter Fuchs. Basel, Switzerland: Birkhäuser, 2001.
Valeria Lieberman. '"Reflections on a Photographic Medium", "Memorial to the Unknown Photographer", or "Visual Diary?": Thomas Ruff's Newspaper Photos', in *Herzog & de Meuron: Eberswalde Library*, edited by Pamela Johnson. London: Architectural Association, 2000.
Gerhard Mack. 'Building with Images', in *Herzog & de Meuron: Eberswalde Library*, edited by Pamela Johnson. London: Architectural Association, 2000.
Gerhard Mack, ed. *Herzog & de Meuron 1978–1981*, vol. 1 of *The Complete Works*. Basel, Switzerland: Birkhäuser, 1997.
Gerhard Mack, ed. *Herzog & de Meuron 1989–1991*, vol. 2 of *The Complete Works*. Basel, Switzerland: Birkhäuser, 1996.
Gerhard Mack, ed. *Herzog & de Meuron 1992–1996*, vol. 3 of *The Complete Works*. Basel, Switzerland: Birkhäuser, 2000.
Gerhard Mack, ed. *Herzog & de Meuron 1997–2001*, vol. 4 of *The Complete Works*. Basel: Birkhäuser, 2009.
Peter McIsaac. *Museums of the Mind: German Modernity and the Dynamics of Collecting*. Philadelphia: University of Pennsylvania Press, 2007.
Erika Mühlthaler, ed. *Lernen von O M Ungers*. Berlin and Aachen, Germany: Arch+, 2006.
Oswald Matthias Ungers. *Architektur 1991–1998*. Stuttgart: DVA, 1998.
Oswald Matthias Ungers. *Architecture as Theme*. New York: Rizzoli, 1982.
Oswald Matthias Ungers. *Die Badische Landesbibliothek Karlsruhe*. Stuttgart: Verlag Gerd Hatje, 1992.
Oswald Matthias Ungers, *10 Kapitel über Architektur*, edited by Anja Sieber-Albers with Jutta Voerhoeve. Köln: Dumont, 1999.
Philip Ursprung. 'Exhibiting Herzog & de Meuron', in *Herzog & de Meuron: Natural History*. Baden, Germany: Lars Muller, 2002.
Philip Ursprung, ed. *Herzog & de Meuron: Natural History*. Baden, Germany: Lars Muller, 2002.

12 Reading *Folk Archive*
On the Utopian Dimension of the Artists' Book

Dan Smith

INTRODUCTION: THE MILIEU OF *FOLK ARCHIVE*

In this chapter, I use artwork to open up passages within the library. 'Folk Archive', an ongoing contemporary art project by Jeremy Deller and Alan Kane, offers a critical intersection with the library as a form, through notions of documentary, photography, taxonomy, and the form of the book itself—titled *Folk Archive*. I privilege the engagement with *Folk Archive* as a book, but one that is contextualised by art gallery exhibitions. Its authors frame this archive as an attempt to consider what constitutes present day folk art in Britain and Northern Ireland—a kind of popular form of practice that can be opposed to corporate and banal forms of representation. The diverse material gathered in Deller and Kane's 'Folk Archive' privileges personal impulse as its organising logic, an admission that must be recognised within the founding of many museums and libraries, because of gestations that are often subject to the preferences, accountabilities, perversions, intentions, and oversights of the founder. This is not stated as an attempt to overly privilege the role of the individual, but to suggest a tension between individual agency and more conventional readings of archives as social structures.[1] 'Folk Archive' resonates in its propinquity to actual institutions by revealing a taxonomical form of holding, subject to generative internal conflicts and oppositions.

Jeremy Deller has achieved an uncommon level of recognition, winning the Turner Prize in 2004, maintaining a high profile beyond the confines of the art world, whilst sustaining favourable critical recognition all round. His projects are always associated with forms of social engagement and participation, while often going so far as to revel in elements of humour and straightforward fun, often grounded by emotive documentary narratives. Part of what makes his level of recognition unusual is that Deller is not a maker, in that he does not paint, draw, sculpt, perform, or even take photographs or make films. His practice is to make use of social elements. For example, 'Acid Brass' is, on one hand, a simple operation, mixing seemingly incongruous musical forms to make an entertaining hybrid. It is a work composed of a series of live performances. Dance music associated with the acid house movement of the late 1980s and early 1990s were played by the William Fairey Brass Band and were subsequently released as an album. For Deller, this act is substantiated by a contextual interest in a social connection between these two forms of music. Essentially, he identified both as forms as forms of class based solidarity against the policies of the Conservative government in the U.K. during the time. Brass bands were a form that Deller associated with trade unions in their battle against the systematic destruction of mining and industrial production during that period, whereas acid house music was at the core of a short-lived celebratory dance culture that was subject to attack from government bills forbidding large unauthorised gatherings.

The 1980s are also revisited in Deller's 'The Battle of Orgreave'. Originally a performance, since made into a documentary by film director Mike Figgis, 'Orgreave' is arguably Deller's most well known and highly regarded work to date. It was staged in June 2001, at the site in South Yorkshire of a conflict between police and miners, seventeen years after the actual event. The use of historical reenactment societies and participants in the initial conflict, in the roles of police and miners, staged an engagement with history and opened up a space of politics, rather than the empty forms of representation that dominate politics. The strike of 1984 was never represented fairly or with any kind of balance. The documentary redresses this with a clear sense of reversing the bias, relying on emotive testimonies that describe the destruction of the mining industry and the working communities in the north of England. However, the work as a whole is a complex and substantial engagement with recent history, memory, social and economic transformation, and alternative acts of representation. A different space of conflict is evoked in 'Baghdad, 5 March 2007'. The work is composed of the remains of a car from a bomb attack in which 38 people died. It is a large ball of mangled wreckage, a readymade artwork with real power, if not the power to shock, then at least to generate reflection and discourse. Deller is not content for the object to sit quietly. It is a catalyst for discussion, for some form of action or thought. Deller took this scorched and twisted ball of metal across the United States, travelling with a U.S. soldier and an artist from Iraq, to form a living process by engaging with audiences and recording ensuing responses and conversations. Art, here, has a function. It is not instrumental, nor is it efficient or measurable. It is qualitative.

His latest high-profile work, 'Sacrilege', lacks the politically charged complexity of engagement offered by some of these projects but is still consistent with the overall territory. It is essentially a bouncy castle for children and adults in the shape of Stonehenge. A work such as this bypasses dependence on reading as an artwork at all—it is simply fun given shape as something relating to history and cultural identity. Deller's 2012 retrospective at the Hayward Gallery in London, 'Joy in People', explored the origins of this practice in recreating his bedroom from 1993, the site of his first exhibition, which signposted his interest in fan culture as a space of quotidian creativity.

226 *Dan Smith*

Visitors moved from here to a cafe serving free cups of tea, another nod to the culture of the ordinary, before having the opportunity to encounter most of the works described and many others. 'Folk Archive' was noticeably absent from this twenty-year survey. Whether this was a curatorial choice, or a pragmatic one, it was absent until the point when visitors walked through the exit, to find themselves in the shop, facing copies of the artwork's book form—*Folk Archive*—lined up on display for sale.

In an introductory essay, which starts on the front cover, Deller and Kane give a brief account of their archive as a celebration of quotidian creativity in Britain and Northern Ireland. It is also framed as an attempt to consider what constitutes present-day folk art—a kind of popular form of practice that can be opposed to the kind of corporate forms of representation once embodied within the Millennium Dome. The material gathered in *Folk Archive* is diverse. Within this collection of images and objects is a recurring emphasis on local festivals, rituals, and contests. Generally orientated around forms of performance, these annual events, often hundreds of years old, evoke the most obvious sense of 'folk' within this visual anthology: gurning, pipe smoking, traditional wrestling, burning barrels, hobby horses, a straw bear, a green man, processions, and seasonal rituals. These strangely exotic forms are somewhat hard to dissociate from the horror film *The Wicker Man* (1973)—the cinematic apotheosis of an imagined fantasy of Britain's folk imagery. However, these practices are collated here as forms that predate capitalist modernity, performed by and for those that the archive casts as 'ordinary'. Although only making up a small proportion of *Folk Archive*, these seemingly archaic practices contextualise the rest of the material as contemporary updates of traditional forms of social practice. The archive manages to hold forms of small-scale (noncorporate) commercial signage together with visual props and techniques of social protest—itself a diverse category that includes handmade banners, a Tony Blair scarecrow, and fake parking tickets designed to embarrass and criticise the drivers of four-wheel-drive cars in London. There are also varied examples of impromptu public display—such as a face scrawled on the back of a dirty van—practical jokes, garden design, Christmas decorations, personal tributes and notices in public spaces, customised cars and bikes, art by prisoners—including not only drawings and paintings but also tattoos and the bricolaged tools used to make them. The copious diversity of the archive also includes fancy dress, graffiti, websites, the Notting Hill Carnival, and a church service held for clowns in Dalston, where the clowns have their own archive of their individual face makeup recorded on eggs.

This nucleus of traditional fairs and ceremonies is evocative of notions of continuity, creative practice, and social engagement that might cut through the alienating and normative fabric of contemporary Britain. There is a direct but unrealised correlation between the activities and artefacts brought together in *Folk Archive* and a significant aspect of the categories assembled by Ernst Bloch across the three volumes of *The Principle of Hope*. As Douglas Kellner describes, *The Principle of Hope* addresses

> the presence of a yearning for something better in the form of a systematic examination of the ways that daydreams, fairy tales and myths, popular culture, literature, theatre, and all forms of art, political and social utopias, philosophy and religion—often dismissed tout court as ideology by some Marxist ideological critique—contain emancipatory moments which project visions of a better life that put in question the organisation and structure of life under capitalism (or state socialism).[2]

Linking *Folk Archive* to the possibility of such emancipatory impulses, and questions relating to the normative orders of modernity, is to begin to activate not just a sense of ethical possibility in this archive, but an explicitly political force within the work. I would like to sustain the presence of this as a latent potential that might be readable, rather than a clear set of intentionalities and deliberate principles inscribed by the authors. The emphasis in *Folk Archive* on a core set of historically absorbed manifestations of practice within British traditions corresponds to a politicized impulse lurking within much of Deller's work. To read this in its most powerful and radical form is to recognise a desire to articulate and facilitate the possibility of social and political resistance.

AESTHETIC AND DOCUMENTARY ASPECTS OF FOLK ARCHIVE AND THEIR RELATION TO THE LIBRARY

Since 2007, 'Folk Archive' has been owned by the British Council, which has chosen to represent it as a set of four virtual rooms navigable via its website. This technological gesture, which feels clumsy and inappropriate, does little to contribute to the ongoing life of 'Folk Archive'. I suggest that it is a mistake to privilege the gallery-based experience (or the British Council's quaint 'virtual' space) over the form as book. Generally, encounters with contemporary art privileges the gallery-based encounter, yet much of the actual operation of the cultural processes that constitute art are dependent on printed forms, such as exhibition catalogues, monographs, and magazines. It is through these that the fleeting encounters with temporary exhibitions are made more permanent. A book such as *Folk Archive*, therefore, should not be approached as a secondary artefact springing from the exhibition, but an object of equal status, or itself the dominant form, as it lives on beyond the temporal and spatial limitations of exhibition practice. The book form could also be argued to be the more successful manifestation of the project. As an exhibition, there is something artless and factual about the presentation of material that lacks any substantial engagement with museological history or display technologies. Similarly, there is little attendance to space, in an abstract, formal, or architectural sense, or in terms of a narrative of movement and navigation. The material is presented and is either of interest or not. The exhibitionary form presents itself as mute. The book, however, addresses photography, documentary, classification, and formal devices within the boundaries of its covers.

'Folk Archive', as an actual holding, contains many different types of material, including some objects, but is generally made up of records and mediated representations of objects. As a book, it is comprised of photographic reproductions, which can read in relation to Douglas Crimp's essay 'The Museum's Old, the Library's New Subject'.[3] In this text, he reflects on the entry of photography into the museum. Crimp likens this to the same move that generated a field of autonomy around painting and sculpture as they were removed from their earlier contexts and divorced from their prior functions: 'when they were wrested from the churches and palaces of Europe and consigned to museums [. . .] so now photography acquires its autonomy as it too enters the museum'.[4] He argues that photography, in entering the museum as a classifiable object, has shifted in status from a form of information, documentation, and evidence. This ghettoisation transforms the plural field of photography, which Crimp suggests offered a form of use within other discursive practices, into a reduced guise. This is described as a 'single, all-encompassing aesthetic'.[5] Significantly, this transformation encompasses the relationship between photography and books. Books about Egypt, Crimp tells us somewhat hysterically, 'will literally be torn apart in order that photographs by Francis Frith may be framed and placed on the walls of museums'.[6] In a tone that appears rather more measured, he reflects on another transformation:

> Whereas we may formerly have looked at Cartier-Bresson's photographs for the information they conveyed about the revolution in China or the Civil War in Spain, we will now look at them for that they tell us about the artist's style of expression.[7]

Crimp assumes that somehow the documentary content of photography is rendered invisible by the privileging of aesthetics and authorship, without thinking that such content will not only be retained but will also continue to be read. He places this historical shift in the viewing of photography as part of a more widespread redistribution of knowledge. This raises the spectre of postmodernism, framed by Crimp as a reactionary force perpetrating myths of artistic freedom.

For Crimp, the transformation of photography into an autonomous form within the museum is a symptom of modernism's demise. Photography, it is pointed out, is neither autonomous, nor is it, strictly speaking, art. The same could be said of the material brought together within *Folk Archive*. That to hold it within a framework that assumes both institutional neutrality and a universal category of art is to reproduce these decadent and reductive forms of modernism that Crimp suggests are responsible for the very demise and discrediting of modernism. It is necessary, according to this argument, to recognize an originary paradox at the core of postmodernism: 'it is photography's reevaluation as a modernist medium that signals the end of modernism. Postmodernism begins when photography comes to pervert modernism'.[8] Although this focuses on a negative understanding of postmodernism as a perversion of modernism, Crimp wishes to offer an alternative in the form of perversion as radicalised practice. This understands the changed status of photography as not just in terms of its introduction into the museum, but also in terms of an equivalence between a shifting classification within the library and the contamination of the purity of modernism's separate categories. Power and fictive autonomy are stripped away from painting and sculpture, yet Crimp fails to recognise this is precisely what is granted to photography in its own right.

Within this essay, frameworks around photography give way to the form of the book as both an organising principle and an object to be organised. Crimp offers an anecdote in which he recalls coming across a copy of Ed Ruscha's *Twentysix Gasoline Stations* (1963) when researching images of transport in the New York Public Library:

> I remember thinking how funny it was that the book had been miscatalogued and placed alongside books about automobiles, highways, and so forth. I knew, as the librarians evidently did not, that Ruscha's book was a work of art and therefore belonged in the art division. But now, because of the reconfigurations brought about by postmodernism, I've changed my mind; I now know that Ed Ruscha's books make no sense in relation to the categories of art according to which art books are catalogued in the library, and that that is part of their achievement. The fact that there is nowhere for *Twentysix Gasoline Stations* within the present system of classification is an index of the book's radicalism with respect to established modes of thought.[9]

There is a failure here to recognise that *Twentysix Gasoline Stations* is no doubt a very useful record of gas stations in the West Coast of the U.S. in the early 1960s. It belongs where Crimp found it, among the documents on transport, not because it is radical but because it can fit into more than one category. This is different from claiming that the book cannot be contained by any one category. Rather it fits into both. It serves as document of the world too. Even if the librarians had recognised the book as artwork, perhaps, understandably, they still considered the book appropriately categorised amongst other books dealing with transport. Similarly, Ruscha's images of car parks must be invaluable historical documents indicating the spaces and patterns of automobile use, despite their production within an art practice. This example offers an indication that the taxonomical determinations of photographic archives in book form are unfixed. The discussion between categories is open and mutually informative. It is within such interstitial spaces within institutional forms that a form of radicalism might be located.

It is in this space that I would argue Deller and Kane situate their material. This is the place in an imaginary library where the copy of their book sits. At the basis of such a claim is that their construction of a taxonomy makes strange the process of ordering itself. Categories appear unnatural, not fixed. In itself, this offers an active image of difference. However, although the book does demonstrate the artificiality of categories, it performs another kind of illusion of a natural set of divisions. The authors of this archive also erase any distinctions between what is collected and art objects. That the activities represented in *Folk Archive* are described as art, albeit of a popular or folk variety, seems odd. It is incongruous with even the most casual acknowledgement that art is constituted through its institutions, discourses, and histories. Problems of classification are not just dramatised by *Folk Archive*, but are also generated by it.

Many artists' books have become precious in their own right. They are held within special collections, and specialist libraries, as valuable works, displayed in glass cases alongside other forms of artworks. This is certainly the case with Rusha's early books, but Deller and Kane's book has yet to achieve this state, because it is still in print and easily available. Although published by Bookworks, specialists in the book as a form for artists to explore as works, this book is presented and treated as a supplementary catalogue, to be to be handled, read, and easily owned. Ruscha's books have long since moved from accessible and intimate objects to special artefacts to be preserved and valued. There may have been a moment before this took place, when there could have been genuine problems of classification, but these have long since passed. The book as artwork has been assimilated into the structures of art, and libraries have become reflexive enough to handle the book as the product of an artist, regardless of apparent subject matter. Ruscha, in an interview from 1989, admitted that his work was not revolutionary. Most of his practice is composed of paintings, which have been commercially successful for decades. However, for a moment, his books were radical, although they too have long since been assimilated:

> I liked the idea that my books would disorient, and it seemed to happen that people would look at them and the books would look very familiar, yet they were like a wolf in sheep's clothing. I felt they were very powerful statements, maybe the most powerful things I've done. I'm kind of considered part of the mainstream of art history now. My work is not revolutionary, but the works that I did were, at that point, a can opener that got into something else. My books were art objects to me, but a lot of people chose not to even accept them, and for this reason they have always been underground—and still are.[10]

Kevin Hatch argues that the inability for the books to fit, at least in relative terms of fitting in comfortably, is a defining characteristic of Ruscha's books—they turn up in unexpected places.[11] Hatch sees the books as challenging, not affirming, divisions, and forging new links between disparate aesthetic practices:

> In the process, they reveal the conventionality underlying the panoply of photography's various functions, from book illustration to objet d'art. In this light, it is perhaps in their guise as 'can opener,' or deconstructive tool, that Ruscha's books have their greatest purchase on our contemporary moment—a moment in which the digital masking of any and all aesthetic sutures has allowed for an unprecedented naturalization of photographic conventions (in film, in print, and online; in art galleries, multiplexes, and shopping malls).[12]

Hatch points out that the works offer a difficulty of classification in how they can be read in relation to his dominant practice, which is painting. They do not characterise the West Coast pop sensibility that has infused that work. Rather they are aligned to a different kind of practice, specifically, as Benjamin Buchloh argues, Conceptual Art.[13] Quotidian subject matter, with a relaxed and direct technical approach are evidenced in Rusha's books, whereas the very form of the book is indicative of an interest of the exploration of modes of distribution demonstrated by Conceptual Art. For Buchloh, Conceptual Art initiated a prohibition of visuality as an aesthetic rule:

> Just as the readymade had negated not only figurative representation, authenticity and authorship while introducing repetition and the series (i.e., the law of industrial production) to replace the studio aesthetic of the handcrafted original, Conceptual Art came to displace even that image of the mass-produced object and its aestheticized forms in Pop Art, replacing an aesthetics of industrial production and consumption with an aesthetic of administrative and legal organization and institutional validation.[14]

Buchloh is describing a radical gesture. When *Twentysix Gasoline Stations* was published in 1963, the book opposed all vestiges of U.S. art in the late 1950s and early 1960s.[15] This was the opening of a space into which works such as Dan Graham's 'Homes for America' started to explore by the mid-1960s. Published as a double-page spread in *Arts Magazine* in 1966, this was a photographic and text-based work focused on suburban housing. Buchloh writes that Graham's 'Homes For America' 'argued for an analysis of (visual) meaning that defined signs as both structurally constituted within the relations of language's system and grounded in the referent of social and political experience'.[16] In addition to the operations relating to language,

232 Dan Smith

signs, and the social, there is a collapsing of the spaces of arts production and reproduction, between primary and secondary information:

> Anticipating the work's actual modes of distribution and reception within its very structure of production, 'Homes for America' eliminated the difference between the artistic construct and its (photographic) reproduction, the difference between an exhibition of art objects and the photograph of its installation, the difference between the architectural space of the gallery and the space of the catalogue and art magazine.[17]

This is the once-radical space that *Folk Archive* now operates within as a normative and familiar territory. A fundamental difference between *Folk Archive* and the conceptual artists of the later 1960s is a rigorous approach to redefining interactions among author, object, and audience:

> all are concerned in the attempt to replace a traditional, hierarchical model of a privileged experience based on authorial skills and acquired competence of reception by a structural relationship of absolute equivalents that would dismantle both sides of the equation: the hieratic position of the unified artistic object just as much as the privileged position of the author.[18]

Buchlow cites Sol LeWitt, from a statement published in 1967, in which he describes the function of the serial artist as that of a clerk, cataloguing the results of a premise, not producing a mysterious or beautiful object.[19] There is no room for taste, for chance, for subjectivity.

Deller and Kane are not serial artists, but are working within conditions that arise out of these contested spaces. Yet theirs is not an objective gaze, a rejection of authorship and subjectivity. It is a reinvestment of these qualities. Hatch's reading of *Twentysix Gasoline Stations* brings us closer to the approach of Deller and Kane than Buchloh's reading of the book as protoform of Conceptual Art. Hatch argues that the arrangement of images is neither random nor 'tactically arranged data, but determined by personal association and autobiography.[20] It is, for Hatch, a smooth meshing of the anonymous and the personal. Not only this, but also 'it is the strangeness of this meshing that gives the book its theoretical charge: it is as if both are acceptable, alternate definitions of photography, like variant dictionary definitions of the same word'.[21] For Hatch, each book is specific and takes on board an element of photographic discourse. This is not due to authorial intention, but emerges across Ruscha's sixteen books from inherent conditions within photography, put into motion by the parameters of each undertaking. He says in terms of the relationship to Conceptual Art, that it is true that there is a system or set of narrow parameters in place, but this is only part of what these books were. So although it is a precedent for Conceptual Art, on one hand, a Ruscha book exceeds this: 'A Ruscha book is Conceptual art with an unruly optical unconscious'.[22] This is an unruliness which creates a sense of discomfort within simple classification schemes and which is carried by Deller and Kane far more than either the short-lived radical transformation of art or the systematic and distanced approach adopted within Conceptual Art. However, this unruliness does not account for the problem of transposing the material collected here and the illusion of transparency performed by Folk Archive.

Things are sought out and collected in Folk Archive that were intended for public display, but not in a gallery, by authors who do not consider themselves artists. But the insistence on this homogenisation of all creativity as art masks some of the problematic aspects of Folk Archive. Deller and Kane claim that they simply transpose the works from one form of public display to another, this being what they call the more traditional presentation of art in a gallery. This act of transposing is presented without any sense of how this might be problematic or even complex as a process. It seems to wilfully ignore any sense of representation as a contested discourse, and is obtuse in its negation of anthropological and ethnographic forms of investigation and debate. This is combined with a slightly disconcerting affirmation of art as something neutral and ahistorical in its constitutive definitions. There is also a subjugation of the roles of art as archival form, material holding, and documentary representation.

That the opposition between art and documentary is an artificial one was a fundamental principle underlying the exhibition 'Making History' at Tate Liverpool.[23] Rather, the two have been mutually informative for a century. Even so, Deller and Kane could still be seen as taking a somewhat leisurely approach to the representation of others. It is perhaps exploitative, both of the accepted propinquity of art and documentary and of the subjects represented. Sarah James's critique of 'Making History' made clear a failure of the show to explore what she described as 'the more difficult depths of documentary'.[24] The same could be said of Folk Archive. Although the book does contain a short interpretative essay by Jeremy Millar, this is a problem compounded, as well as illustrated, by the absence of either a sustained and reflective account of their project or any critical and reflexive formal mechanism within the display of the archive.

In contrast, Martha Rosler's photographic project 'The Bowery in Two Inadequate Descriptive Systems' (1974–75) addresses itself as a problematic form of representation through the use of two forms of signifier: text and image. It is also contextualised by Rosler's own writing around her practice. She has argued that documentary photography belongs to the New Deal sense of progressive and liberal sensitivity in the U.S., and she is critical of a justification for documentary that advocates a disengagement from a social cause.[25] Documentary cannot precede or transcend activism. A similar impulse is present in Stephen Willats's works from the early 1970s, including 'The West London Social Resource Project', collated in the book Art and Social Function.[26] He describes the book as a manual for artists wanting to intervene in the broader fabric of society. Willats positioned his projects as attempts to expand the concerns of art practice together with the social territory in which it functioned, and combined documentary tendencies with forms of sociological fieldwork. Intention, context, and audience are not only addressed by Willats but are also explicated in stifling detail.

Within Deller's own practice, complex and varied forms of social engagement are the primary concerns of the work. Perhaps this does not constitute activism, but certainly a set of intriguing and active engagements that explore documentary in relation to art and social responsibility. Rosler, however, problematises the 'every day' as a theme within documentary: the representation of the commonplace is only justifiable if adequately theorised. This is to counteract the possibility of such practices becoming purely exploitative—either ethically or commercially. Within and around *Folk Archive* is a sense of resistance to the historical and theoretical discourses that it might evoke. However, through the apparently straightforward approach adopted here, and by artificially homogenising the contents of *Folk Archive*, Deller and Kane risk aligning themselves with the wordless power of institutional authority. John Tagg argues that photography, the principle medium of *Folk Archive*, is granted its authority by its relationships with institutional spaces.[27] The power of photography is not the power of the camera, but that of the apparatuses that deploy it. As authors of an artwork displayed in public spaces, and now owned by the British Council and touring the globe, Deller and Kane are implicated in this alignment. The artists wield authority, with the legitimacy of state apparatuses, over those they represent.

Closely aligned to Tagg's positions on photography, and similarly influenced by Marx, Barthes, and Foucault, is Alan Sekula—known equally for his documentary practice, manifested in both gallery works and books and his critical writings. He argues that archives by their very structure maintain a hidden connection between knowledge and power. Archives are not neutral. Rather, they appeal to institutions of modernity for their authority and embody the power inherent in accumulation, as well as the power inherent in the command of language. An artwork in an archival and documentary form must be interrupted by criticism if it is not to reinforce the naturalisation of the cultural: 'Any discourse that appeals without scepticism to archival standards of truth might well be viewed with suspicion'.[28] That *Folk Archive* seems not to interpret, or to interrupt itself, through critical contextualisation, is perhaps what is troubling about it.

Sekula also raises the problem of a refined sensibility, the look of a sophisticated viewer constructed in relation to a preceding inferior one. Images in the archive become objects of a secondary voyeurism, which preys on, and claims superiority to, a more naïve and primary act of looking. Sekula's solution to the taint of 'intellectual and aesthetic arrogance' that might permeate an archive such as this is that it must be read from below, from a position of solidarity with those who have suffered from the machineries of progress.

This possibility of a form of solidarity, a sense of shared participation, characterises much of Deller's own practice, but is less obvious in *Folk Archive*.

CONCLUSION: THE UTOPIA OF THE LIBRARY

Characterised by a disturbing ambivalence, an enabling tension brings about a meditation on the act of recording and presenting this material. *Folk Archive* is able to operate in exteriority to a social science, social history display, or mainstream entertainment. This book also demonstrates a resistance to any easily satisfying relationship with textual, or theoretical, discourse. This is both what might be wrong with *Folk Archive* and what is most essential. Nevertheless, the challenge to relationships between theory and practice enacted here are also subject to an interpretative metaphor in the form of the library. The model of the library here is borrowed from Walter Benjamin, whose short essay 'Unpacking My Library' of 1931 reflected on the reunion with his book collection after a hiatus of two years. He describes the chaotic mess of books spilling out from open crates, not yet touched by 'the mild boredom of order'.[29] Rather, the order of the collection, held in place by the passion of the collector, is intuitive and irrational. Within this private library, the objects of the collection do not come to life in the collector. Rather, the collector lives in them, disappearing into an edifice built from the archive of books. Benjamin reveals a personal, rather than purely institutional, aspect of representation in *Folk Archive*, in which the artists inhabit the collection.

It is hard to reject outright that Deller and Kane are engaging in a troubling form of exploitative fetishism, a romantic objectification of both people and practices, or positioning a sophisticated look in relation to a crude one. Yet they have put together a form of reflection on archival holdings and documentary practices that intersects with the book and the library. The illusion of transparency is replaced by personal and idiosyncratic preference, echoing Benjamin's selfishly activated library that, nevertheless, through the accountability of the library's owner, becomes an ethical and redemptive practice. It is redemptive because the library becomes a space of active agency, resistant to the homogenising and alienating forces of capitalist modernity. It is an ethical practice in the sense that the collector must establish and maintain a relationship not just with the books but also with those who may one day encounter them: 'the most distinguished trait of a collection will always be its transmissibility'.[30] The collector assumes a responsibility that is not predetermined, which is not bound to institutional needs, 'For a collector's attitude toward his possessions stems from an owner's feeling of responsibility toward his property'.[31] Both Benjamin's library and *Folk Archive* point to the presence of forms of utopian imagination and impulse within the everydayness as an operation simultaneous with its questioning of archival construction.

A useful point of reference here is Hal Foster's essay 'An Archival Impulse', which has served as a much-needed point of focus in recent years.[32] Foster brings together Thomas Hirschhorn, Sam Durant, and Tacita Dean as artists whose work appears disparate but who 'share a notion of artistic practice as an idiosyncratic probing into particular figures, objects, and events in modern art, philosophy, and history'.[33] These practices also share a paranoiac dimension, a will to connect what cannot be connected. The combinations may be 'forced' or 'bad,' but in their perversity, these private orders disturb those of symbolic and public realms.[34] In sympathy with Foster's archival impulse, within *Folk Archive* is a destabilizing of the authoritative alignment of state apparatuses that offers a gesture towards a disturbance of the symbolic order at large. The critical intersection between the two archives under discussion here, between artwork and library, corresponds with the plaintive conclusion of Foster's 'An Archival Impulse', in which the no-place of the archive makes possible the retrieval of the no-place of utopia.

The no-place of the archive can also be read through Fredric Jameson's 'Reification and Utopia in Mass Culture'.[35] Building on a reading of Ernst Bloch, Jameson argues that despite being dependent on different social realities, and being the product of distinct social communities or castes, mass culture cannot be thought of without taking into account folk culture and the popular art of the past. More significant is the Blochian recognition of what Jameson calls the 'Utopian or transcendent functions of mass culture' which needs to be recognised in simultaneity with the ideological.[36] Ignoring this Utopian dimension results only in 'the empty denunciation of the latter's manipulatory function and degraded status'.[37] The very practical yearning that Bloch identifies as a utopian impulse must be recognised and taken into account. In short, embodied as a book—an organising device subject to the library—*Folk Archive* captures historically changing forms of tradition, inventions of resistance and protest, constructions of narratives of past, and present moments and hopeful futures—notions of continuity beyond ideological hegemony. Rather than functioning merely as an officially sanctioned promotional tool, in the manner of a conventionally determined artist in residence working with an institution such as a museum or a library, *Folk Archive* engages in a sympathetic, imaginative, and indirect form of communication rather than a pure exploitation of both holdings and subjects.

NOTES

1. The book is also contextualised by its relationship to another archival holding, the Vaughn Williams Memorial Library, housed in Cecil Sharp House in London. There is an issue shared by these institutions: that of objectification—the constitutive and manipulative representation of social alterity within the archive. Nevertheless, my interest here is in exploring relationships between photography, archives, documentary, ethics, and representation. The concept

of folk is at its most loaded in accentuating the divide between art and nonart, between specialist and amateur.
2. Douglas Kellner, 'Ernst Bloch, Utopia and Ideology Critique', in *Not Yet: Reconsidering Ernst Bloch,* ed. Jamie Owen Daniel and Tom Moylan (London and New York: Verso, 1997), p. 81.
3. Douglas Crimp, 'The Museum's Old, the Library's New Subject', in *On The Museum's Ruins* (Cambridge, MA, and London, UK: MIT Press, 1993), pp. 66–83.
4. Ibid., p. 75.
5. Ibid.
6. Ibid.
7. Ibid.
8. Ibid., p. 77.
9. Ibid., p. 78.
10. Quoted in Bernard Blistene, *Edward Ruscha:Paintings* (Rotterdam: Museum Boymans-van Beuningen, 1989), p. 134.
11. Kevin Hatch, 'Something Else: Ed Ruscha's Photographic Books', *October* 111 (Winter 2005), pp. 107–226.
12. Ibid., p. 109.
13. Benjamin Buchloh, 'Conceptual Art 1962–1969: From the Aesthetics of Administration to the Critique of Institutions', *October* 55 (Winter 1990), pp. 105–43.
14. Ibid., p. 119.
15. Buchlow keeps this context very much North American, not considering any possible precedents or correlations that may have been active elsewhere: the Bechers, Boetti, On Kawara, Social realism, and British examples of the relation between art and documentary do not feature at all. Likewise, Soviet precedents, German precedents, and Surrealism are all largely absent. Broadly speaking, he misses a far more politicised and interesting role for the book, rather wanting to create a micro myth of origins and, of course, a privileging of art, despite a rhetoric of a leveling out of media, processes and technology.
16. Buchlow, 'Conceptual Art', p. 124.
17. Ibid.
18. Ibid., p. 140
19. Ibid.
20. Hatch, 'Something Else', p. 110
21. Ibid.
22. Ibid., p. 124
23. 'Making History: Art and Documentary in Britain from 1929 to Now', Tate Liverpool, 3 February to 24 April 2006.
24. Sarah James, 'Documenting Documentary', *Art Monthly* 295 (April 2006), p. 3.
25. See Martha Rosler, *Decoys and Disruptions, Selected Writings 1975–2001* (Cambridge, MA, and London, UK: MIT Press, 2004).
26. Stephen Willats, *Art and Social Function* (London: Ellipsis, 2000).
27. John Tagg, 'A Means of Surveillance: The Photograph as Evidence in Law', in *The Burden of Representation: Essays on Photographies and Histories* (Amherst: University of Massachusetts Press, 1998), pp. 66–102.
28. Allan Sekula, 'Reading an Archive: Photography Between Labour and Capital', in *The Photography Reader*, ed. Liz Wells (London: Routledge, 2003), p. 447.
29. Walter Benjamin, 'Unpacking My Library', in *Illuminations* (London: Fontana, 1973), p. 59.
30. Ibid., p. 66.

31. Ibid.
32. Hal Foster, 'An Archival Impulse', *October* 110 (Fall 2004), pp. 3–22. This article has served as the point of departure for numerous conference panels and symposia, for example, Tate Britain's 'The Archival Impulse' event in November 2007 and a session at the 2008 Association of Art Historians' Conference.
33. Ibid., p. 3.
34. Ibid., p. 21.
35. Fredric Jameson, 'Reification and Utopia in Mass Culture', *Social Text* 1 (Winter 1979), pp. 130–48.
36. Ibid., p. 144.
37. Ibid., p. 145.

BIBLIOGRAPHY

Walter Benjamin. 'Unpacking My Library', in *Illuminations*. London: Fontana, 1973.
Bernard Blistene. *Edward Ruscha: Paintings*. Rotterdam: Museum Boymans-van Beuningen, 1989.
Benjamin Buchloh. 'Conceptual Art 1962–1969: From the Aesthetics of Administration to the Critique of Institutions'. *October* 55 (Winter 1990).
Douglas Crimp, 'The Museum's Old, the Library's New Subject', in *On The Museum's Ruins*. Cambridge, MA, and London, UK: MIT Press, 1993.
Hal Foster. 'An Archival Impulse'. *October* 110 (Fall 2004).
Kevin Hatch. 'Something Else: Ed Ruscha's Photographic Books'. *October* 111 (Winter 2005).
Sarah James. 'Documenting Documentary'. *Art Monthly* 295 (April 2006).
Fredric Jameson. 'Reification and Utopia in Mass Culture'. *Social Text* 1 (Winter 1979).
Douglas Kellner. 'Ernst Bloch, Utopia and Ideology Critique', in *Not Yet: Reconsidering Ernst Bloch*, edited by Jamie Owen Daniel and Tom Moylan. London and New York: Verso, 1997.
Martha Rosler. *Decoys and Disruptions, Selected Writings 1975–2001*. Cambridge, MA, and London, UK: MIT Press, 2004.
Allan Sekula. 'Reading an Archive: Photography between Labour and Capital', in *The Photography Reader*, edited by Liz Wells. London: Routledge, 2003.
John Tagg. 'A Means of Surveillance: The Photograph as Evidence in Law', in *The Burden of Representation: Essays on Photographies and Histories*. Amherst: University of Massachusetts Press, 1998.
Stephen Willats. *Art and Social Function*. London: Ellipsis, 2000.

13 The Archive and the Library in V. Y. Mudimbe's *The Rift*

Wendy W. Walters

INTRODUCTION

Postcolonial literature often enters into the colonial library in order to question the archive housed there. What is this archive? In *The Imperial Archive: Knowledge and the Fantasy of Empire*, Thomas Richards refers to a 'paper empire' of data collected by the British Museum, the Royal Geographical Society, the India Survey, and British universities. Richards suggests that the archive in Victorian England 'was not a building, nor even a collection of texts, but the collectively imagined junction of all that was known or knowable, a fantastic representation of an epistemological master pattern, a virtual focal point for the heterogeneous local knowledge of metropolis and empire'.[1] Richards here describes the archive in a Foucauldian way, because by the term *archive*, Foucault '[does] not mean the sum of all the texts that a culture kept upon its person as documents attesting to its own past or as evidence of a continuing identity'. Rather, Foucault reads the archive as the 'first the law of what can be said, the system that governs the appearance of statements as unique events'.[2] Richards's study identifies the specific archival technologies of power that the British Empire deployed in relation to its colonies. In questioning this archive, many black international writers attempt to deconstruct these technologies of power. Indeed, the work of V. Y. Mudimbe, as a novelist and a philosopher, is marked by just such a questioning of the archive. Explaining its power, he writes, in *The Idea of Africa*, that 'To comprehend the archaeological organization of this very idea of Africa and its resonances, it seems to me, it is impossible not to consider Western literature and, particularly, its culmination in the "colonial library"'.[3] In placing the 'colonial library' in quotes, Mudimbe refers beyond a singular, physical space, beyond one building, and out towards a more general archive governing the epistemological bases of various disciplines producing knowledge about Africa.

Mudimbe's geographical biography traces a path from colonial Zaire, France, Belgium, to the U.S. He has described himself as 'an international person, in fact [. . .] a nomad'.[4] Mudimbe is the author of at least fourteen book-length theoretical treatises (spanning the linguistic, philosophical, and sociological genres), three novels, three books of poetry, and many other coauthored and edited volumes as well. As Bennetta Jules-Rosette states, 'Mudimbe is a product of several cultural environments and speaks in different registers and a concatenation of discourses, while sustaining a consistent critique of the limitations of classical anthropology'.[5] Mudimbe's novel, *The Rift* (1993), published originally in French as *L'Ecart* (1979), represents the diary of Ahmed Nara, a postcolonial, Paris-educated African doctoral student living between multiple worlds. Situated geographically between an unnamed African country and France, he also exists between relationships with women and men, Africans and Europeans. Perhaps his most important liminal location is his own agonized subjectivity, because it is represented in his diary entries that counterpose his academic work in reconstructing the history of an ancient African people, the Kuba. Mudimbe's novel signals the performative, constructed nature of both the historiographic project and the writing of a life, as the reader shuttles between Nara's fragmented thought processes. *The Rift* is an important piece of Mudimbe's intellectual oeuvre because it raises critical questions about the nature of an archive and frames a postcolonial critique of the imperial archive. The novel also links archival research and psychoanalysis. In its attention to the concept of the archive, Mudimbe's novel draws on the work of Foucault; indeed, as Manthia Diawara's 1990 article title indicates, much of Mudimbe's intellectual work can be seen as 'reading Africa through Foucault'.[6] Scholarship on *The Rift* typically addresses the questions Mudimbe raises about the discourses of anthropology, the creation of an African gnosis, and the position of European-educated postcolonial African intellectuals. This chapter continues these questions, foregrounding Mudimbe's critique of the imperial archive and demonstrating the centrality of the concept of archive in Mudimbe's work, partly by reading the fictional Nara's diary about his own work in a specific library.

NARA'S DIARY

To briefly summarize the novel, an anonymous publisher introduces the text of (recently deceased) Ahmed Nara's diary, as given to him by Salim, the archivist employed in the African library where Nara frequently worked (or, rather, suffered writer's block): Nara's intellectual production is characterized by inaction, fits, starts, and silence. When his diary entries commence, he has been working on his dissertation for ten years, suffering also from an acute work stoppage during which he was away from the library for nine months, a significant period in that his absence gave birth to nothing. Thus, an existential angst is a central aspect of Nara's character, and Nara, the diarist, frequently quotes French existential philosopher Emile Cioran. Nara's writer's block can be linked to the concept of *blocage*, which Mudimbe describes in his theoretical volume *L'odeur du père* (*The Smell* of the Father). Jules-Rosette summarizes Mudimbe's position in L'odeur: 'the African intellectual criticized by Mudimbe is trapped in a self-imposed and self-regulated prison. Escape necessitates throwing off the "smell of the father" (colonial cultural patrimony), as well as a rupture with foreign customs, received knowledge, and social complacency. According to Mudimbe, anthropology as a discipline finds itself similarly imprisoned and subject to *blocage*'.[7] My reading of *The Rift* proposes that Mudimbe is critical of Nara, showing his method to be stuck in a place which Mudimbe's own scholarship avoided, and this will become clearer as I further discuss parallels between Nara's scholarly process and Mudimbe's. William Slaymaker states that 'Like [Kwame Anthony] Appiah, Mudimbe is seeking some way to transcend the contradictions of his own position between colonized subject and librarian of the master narratives—the Western ones that are a part of his own archives'.[8] Both Mudimbe's own critical work and scholarship about his work speak in metonymic terms about libraries and archives. *The Rift* adds to this complication in that Nara works inside a specific library, yet is also paralyzed by what Mudimbe has referred to as a more general 'colonial library', meaning the history of European discourse about Africa.

However, because the narrator who introduces Nara's diary is asked by Nara's friend, Salim, the archivist, to discover its truth, the reading of the diary repeatedly throws the very concept of truth into question, portraying the pursuit of historical truth as a doomed and perhaps mad enterprise. The diary form itself, a genre on which historical reconstruction often relies, is here depicted as performance of psychological imbalance, the paper space between madness and sanity. We know that a diary is both a reflection of an interior mental state, and is often part of the substance of an archive, as researchers pore over the pages of diaries to find out some 'truths' about history. Mudimbe's novel then gives us a young historian, working in the library to gain access to historical truth, even as he is simultaneously recording his own diaristic archive, which we are reading (potentially as researchers). Thus, Mudimbe throws our own reading into question.

Cathy Davidson reminds us that 'poststructuralist critics have long since deconstructed the methods of historical reconstruction by asking Foucauldian questions about the reliability, inclusiveness and generalizability of any archive and by showing how the most intimate writing of a diary can be a narrative performance'.[9] Indeed, much of Mudimbe's theoretical work, especially *The Invention of Africa*, is also a Foucauldian critique of anthropological discourses about Africa, and he has stated in an interview that *The Rift* is his attempt to make the theoretical issues of *The Invention of Africa* 'more transparent'.[10] Throughout *The Rift*, Ahmed Nara alternately mocks, revises, is captured by, and wars against an archive of Africanist discourse written by Europeans with which his own work is in dialogue. Mudimbe uses the diary form as our way to know Ahmed Nara specifically for the purpose of calling attention to textuality, and the narrative representation of history as it exists in archives and libraries. Quite pointedly, Mudimbe's protagonist's last name is itself the acronym for the National Archives and Records Administration in the U.S., and this archive is most frequently referred to as NARA. Yet Nara, the specific character, resists the specificity of the physical library in which he works, paralyzed by the more universal archive of colonial scholarship which precedes his own work. His notebooks state, 'In the courtyard I came upon a broom, a bucket, an old abandoned crate. On a board you could still read BIBLIOTHÈQUE NAT [. . .] I knew very well that I should finish the word off, refused to, though I'd already done so at the beginning. Finish off would surely mean an address or a body. But to what end?'[11] Indeed, *The Rift* never fully finishes the phrase 'Bibliothèque Nationale de France', also known as the BNF, the French National Library located in Paris. Mudimbe shifts the proper name of his fictional library only slightly, so that this library bears the trace of empire, but is here in all caps and refers to the library in Mudimbe's fictional African city of Krishville.

The fictional publisher of Nara's diary tells us that he titles the diary 'The Rift' in order to 'bring together [. . .] Ahmed Naras questioning and the uncanny split in his being'.[12] Perhaps what is suggested here is that publishing, or the act of diaristic writing itself, is a way of constructing a seamless identity. But the text we read in no way accomplishes such a unified construction. Davidson's suggestion that diary writing is a narrative performance implicates both the reader *and* the narrator as potential audiences. The narrator/publisher tells us that Nara's diary was marked as if he planned to revise it (an act ultimately aborted by his unexplained death). Following Davidson, we can identify at least three Ahmed Naras in Mudimbe's text: Nara the author of the diary, Nara the character in the diary, and Nara the implied future reader of the diary. Mudimbe's use of this split and multiple positioning inherent in the diary form sheds light on the multiplicity Nara experiences as a European-educated African doctoral student writing a historical thesis on an African people, the Kuba. Also, Mudimbe here posits diary writing as a mirror for anthropological writing as well as for the psychoanalytic process: all discursive practices concerned with constructing a narrative of (a) life.[13] The publisher within the novel questions Nara's purpose in writing the diary:

> the only thing that is certain is that he was not planning to surrender his notes as they stood. Indeed, there are throughout his notebooks very specific notations, such as *to think about . . ., to be developed . . . to be remembered,* clearly indicating that the author was thinking of rewriting his journal one day [. . .] What this amounts to, then, is that the book published by me is not what the author would have published.[14]

Thus, not only are we reminded to question the reliability of the diary form as a portraiture or a mirror of reality, but so too does the text lead us to question the truth claim of any historical archive. In his reading of this novel, Diawara states that 'clearly what Nara is doing at the *Bibliothèque Nationale* is appropriating the archives and constructing his own regime of truth'.[15] Certainly this seems to be Nara's goal.

The text of Nara's diary, in fact, self-consciously makes connections between the acts of ordering, classifying, and categorizing which support the construction of academic historical discourse, and the acts of writing which support a diaristic performance of self. In his diary, Nara records, 'Soon it will be ten in the evening . . . I am caught in these memories, am going in circles. As I was leaving my hotel this morning, I thought I could catch up on the time I've lost . . . .Work on putting my card file in order [. . .] The utter boredom of the daily ritual [. . .] What to do? At least noting down these few dead-end alleys where my helplessness leads me gives me something to do, and it consoles me that I am still able to name some of my longings'.[16] Here the act of writing itself, alongside the acts of categorizing (card files), is highlighted as sense-making. Mudimbe's novel focuses on science and self, raising questions not only about the assumed objectivity of historical research but importantly about the very concept of intellectual production in relation to the body also. The text teases the traditional mind/body split. Tormented by a 'self' ever in danger of splitting, Nara seeks refuge in a scientific method he assumes can be free of himself. Yet his very corporeality is implicated in the materiality of his work:

> I took my index cards from my briefcase. I looked at the hand-writing; it's small and I hate it [. . .] What to do? Where to pick up the dialogue again with these notes that open a whole universe of contradictions for me? [. . .] It was important for me to find a rhythm again, to prescribe a specific movement for myself: reread, correct, see what merited revision and completion. Then, establish a daily work schedule and specific criteria for the interpretation of the data.[17]

Nara's diary reveals the complicated ways he uses his academic research as an attempt to lose himself and the simultaneous fact of his ever-presence in this process. The following diary entry shows both the fantasized absence of a willed self and the physical sensuality which Mudimbe's text invites us to consider as a fantasy of scholarship:

> Worked very well today. From the moment the library opened, I delved into the reconstruction of the historical relationship between the Lele and the Kuba. My notes were multiplying. Veritable caresses. Excitement. For hours on end I was under the clear impression that I was inside a fire. It felt gentle to me. A body that gave me nourishment. Its strength was flowing through me. My communion with it was profound. Ideas came to me, my hand took control of them, and they wrote themselves, as it were, on my index cards.[18]

Thus, when his work is progressing, Nara's pleasure is physical and sensual; his own body an intimate extension of his work itself. Helen Freshwater's article 'The Allure of the Archive' cites an 1827 letter by German historian Leopold von Ranke referring quite similarly to a morning's work in an Italian archive: 'Yesterday I had a sweet, magnificent fling with the object of my love, a beautiful Italian, and I hope that we produce a beautiful Roman-German prodigy. I rose at noon, completely exhausted'.[19] Perhaps Nara too is seduced 'the allure of the archive', and perhaps by what Foucault refers to as the 'fantasia of the library'. Foucault describes 'the visionary experience [that] arises from the black and white surface of printed signs, from the closed and dusty volume that opens with a flight of forgotten words; fantasies are carefully deployed in the hushed library, with its columns of books, with its titles aligned on shelves to form a tight enclosure, but within confines that also liberate impossible worlds'.[20]

AFRICAN HISTORY AND THE ARCHIVE

Part of the reason for Nara's writer's block, however, for the fact that most of the time his work does not progress, is his intellectual understanding not only of the colonizing nature of anthropological discourse written by Europeans but also of his own discursive practices as well. He writes in a previous entry:

> I would like to start from scratch, reconstruct the universe of these peoples from start to finish: decolonize the knowledge already gathered about them, bring to light new, more believable genealogies, and be able to advance an interpretation that pays more careful attention to their environment and their true history. Often I find myself to be surprisingly hesitant. At such moments I feel like making fun of this unyielding ambition to make new inroads.[21]

Aware of the potentially colonizing power of anthropological writing as it 'makes new inroads,' Nara implicitly questions his own perhaps ambivalent cultural positioning as insider or outsider. According to Mudimbe in *L'odeur du pere*,

> The African [who would write a new ethnology] must assume his/her freedom as a subject and speak to be heard. This insurrection against the Western ethnocentrism enables him/her to push sciences forward, to 're-analyze for our benefit the contingent supports and the areas of enunciation; to know what new meaning and what road to propose to our quest so that our discourse can justify us as singular beings engaged in a history that is itself special'.[22]

Nara's scholarly motivation is driven by his (correct) conviction that much previous scholarship on Africa, especially European-authored Africanist discourse, is biased, inherently incomplete, nonspecific, and so on. Here Mudimbe's novel echoes his work in *The Invention of Africa* in presenting a critique of the Euro-centred knowledge systems which structure the foundational discourses of anthropology.

Nara's diary describes his ordering process, the categorization of index cards which is a part of his scholarly work. In the *Invention of Africa*, Mudimbe states, 'Colonialism and colonization basically mean organization, arrangement. The two words derive from the latin [*sic*] word, *colere*, meaning to cultivate or design [. . .] the colonists (those settling a region), as well as the colonialists (those exploiting a territory by dominating a local majority) have all tended to organize and transform non-european [*sic*] areas into fundamentally European constructs'.[23] Mudimbe uses the diary form in order to raise questions about the process of ordering and classification, to expose what he sees as the discursive violence at the base of this classifying project. Mudimbe's position in *L'autre face du royaume* is that 'the theoretical 'violence' of scientific colonialism [. . .] rests on an attempt to describe idyllic conditions of existence prior to colonization, while destroying those very conditions in the name of progress and civilization'.[24] In *Culture and Truth*, Renato Rosaldo calls this mode of inquiry 'Imperialist Nostalgia'.[25]

Let us turn for a moment to another theoretical text by Mudimbe, *Parables and Fables: Exegesis, Textuality and Politics in Central Africa*. In this text, Mudimbe studies the Luba genesis charter, as well as earlier anthropological treatises on the Luba people. (The diarist in *The Rift*, Ahmed Nara, is studying the Kuba people.) In the introduction to *Parables and Fables*, Mudimbe reinvokes a question he asked in *L'odeur du pere*: 'How does one think about and comment upon alterity without essentializing its features? Second, in African contexts, can one speak and write about a tradition or its contemporary practice without taking into account the authority of the colonial library that has invented African identities?'[26] Here Mudimbe uses the phrase 'the authority of the colonial library' as a synonym for what Richards alternatively calls 'the imperial archive'.[27] Mudimbe's fictional character, Nara, is trapped then, within both the specific library of the *Bibliothèque Nationale* and within this larger archive of discourse about 'African identities'. In *Parables and Fables*, however, Mudimbe proposes a method to avoid essentializing, stating the need to '[face] local speeches and texts by themselves as simple contingencies [. . .] and to read them without necessarily confronting them as true or false historical documents'.[28] Mudimbe rejects the truth claims made by scientific paradigms such as classical anthropology and locates all texts, including the Luba genesis charter, at the level of evolving discourse, rejecting an originary object to which anyone could propose to have recourse. Of the charter he states, 'I propose to consider this memory-text as a theoretical discourse which validates a human geography, its spatial configuration, and the competing traditions of its various inhabitants, simultaneously cementing them via this retelling of the genesis of the 'nation' in its social organization'.[29] Mudimbe's fictional character, Nara, has not yet seen his way through to a liberating scholarship.

Working in the library, Nara mocks 'the level of seriousness of Western scholars experienced in African matters' to his friend Salim, making a joking game of quoting passages by European scholars, about African societies, substituting Spanish for the Lele and Portuguese for the Kuba.[30] Nara knows his task must be to throw off this false patrimony of scholarly predecessors: 'Look, Salim, that is what my mentors say! About Africa. The game I'm presenting is most edifying [. . .] Now let them tell me that history is a rigorous discipline'.[31] In *The Rift*, Mudimbe opens up the term *archive* through Nara's critique of his own mentors. The following quote from his journal is important:

> Virgin Africa, without archives recognized by their scholarship, is an ideal terrain for all illicit trade. The discipline I was used to, thanks to their own standards, gave me the right to demand something other than pretty embellishments concerning the civilizations of the oral tradition. A vile qualification! As if there were a single culture in existence not supported surreptitiously by the spoken word! As if the concept of archives should coincide at all times with the specific expressions brought up to date by the short history of Europe.[32]

The original French of this passage refers to a singular *concept d'archive*, indicating the novel's Foucauldian critique, not of the physical space of a singular archive but rather to a system of statements. Claiming he would like to be 'un historien nègre', Nara here argues for including oral cultures within the concept of archive. But he is also faced with the difficulty of how to record, study, and analyze the Kuba culture outside of the methodologies of European anthropology.

The novel asks whether there is a way out of this discursive trap. Jules-Rosette states that Mudimbe's own anthropological narrative process 'shifts the source of cultural attribution from the European ethnologist to the indigenous producers of African knowledge systems. When this shift in the configuration of power and knowledge has been accomplished, empirical studies are possible. As long as the epistemological base of classical anthropology remains unchallenged, however, empirical studies are merely external chronicles of cultural otherness and applied exercises in hegemonic domination'.[33] Through its inscriptions of Ahmed Nara's doubts, however, *The Rift* questions the postcolonial complications in this shift from European ethnologist to indigenous producer of African knowledge systems. Where would European-educated Ahmed Nara be in such a shift? Perhaps Nara's own psychological torment reflects his unstable positioning as a postcolonial intellectual both inside and outside Western discourse. In his academic work, he attempts to respect and represent the local knowledge of Kuba culture, basing his work on oral histories he recorded during thirty-five months he spent with two Kuba people. Working in the library in Krishville, he consults his own records of 'the oral tradition' of Kuba history, describing this material as 'an unfamiliar library with whose organization of treasures I'm not at all sure I am perfectly familiar'.[34] The experience of the Kuba has here entered into a new form and space, marked down now as writing on Nara's notecards in the library. With some comparability, Paul Ricoeur warns that '[a] vigilant epistemology will guard [. . .] against the illusion of believing that what we call a fact coincides with what really happened, or with the living memory of eyewitnesses, as if the facts lay sleeping in the documents until the historians extracted them'.[35]

In what way can Nara represent the histories of the Kuba? At the end of *Parables and Fables*, Mudimbe answers this question:

> An interpretation of the relation between a lived and an oral or written narrative witnessing to it can only be a reduction to a theoretical synthetic unit. It signifies both a simplification of the complexity of the dynamics of the lived in the real place and jumps from the rules of the place to those of an intellectual space in which observed facts and behaviors are submitted to a context of theory and the logic of a scientific discourse and its procedures.[36]

Nara records his own conundrum in the pages of his diary: 'Once again I found the path of silence and sympathy. The contact with a tradition and the practice of its rigors had to subject me to its norms so that my words could represent them faithfully'.[37] Because there is no way for the researcher to absent his or her subjectivity, to 'speak silently', Nara's body and intellect are implicated in what he would like to see as a 'faithfully' nonsubjective process. Nara is so angst-ridden because he is fully aware of this circularity. He writes, 'From eight in the morning until six in the evening I worked without interruption, prey to a veritable rage: to reconstruct the course of the Kuba as best and as quickly as possible. Is it an attempt to create a world? Or, more simply, am I possessed?'[38] Nara's question to himself, recorded in his diary, reminds us that historiography is world making, as perhaps so too is diary inscription. What is so compelling about this novel, is that Mudimbe precisely places his reader in this same position, as we are faced with the mediated text of Nara's diary—can we somehow see past the publisher/introducer's own organization of it? Can we ever have direct access to a subject called Nara, or narrator, who presents himself to us in so many levels of mediation? For whom does Nara create the Kuba world? For whom does he narrate his own trajectory? In fact, Nara admits to his aptly named psychoanalyst, Dr. Sano, that perhaps he is using the Kuba miracle to save himself from Isabelle and 'all the lies'.[39]

PSYCHOANALYSIS AND PERSONAL HISTORY

The Rift presents readers with not only Nara's educational history but his sexual history as well. Isabelle is a white European woman with whom Nara has a relationship while studying in Paris. In Nara's diaristic recollections of their discussions (keeping in mind the unreliable nature of Nara as narrator), Isabelle exists as a parallel to European anthropologists, seeing him as an incarnation of Africa, her refuge. Nara makes the equation in his diary: 'This blonde, always with the same old story [. . .] To use Africa as a refuge is amusing. Obviously she could bring me hundreds of scholarly works to substantiate doing so . . . Entire libraries . . . Africa dancing . . . The Africa of emotions, of desire'.[40] According to Nara, Isabelle's desire determines his subjectivity as a beast and reduces his identity to a phallus.[41] In Isabelle, we read echoes of Fanon's analysis of European attitudes toward 'the Negro' when he states in *Black Skin, White Masks* that 'The Negro symbolizes the biological'. Fanon adds that within certain French literary discourses 'the Negro is eclipsed. He is turned into a penis. He is a penis'.[42]

Isabelle's alter ego is Aminata (and both their names, like most of the names in the novel, may be read as homonyms), an African woman, a single mother of two boys who works in the library in Krishville and who takes Nara under her wing, so to speak, in a relationship marked by ambiguity, but which appears primarily maternal and platonic. In his diary, Nara describes Aminata's solicitous concern for him as both his refuge and his cage. His fragmented diary entries alternately recall conversations and interactions with both women, who seem to represent for Nara, Europe and Africa, which for him exist in a binary relationship. This binary structure also characterizes the way he perceives his education and upbringing. Early in his diary Nara describes a typical experience of the violence of colonial education: 'first of all there was language, French . . . A disarray into which I had to inscribe my anguish . . . The sun everywhere, the putrid alleys of my neighborhood, the distorted mirrors of the stories told around the fire in the evenings became forbidden roads from one year to the next [. . .] I was to become the son of a newly acquired knowledge'.[43] As we often see in postcolonial literature, Nara here records the ways that the patrimony of colonial education separates the child from the natal/oral culture, replacing this familial education with the initial alienation of both writing and European language. Indeed, in a closely following passage, Nara recounts a dream of black-and-white images, reinforcing the binary opposition he feels between Europe and Africa and symbolizing his burying of his father in acquiring 'Europeanness' as equivalent to burying his own natal 'self'. 'I moved forward to the grave . . . It was already half-filled with earth and snow . . . All in black, her body rigid, her eyes hard and dry, my mother looked at me: "Come on, quickly, throw your bit of soil and disappear . . ." Should I listen to her? Right away I understood that I was going to disappear underneath a mound of earth'.[44] Nara sees the acquisition of a European education as responsible for the death of his indigenous self, witnessed, perhaps foretold, by his mother. Perhaps Nara's angst is caused by his own binaristic perceptions of cultural identities which are in fact more complex and multiple.

Importantly, however, the text also posits Nara's mother, or by extension, mother culture, as responsible for the repression of his gay identity. Sexual identity is a topic in *The Rift* that is relatively silenced in the small corpus of critical work on this novel. Scholars do address sexuality in Mudimbe's work, though not often in explicit terms, and not regarding this novel. In '*Le bel immonde*: African Literature at the Crossing', Kenneth Harrow argues that the 'stratum that undergirds' all of Mudimbe's novels is 'the place of love'. Harrow reads *Le bel immonde* as 'a modern myth of love in a world that refuses it'.[45] Although Harrow's article does not explicitly mention a reading which would allow for homosexuality in any of Mudimbe's novels, he does reduce *Le bel immonde* to 'only one essential question—not how one can combat injustice, but how one can be free to love'.[46] Mudimbe himself says that Belle, the prostitute in *Le bel immonde*, is a lesbian.[47] In 'The Archaeology of Invention: Mudimbe and Postcolonialism', B. Jewsiewicki briefly refers to the role of sexuality in Mudimbe's fiction: '*Le bel immonde* already foreshadowed this investigation of the being who looks at herself/himself and lives his or her life more deeply than the social form of her or his identity. Mudimbe chose to illustrate this with the borderline case of sexual identity'.[48]

In *The Rift*, Nara recounts a formative nightmarish childhood moment to Dr. Sano when his mother mistakenly punished him (his older brother being at fault) by locking him in the tool closet, forgetting him for an entire day, which seemed like a night. Adding to the horror of his misplaced punishment, there was a rat inside the closet. When she did retrieve her son, his mother, in tears, apologized, telling him that she has just learned his father is dead. In his therapy sessions with Dr. Sano, Nara recalls these experiences as explanation for his fear of rats, the night, and women. Another way to read this childhood experience is that Nara's mother effectively put him 'in the closet' in a homophobic silencing of a potential gay identity. Very late in his diary, he recalls, 'It was my mother. A very long time ago, something to do with a whim, long lost in the past. "You can't always have it your way in life, Nara . . .". I never forgot that . . . That's why I'm here, busy reconstructing my life'.[49] This passage naming his mother's role in repressing his sexuality comes just after he has recorded a version of his life history as told to Aminata one night in a bar, in internal mental response to her invitation, '"Tell me about yourself"'. In response, he thinks, 'A blow . . . a feeling . . . A past . . . hideous . . . The turmoil of a miserable childhood . . . A brainwashing they call education . . . Some vague studying of history . . . A diploma . . . The anus open to the explosion of haphazard lovers . . . And then getting to like men'.[50] The violence of Nara's maturation is thus doubled; although he describes his European education as a brainwashing away from his natal culture, it is also his mother and the culture she represents which put him in the closet, forcing him to repress his potential desires.

Perhaps homosexuality functions in this text as 'the sign of a prior violence, the violence of boundarylessness, or cultural eclipse'.[51] In his study of masculinity and abjection in Puerto Rican literature Arnaldo Cruz-Malave cites recent analyses of Fanon's *Black Skin, White Masks* which show that 'much despite the vigilance with which Fanon turns to his own body in order to unveil the masks of his complicity with the structures that oppress him [...] his efforts to transcend the binary relations of expiation are also built on the expulsion of the other—of the homosexual'.[52] Perhaps we can read the mother's closeting of Nara as part of the maintenance of a cultural boundary which must place homosexuality on the outside. In 'Interior Colonies: Frantz Fanon and the Politics of Identification', Diana Fuss also asks important questions about the culturally specific labels we ascribe to sexual behaviors: 'Is it really possible to speak of "homosexuality", or for that matter "heterosexuality" or "bisexuality", as universal, global formations? Can one generalize from the particular forms sexuality takes under Western capitalism to sexuality *as such?* What kinds of colonizations do such discursive translations perform on "other" traditions of sexual differences?' [53] Is sexual identity buried like a secret not only in the dialogue of Nara's psychoanalysis but also in the diary he is attempting to write?

Toward the end of this passage where Nara recounts his life history, Aminata and Isabelle merge in Nara's diary. Perhaps we may also read Dr. Sano as Nara's alter ego, a 'sane' or rational part of himself attempting to mollify his fears and obsessions. In conversation with the psychoanalyst, he says, 'So, tell me why you're hiding, Dr. Sano... There behind me'.[54] Thus, several important characters actually are potentially their own doubles. Mudimbe's text moves toward this multiplicity as Nara at one point explains: 'The difference, Isabelle, the difference is that Europe is, before anything else, an idea, a legal institution . . . while Africa . . . Africa is perhaps primarily a body, a multiple existence'.[55] In 'The Postcolonial and the Postmodern,' Kwame Anthony Appiah reads this passage as indicative of 'the essential ambiguity of the postcolonial African intellectual's relation to Africa'.[56] Here I want to try to be more specific, if possible, about the ambiguity Appiah names. In saying that Africa is both a body and a multiple existence, Nara brings together the splits which have hitherto seemed to characterize his conceptualizations. On one hand, influenced by his relationship with Isabelle, he contrasts Africa as body to Europe as mind. But in seeing Africa also as a multiple existence, perhaps Nara incorporates the disparate parts of his identity as postcolonial African intellectual: gay/straight, local knowledge/ European archive, writing/orality, Paris/Krishville, and madness/sanity. These are the binaries which have long characterized Eurocentric discourses

The Archive and the Library in V. Y. Mudimbe's The Rift 251

about sexuality, identity, and culture, and Nara represents a scholar whose own life exceeds these boundaries, yet whose thinking is in many ways trapped and defined by them. Appiah cites Mudimbe's later novel *Entre les eaux* (*Between Tides*) as providing a way out of the manicheism in which Nara is trapped: '*Entre les eaux* provides a powerful postcolonial critique of this binarism: we can read it as arguing that if you postulate an either-or choice between Africa and the West, there is no place for you in the real world of politics, and your home must be the otherworldly, the monastic retreat'.[57]

DEATH AND THE ARCHIVE

In *The Rift*, Mudimbe opens up questions about the nature of several archives. One relationship between subject and archive is achieved via Dr. Sano, for is not the psychoanalytic process an attempt to enter into dialogue with the archive of one's unconscious past? Sven Spieker notes that 'there may be an archive implicit in Freud's theory of the unconscious and the way it stores traces of the past'.[58] As a patient, Nara is attempting to reorder and 'make sense of' the events of his past (his being locked in the closet, the death of his father, his French education, a gay sexuality) in order to create a narrative of himself. Mudimbe has said that all archives are violence. Does Nara die at the end of the novel because of the ultimate violence to the self which his own archiving represents? At the very end of his diary, Nara recalls a conversation with Dr. Sano in which he tells the psychoanalyst, 'The text of life is black. No matter what written text proves that. Erase the black and you will understand that letters kill. The night is a letter. Like the Negro. Tell me which fault of his it is that can explain his degradation [. . .] I can also write with my blood. One little cut, a pen, and a white sheet of paper is all it takes'.[59] Fanon describes his own imprisonment by the gaze of 'the white man': 'I took myself far off from my own presence, far indeed, and made myself an object. What else could it be for me but an amputation, an excision, a hemorrhage [*sic*] that spattered my whole body with black blood?'[60] The literal gaze recorded by Fanon echoes the violence represented by the imperial archive of European anthropological gazes on Africa. A few pages later, Nara mentally addresses Aminata: 'You belong to the first line of a paragraph [. . .] Tomorrow, can I still offer you the letter of my body'. And two pages later, 'Just erase me'.[61] This desire for erasure perhaps chimes with Derrida's link between 'archive fever' and the death drive: as he wrote, 'there is no archive fever without the threat of this death drive, this aggression and destruction drive'.[62]

Nara's diary ends with an ellipsis, and his unexplained death. Perhaps we can turn again to Fanon to help us solve the mystery of Nara's death: 'In the white world the man of color encounters difficulties in the development of his bodily schema. Consciousness of the body is solely a negating activity. It is a third-person consciousness'.⁶³ Nara's end may ultimately be the result of his inability to avoid participating in a discourse which negates himself. Christopher Miller's *Blank Darkness* recounts the multiple ways in which French discourse on Africa presents Africa as null: 'European discourse projects an object onto the unknown, an object of impossible nullity'.⁶⁴ Unlike his creator, Mudimbe, Ahmed Nara is trapped by the binarism in which he was trained. Yet, in 'The Human Sciences', Foucault sees psychoanalysis and ethnology as '"counter-sciences"[,] which does not mean that they are less "rational" or "objective" than the others, but that they flow in the opposite direction, that they lead them back to their epistemological basis, and that they ceaselessly "unmake" that very man who is creating and re-creating his positivity in the human sciences'.⁶⁵ Likewise, Jules-Rosette has said that the 'hybrid legacy' of Mudimbe's own genealogy—'African, European and classical in every sense of the term— allows Mudimbe to stand at the crossroads as an interpreter of his local culture and hidden history, as they are remembered and transformed into a universal knowledge system'.⁶⁶ Indeed, she argues that in *Parables and Fables*, Mudimbe effectively transforms Luba cosmology 'from a series of exotic folktales [. . .] into a universal mythos and the basis for a new African practice of anthropology'.⁶⁷

It seems clear that Mudimbe succeeds where Nara fails. Mudimbe's own prolific compilation of multiple discursive inroads succeeds not only in creating a new archive but also works between and amongst multiple archives, teasing out the discourses of their very formation. Whereas Nara is paralyzed by his own recording of Kuba traditions, Mudimbe's *Parables and Fables* presents a method whereby 'we can read and comment about the passions present in transcribed oral traditions, written texts, and performances in African or European languages and, indeed, reconstruct, or deconstruct the history, arguments, and paradigms of the anthropological and colonial libraries'.⁶⁸ Mudimbe's novel not only critiques the authority of the colonial library but also places both his narrator and his reader within the specific library spaces frequented by historical researchers, spaces whose character are indicated by the unfinished signpost of the 'BIBLIOTHEQUE NAT . . .' and the seven unfinished notebooks of Ahmed Nara.

NOTES

1. Thomas Richards, *The Imperial Archive: Knowledge and the Fantasy of Empire* (London: Verso, 1993), p. 11.
2. Michel Foucault, *The Archaeology of Knowledge and the Discourse on Language* (New York: Pantheon, 1972), pp. 128–29.
3. V. Y. Mudimbe, *The Idea of Africa* (Bloomington: Indiana University Press, 1994), p. 213.
4. Guarav Desai, 'V.Y. Mudimbe: A Portrait', *Callaloo* 14, no. 4 (1991), p. 933.

5. Bennetta Jules-Rosette, 'Speaking about Hidden Times: The Anthropology of V.Y. Mudimbe', *Callaloo* 14, no. 4 (1991), p. 954. A special issue of the African diasporic journal *Callaloo,* volume 14, issue 1 (1991), focuses on the varied oeuvre of Mudimbe.
6. Manthia Diawara, 'Reading Africa through Foucault: V. Y. Mudimbe's Reaffirmation of the Subject', *October* 55 (1990), pp. 79–92.
7. Jules-Rosette, 'Speaking about Hidden Times', p. 948.
8. William Slaymaker, 'Agents and Actors in African Antifoundational Aesthetics: Theory and Narrative in Appiah and Mudimbe', *Research in African Literatures* 27, no. 1 (1996), p. 124. Neil Lazarus reads *The Rift* as an 'inversion of the strategy through which colonialist discourse had tended to represent Africa', such that 'the notorious excess of signification' in Conrad 'becomes in Mudimbe's novel a self-conscious inarticulacy, emblematic of an equally unfulfillable desire *not* to taxonomise a presence'. See Neil Lazarus, 'Representation and Terror in V.Y. Mudimbe', *Journal of African Cultural Studies* 17, no. 1 (2005), p. 93.
9. Cathy Davidson, 'Critical Fictions', *PMLA* 111, no. 5 (1996), p. 1070.
10. Faith Smith, 'A Conversation with V.Y. Mudimbe', *Callaloo* 14, no. 4 (1991), p. 983.
11. V. Y. Mudimbe, *The Rift*, trans. Margolin de Jager (Minneapolis: University of Minnesota Press, 1993), p. 11.
12. Ibid., p. 4.
13. In *The Rift*, Nara is described as a historian, writing a history of the Kuba people, reconstructing 'the historical relationship between the Lele and the Kuba' (p. 43). Thus, his work may be seen as ethnology, and he identifies his academic precursors as ethnologists (in this regard, see V. Y. Mudimbe, *L'écart* [Paris: Presence Africaine, 1979], p. 26).
14. Mudimbe, *The Rift,* p. 3.
15. Diawara, 'Reading Africa through Foucault', p. 91.
16. Mudimbe, *The Rift,* pp. 12–13.
17. Ibid., p. 10.
18. Ibid., p. 43.
19. Helen Freshwater, 'The Allure of the Archive', *Poetics Today* 24, no. 4 (Winter 2003), p. 734n10. Ranke's comments are also cited by Bonnie Smith, who notes that Ranke's letter goes on to refer to another archival collection as 'absolutely a virgin. I long for the moment when I have access to her'. See Bonnie G. Smith, *The Gender of History: Men, Women, and Historical Practice* (Cambridge, MA: Harvard University Press, 1998), p. 119.
20. Michel Foucault, 'Fantasia of the Library', in *Language, Counter-Memory, Practice: Selected Essays and Interviews*, ed. and trans. Donald F. Bouchard (Ithaca, NY: Cornell University Press, 1977), p. 90.
21. Mudimbe, *The Rift,* p. 13.
22. Cited in Manthia Diawara, 'The Other('s) Archivist', *Diacritics* 18, no. 1 (1988), p. 73.
23. V. Y. Mudimbe, *The Invention of Africa: Gnosis, Philosophy and the Order of Knowledge* (Bloomington: Indiana University Press, 1988), p. 1.
24. Jules-Rosette, 'Speaking about Hidden Times', p. 947.
25. See Renato Rosaldo, *Culture and Truth: The Remaking of Social Analysis* (Boston: Beacon Press, 1989).
26. V. Y. Mudimbe, *Parables and Fables: Exegesis, Textuality, and Politics in Central Africa* (Madison: University of Wisconsin Press, 1991), p. xi.
27. Richards, *The Imperial Archive*.
28. Mudimbe, *Parables and Fables*, p. xi.
29. Ibid., p. 89.

30. Mudimbe, *The Rift*, p. 44.
31. Ibid., p. 45.
32. Ibid., p. 46.
33. Jules-Rosette, 'Speaking about Hidden Times', p. 956.
34. Mudimbe, *The Rift*, p. 86.
35. Paul Ricoeur, *Memory, History, Forgetting*, trans. Kathleen Blamey and David Pellauer (Chicago: University of Chicago Press, 2004), p. 178.
36. Mudimbe, *Parables and Fables*, p. 192.
37. Mudimbe, *The Rift*, p. 14.
38. Ibid., p. 113.
39. Ibid., p. 116.
40. Ibid., p. 84.
41. Ibid., p. 19.
42. Frantz Fanon, *Black Skin, White Masks*, trans. Constance Markmann (New York: Grove, 1967), pp. 167, 170.
43. Mudimbe, *The Rift*, p. 17.
44. Ibid, p. 17.
45. Kenneth Harrow, '*Le bel immonde*: African Literature at the Crossing', *Callaloo* 14, no. 4 (1991), p. 990.
46. Harrow, '*Le bel immonde*', p. 991.
47. Smith, 'A Conversation with V.Y. Mudimbe', p. 977.
48. B. Jewsiewicki, 'The Archaeology of Invention: Mudimbe and Postcolonialism', *Callaloo* 14, no. 4 (1991), p. 964.
49. Mudimbe, *The Rift*, p. 120.
50. Ibid., p. 119.
51. R. Reid-Pharr, 'Tearing the Goat's Flesh: Homosexuality, Abjection, and the Production of a Late-Twentieth-Century Black Masculinity', in *Novel Gazing: Queer Readings in Fiction*, ed. Eve Sedgwick (Durham, NC: Duke University Press, 1997), p. 354.
52. Arnold Cruz-Malave, '"What a Tangled Web!": Masculinity, Abjection, and the Foundations of Puerto Rican Literature in the United States', *Differences: A Journal of Feminist Cultural Studies* 8, no. 1 (1996), p. 138.
53. Diana Fuss, 'Interior Colonies: Frantz Fanon and the Politics of Identification', *Diacritics* 24, no. 2–3 (1994), p. 33.
54. Mudimbe, *The Rift*, p. 122.
55. Ibid., p. 88.
56. Kwame Anthony Appiah, *In My Father's House: Africa in the Philosophy of Culture* (New York: Oxford University Press, 1992), p. 153.
57. Appiah, *In My Father's House*, p. 155.
58. Sven Spieker, 'Freud's Files', in *The Big Archive: Art from Bureaucracy* (Cambridge, MA: MIT Press, 2008), p. 36.
59. Mudimbe, *The Rift*, p. 121.
60. Fanon, *Black Skin, White Masks*, p. 112.
61. Mudimbe, *The Rift*, pp. 123, 125.
62. Jacques Derrida, 'Archive Fever: A Freudian Impression', *Diacritics* 25, no. 2 (1995), p. 19.
63. Mudimbe, *The Rift*, p. 110.
64. Christopher Miller, *Blank Darkness: Africanist Discourse in French* (Chicago: University of Chicago Press, 1986), p. 27.
65. Michel Foucault, *The Order of Things: An Archaeology of the Human Sciences* (New York: Vintage, 1994), p. 379.
66. Jules-Rosette, 'Speaking about Hidden Times', p. 956.
67. Ibid., pp. 956–57.
68. Mudimbe, *Parables and Fables*, p. 193.

BIBLIOGRAPHY

Kwame Anthony Appiah. *In My Father's House: Africa in the Philosophy of Culture.* New York: Oxford University Press, 1992.
Arnold Cruz-Malave. '"What a Tangled Web!": Masculinity, Abjection, and the Foundations of Puerto Rican Literature in the United States'. *Differences: A Journal of Feminist Cultural Studies* 8, no. 1 (1996).
Cathy Davidson. 'Critical Fictions'. *PMLA* 111, no. 5 (1996).
Jacques Derrida. 'Archive Fever: A Freudian Impression'. *Diacritics* 25, no. 2 (1995).
Guarav Desai. 'V.Y. Mudimbe: A Portrait'. *Callaloo* 14, no. 4 (1991).
Manthia Diawara. 'The Other('s) Archivist'. *Diacritics* 18, no. 1 (1988).
Manthia Diawara. 'Reading Africa through Foucault: V.Y. Mudimbe's Reaffirmation of the Subject'. *October* 55 (1990).
Frantz Fanon. *Black Skin, White Masks*, translated by Constance Markmann. New York: Grove, 1967.
Helen Freshwater. 'The Allure of the Archive'. *Poetics Today* 24, no. 4 (Winter 2003).
Michel Foucault. *The Archaeology of Knowledge and the Discourse on Language.* New York: Pantheon, 1972.
Michel Foucault, 'Fantasia of the Library', in *Language, Counter-Memory, Practice: Selected Essays and Interviews*, edited and translated by Donald F. Bouchard. Ithaca, NY: Cornell University Press, 1977.
Michel Foucault. *The Order of Things: An Archaeology of the Human Sciences.* New York: Vintage, 1994.
Diana Fuss. 'Interior Colonies: Frantz Fanon and the Politics of Identification'. *Diacritics* 24, no. 2–3 (1994).
Kenneth Harrow. '*Le bel immonde*: African Literature at the Crossing'. *Callaloo* 14, no. 4 (1991).
B. Jewsiewicki. 'The Archaeology of Invention: Mudimbe and Postcolonialism'. *Callaloo* 14, no. 4 (1991).
Bennetta Jules-Rosette. 'Speaking about Hidden Times: The Anthropology of V.Y. Mudimbe'. *Callaloo* 14, no. 4 (1991).
Neil Lazarus. 'Representation and Terror in V.Y. Mudimbe'. *Journal of African Cultural Studies* 17, no. 1 (2005).
Christopher Miller. *Blank Darkness: Africanist Discourse in French.* Chicago: University of Chicago Press, 1986.
V.Y. Mudimbe. *The Idea of Africa.* Bloomington: Indiana University Press, 1994.
V.Y. Mudimbe. *The Invention of Africa: Gnosis, Philosophy and the Order of Knowledge.* Bloomington: Indiana University Press, 1988.
V.Y. Mudimbe. *L'écart.* Paris, Presence Africaine, 1979.
V.Y. Mudimbe, *Parables and Fables: Exegesis, Textuality, and Politics in Central Africa.* Madison: University of Wisconsin Press, 1991.
V.Y. Mudimbe. *The Rift,* translated by Margolin de Jager. Minneapolis: University of Minnesota Press, 1993.
R. Reid-Pharr. 'Tearing the Goat's Flesh: Homosexuality, Abjection, and the Production of a Late-Twentieth-Century Black Masculinity', in *Novel Gazing: Queer Readings in Fiction*, edited by Eve Sedgwick. Durham, NC: Duke University Press, 1997.
Thomas Richards. *The Imperial Archive: Knowledge and the Fantasy of Empire.* London: Verso, 1993.
Paul Ricoeur. *Memory, History, Forgetting,* translated by Kathleen Blamey and David Pellauer. Chicago: University of Chicago Press, 2004.
Renato Rosaldo. *Culture and Truth: The Remaking of Social Analysis.* Boston: Beacon Press, 1989.

William Slaymaker. 'Agents and Actors in African Antifoundational Aesthetics: Theory and Narrative in Appiah and Mudimbe'. *Research in African Literatures* 27, no. 1 (1996).
Bonnie G. Smith. *The Gender of History: Men, Women, and Historical Practice.* Cambridge, MA: Harvard University Press, 1998.
Faith Smith. 'A Conversation with V.Y. Mudimbe', *Callaloo* 14, no. 4 (1991).
Sven Spieker. 'Freud's Files', in *The Big Archive: Art from Bureaucracy,* Cambridge, MA: MIT Press, 2008.

14 Digital Libraries and Fantasies of Totality

Andrew White

INTRODUCTION

The massive increase in the processing power of computers over the last decade or so and the development of new digital storage forms, such as cloud computing, may seem to offer an almost unlimited capacity for the archiving and dissemination of academic texts. Hence, the realisation of the long-held dream of a universal library, albeit in digital form, does not seem entirely implausible. One corporation that is determined to make this happen is Google. Like the great national legal deposit libraries, Google's mission is to 'organise the world's information and make it universally accessible and useful'.[1]

In its effort to achieve this goal, it has established agreements with many of the world's leading educational and research libraries to digitise their books.[2] Many commentators have discussed the purely technical, legal, and economic aspects of these projects, highlighting some of the factors that could potentially retard or even derail them.[3] But, interesting though they are, it is not my intention here to look at these particular issues. Indeed, what is fascinating is the extent to which the universal library project endures despite such formidable obstacles. That the most zealous advocates of the universal library are unmoved when presented with evidence that challenges their vision is a story in itself; what I want to argue is that this disposition is best explained as a type of utopianism. In this context, this chapter begins by looking at the genesis of the idea of the universal library, and then investigates the rise of utopian literature and its relationship to knowledge, particularly from the nineteenth century onwards. Although this provides intellectual ballast for the universal library, the early-nineteenth-century romantic movement inspired—and still inspires—a rich literature that is of a more critical nature. A survey of both types of literature will be helpful in providing us with a clearer understanding of the universal library in its proposed digital form.

THE UNIVERSAL LIBRARY

The universal library as a concept is around two millennia old: the Ptolemaic project to gather as many manuscripts as possible at the library at Alexandria in the first century AD being commonly considered the first attempt to put this idea into practice.[4] The eventual destruction of the Alexandrian library did not quench this thirst for totality:

> It underlay the constitution of great princely, ecclesiastical, and private 'libraries'; it justified a tenacious search for rare books, lost editions, and texts that had disappeared; it commanded architectural projects to construct edifices capable of welcoming the world's memory.[5]

But what thwarted the realisation of this dream, from the Middle Ages onwards, was the print revolution, which disgorged so many different titles and editions that it was difficult to find any institution large enough to house them all.[6] Despite this, valiant attempts have been made in the form of national libraries. In the U.K. and Ireland, for instance, all publications should be deposited in the six legal deposit libraries that cover both jurisdictions. Such is the proliferation of publications that it is impossible to keep all this material at one site: visitors to the British Library will often discover that the items which they have requested will take two days to arrive at their desk from an offsite location in Boston Spa, Yorkshire.

Perhaps in recognition of this attenuation of universalism in practice, corporations such as Google, Yahoo!, and MSN have been involved in initiatives to digitise the holdings of many of the world's major research libraries. In continuing the long-held desire for universality or totality, the champions of the universal digital libraries invest their faith in new media technologies. One of the most vociferous of these champions is online magazine *Wired*'s self-styled 'senior maverick' Kevin Kelly. For him, however, the digital library is not merely a means of delivering what was in the past quantitatively impossible but offers a qualitatively transformative experience too:

> Search engines are transforming our culture because they harness the power of relationships, which is all links really are. There are about 100 billion Web pages, and each page holds, on average, 10 links. That's a trillion electrified connections coursing through the Web. This tangle of relationships is precisely what gives the Web its immense force. The static world of book knowledge is about to be transformed by the same elevation of relationships, as each page in a book discovers other pages and other books. Once text is digital, books seep out of their bindings and weave themselves together. The collective intelligence of a library allows us to see things we can't see in a single, isolated book.[7]

These ideas cannot be summarily dismissed as the whimsical reflections of a maverick journalist, because, for example, Google itself subscribes too much of Kelly's futurism:

[Google] seek[s] to develop 'the *perfect* search engine', which it defines as something that 'understands *exactly* what you mean and gives you back *exactly* what you want'. [. . .] In a 2004 interview with *Newsweek*, Brin [Sergey] said: 'Certainly if you had all the world's information directly attached to your brain, or an artificial brain that was smarter than your brain, you'd be better off'.[8]

This type of thinking is often derided as technological determinism. However, I am not convinced that this is what it constitutes. After all, whether we agree with it or not, technological determinism sometimes offers a valid explanation of certain phenomena, for example, arguing that the invention of the nuclear bomb has utterly altered international relations is eminently plausible. Whatever one thinks of this argument, it at least has some empirical validity. Conversely, Kelly's argument and Google's ambitions are more speculative: the notion that the web constitutes a form of collective intelligence does not appear to have any basis in science. Rather, as Fred Turner has skilfully explicated, Kelly's views grow out of 1960s Californian counterculture's search for universal harmony.[9] Originally, this condition was sought through the use of experiments in LSD and the arts. But by the 1980s, a technological component of this dream had also eclipsed the other elements. Such was the power of the myth that it effectively sidelined politics too. Therefore, the pursuit of universal harmony became merely a technical exercise in which the key to its realisation was the discovery of the most appropriate form of technology: in Kelly's case, the personal computer. Others, too, such as the head of MIT's MediaLab, Nicholas Negroponte, wrote visions of the future in which a politically frictionless and resource abundant society would emerge from digital technology.[10]

It is often argued that these visions were inspired by cyberpunk fictions such as William Gibson's *Neuromancer*, famous for its invention of the word *cyberspace*. But much of this fiction does not share the optimism of the digital visionaries. For Gibson, cyberspace is a relatively dark and dismal place in which his disembodied characters face a grim struggle for survival.[11] Gibson's understanding of computer technology was rudimentary to say the least:

> It wasn't until I could finally afford a computer of my own that I found that there's a drive mechanism inside this little thing that spins around. I'd been expecting an exotic crystalline thing, a cyber-space deck or something, and what I got was a little piece of Victorian engine that made noises like a scratchy old record player. That noise took away some of the mystique for me; it made computers less *sexy*. My ignorance had allowed me to romanticize them.[12]

In this, Gibson locates himself within the mainstream of technological dystopias ranging from the writings of Aldous Huxley to Philip K. Dick. But this does not mean that notions of perfect societies based on digital technologies have no literary antecedents. What is argued here is that, despite its thoroughly modern vision—some would even argue that it is postmodern—the ideas on which it is based are of a much earlier vintage. The idea of universal harmony is clearly utopian and therefore can be placed within that genre. The specific association of technology and utopianism began with Francis Bacon's *New Atlantis*, published in 1627, but it was not until the late nineteenth century that a spate of technology-centred utopias propelled this conjunction into the mainstream of utopian writing. But this association often obscures a much more foundational element of these utopias, the idea that the perfect society can only be delivered by the application of perfect knowledge. For sure, this perfect knowledge is often to be developed by technical means—in the late nineteenth century with the use of manufacturing technologies and scientific technique, in the early twenty-first century by digital technology—but that is a reflection of the tendency of humankind to invest faith in transient technologies to deliver seemingly timeless goals.[13] In contemporary Western society, digital technology is the supposedly omnicompetent technology that can deliver the timeless goal of perfect knowledge, the prerequisite for a perfect society. In order to understand this mind-set, it would be useful to briefly survey utopian literature, an exercise to which I now turn.

UTOPIAN LITERATURE AND THE SEARCH FOR PERFECT KNOWLEDGE

Published in 1517, Thomas More's *Utopia* (literally 'no place') has spawned many imitators.[14] The book is in two parts, the second part of which features an acquaintance of the narrator named Hythloday who describes his visit to an island called Utopia. What was remarkable about More's text was the extent to which it prefigured debates about penal reform and the common ownership of property that were to become all too familiar centuries later.[15] This prescience is indicative of the capacity of the most impressive utopian fiction to offer a vision of the future which, although ridiculed contemporarily, contains significant elements which reach fruition over time. Although technology did not really feature in More's *Utopia* (it is not even clear how this society came into being), it established what would eventually become common elements of most literary utopias.

For Fredric Jameson, the most significant aspect of More's *Utopia* is its location on an island separated by a moat from the mainland.[16] This has an epistemic rather than solely aesthetic or descriptive function:

> the properly Utopian program or realization will involve a commitment to closure (and thereby to totality): was it not Roland Barthes who observed, of Sade's Utopianism, that 'here as elsewhere it is closure which enables the existence of system, which is to say, of the imagination?'[17]

Here, Jameson is suggesting that totality cannot be attained without closure. In this sense, utopia is an enclave cut off from the rest of society. The perfect society that exists inside the enclave is characteristically eternal and unchanging, and devoid of politics; Jameson uses the example of the law court is just such an enclave.[18] Within this enclave, in place of politics, lies a simple belief that all social and political ills can be dealt with in composite fashion; that is to say that there is a single solution for all society's problems; the trick is to discover that solution and employ the best means of delivering it. And, of course, once that solution is found all political debate will end. But there is an epistemological problem here, in that totality can only be achieved *within* the enclave, suggesting that utopia cannot be universal. This paradox in relation to the limitations of the universal library is explored in more detail later.

In terms of digital utopianism, as significant as the emphasis on technology is the centrality of knowledge. The discovery of ancient Greek and Latin texts during the fifteenth-century Renaissance led to an upsurge in utopian writing.[19] The most likely reason for this is the notion that these texts contained some long lost wisdom which could help contemporary humankind. In short, the acquisition of knowledge and the application of reason were reckoned to be the crucial elements of the single solution to all social ills. The figure whose incorporation of these elements into his work made him one of the most influential utopians was philosopher and former Lord Chancellor of England Francis Bacon.

Bacon's significance derives from his location at the nexus of scientific, philosophical, and utopian thought. Bacon is probably best known for his pioneering work on experimental philosophy, introducing the concept of 'induction' (the notion that scientific theory should be based on the observation of particular experiments or data); with the deductive method, the theory or hypothesis *precedes* the particular observation. Although Bacon's legacy is open to debate, his influence on the Royal Society of London, established in 1662 and includes pioneering scientists such as Robert Boyle and Robert Hooke, is not.[20] As David Hand has pointed out, Bacon's experimental philosophy is based on the collection of large amounts of accurate data.[21] Thus, we can discern an explicit link between scientific method and the desire to accumulate a totality of information. In common with later digital visionaries who champion a form of collective intelligence, Bacon rejected the Renaissance concept of individual genius, advocating a more collaborative method of inquiry[22]:

> Two other practical inventions, printing and navigation, had contributed to the possibility for a cooperative research effort by producing an 'openness of the world' and disclosing 'multitudes of experiments, and a mass of natural history' (vol. 3, 476; cf. Book One, aphorisms 84 and 110). Bacon argued that to make the best use of this situation, the 'great storehouse of facts should be accumulated' and added that

because 'the materials on which the intellect has to work are so widely spread, one must employ factors and merchants to go everywhere in search of them and bring them in' (vol. 4, 251–52).[23]

The supposition that Bacon intended this type of 'storehouse' to be a universal library does not appear to be in doubt:

> Once gathered, this experience had to be compiled into organized national histories, that could be printed and distributed throughout the learned world and thus could foster communication and the free exchange of ideas and information. As early as his advice to Elizabeth I in the 1590s, he had been urging the establishment of institutions that would advance this goal, such as *'a most perfect and general library,' containing all 'books of worth' whether ancient or modern, printed or manuscript, European or of other parts'; a botanical and zoological garden for the collection of all plants as well as rare beasts and birds; a museum collection of all things that had been produced 'by exquisite art or engine'; and a laboratory 'furnished with mills, instruments, furnaces and vessels* (vol. 8., 334–35).[24]

This combination of universality and systematicity is similar to Diderot's eighteenth-century alphabetic *encyclopedie*; indeed, Warman argues that Diderot's project was very much inspired by Bacon's ideas about knowledge.[25] Bacon's contribution to utopian literature, *New Atlantis*, is replete with these themes too. However, in the preceding passage, the universal library can only be attained if it is supplemented by objects from other institutions, such as museums and laboratories. Like Jameson's identification of traditional utopianism with the enclave, this illustrates the epistemological problem with the concept of the universal library.

Although Bacon's expositions on the relationship among knowledge, science, and power resonate even today, there was a religiosity to his work which, without acknowledgement, we cannot really gain a full appreciation of the complexity of his thought. Perhaps one of the reasons that this is underplayed in contemporary commentary on Bacon's work is because of the modern tendency, best exemplified by Darwinist scientist Richard Dawkins, to view science as a replacement for religious beliefs and magic. Conversely, many academics have demonstrated the occult origins of modern science.[26] This means not only that scientists of Bacon's vintage saw no incompatibility between their religious beliefs and science but that they were also more often than not inspired by visions that were magical or religious in origin. And what of Bacon himself? Well, Bacon's thought has often been linked to the Puritanism that reached its apotheosis in England during the Civil War in the mid-seventeenth century.[27] A related idea is that humankind had perfect knowledge before the Fall of Adam and that it should be possible to return to that state through the proper application of a knowledge-based science.[28] These ideas all appear in Bacon's *New Atlantis*, with its references to Adam and Solomon and its emphasis on the Christianity of the utopian scientific community on which his narrator stumbles. Significantly, central to the maintenance and development of the island are the twelve Merchants of Light who, disguised, travel to other lands to gather as much knowledge as possible.[29] The word *light*, a metonym for knowledge, is a crucial element of the story.[30]

Two other important utopias were written around the same time, both of which shared the basic architecture of *New Atlantis* and in that sense instrumental in shaping the utopian genre. Andreae's *Christianopolis*, published in 1619, was another attempt to establish a perfect community that married scientific thought with religion and magic.[31] Like other thinkers at this time, Andreae reconciled his religious belief with his science by arguing that God was the designer of nature, and it was with the aid of science that we would properly understand that nature and hence God's work:

> The inhabitants [of Christianopolis] believe that the Supreme Architect of the Universe did not make his mighty mechanism haphazard but completed it most wisely by measures, numbers, proportions, and added to it the element of time, distinguished by a wonderful harmony.[32]

The emphasis here on mechanism and numbers is a reflection of the moves in science at that time towards the notion that all nature, including humankind, was literally run like clockwork and, hence, was measurable in the numeric sense. It could even be argued that today's digital utopians are similar in their valorisation of binary data.

Shortly afterwards, in 1623, Comenius's *Labyrinth of the World* appeared. The author's views can be inferred from his *Way of Light* written in 1641, in which he advocates 'universal' books as a means of attaining universal wisdom.[33] Similarly, his 1623 work lays out a labyrinthine architectural memory system in which the streets are essentially an encyclopaedia of sciences, learning, and occupation. But what is interesting is the way in which this intricately ordered intellectual system is a failure:

> Such a city ought to be at the same time a Utopia, an ideal city, a blueprint for a reformed world of the future. But Comenius is in reaction against the delusive hopes of preceding years; his city as a labyrinth reverses Utopia, because in this labyrinth everything is wrong. All the sciences of man lead to nothing, all his occupations are futile, all his knowledge is unsound. The book represents the state of mind of a thoughtful and idealistic person after the beginning of the Thirty Years War.[34]

Although Yates's pinpointing Comenius's disillusionment with a Europe on the verge of conflagration seems a plausible explanation of his critique of his own utopian design, the question remains: Why write something that undermines much of the then prevailing philosophical consensus (including, presumably, his own)? Could it stem from recognition of the epistemological problem of the concept of universality already identified in this chapter? Whatever the answer, Comenius's self-doubt is an early and, at the time, rare admission that universal knowledge does not inevitably lead to universal harmony.

NINETEENTH-CENTURY UTOPIAN LITERATURE

The nineteenth century, particularly towards it end, was a fertile time for utopian writing. Although the importance of technology to utopias was, as we have seen, already well established, the industrialisation of Western Europe and North America cemented its position at the centrality of this genre. This changed the nature of utopias: advances in technology have made it impossible to achieve closure, an intrinsic part of Jameson's notion of the enclave. This, then, might enable us to overcome the intellectual contradiction of a 'bounded' universality; rather than disappearing, the enclave became in the nineteenth century boundless, or universal:

> A certain amount of claustrophobia enters this argument when it is realized, as it is from about 1850 on, that technology tends to unify the whole world. The conception of an *isolated* utopia like that of More or Plato or Bacon gradually evaporates in the face of this fact. Out of this situation comes two kinds of utopian romance: the straight utopia, which visualizes a world-state assumed to be ideal, or at least ideal in comparison with what we have, and the utopian satire or parody, which presents the same kind of social goal in terms of slavery, tyranny or anarchy.[35]

Highly accurate cartography and western circumnavigation of the globe undermined the spatial utopia; the notion that there were long-lost worlds yet to be discovered not only stretched credulity but had also been rendered less exotic by the new technologies. For this reason, the genre gradually shifted its register from the spatial to the temporal. As humankind conquered place, its inability to master time became ever more acute. Now, rather than finding a previously hidden location by accident, it was increasingly common for protagonists in utopian novels to find themselves being transported through time, Edward Bellamy's *Looking Backwards 2000–1887* and H. G. Wells's *The Time Machine* being two famous examples.

Set free from its spatial constraints, the utopian novel became totalising in tenor. Its projection into the future gave its writers more room for invention as their blueprints could not easily be contradicted. This was mirrored by developments in history, from philosophers such as Vico, Condorcet, Fourier, Marx, and Comte, who offered teleological accounts of human life—the notion that humankind would progress to a desired endpoint sometime in the future when all political complexities would be ironed out.[36] But this does not mean that the thread that ran from Francis Bacon's *New Atlantis* was necessarily broken. Although it could be said that Bacon's approach was not strictly teleological—after all, he wanted in a sense to go backwards, to return to a world that existed before the Fall—many of the earlier utopias were millenarian in character: Andreae and Comenius, for example, believed that universal enlightenment would presage the end of the world, essentially the Second Coming of Jesus Christ.[37] In order to emphasise the importance of technology many of the late-nineteenth- and early-twentieth-century utopias satirised those who did not fully grasp the usefulness of technology. In H. G. Wells's *A Modern Utopia*, the chapter titled 'The Voice of Nature' features an appropriately blond-haired straw man whose simplistic arguments against science are obviously intended to demonstrate the ineluctable logical of the vision that the author offers.[38]

THE ROMANTIC TURN

But there was another strand of nineteenth-century thought which challenged both the idea of history as a grand narrative and the notion that scientific and technological development could lead to a state of perfect knowledge. The seeds of this understanding in romanticism were sown in Germany by philosophers such as Immanuel Kant, who sought to establish humankind's detachment from nature. Yet the concept of a universal solution applicable to all times and all places was undermined by Herder's insistence that cultures were individually unique.[39] Romanticists rejected the systemic and totalising character of Western philosophy in favour of pluralism and an emphasis on the will of the individual. German romantic plays and novels depicted, even celebrated, the unstable nature of human life. This had a considerable impact on the modernist novel generally and utopias specifically:

> Whatever the political theorists may have taught, the imaginative literature of the nineteenth century, and ours too, which expresses the moral outlook, conscious and unconscious, of the age, has (despite the apocalyptic moments of Dostoevsky or Walt Whitman) remained singularly unaffected by Utopian dreams. There is no vision of final perfection in Tolstoy, or Turgenev, in Balzac or Flaubert or Baudelaire or Carducci. Manzoni is perhaps the last major writer who lives in the afterglow of a Christian-liberal, optimistic eschatology. The German romantic school, and those it influenced, directly and indirectly, Schopenhauer, Nietzsche, Wagner, Ibsen, Joyce, Kafka, Becket, the existentialists, whatever fantasies of their own they may have generated, do not cling to the myth of an ideal world.[40]

Some of these writers presented the epistemological obstacles to the dream of a knowledge-based utopia. Following Comenius in his questioning of the axiom that greater knowledge and the application of reason of necessity leads to universal harmony, Flaubert, Dostoevsky and Sartre wrote elaborate satires on the futile search for perfect knowledge. Flaubert's *Bouvard and Pécuchet* satirises the hapless attempts by two friends to use their experimental knowledge to take up a number of different occupations. The failure of all these ventures lead them to pursue knowledge for its own sake, in which, in a parody of the accumulation of books and documents that the construction of the universal library involves, they are reduced to the fanatical copying of everything they can get their hands on. In an introduction to the book, Mark Polizzotti encapsulates the early modernist view that the pursuit of perfect knowledge not only was unattainable but could conceivably be dangerous as well:

> To the majority who clung to the belief that science and industry were all to the good, Flaubert countered with the absurd sight of his two characters chasing after a hunk of knowledge, swallowing it whole, and having nothing to show for it but indigestion. But more than this, he unearthed a darker truth of scientific progress, one as yet largely unsuspected, and in our century all too familiar: that experimental dispassion so easily shades into depraved indifference. Through nineteenth-century eyes, the novel's most horrific moment is no doubt when the child Victor boils his pet cat just to see what will happen, a scene that still elicits a revulsion only partly tempered by the boy's youth and background. But the years have added their own patina to the story: for if the image of Bouvard and Pécuchet similarly experimenting on their patients, human and animal, with little regard for their well-being, once suggested a portrait of laughable ineptitude, what it now can't help calling to mind is the ghoulish profile of a Josef Mengele, a Harold Shipman, or the 'torture doctor' H.H. Holmes. From a perceived lack of method, our science has been proven to have far too much method, especially when turned against us.[41]

In tandem with this view is Flaubert's assertion that there was no perfect state of humankind before the Fall, Bouvard citing the existence of volcanoes and wild beasts as evidence of evil at that time.[42] In Jean-Paul Sartre's *Nausea*, the fanatical accumulation of knowledge is also ridiculed through its pursuit by the Autodidact, an odd character whose increased learning does not lead to greater understanding. In particular, he cannot comprehend aesthetic pleasure. He cannot appreciate painting, music and dancing, but does 'possess a certain amount of knowledge':

> Well, believe it or not, I have seen some young people who didn't know half as much as I do, and who, standing in front of a painting, seemed

to be experiencing pleasure. [. . .] What upsets me is not so much being deprived of a certain type of pleasure, it's rather than a whole branch of human activity should be foreign to me [. . .] yet I am a man and it is *men* that have made those pictures.⁴³

To emphasise the potential damage that the pursuit of knowledge at the expense of all other realms of human activity can cause, Sartre conjures an ignominious and hugely symbolic violent ejection of the Autodidact from the library.⁴⁴
One of the more explicit rejections of the world as a harmonious whole that can be restored to its pre-Fall state is Dostoevsky's *The Dream of a Ridiculous Man*.⁴⁵ The short story's main character resiles from committing suicide after an encounter with a terrified young girl shouting for her mother. The dream that follows is of a perfect society which eventually is defiled, the intervention of Dostoevsky effectively precipitating the Fall. Interestingly, despite the chaos that ensued, the inhabitants of this society did not wish to return to their former state but do seek to construct a perfect society by using reason. As Leatherbarrow argues in his introduction, the Ridiculous Man was saved not by exposure to this utopia but by the compassion he felt for a small child, a compassion that is seemingly outside the realm of reason.⁴⁶
One of the Ridiculous Man's misunderstandings with the inhabitants of his dream's perfect society centres on the latter's incomprehension of the duality of values, in other words, the impossibility of having a positive value without its polar opposite; Dostoevsky's example in the story being love and hate.⁴⁷ In commenting on the romantic challenge to utopianism, philosopher Isaiah Berlin was also concerned with duality, but in a far more subtle way. Berlin argued that there are dualities of competing 'goods'. That is to say that one cannot have both complete justice *and* complete mercy, complete liberty, *and* complete equality. Indeed, Berlin famously argued that 'total liberty for wolves is death to the lambs'.⁴⁸ This is the foundation of Berlin's attack on what he insists are the three elements of the Platonic ideal that underpins Western philosophy.⁴⁹ This demonstration of the epistemic impossibility of making all social goods compatible with each other constitutes a devastating critique of utopias.⁵⁰

WHAT IS TO BE DONE WITH THE DIGITAL LIBRARY?

How, then, does all this relate to our understanding of digital libraries? Well, to the extent that the most ambitious projects are universal in scope and zealous in their advocacy of perfect knowledge, they can be described as utopian. It has already been noted that one of the most vociferous champions of the universal library is *Wired* magazine's Kevin Kelly. Fred Turner has identified the role of the magazine and its antecedents—Kelly's participation in all this being more than that of a mere footnote—in the proselytising of the personal computer as a perfect countercultural tool. Interestingly, the Californian counterculture originally gained its strength from its antipathy towards technology. This movement was utopian in nature and, like earlier socialist and Christian dreamers, established communes all over the country.[51] But the story of this period in American history certainly seems to be compatible with Northrop Frye's earlier observation that the imperial reach of new technologies made the existence of isolated enclaves all but impossible. Thus, when the communes dissolved, the utopian impulse was not ditched but instead was universalised. This universalism was based on the very technologies from which the communes were supposedly retreating. For former commune dweller and Internet pioneer Stewart Brand, the personal computer was the tool that would deliver freedom.[52]

Among Brand's followers and acolytes were people such as Kevin Kelly, Nicholas Negroponte, and John Perry Barlow.[53] Kelly's proselytising of the universal library in digital form has already been noted, but it is worth considering Negroponte's and Barlow's views too. Negroponte is famous for his book *Being Digital*, which seemed to capture the zeitgeist of the early years of the World Wide Web. Like all good digital utopians, his vision of cyberspace was imperial in scope:

> Today when 20 percent of the world consumes 80 percent of its resources, when a quarter of us have an acceptable standard of living and three-quarters don't, how can this divide possibly come together? While the politicians struggle with the baggage of history, a new generation is emerging from the digital landscape free of many of the old prejudices. These kids are released from the limitation of geographic proximity as the sole basis of friendship, collaboration, play and neighbourhood. Digital technology can be a natural force driving people into greater world harmony.[54]

This is classical utopianism in its eliding of the messy business of political choices, its evocation of world harmony, and its representation of technology as a 'natural force'. This desire to use computer technology as a means to move beyond politics was superficially a motivation for John Perry Barlow too. In 1996, his 'Declaration of the Independence of Cyberspace' was an attack on the U.S. Congress's passing of the *Telecommunications Act* and a rider, the *Communications Decency Act*, whose aim was to restrict Internet pornography.[55] Barlow's was a clarion call for freedom of speech and was very much grounded in the counterculture's suspicion of bureaucracy.

Philosopher John Gray views all types of utopianism, even and perhaps especially in a secular guise, as rehashed millennarianism.[56] For this reason, he retracts from all utopian schemes. But this seems to me to succumb to fatalism: how can we fashion a politics without grand, sweeping visions? Despite her criticism of the tendency of utopians to employ science in an omnicompetent manner, Mary Midgley does not believe it possible to comprehend the world around us without the aid of mental maps, however simplistic they may be.[57] Like Midgley's, Berlin's scepticism of utopian thinking does not prevent him from commenting that 'Utopias have their value—nothing so wonderfully expands the imaginative horizons of human potentialities'.[58]

One way of appreciating the usefulness of utopias without subscribing to some of their wilder proposals is to adopt Paul Ricoeur's dialectic between utopia and ideology.[59] Put simply, there is an antagonistic relationship between ideology and utopia which is subject to an ongoing dialectic, through which coherent political programmes are fashioned. Although this chapter has addressed the problem of being seduced by utopian projects, as Ricoeur illustrates, a complete rejection of them runs the risk of merely endorsing the existing prevailing ideology:

> My own conviction is that we are always caught in this oscillation between ideology and utopia. There is no answer to [Karl] Mannheim's paradox except to say that we must try to cure the illnesses of utopia by what is wholesome in ideology—by its elements of identity, which is once more a fundamental function of life—and try to cure the rigidity, the petrification, of ideologies by the utopian element.[60]

This is a useful way of thinking about the success of the counterculture movement in embedding the idea of 'open source' software beyond its immediate audience.[61] This is an idea that could never have taken root in our increasingly commercialised world without the missionary zeal of digital utopians. Another example is Nicholas Negroponte's project to deliver $100 laptops to millions of children in developing nations. As a means of promoting constructionist learning, this approach could be deemed naïve in its supposition that the provision of laptops alone could radically transform the education of these children, while it is also ignorant of the political realities of this type of intervention. But only after its ideas were adopted, the project was thwarted by large competitor corporations—proof that digital utopianism contains elements worth pilfering.[62]

Patrice Flichy argues that although Ricoeur's dialectic is useful, we should not perceive it in terms of a linear continuum. Instead, he takes a transformative approach in which utopia can mutate into ideology. Flichy argues that once utopian projects are subjected to experimentation then that lends them a certain scientific credibility. The success of what is essentially a local experiment will assume a mythos that enables the utopian to disseminate the innovation far and wide. Aspects of social reality that do not conform to this myth—for example, the fact that the experiment may only have local rather than universal applicability—are jettisoned by the need to expand the utopian project beyond its local audience. Flichy refers to this as a *mask ideology*.[63] An example of this transformation of utopia into mask ideology can be seen in relation to the Internet. Originally, the Internet was a construction that contained a series of self-created communities of people with similar interests and ideas, most of whom were from similar backgrounds. These communities, mainly run within universities, could be said to constitute a new online public sphere, certainly within academia, underpinned by communicative action free from the state and commercial corporations in the true Habermasian sense. As many academics have pointed out, the World Wide Web that we know today does not conform to that model, and yet the mask ideology is successful in framing many debates about the Internet within the 'public sphere' framework.[64]

Another example, more pertinent in the sense that it involves many of the activists who inspire the digital utopians at *Wired* magazine, is of the counterculture movement itself. The notion of free speech that prevailed in the utopian communes of the 1960s was probably only suitable for the peculiar circumstance in which the commune dwellers found themselves. And what were these circumstances? Well, although they railed against the violence and bureaucracy of mainstream U.S. society, their own communes relegated women to a subordinate role and failed to resolve the ethnic tensions that prevailed outside their borders.[65] Once they returned to mainstream society, it is questionable whether their ideas of unlimited freedom of speech could survive in a society which was multiracial in actuality as well as ethos and where language appeared to be increasingly gender neutral. This free speech utopianism masked a distinct New Right ideology.[66] More significant than that, however, was the tendency to mask the activities of large multinational corporations in this utopian schema.[67] As no doubt Isaiah Berlin would argue, the elision of politics does not lead to universal harmony, and the fiction that technology can solve all political problems only masks the ideology, namely, neoliberal capitalism, that underpins the computing industry.

The notion that universal knowledge can lead to a universal harmony free from politics is fundamentally flawed. That said, we should not reject anything that advances the cause of education, as long as it is not acknowledged as a panacea. In this sense, in its capacity to widen access and make textual searching easier, the concept of the digital library should be supported. However, public institutions should not lose sight of the values that make them different from private corporations. They should not embark on a futile endeavour for a perfect knowledge that does not exist, especially when that pursuit masks an ideology that champions the transferring of publicly owned information to the private sector.

NOTES

1. Patrick J. Carr, 'The Brain Drain', *The Independent* [London], 18 July 2008 (*Extra* section), p. 4.

2. Microsoft and Yahoo! signed similar contracts with other libraries as well, but their programmes did not develop as much as Google's; indeed, in May 2008, the former announced the termination of its book-scanning programme (Randall Stross, *Planet Google* [New York: Free Press, 2008], p. 106). See also Andrew White, 'Digital Britain: New Labour's digitisation of the UK's cultural heritage', *Cultural Trends* 20, no. 3–4 (2011), for a contemporary review of the Google Books project.
3. See: Paul Duguid, 'Inheritance and Loss? A Brief Survey of Google Books', *First Monday*, 12, no. 8 (2007), accessed 30 March 2013, www.firstmonday.org/htbin/cgiwrap/bin/ojs/index.php/fm/article/view/1972/1847; Jean-Noël Jeanneney, *Google and the Myth of Universal Knowledge [a View from Europe]*, trans. Teresa Lavender Flanagan (Chicago and London: University of Chicago Press, 2007); Andrew White, 'Understanding Hypertext Cognition: Developing Mental Models to Aid Users' Comprehension', *First Monday*, 12, no. 1 (2007), accessed 30 March 2012, www.firstmonday.org/htbin/cgiwrap/bin/ojs/index.php/fm/article/view/1425/1343; and White, 'Digital Britain'.
4. Mathew Battles, *Library: An Unquiet History* (London: Vintage, 2004), pp. 22–26, 29–31.
5. Roger Chartier, *The Order of Books*, trans. Lydia G. Cochrane (Cambridge, UK: Polity Press, 1994), p. 62.
6. Ibid., p. 63.
7. Kevin Kelly, 'Scan this Book!' *New York Times*, 14 May 2006, accessed 30 March 2012, www.nytimes.com/2006/05/14/magazine/14publishing.html?ex=1305259200&en=c07443d368771bb8&ei=5090.
8. Carr, 'The Brain Drain', p. 4, emphasis added.
9. Fred Turner, *From Counterculture to Cyberculture* (Chicago and London: University of Chicago Press, 2006), p. 201.
10. Nicholas Negroponte, *Being Digital* (London: Hodder and Stoughton, 1995).
11. Turner, *From Counterculture to Cyberculture*, pp. 162–63.
12. Larry McCaffery, 'An Interview with William Gibson,' in *Storming the Reality Studio: a Casebook of Cyberpunk and Postmodern Science Fiction*, ed. McCaffrey (Durham, NC: Duke University Press, 1991), p. 269, cited in Richard Coyne, *Technoromanticism: Digital Narrative, Holism and the Romance of the Real* (Cambridge, MA, and London: MIT Press, 1999), p. 290.
13. Mary Midgley has argued that successful contemporary technologies tend to be commandeered by utopians who make them imperial in their application and scope. Thus, at various periods in history, we have witnessed the Bronze Age, the Atomic Age, the Space Age, and the Information Age. Like all imperia, once these seemingly omnipotent technologies are proved fallible, they are replaced by other technological regimes, but the idea of omnicompetence still remains. See Mary Midgley, *The Myths We Live By* (London and New York: Routledge, 2003).
14. It could be argued that Plato's *Republic*, which undoubtedly had an influence on More's text, was the first utopia. However, the former text did not really lead to a spate of utopias in the same way that More's did.
15. Thomas More, *Utopia: A Revised Translation, A Norton Critical Edition, Second Edition*, trans. Robert M. Adams (New York and London: Norton, 1991).
16. Frederic Jameson, *Archaeologies of the Future: The Desire Called Utopia and Other Science Fictions* (London and New York: Verso, 2005), pp. 4–5.
17. Roland Barthes, *Sade, Fourier, Loyola* (Paris, 1971), p. 23, cited in Jameson, *Archaeologies*, p. 5.
18. Jameson, *Archaeologies*, p. 15.
19. Isaiah Berlin, *The Crooked Timber of Humanity* (London: Fontana Press, 1991), p. 27.

20. The Royal Society was explicitly based on the scientific society in Bacon's utopian novel *New Atlantis*. See also Rose-Mary Sargent, ed., *Francis Bacon: Selected Philosophical Works* (Indianapolis, IN: Hackett Publishing Company, 1999), p. xxii
21. David J. Hand, *Information Generation: How Data Rule our World* (Oxford, UK: Oneworld, 2007), pp. 41–43.
22. Sargent, *Francis Bacon*, p. xx. For one of the best accounts of the collaborative working practices and associated philosophies of the Californian counterculture that were central to the building of the World Wide Web, see Turner, *From Counterculture to Cyberculture*.
23. Sargent, *Francis Bacon*, p. xx.
24. Ibid., emphasis added.
25. M. J. Bragg, J. Hawley, C. Warman and D. Wootton, *In our Time*: 'The Encyclopedie', London: BBC Radio 4, 26 October 2006.
26. See Hand, *Information Generation*; Midgley, *The Myths We Live By*; and Francis Yates, *The Rosicrucian Enlightenment* [1972] (London and New York: ARK Paperbacks), 1986.
27. Battles, *Library*, p. 84.
28. Ibid., p. 84; and Yates, *The Rosicrucian Enlightenment*, p. 97.
29. Sargent, *Francis Bacon*, p. 267.
30. Ibid., pp. 239–68.
31. Edward Rothstein, Herbert Muschamp, and Martin E. Marty, *Visions of Utopia* (Oxford, UK, and New York: Oxford University Press, 2003), p. 79.
32. Yates, *The Rosicrucian Enlightenment*, p. 148.
33. Ibid., p. 179.
34. Ibid., p. 161.
35. Northrop Frye, 'Varieties of Literary Utopias', in More, *Utopia*, p. 208.
36. Edward Bellamy, *Looking Backward 2000–1887*, ed. by John L. Thomas (Cambridge, MA: The Belknap Press of Harvard University Press, 1967), p. 42.
37. Yates, *The Rosicrucian Enlightenment*, p. 178.
38. H.G. Wells, *A Modern Utopia* [1905] (London and New York: Penguin Classics, 2005), pp. 81–94. A cautionary note should be offered here because it is sometimes not clear when modernist utopias are genuine and when they are subtly satiric of the utopian genre as such.
39. Berlin, *The Crooked Timber*, pp. 217, 224.
40. Ibid., p. 236.
41. Mark Polizzotti, 'Stan and Ollie in the Lab', in Gustave Flaubert, *Bouvard and Pécuchet* [1881], trans. by Mark Polizzotti (Paris: Dalkley Archive Press, 2005), p. xv.
42. Flaubert, *Bouvard and Pécuchet*, p. 224.
43. Jean-Paul Sartre, *Nausea* [1938], trans. Robert Baldick (London: Penguin, 1963), p. 157.
44. Ibid., pp. 235–39.
45. Fyodor Dostoevsky, 'The Dream of a Ridiculous Man', in Fyodor Dostoevsky, *A Gentle Creature and Other Stories*, trans. Alan Myers (Oxford, UK: Oxford University Press, 2009), pp. 107–28.
46. William Leatherbarrow, 'Introduction', in Dostoevsky, *A Gentle Creature*, p. xxiii.
47. Leatherbarrow, 'Introduction', p. 122.
48. Berlin, *The Crooked Timber*, p. 12.
49. These are (1) all questions must each have only one true answer, (2) there must be a dependable path or methodology leading to these truths, and (3) all the answers are compatible with each other and thus form a uniform whole. See Berlin, *The Crooked Timber*, pp. 5–6.

50. The choices that need to be made between competing social goods can be conceptualised as the exercise of 'free will', a notion which is explored in twentieth-century novels such as Anthony Burgess's *A Clockwork Orange* and Aldous Huxley's *The Doors of Perception* and its sequel *Heaven and Hell*. Like Berlin, both Burgess and Huxley argue that negative side effects are an integral part of even the most positive 'choices' that we make when we exercise our free will, and which therefore demonstrate the epistemological and practical impossibility of realising utopia.
51. To give two examples: John Humphrey Noyes established a Christian commune named Oneida in New York state in 1848, following the even earlier New Harmony at Harmonie, Indiana, established by a British industrialist and socialist. See John Gray, *Black Mass: Apocalyptic Religion and the Death of Utopia* (London: Allen Lane, 2007), pp. 15–16. Turner, cites Judson Jerome's estimation that by the early 1970s, there were around 10,000 communes throughout America, housing some 750,000 people. See Turner, *From Counterculture to Cyberculture*, p. 32.
52. Brand established the *Whole Earth Catalog* in 1968, a document that Turner describes as 'one of the defining documents of the era' (Turner, *From Counterculture to Cyberculture*, p. 32).
53. Space does not permit a detailed overview of the relationship between all the digital utopians, but suffice it to say that *Wired* magazine and Stewart Brand's *Whole Earth Review* were both at one time edited by Kevin Kelly, and both shared the same cohort of techno-enthusiasts. Negroponte was the director of MIT's Media Lab and was, and still is, a charismatic and proactive digital utopian. John Perry Barlow's digital utopianism was differentiated from the others by virtue of being explicitly political: his establishment of the Electronic Frontier Foundation was a sophisticated campaign for free speech which he took to the heart of Washington.
54. Negroponte, *Being Digital*, p. 230.
55. Turner, *From Counterculture to Cyberculture*, p. 13.
56. Gray, *Black Mass*, p. 1.
57. Mary Midgley, *Utopias, Dolphins and Computers* (London and New York: Routledge, 1996), pp. 23, 25.
58. Berlin, *The Crooked Timber*, p. 15.
59. See Paul Ricoeur, *Lectures on Ideology and Utopia*, ed. George H. Taylor (New York: Columbia University Press, 1986).
60. Ricoeur, *Lectures on Ideology and Utopia*, p. 312.
61. For a discussion of open source, see Thomas Friedman, *The World is Flat* [2005] (London: Penguin, 2006).
62. Brian Appleyard, 'Computers Say No', *The Sunday Times* [London], 10 August 2008 (*Magazine* section), pp. 24–31.
63. Patrice Flichy, *The Internet Imaginaire* (Cambridge, MA, and London: MIT Press, 2007), p. 11.
64. Jill Walker Rettberg, *Blogging* (Cambridge, UK, and Malden, MA: Polity Press, 2008), p. 46.
65. Turner, *From Counterculture to Cyberculture*, pp. 76–78.
66. For the links between *Wired* writers and Republican libertarians in the 1990s, including the then Speaker of the House of Representatives Newt Gingrich, see Turner, *From Counterculture to Cyberculture*, pp. 222–32.
67. In this regard, questions about the pricing model that corporations will adopt to provide digital texts are often not asked. For a discussion of this, see Robert Darnton, 'Who Will Digitize the World's Books? An Exchange with Jean-Claude Guédon and Boudewijn Walraven', *The New York Review of Books* 55, no. 13 (August 2008), p. 72.

BIBLIOGRAPHY

Mathew Battles. *Library: An Unquiet History*. London: Vintage, 2004.
Edward Bellamy. *Looking Backward 2000–1887*, edited by John L. Thomas. Cambridge, MA: The Belknap Press of Harvard University Press, 1967.
Isaiah Berlin. *The Crooked Timber of Humanity*. London: Fontana Press, 1991.
Roger Chartier. *The Order of Books*, translated by Lydia G. Cochrane. Cambridge, UK: Polity Press, 1994.
Richard Coyne. *Technoromanticism: Digital Narrative, Holism and the Romance of the Real*. Cambridge, MA, and London: MIT Press, 1999.
Robert Darnton. 'Who Will Digitize the World's Books? An Exchange with Jean-Claude Guédon and Boudewijn Walraven'. *The New York Review of Books* 55, no. 13 (August 2008).
Fyodor Dostoevsky. 'The Dream of a Ridiculous Man', in Fyodor Dostoevsky, *A Gentle Creature and Other Stories*, translated by Alan Myers. Oxford, UK: Oxford University Press, 2009.
Paul Duguid. 'Inheritance and Loss? A Brief Survey of Google Books'. *First Monday* 12, no. 8 (2007). www.firstmonday.org/htbin/cgiwrap/bin/ojs/index.php/fm/article/view/1972/1847.
Thomas Friedman. *The World is Flat* [2005]. London: Penguin, 2006.
Gustave Flaubert, *Bouvard and Pécuchet* [1881], trans. by Mark Polizzotti. Paris: Dalkley Archive Press, 2005.
Patrice Flichy. *The Internet Imaginaire*. Cambridge, MA, and London: MIT Press, 2007.
Northrop Frye. 'Varieties of Literary Utopias', in Thomas More, *Utopia: A Revised Translation, A Norton Critical Edition, Second Edition*, translated by Robert M. Adams. New York and London: Norton, 1991.
John Gray. *Black Mass: Apocalyptic Religion and the Death of Utopia*. London: Allen Lane, 2007.
David J. Hand. *Information Generation: How Data Rule our World*. Oxford, UK: Oneworld, 2007.
Frederic Jameson. *Archaeologies of the Future: The Desire Called Utopia and Other Science Fictions*. London and New York: Verso, 2005.
Jean-Noël Jeanneney. *Google and the Myth of Universal Knowledge [a View from Europe]*, translated by Teresa Lavender Flanagan. Chicago and London: University of Chicago Press, 2007.
William Leatherbarrow. 'Introduction', in Fyodor Dostoevsky, *A Gentle Creature and Other Stories*, translated by Alan Myers. Oxford, UK: Oxford University Press, 2009.
Larry McCaffery. 'An Interview with William Gibson,' in *Storming the Reality Studio: A Casebook of Cyberpunk and Postmodern Science Fiction*, edited by McCaffrey. Durham, NC: Duke University Press, 1991.
Mary Midgley. *The Myths We Live By*. London and New York: Routledge, 2003.
Mary Midgley. *Utopias, Dolphins and Computers*. London and New York: Routledge, 1996.
Thomas More. *Utopia: A Revised Translation, A Norton Critical Edition, Second Edition*, translated by Robert M. Adams. New York and London: Norton, 1991.
Nicholas Negroponte. *Being Digital*. London: Hodder and Stoughton, 1995.
Mark Polizzotti. 'Stan and Ollie in the Lab', in Gustave Flaubert, *Bouvard and Pécuchet*, translated by Mark Polizzotti. Paris: Dalkley Archive Press, 2005.
Jill Walker Rettberg. *Blogging*. Cambridge, UK, and Malden, MA: Polity Press, 2008.
Paul Ricoeur. *Lectures on Ideology and Utopia*, edited by George H. Taylor. New York: Columbia University Press, 1986.

Edward Rothstein, Herbert Muschamp and Martin E. Marty. *Visions of Utopia*. Oxford, UK, and New York: Oxford University Press, 2003.
Rose-Mary Sargent, ed. *Francis Bacon: Selected Philosophical Works*. Indianapolis, IN: Hackett Publishing Company, 1999.
Jean-Paul Sartre. *Nausea* [1938], translated by Robert Baldick. London: Penguin, 1963.
Randall Stross. *Planet Google*. New York: Free Press, 2008.
Fred Turner. *From Counterculture to Cyberculture*. Chicago and London: University of Chicago Press, 2006.
H. G. Wells. *A Modern Utopia* [1905]. London and New York: Penguin Classics, 2005.
Andrew White. 'Digital Britain: New Labour's Digitisation of the UK's Cultural Heritage'. *Cultural Trends* 20, no. 3–4 (2011).
Andrew White. 'Understanding Hypertext Cognition: Developing Mental Models to Aid Users' Comprehension'. *First Monday* 12, no. 1 (2007). www.firstmonday.org/htbin/cgiwrap/bin/ojs/index.php/fm/article/view/1425/1343
Francis Yates. *The Rosicrucian Enlightenment* [1972]. London and New York: ARK Paperbacks, 1986.

Contributors

Geoffrey Bennington is Asa G. Candler Professor of Modern French Thought in the Department of French and Italian at Emory University. He is the translator of works by Derrida, Lyotard, and other French thinkers, and the author of more than one hundred essays published as chapters in books, or as articles in journals, including *Diacritics*, *Le contretemps*, *French Studies*, the *Journal of the British Society for Phenomenology*, *Oxford Literary Review*, *Paragraph*, *Parallax*, *Poétique*, and *Ratio*. He is the author of *Lyotard: Writing the Event* (1988); *Jacques Derrida*, with Jacques Derrida (1991); *Legislations: the Politics of Deconstruction* (1995); *Interrupting Derrida* (2000); *Frontières kantiennes*, 2000; *Frontiers (Kant, Hegel, Frege, Wittgenstein* (2003); *Other Analyses: Reading Philosophy* (2005); *Open Book / Livre Ouvert* (2005); *Deconstruction is Not What You Think* (2005); *Late Lyotard* (2005); and *Not Half No End* (2010). He is also a member of the French editorial team preparing Jacques Derrida's seminars for publication, and general editor (with Peggy Kamuf) of the English translation of those seminars.

Emily Bowles is a senior lecturer in English and Women's Studies at the University of Wisconsin–Fox Valley. She also volunteers for the Sexual Assault Crisis Center-Fox Cities. Publications include: 'You have not what you ought to have: Gender and corporeal intelligibility in Henry Fielding's The Female Husband', in *Genders* (2010); 'Stitched into the skin: Needlework and the embodiment of female authority in Aphra Behn's Oroonoko and The History of the Nun', in the special issue of *In-between: Essays & Studies in Literary Criticism* on early modern women's writing (summer 2009); 'Perfect Patterns of Conjugal Love and Duty: The Imprint of George Ballard's Domestic Ideologies on his Representations of Elizabeth Egerton and Margaret Cavendish', in The *Age of Johnson: A Scholarly Annual* 19 (2008); and *Triumphant Bodies: Sexual-Political Conquest in British Women's Published Writing, 1660–1763* (2007).

Tom Cohen is Professor in the College of Arts and Sciences at the University of Albany, SUNY. His work began in literary theory and cultural politics and traverses a number of disciplines—including critical theory, cinema studies, digital media, American studies, and, more recently, the contemporary shift of twenty-first-century studies in the era of climate change. His *Ideology and Inscription—'Cultural Studies' after Benjamin, de Man, and Bakhtin* (1998) examined modes of thinking cultural and interpretive politics in relation to scriptive memory. In this context, he is the author of a number of books on the archival wars and confluences of contemporary technics. These include *Anti-Mimesis* (1994), *Ideology and Inscription* (1998), and the two-volume *Hitchcock's Cryptonymies* (2005) and is coauthor of *Theory and the Disappearing Future* (2012). His edited and coedited volumes include *Material Events* (2001) and *Jacques Derrida and the Humanities* (2002). He is currently interested in the cognitive mutations implied by the logics of climate change and is founder of the Institute on Critical Climate Change (IC3).

Rick Crownshaw is Senior Lecturer in the Department of English and Comparative Literature, Goldsmiths, University of London, where he teaches mainly American literature. He is author of *The Afterlife of Holocaust Memory in Contemporary Literature and Culture* (2010); coeditor, with Antony Rowland and Jane Kilby, of *The Future of Memory* (2010); and contributing editor of a special edition of the journal *Parallax* on the topic transcultural memory (2011). His currently working on several monograph-length projects: global memory in recent American fiction and the idea of the secret in contemporary American fiction.

Elizabeth Evenden is a Marie Curie International Outgoing Fellow in the History Department at Harvard University. Her main areas of research are the creation and dissemination of religious propaganda in England, Portugal, and Spain, and the impact of printing in the dissemination of information and misinformation to an increasingly literate laity during the early modern period. Her publications include *Patents, Pictures and Patronage: John Day and the Tudor Book Trade* (2008) and *Religion and the Book in Early Modern England: the Making of John Foxe's Book of Martyrs* with Thomas S. Freeman (2011).

Suzanne Keen is Thomas Broadus Professor of English at Washington and Lee University, where she teaches modern and contemporary fiction in English, and past president of the International Society for the Study of Narrative Literature. Her books include *Victorian Renovations of the Novel: Narrative Annexes and the Boundaries of Representation* (1998), *Romances of the Archive in Contemporary British Fiction* (2001), *Narrative Form* (2003); *Empathy and the Novel* (2007), and a volume of poetry, *Milk Glass Mermaid* (2007). Her essays include 'A Theory of Narrative Empathy' in *Narrative* (October 2006); 'The Historical Turn in British Fiction' in *The Blackwell's Companion to Contemporary British*

Fiction, ed. James English (2006); and 'Strategic Empathizing: Techniques of Bounded, Ambassadorial, and Broadcast Narrative Empathy' in *Deutsche Vierteljahrs Schrift* (2008). She is guest editor of *Narrative and the Emotions*, a double special issue of *Poetics Today* (2011). Her chapter on twentieth-century trilogies and sequences is published in *The Cambridge History of the English Novel* (2012).

Michelle Kelly is a Research Assistant with the Institute for Culture and Society at the University of Western Sydney. She graduated with a BA (Hons) and a University Medal in 2003 and was awarded her PhD from the Department of English at the University of Sydney for her thesis 'Library Encounters: Textuality and the Institution' (2012). She is coeditor of *The Politics and Aesthetics of Refusal* (2007) and a cofounder and senior editor of the postgraduate journal *Philament* from 2003 to 2007. Her work has appeared in *Rhizomes: Cultural Studies in Emerging Knowledge*, *M/C Journal*, *Australian Book Review*, *API Review of Books*, and *Colloquy*.

Sas Mays is Senior Lecturer in Cultural and Critical Theory in the Department of English, Linguistics, and Cultural Studies at the University of Westminster, London. He leads the sporadic online and off-line research events and publications project 'Archiving Cultures', which is located within Westminster's Institute for Modern and Contemporary Culture. He has been an invited speaker at, and the developer of, a number of conferences and colloquia intersecting with his overall research interest in the mediation of cultural memory through technological and archival forms, from the textual to the visual and from the analogue to the digital. His publications related to this research area include 'Ansel Adams: The Gender Politics of Photographic and Literary Archives', in *Literature and Photography in the Twentieth Century*, edited by Cunningham, Fisher, and Mays, (2005); 'Consigning Badiou to the Past: the Encyclopaedia and Philosophy's Gendered Thought of the Endless Archive', in *Cultural Politics* (2009); 'Between Pandora and Diogenes: On the Gender Politics of the Archive in the Visual and Textual Practices of W. H. F. Talbot', in *Journal of Visual Culture* (2103); 'Witnessing the Archive: Art, Capitalism and Memory', in *All this Stuff: Archiving the Artist*, edited by Judy Vaknin (2013); and the coedited volumes *Materialities of Text*, a special issue of *New Formations* (2013), and *The Machine and the Ghost: Technology and Spiritualism in 19th to 21st Century Art and Culture* (2013).

Martin McQuillan is Dean of the Faculty of Arts & Social Sciences at Kingston University, London, where he is also codirector of The London Graduate School. He works in the spaces between literary theory, art theory, cultural studies and continental philosophy, and writes on the work of Jacques Derrida, Hélène Cixous, and Paul de Man. He was the editor of *The Year's Work in Critical and Cultural Theory* (2003–05), the journal *Parallax* (2000–10), and has edited volumes of the *Oxford Literary Review* and *Derrida Today*. He is also the editor of *The Frontiers of Theory* series for Edinburgh University Press. His monographs include *Deconstructing Disney* (1999), with Eleanor Byrne; *Paul de Man* (2001); *Deconstruction after 9/11* (2009); and *Roland Barthes: Or the Profession of Cultural Studies* (2011). His edited volumes include *Deconstruction: A Reader* (2000); *The Politics of Deconstruction: Jacques Derrida and the Other of Philosophy* (2007); *The Portable Rousseau,* edited by Paul de Man (2010); and *Textual Allegories,* by Paul de Man (2010).

Kaye Mitchell is Lecturer in Contemporary Literature and Programme Director of the MA Contemporary Literature and Culture at the University of Manchester. She is the author of *A.L. Kennedy* (2007) and *Intention and Text* (2008), the editor of *Sarah Waters: Contemporary Critical Perspectives* (2013), and has published numerous articles and chapters on contemporary literature, critical theory, and gender and sexuality, including B. S. Johnson's *The Unfortunates* and hypertext; gender and technoculture; Alan Hollinghurst and homosexual identity; Judith Butler and the politics of unintelligibility; contemporary erotic memoirs and sex blogs by women; and 1950s pulp sexology. Her current work in progress is a monograph on the politics, poetics, and erotics of shame in literature since the 1990s.

Simon Morgan Wortham is Professor of English at Kingston University and the author of *Rethinking the University: Leverage and Deconstruction* (1999), *Samuel Weber: Acts of Reading* (2003), *Counter-institutions: Jacques Derrida and the Question of the University* (2006), *Derrida: Writing Events* (2008), and *The Derrida Dictionary* (2010). He is coeditor of *Experimenting: Essays with Samuel Weber* (2007) and *Encountering Derrida: Legacies and Futures of Deconstruction* (2007). He has also edited special issues of *Angelaki, Culture Machine,* and *Textual Practice* and has published numerous essays in journals including *Diacritics, New Literary History, Cultural Critique,* and *New Formations*.

Andrew Peckham lectures in architecture in the School of Architecture and the Built Environment at the University of Westminster. His current research interests focus on the publication of architecture and the culture of rationalism. 'Moneo, Libeskind and a Question of Influence' was published in the *Journal of Architecture* (2008), and 'Questions of Authenticity: Brickwork and Found Space' was published in *Architectural Research Quarterly* (2011). He is the coeditor of *Narrating Architecture* (2006) and of *The Rationalist Reader: Architecture and Rationalism in Western Europe 1920–1940 and 1960–1990* (2013). He is currently working on a second book, *Architecture and its Imprint*.

Dan Smith is Senior Lecturer in Fine Art Theory at Chelsea College of Art and Design, University of the Arts London, and editor of the online publication *Altertopian*. His book *Traces of Modernity* was published in 2012 by Zero Books. Recent work includes 'Wells' First Utopia: Materiality and Portent', a book chapter in *Exploring the Utopian Impulse: Essays on Utopian Thought and Practice*, edited by Michael J. Griffin and Tom Moylan (2007), and 'Horizontality' in *Art Monthly* (2008). His *A World of Uncertain Seasons*, a book on contemporary art and utopia, is published by Peter Lang and *Agamben Reframed* is published by I. B. Tauris, both in 2013.

Wendy W. Walters is an Associate Professor in the department of Writing, Literature & Publishing, at Emerson College, Boston, MA. In 2001–2002 she was a nonresident fellow at the W. E. B. Du Bois Institute for Afro-American Research at Harvard. She is the author of the book *At Home in Diaspora: Black International Writing* (2005) and has an article in *American Literature*, '"Object Into Subject": Michelle Cliff, John Ruskin, and the Terrors of Visual Art' (2008). Some of her other publications include an article on V. Y. Mudimbe in *Critical Arts*, an article on Chester Himes in *African American Review*, a chapter on writing diaspora in *Diasporic Africa: A Reader*, and an article on the Legend of the Flying Africans in *MELUS*.

Andrew White is Lecturer in Digital Media and Mass Communications at the University of Nottingham Ningbo, China, and has previously held research posts at Belfast's Linen Hall Library, Queen's University Belfast, and the University of Ulster. His background is in contemporary Northern Irish politics and much of his research reflects that. His main research interest, however, is on the impact of digital media on contemporary society. His current research is focused mainly on the relationship between new media technologies and knowledge, exploring concepts like the universal library and utopianism in relation to the World Wide Web. He has published many papers in edited collections and journals, including *The International Journal of Media and Cultural Politics*, *First Monday*, the *Irish Journal of Sociology*, and *Identities*. He is a member of the editorial board of *Multicultural Education and Technology Journal* and a national committee member of the *Association of History and Computing* (UK). Publications relevant to this contribution include 'The Development of Digital Resources by Library and Information Professionals and Historians: Two Case Studies from Northern Ireland', in *Program: Electronic Library and Information Systems* (2005), and 'The Return to Orality: Digital Texts and their Impact on Literacy', *The Hand of the Interpreter: Essays on Meaning After Theory*, edited by M. Mitrano and E. Jarosinski (2009).

Index

9/11 12, 187

account books 41, 181n6
Adkins, Denice 142n12
aesthetic 47, 57, 85, 88, 103–4, 106,
    112n55, 160, 207, 212, 216,
    228, 231, 234, 260, 266
Agamben, Giorgio 87–8, 93–4
AIDS 165, 182n31
alienation 50, 142n3, 221n46, 226,
    235, 248
alphabet 16, 56, 135, 136, 141,
    144n32, 145n42, 146n53, 212,
    262
Althusser, Louis 157, 159
Amazon 125, 131, 146n52
Andreae, Johannes Valentinus 263, 265
anthropocene 74, 78n23
anthropology 14, 233, 240–2, 244–6,
    248, 251–2
aporia 73, 187–8, 197
Appiah, Kwame Anthony 241, 250
Appleyard, Brian 273n62
archival research 14, 15, 107, 115–27,
    167–8, 170, 229, 240–1, 243
archive fever 69, 152, 176, 251
archiving archive 69, 71–2, 169, 190
archivist(s) 59, 86, 117, 123, 170,
    240–1
Arendt, Hannah 159
Attridge, Derek 193–4
authority 7, 52, 58, 84, 86, 98–9, 105,
    106, 123, 142n6, 151, 153, 156,
    164, 165, 172, 175, 207, 234,
    236, 245, 252,
autoimmunity 77n16, 152

Bacon, Francis 260–5
Baker, E. A. 133
Baker, Sharon L. 135

Balibar, Etienne 95n31
Balzac, Honoré de 8, 10, 265
Barlow, John Perry 268, 273n53
Barthes, Roland 1, 4–5, 7, 9, 16, 234,
    260
Bartky, Sandra Lee 40
Bass, Alan 156
Bass, Saul 61
Battles, Mathew 17n4, 219n18,
    222n50, 271n4
Baudelaire, Charles 265
Bayard, Louis 118
Beck, John 86–7, 91
Beghtol, Clare 133, 134, 136–7, 138,
    143n20, 144n40, 145n47,
    147n65
Bellamy, Edward 264
Benjamin, Walter 4, 5–10, 14, 16, 57,
    88, 186, 203–4, 206, 216, 235
Berlin, Isaiah 267, 270
Bernier, Charles L. 20, 22, 24
Bible 106
biblion 12, 194–5
bibliothèke 13, 195, 214
Bjorklund, Nancy Basler 109n14
Blair, Lowell 157
Blair, Tony 226
Blanchot, Maurice 193
Blistene, Bernard 237n10
Bloch, Ernst 227, 236
body (corpus) 6, 42, 45, 58, 87, 107,
    188, 193, 210, 214
body (human) 28, 40, 41, 44, 73, 82–4,
    86, 91, 93, 115–16, 124, 126,
    188, 242–4, 247–51
book, era of 56–8, 63, 67–74 *passim*
book, materiality of 69, 71, 75, 97, 120,
    171, 177, 195, 212; notebooks
    171, 174, 196, 242–52 *passim*;
    see also diary

Index

book binding 102–8, 118, 132, 204, 258
book-case 168–9, 206
Book Depository, The 131
book form 1–2, 4–10 passim, 11–16 passim, 102, 158, 195, 227–9, 231, 258
book selection 11, 101, 132–4, 156, 158, 161, 165
bookshelf 5, 9, 16, 17n6, 81, 131, 135, 137, 151, 175, 203–4, 206, 244
bookshop/bookstore 4–5, 9, 59, 61, 71, 226
book stacks 16, 81, 125, 202, 203, 214, 219n19, 202, 214
Bordo, Susan 41, 45
Borges, Jorge Luis 91, 156
Borko, Harold 20, 22, 24
Borradori, Giovanna 187
Bossaller, Jenny E. 142n12
Boulée, Étienne-Louis 214
Bouman, Ole 221n33
bourgeois 4–10 passim, 85
Boyle, Robert 261
Bragg, Melvin 272n25
Brand, Stewart 268
British Empire 65, 67, 102–3, 239; see also empire
Brontë, Emily 121
Brouillette, Sarah 117
Brown, Dan 118, 128n25
Buchloh, Benjamin 231–2
bureaucracy 268, 270
Burgess, Anthony 273n50
Burt, Ellen 158–9
Burton, Antoinette 167
Buxton, Jackie 118
Byatt, A. S. 115, 117, 118–19

Cadava, Eduardo 57–8
Calvino, Italo 125, 206
Cameron, Alastair 145n27
capitalism 4, 6, 8, 11–12, 56, 59, 76, 78n26, 85, 86–7, 91, 226–7, 235, 250, 270; see also neoliberalism
Carducci, Giosuè 265
Carr, Patrick J. 270n1
Cartesian 82, 84–5, 89, 90–1, 206, 221n42; see also Descartes, René
Cartier-Bresson, Henri 228
Casanova, Giacomo 160–1
Cassiodorus, Flavius Magnus Aurelius 97–8
Casson, Lionel 210
catalogue 3–5 passim, 12, 16, 21–2, 24, 26, 49, 92, 102, 103, 107, 131, 146n58, 146n59, 168–77 passim, 202–7 passim, 212–13, 216, 227, 229–32 passim
catastrophe 76, 82–94 passim
categorisation 8, 10, 14, 48–9, 82, 116, 133–7 passim, 170, 173, 193–4, 220n24, 226, 229–30, 243–5
Catholic 99, 100, 107
Cepl, Jasper 203, 206
Chan, Lois Mai 142n6, 145n42, 145n44
Chartier, Roger 195, 220n24, 271n5
Chase, Cynthia 158
Chedgzoy, Kate 178
Christian/Christianity 75, 85, 97–108 passim, 263, 265, 268, 273n51
cinema 11, 56–76 passim, 226
Cioran, Emile 240
civil war 87; English 41, 50–2, 262; Spanish 228
Cixous, Hélène 13, 196–9
Clark, Timothy 193–4
classification 2, 4–6, 10, 12, 83, 130–41 passim, 159, 170, 195, 228–33 passim, 245; card classification 131; shelf classification 2, 131, 137, 139, 229
codex, codices 3, 10, 11, 16, 17n5, 97–108 passim, 139
collection(s) 1–15 passim, 23, 40–1, 56, 59, 65, 86, 92, 99–108 passim, 116–17, 120, 124–5, 130–41 passim, 153, 155–60 passim, 165–7, 170, 176–8, 195, 199, 202–18 passim, 226, 230, 235, 239, 261–2; private 8, 14, 40, 98, 115, 124, 202; public 170
collector(s) 5–16 passim, 98–105 passim, 115, 125, 165, 203–6, 213, 218, 235
Collins, Wilkie 125
Comenius, Jon Amos 263–6 passim
community 115, 165–9 passim, 173, 179–80, 181n6, 263
computer(s) 9, 22, 71, 124, 133, 154, 190, 195, 199, 257–9, 268
Comte, Auguste 264
Conan Doyle, Arthur 124
conceptual art 13, 231–5 passim
Condorcet, Marquis de 264

Conrad, Joseph 78n24, 253n8
Cook, Terry 17n2
Cornwell, Patricia 119
corporate 117, 224, 226
corporation(s) 257–8, 269–70
Cosgrove, Mary 90
counter-archive 13
counterculture 12, 259, 268–70
Coyne, Richard 271n12
Crimp, Douglas 228–9
Croghan, Antony 145n47
Crone, Rosalind 17n4
Cruz-Malave, Arnaldo 250
Cvetkovich, Ann 165–6, 171, 174
cyber-space 259, 268

Darnton, Robert 17n5, 273n67
data 16, 46, 76, 107, 131, 203, 232, 239, 243, 261, 263
database 116, 145n52
datascape 203
Davidson, Cathy 241–2
Davidson, Jenny 115, 119–20, 121–3, 126
Davies, Richard 146n53
Dawkins, Richard 262
Dean, Tacita 94n10, 236
death drive 70, 182n48, 197, 199, 251
deconstruction 9, 10, 30, 67, 91, 151–4
Defoe, Daniel 121
de Groot, Jerome 181n6, 181n11
Deleuze, Gilles 77n9
Deller, Jeremy 224–237 *passim*
de Man, Patricia 157–9
de Man, Patsy 158
de Man, Paul 11, 157–60, 161
democracy 15, 164–5, 203
Derrida, Jacques 4, 8–10, 11, 12, 21, 23, 29–38 *passim*, 62, 68–73 *passim*, 150–7, 159, 161, 164–6, 169, 180, 185–99 *passim*, 251;
   Derridean 15, 73
Desai, Guarav 252n4
Descartes, René 33, 82
desire 4, 8, 13, 15, 107, 123, 152, 156, 168–80 *passim*, 185, 227, 248–51, 258, 261, 265, 268
Dewey Decimal Classification (DDC) 16, 136, 145n42
DeZelar-Tiedman, Christine 139
diary 14, 62, 83, 170–1, 240–52 *passim*
Diawara, Manthia 240, 243
Dick, Philip K. 259
Dickins, Bruce 109n14

dictionary 26–8, 36, 160–1, 232
Diderot, Denis 159, 262
Diers, Michael 94n4
digital 3–4, 8–10, 11–13 *passim*, 56–7, 68, 75–6, 108, 126, 131–2, 141, 156–60 *passim*, 210–12, 231, 257–70 *passim*
Dinshaw, Caroline 171
disorder 5–6, 14, 40, 43–4, 86, 91; *see also* order
DNA 117, 211
document(s) 15, 47, 50, 97, 100–1, 107, 116, 122, 125–6, 133, 138, 140, 165–80 *passim*, 182n31, 195, 239, 245, 247, 266
documentary 13, 15, 70, 83, 107, 168, 197, 224–36 *passim*
documentation 202–3, 207–8, 212, 216
domestic 7, 41, 46–52 *passim*, 56, 74, 180, 185, 203
Dostoevsky, Fyodor 265–7
Duguid, Paul 271n3
Duncker, Patricia 182n31
Durant, Sam 236
Durkheim, Émile 133–4

early modern 97–108 *passim*
Eco, Umberto 118
ecology 11; ecological 56, 76; ecosystem 9–10, 71–2
economic 1, 4, 116, 138, 185, 188, 197, 225, 257
Edelman, Lee 182n48
Eisenstein, Elizabeth L. 42, 53n7
Electronic Frontier Foundation 273n53
Elizabethan 99, 106, 123, 124
Elsner, John 203, 218
E-mail 190
Emden, Christian J. 80
empire 67, 239, 242; *see also* British Empire
encyclopaedia 263; encyclopaedic 11, 151–62 *passim*; *encyclopedie* 262
Enlightenment 12, 14, 69, 78n24, 86, 153; enlightenment 222n50, 265
ephemera 15, 165, 167, 181n6
epistemological 2, 14, 57, 68, 82–3, 239, 246–7, 252, 261–2, 264, 266
e-publishing 76
Eriksson, Rune 134, 135, 137
ethics 37, 82, 93, 121, 227, 234, 235, 236n1

ethnography 166, 233
Eurocentric 250
Europe 15, 40, 116, 120, 161, 228, 263–4; European 12, 14, 40, 82, 118, 126, 240–52 passim, 262
Evelyn, John (Duke of Newcastle) 40–1, 45–53 passim
evidence 101, 107, 116, 127n8, 130, 165, 170, 178–9, 185, 186, 228, 231, 239, 257, 266

Fairfield, Leslie P. 109n15
Fanon, Frantz 248, 250–1
feminine 49, 52; see also masculine
femininity 14, 41; see also masculinity
Ferraris, Maurizio 77n15
Fforde, Jasper 127n9
Fielding, Henry 43, 121
film 11, 56–76 passim, 219n19, 231
Fischer, Steven Roger 17n4
Fitzgerald, Edward 87
Flanagan, Teresa Lavender 271n3
Flaubert, Gustave 86, 160, 265, 266
Flichy, Patrice 269
Foster, Hal 236
Foucault, Michel 17n3, 53n1, 77n13, 83, 164–7, 171, 182n31, 234, 239–44 passim, 252; Foucauldian 14, 15, 239, 241, 246
Fourier, Joseph 264
Frampton, Kenneth 221n37
Freeman, Thomas 112n56
Frege, Gottlob 31–7
Freshwater, Helen 244
Freud, Sigmund 77n16, 156, 192, 197, 251; see also death drive; psychoanalysis
Friedman, Thomas 273n61
Friedrichmeyer, Sara 95n49
Frith, Francis 228
Fritzsche, Peter 90
Frizzell, Robert Alan 127n6
Frye, Northrop 268
Fuchs, Anne 82–3
Fuss, Diana 250
future 10, 13, 16, 71, 74, 77n8, 77n15, 164, 169, 173, 182n48, 186, 188–99 passim, 216, 236, 242, 259–65 passim; future generations 97, 98, 102, 126, 157

Gadamer, Hans-Georg 193
gender 6, 13, 15, 40–53 passim, 63, 116, 118, 179, 193, 270

Genette, Gérard 20, 21
Gerhardt, Ernst 109n15
Gibson, William 259
Given, Lisa 17n1
globalization 68, 188
Goethe, Johann Wolfgang von 159
Google 131, 257–9
Graham, Dan 231
Graham, Timothy 104
grammarians 43; grammatical 28, 36
Gravagnuolo, Benedetto 221n36
Gray, John 268
Greenhalgh, Liz 142n4
Greimas, Algirdas J. 117
Grenville, Kate 118
Guattari, Fèlix 77n9
Guillory, John 147n67, 147n68
Gutenberg, Johannes 17n5, 108

Habermas, Gary 78n25
Habermas, Jürgen 77n16, 270
Hackel, Heidi Brayman 53n5, 53n15
Halberstam, Judith 166–7, 174
Hall, Radclyffe 15, 168
Halsey, Katie 17n4
Hamilton Findlay, Ian 206
Hand, David J. 261
Haraway, Donna 41
Harrel, Gail 133, 135–7
Harrow, Kenneth 249
Hartley, A. J. 119
Hatch, Kevin 231–2
Hawisher, Gail E. 147n66
Hawley, Judith. 272n25
Hayes, Christa-Maria L. 82
Hayes, Susan 133, 140
Hayles, N. Katherine 141
Hegel, G. W. F. 6–7, 29, 30, 34, 36, 159
Heidegger, Martin 27, 193
Herder, Johann Gottfried 265
heritage 13, 18n23, 99, 115–16, 126–7, 271n2
Herzog and de Meuron 15, 202–18 passim
Hidderley, Rob 147n65
Hillis Miller, J. 76n4, 193
Hirschhorn, Thomas 236
historians 43, 49, 52, 81, 124–7, 241, 247
historiography 17n4, 120, 192, 194, 247
history: cultural 80–94 passim, 181n11; ecclesiastical 97–108 passim; of classification 132–4; official 165; of sexuality 164–70; of

technology 8–9, 56, 65, 68, 155–6, 160, 188
Hitchcock, Alfred 11, 56–76 *passim*
Hitler, Adolf 87
Hjørland, Birger 131
Höfer, Candida 204
Holbein, Hans 85
Hölderlin, Friedrich 159
Hollinghurst, Alan 15, 170–4 *passim*
Holmes, H. H. 266
Holocaust 83, 90, 121; holocaust 198
homosexual 167–80 *passim*;
    homosexuality 15, 167, 249–50;
    see also lesbian
Hooke, Robert 47, 261
Hugo, Victor 202
Husserl, Edmund 24, 29–32, 37
Huxley, Aldous 259

Ibsen, Henrik 265
identity 8, 28, 37, 51, 118, 166–80 *passim*, 193, 205, 225, 239, 242, 248–51, 269
ideology 1, 4, 5, 41, 49, 52, 85, 87, 95n31, 160, 166–7, 227, 236, 269–70
Iivonen, Mirja 135
index card 14, 153, 243–5
index 12, 20–38 *passim*, 56–7, 175, 202, 210, 229, 285; *indexing* 67, 137, 138; indices 3, 12, 105
index nominorum 22–3, 26
index rerum 22–3
information 12, 83, 97–100 *passim*, 116, 126, 131–3, 139, 140, 167, 169, 181n11, 188–9, 203, 210, 228, 257–62 *passim*, 270
inheritance 6, 125, 151–3, 156
institutions 9, 12, 13, 44–5, 48, 58, 74–6 *passim*, 84, 155, 164, 167, 176, 180, 185, 190–7 *passim*, 208, 224–36 *passim*, 250, 262, 270; *see also* library as an institutional form
Internet 17n5, 76, 78n27, 126, 158, 268–70
Interregnum 15, 40–2
inventory 41, 44, 92–3, 160, 207, 212–13, 221n32
irrational 85, 91, 196, 235 *see also* rational

Jakobson, Roman 28
James, M. R. 111n46

Jameson, Frederic 236, 260–4
Jeanneney, Jean-Noël 271n3
Jesus 75, 265
Jewish 14, 87, 91, 192–3
Jewsiewicki, B. 249
Jones, Norman L. 109n15
Josten, C. H. 162n9
Joyce, James 9, 265
Juhasz, Alexandra 166
Jules-Rosette, Bennetta 240–1, 246, 252

Kafka, Franz 88, 160, 265
Kane, Alan 13, 224–36 *passim*
Kant, Immanuel 159, 265
Kellner, Douglas 227
Kelly, Kevin 258, 267–8
khora 62, 68–9, 73
Kilbourn, Russel 85–6, 88, 93
Klingmann, Anna 219n2
knowledge 2, 6, 8, 11–14, 21, 35–6, 42, 58, 81, 107, 140, 174, 185, 196, 228, 239–41, 257–70 *passim*; archival 68, 83–8, 89–93, 115–16, 125–6, 151, 164–80 *passim*, 234, 244–42 *passim*; digital 76, 108; historical 80; preservation of 97–8; textual 56
Kolbowski, Silvia 221n37
Koolhaas, Rem 211
Kostova, Elizabeth 115, 119, 120, 125–7
Krafft-Ebing, Richard Von 168

Labrouste, Henri 214
Langridge, D. W. 138, 146n55
Larkin, Phillip 115–17, 126, 127n1, 128n28
law(s) 6–7, 12, 30, 37, 69, 81, 87–8, 102, 155–6, 164, 180, 185, 191, 195–6, 231, 239, 261; lawyers 43; *see also* legal
Lazarus, Neil 253n8
legal 5, 7, 68, 87–8, 185, 192, 194, 231, 250, 257–8 *see also* law; legislate, legislator
Leatherbarrow, William 267, 272n47
legislate, legislator 38, 69, 169; *see also* law; legal
Lepik, Andres 203, 219n5
Lerner, Fred 17n4, 98–9, 108n6, 109n13
lesbian 15, 164–80 *passim*, 249
Lesbian Herstory Archives (LHA) 164–5

Index

Le Witt, Sol 232
librarian(s) 12, 80, 82, 102, 120, 123, 126, 130–41 *passim*, 152, 161, 173, 229, 241
libraries: Alexandrian Library 258; Baden State Library 212; Bibliotèque nationale de France (BNF) 13, 195–8, 242, 252; British Library, London 66–7, 115, 123, 258; Bodleian Library, University of Oxford 11, 150–6, 197; Bradenburg Technical University Library 210–11; Butler Library, Columbia University 123; Cambridge University Library, University of Cambridge 42, 48, 104, 105; Duke Humphrey's Library, University of Oxford 153; Fachhochschule Library, Eberswalde 208–9; Ptolemaic Library 12, 257; Sterling Library, Yale University 123; Widener Library, Harvard University 123
library: as an institutional form 2–4, 9, 12–13, 14, 16, 42–4, 56, 76, 133–4, 202, 208, 213; destruction of 58, 70, 98–9, 102, 106, 177, 197–8; private 6–7, 14–15, 40–2, 49, 98, 170, 202, 235, 258; public 15, 58–9, 130, 133, 135–6, 161, 169, 170, 213, 229; *see also* private collector/collection; public collector/collection
Library of Congress Classification (LCC) 136, 145n44
Liew, Chern Li 143n13
Long, J. J. 83, 85–6, 93, 94n11, 94n12
Longfellow, Erica 51, 54n33
Love, Heather 169, 182n28
LSD 259
Lucas, Peter 110n27
Lutheran 99
Lyotard, Jean-François 22–38, 38n9, 38n11

McCaffrey, Larry 271n12
Macherey, Pierre 95n31
McIsaac, Peter 221n32
Mack, Gerhard 207–8, 219n14
Malabou, Catherine 78n26
Mannheim, Karl 269
manuscript (general form of) 11, 13, 52, 108, 115, 117, 120, 262

manuscripts (particular) 42, 44, 47, 97–108 *passim*, 116, 121–6 *passim*, 150–62 *passim*, 199, 216, 257
Manzoni, Allesandro 265
Marlowe, Christopher 120, 123–4
Mars-Jones, Adam 182n31
Martin, Valerie 127n9
Marx, Karl 159, 227
masculine 15, 47, 49, 118, 175
masculinity 250, 254n51
Mauss, Marcel 133–4, 143n15
media 8, 11, 58, 61–2, 69, 75–6, 85, 141, 186–8, 199, 203, 211, 237n15, 258; mass media 81, 187
melancholia 10, 80, 85 *see also* mourning
Mengele, Josef 266
Merleau-Ponty, Maurice 31
metaphysics 30–2, 91–3, 151
Michaud, Phillipe-Alain 81, 94n6
Midgley, Mary 269, 271n13, 271n26
Miksa, Francis 142n6
Miller, Christopher 252, 254n64
Miller, David P. 142n6
Mills, Robert 179, 183n81
mnemonic 56–9, 65, 68, 72, 74
mnemotechnic 56, 61, 67, 69–70, 74–6
modern(ism) 47, 81–3, 85–8, 91–3, 117, 122, 133–4, 167, 228–9, 236, 249, 260–2, 265–6; modernity 14, 72, 82–3, 85–8, 90, 93–4, 226–7, 234–5; *see also* early modern; postmodern(ism)
monograph 108, 202, 207, 227
monotheism 56
Moore, Nick 142n5
More, Thomas 260, 264, 271n14, 271n15
Morris III, Charles E. 166, 181n14
mourning 46, 71, 80, 85, 187; *see also* melancholia
Moyer, Jessica E. 135, 137, 144n33, 145n50
MSN (MicroSoft Network) 258
Mudimbe, V. Y. 14–15, 239–52, 252n3
Mühlthaler, Erika 221n31
museum 65, 67, 84, 85, 203, 208, 224, 228–9, 236, 262
museums: Ashmolean 153; British 65, 67, 122, 239; Hunterian 119, 123
myth(s)/mythic 75, 88, 156, 227–8, 237n15, 249, 252, 259, 265, 269; mythology 80, 87

Index 287

narrative 16, 72, 75–6, 80, 132, 139, 152, 169, 179, 218, 228, 246–7, 251; anthropological 246; autobiographical 16, 242, 251; documentary 224; grand 265; historical 51, 174–5, 236, 241–2; master 169, 241; personal 52; philosophical 206; of the decline of the library 48–52; *see also* narrative fiction
narrative fiction 12, 40, 44, 48–52, 82–93 *passim*, 116–27 *passim*, 134
nature 59, 82–3, 89–94 *passim*, 212, 244, 263, 265
Negroponte, Nicholas 259, 268, 269, 271n10
neoliberal 1, 270
Neville, Katherine 118
New World 13, 116; *see also* Old World
Nietzsche, Friedrich 59, 265
North America 237n15, 264; *see also* U. S.
Noyes, John Humphrey 273

O'Brien, Ann 133, 135–6, 143n22
Oedipal 72, 77n8
Old World 13, 116, 126; *see also* New World
Ong, Walter J. 139, 146n63
online 131–2, 142n12, 145n52, 156, 158–9, 231, 258, 270
Ooi, Kamy 143n13
oral culture 97, 246, 248
order/ordering 3, 4, 10, 11, 28, 43, 86, 91, 151, 158, 180, 190, 195, 203, 206, 218, 230, 243–5, 251, 263; alphabetical 16, 135–6; archival 14, 65, 68–9, 169; boredom of 5–6, 203, 216, 235; desire for 4; mania for 176; normative 227; shelf order 5, 9, 130–41 *passim*; social 92; symbolic 236; textual 132; *see also* disorder; taxonomy/taxonomic

Page, Raymond I. 110n28
panoptic 77n5, 83, 167
paper 2, 3–4, 8–13 *passim*, 44, 58, 71, 86, 106, 131–2, 139, 156, 177, 186–8 *passim*, 195–7, 208, 239, 251; papers 115–16, 120–7 *passim*, 156–7, 160, 167–8, 204

paratext 38n1, 44–5, 48–9, 91, 123, 139
Paris, Matthew 150, 151, 152, 155, 197
Parker, Matthew (Archbishop) 98–108, 108n7, 109n10, 112n54
Parkes, M. B. 110n30
Pejtersen, Mark 136, 137, 144n32, 145n47
Pepys, Samuel 40
Perkins, David 141n1
photography 7, 57–8, 72, 77n21, 89, 122, 170–4, 203–4, 208, 217, 224, 228–34
Plato 11, 62, 150–4, 197, 198, 264, 271n14
Pogorelec, Andrej 135, 144n35
political 1, 3, 8, 11, 18n23, 41, 48, 51–2, 57, 103, 158, 164–79 *passim*, 185, 188–9, 194, 208, 227, 231, 265–70; biopolitical 56, 82–9 *passim*
politics 37, 40, 74, 151, 153, 225, 251, 259, 261; cultural 193; of memory 56
Polizzotti, Mark 267, 272n41
Pop Art 231
postmodern(ism) 1, 12, 116, 118, 153, 168, 203, 213, 229, 250, 260; *see also* modern(ism)
power 8, 15, 69, 71, 74, 83–93 *passim*, 164–7, 234, 239–51 *passim*, 262
print 17n5, 41–49 *passim*, 53n7, 57–9, 76, 169, 190–1, 202, 211, 227, 258, 261–2; early modern 98–108; printed fiction 130–41
print on demand 76
Prosser, Jay 168, 182n26
psychoanalysis 71, 77n8, 169, 190–3, 197, 240–52; *see also* Freud, Sigmund
publishing 49, 76, 119, 202, 242

Rafferty, Pauline 140, 147n65
Ranke, Leopold von 244, 253n19
Ranta, Judith A. 147n65
rational 11, 14, 15, 61, 82, 85–91 *passim*, 133–4, 181n24, 186, 202–18 *passim*, 250, 252; *see also* irrational
Reid-Pharr, R. 254n51
Rembrandt van Rijn 82–6
Renaissance 4, 80, 85, 120, 124, 126, 141, 261
repository 58, 65, 107, 167

288 *Index*

Restoration 15, 40–1
Rettberg, Jill Walker 273n64
Richard, Amy J. 136, 144n37
Richards, Thomas 239, 245, 252n1
Richardson, Ernest Cushing 131, 142n7
Ricoeur, Paul 31, 247, 254n35
Roberts, Colin H. 108n3
Rosaldo, Renato 245, 253n25
Rosler, Martha 233, 234, 237n25
Roudinesco, Elizabeth 189, 190
Rousseau, Jean-Jacques 157–62, 162n20
Ruff, Thomas 208, 210, 219n19
Ruscha, Ed 229–33, 237n11

Saarti, Jarmo 133, 137, 138, 143n23, 143n25, 144n39, 145n52
Sade, Marquis de 260, 271n17
Santner, Eric 88, 96n37
Sapp, Greg 130, 134, 136, 137, 138, 142n2, 143n25
Sartre, Jean-Paul 266, 267, 272n43,
Šauperl, Alenka 135, 144n35, 146n52
Saussure, Ferdinand de 28, 30–1, 37, 38n9
Schopenhauer, Arthur 265
Schwartz, Joan M. 17n2
science(s) 81, 120, 122, 156, 166–7, 192–4 *passim*, 235, 243–4, 252, 259; scientific 16, 46–8, 138, 169, 192, 245, 247, 260–70 *passim*; science fiction 119, 121, 135
scroll/roll 3, 11, 16, 46–7, 97, 211–12, 214, 217–18
secrecy 13, 46, 52, 68, 71, 92, 118, 120, 150–1, 153, 173–7 *passim*, 185, 196–8, 250; secret histories 170; secret library 168–9, 175
secular 93, 97, 155, 268
Sedgwick, Eve 254n51
Sekula, Alan 234
Selfe, Cynthia L. 147
Semper, Gottfried 210
Sergey, Brin 259
sexology 169–70
Shakespeare, William 41, 46, 54n21
Shepherd, Gay W. 135, 143n29
Shipman, Harold 266
Sieber-Albers, Anja 220n28
Silbert, Leslie 115, 119, 120, 123, 124, 126, 127n13
Singleton, David W. 144n37
Skeat, T. C. 108n3, 108n4
Slaymaker, William 241, 253n8

Smith, Bonnie G. 253n19
Smith, Faith 253n10
Soane, John 203, 218
Socrates 11, 150, 151, 152, 154, 155, 157, 160, 197, 198
Sosnoski, James 147
Spieker, Sven 251, 254n58
Springer, Carl P. 110n29
Steedman, Caroline 180, 180n1
Stewart, Garrett 142n3
Stiegler, Bernard 195
Stoker, Bram 120, 121, 125
Stoppard, Tom 124
storage 3, 9, 56, 59, 63, 67, 71, 76, 83, 97, 103, 107, 187–8, 195–6, 207, 210, 217, 251, 257; storehouse 98, 125, 261–2; *see also* repository
Strauss, Leo 159, 162n20
Striphas, Ted 17n5
Stross, Randall 271n2
subject (subject matter) 16, 48, 118, 134, 134–41 *passim*, 228–33 *passim*
subjectile 9, 69, 71, 188
subjectivity 6–8, 23, 29–33 *passim*, 36, 58, 61–5 *passim*, 68–74 *passim*, 80–7 *passim*, 172, 179, 186, 232, 240–52 *passim*
symbolic 15, 30, 115, 176, 178–9, 202, 236
symbolism 80, 248, 267

tablet 3, 11, 13, 16, 75, 97, 195, 210, 217–18
Tagg, John 234, 237n27
taxonomy 2, 4, 11–16 *passim*, 86, 130–1, 159–61, 170, 175, 224, 229–30, 253n8
Taylor, Arlene G. 142n6
Tey, Josephine 127n12
Thomas, John L. 272n36
Tolstoy, Leo 265
Toorn, Roemer van 221n33
Towheed, Shafquat 17n4
Turgenev, Ivan 265
Turner, Fred 259, 267, 271n9, 272n22, 273n51
typewriter 199
typography 212, 220n27

U. S. (United States of America) 13, 16, 73, 115, 123–4, 135–6, 187, 225, 229–34 *passim*, 239,

242, 268, 270; *see also* North America
Ungers, Liselotte 204
Ungers, O. M. 15, 202–18, 219n11, 220n28, 221n32, 222n51
Ursprung, Philip 216, 219n1
utopia 11–13, 224–36 *passim*, 257, 260–70 *passim*

Vandendorpe, Christian 17n5
Vernitski, Anat 140, 145n51, 147n65
Vicinus, Martha 178, 183n77
Vico, Giambattista 264
Voerhoeve, Jutta 220n28

Walker, R. S. 133, 143n18
Warburg, Aby 80, 81–3, 86, 88, 89, 94n2
Warman, C. 262, 272n25
Waters, Sarah 15, 174–9, 183n54
Weber, Samuel 186, 199n2
Wells, H. G. 264, 265, 272n38

Wheatley, Henry B. 20, 21, 22, 38n2
Whitman, Walt 265
Wilde, Oscar 173
Willats, Stephen 233, 234, 237n26
Winterson, Jeanette 120
Wittgenstein, Ludwig 20, 26–7, 32–3, 35–8, 38n5
Wootton, D. 272n25
word processor 199
World Wide Web 126, 268, 270, 272n22
Worpole, Ken 142n4
Wright, C. E. 109n8

Yahoo! 258, 271n2
Yates, Frances 263, 272n26
Yerushalmi, Yosef Hayim 192
Yu, Liangzhi 133, 135, 136, 143n22, 145n41

Zaug, Rémy 208

For Product Safety Concerns and Information please contact our EU
representative GPSR@taylorandfrancis.com
Taylor & Francis Verlag GmbH, Kaufingerstraße 24, 80331 München, Germany

www.ingramcontent.com/pod-product-compliance
Lightning Source LLC
Chambersburg PA
CBHW050432240426
43661CB00055B/2353